The Protection of Human Rights in the Administration of Criminal Justice

A Compendium of United Nations Norms and Standards

By
M. Cherif Bassiouni

With the Collaboration of
Alfred de Zayas

Transnational Publishers, Inc.
Irvington-on-Hudson, New York

Centre for Human Rights
United Nations, Geneva

M. Cherif Bassiouni is Professor of Law, President, International Human Rights Institute, DePaul University, Chicago, Ilinois; President, International Association of Penal Law; President, International Institute of Higher Studies in Criminal Sciences, Siracusa, Italy.

Alfred de Zayas is Visiting Professor, DePaul University.

Library of Congress Cataloging-in-Publication Data

The Protection of human rights in the administration of criminal justice : a compendium of United Nations norms and standards / by M. Cherif Bassiouni.
p. cm.
ISBN 0-941320-87-1
1. Criminal procedure. 2. Criminal justice, Administration of. 3. Human rights. I. Bassiouni, M. Cherif, 1937-
K5452.P76 1994
345' .05--dc20
[342.55] 93-41135
CIP

Manufactured in the United States of America

Dedication
to
Kemoko Keita

He was presumed dead seven years after being secretly taken by the security forces of Guiné in the late sixties to a prison later known to hold those that the despotic president wanted eliminated. At the time he was taken to what was to be his certain death, he was a respected and esteemed career judge, totally uninvolved in politics, and recently appointed deputy Procurateur-General.

For more than ten years, Keita (as he was called by everyone except his close family and friends who called him Kemo) served as a judge in the provincial town of Kankan. From there, he travelled his circuit to the neighboring villages and tribes to dispense justice in a mixture of modern and tribal ways.

A humble, sensitive and learned man, he was dedicated to his people in every sense of the word. His hobby was soccer and he organized youth teams in his hometown of Kankan and in the neighboring villages, frequently umpiring the games between these teams. In this way, he brought to his people more than the application of the law. He sowed harmony and instilled a subdued sense of order and discipline to those he cared for so much.

Keita became so renowned that he was repeatedly called on to serve in high judicial positions in the capital, Conakry. But he always refused because he wanted to stay where he could best serve those with the greatest needs. The time came when he could no longer avoid promotion and transfer. But for a man of integrity and dedication, there could be no survival under the violent and repressive dictatorship of that time. Shortly after he assumed his new post of Deputy Procurateur-General in Conakry, he disappeared, never to be seen alive again.

The son of a Kankan-based part-time jungle truck driver with a large family, he was the only one who went beyond grade school. He won several scholarships that led him to Dijon University Law School in the early days of the struggle for African decolonization, as a bright, hard-working, poor and dignified Black African.
When he graduated in 1958, he was offered a scholarship to pursue a doctorate. Without the slightest hesitation or hint of regret, he humbly and gratefully turned it down to return to Kankan to serve his people.

We were classmates at Dijon Law School and shared the same two-person bench and desk. We ate at the same table at the university's modest dining refectory. We ritualistically sat together at a nearby café every day after lunch to debate every imaginable legal, social, cultural, historical, and above all, political subject. Two coffees a day were Kemo's only vice. Indeed, he could afford no more.

He was everything that I was not, but we stood for the same things. We became soul-brothers. For years, I hoped he would suddenly reappear as he had suddenly disappeared . . . friendly, level-headed, human, and sensitive as he always was. But by the mid-seventies, it was clear that no hope was left. It took time for the realization to sink in that he is gone . . . a victim of the very things we had so frequently spoken of -- injustice. We had dedicated our lives to eradicate injustice. He died doing it and I am left only writing about it. And that is why I now dedicate this book to his memory. A man of greatness marked by simple dedication to his fellow-man, serving his people as best he knew . . . through the law. But the law he served did not serve him well. He was the victim of the most common and frequent of human rights abuses: arbitrary arrest and detention and summary extra-judicial execution. I can only hope that it did not include torture.

A *post-scriptum* which may surprise many: every day of the week, after lunch, we would sit at the café and this man who had to count his pennies indulged in his only pleasure. He would put a coin in the jukebox to listen to Paul Robeson's rendition of "Old Man River." Kemo spoke no English, but profoundly understood and felt the deep meaning of this song. It was to him somewhat of a reminder of who he was, where he might have been, and above all, what he had to do to prevent others from suffering the fate of slavery and its related contemporary practice which he dreaded most.

May there be many others like him to pick up where he and his likes have left off. And may we never forget that such abhorrent practices still go on and that their authors in so many parts of the world still enjoy impunity.

Last I heard, his wife and son lived in France and I hope that someday his son may stumble over this dedication and feel inspired by the memory of his father.

M. Cherif Bassiouni
Wilderness Dunes, Michigan, June 27, 1993

CONTENTS

TABLE OF AUTHORITIES

Application of the International Covenant on Civil and Political Rights under the Optional Protocol by the Human Rights Committee, Centre for Human Rights Reprint No.1 (December 1991).

Basic Principles for the Treatment of Prisoners [*adopted by* Eighth Congress on the Prevention of Crime and the Treatment of Offenders (Annex), Havana, Cuba, 27 August-7 September 1990, U.N. Doc. A/Conf. 144/28/Rev.1, I.A.5.], G.A. Res. 45/111, 14 December 1990, 45 U.N. GAOR Supp. (No. 49A) 199, U.N. Doc. A/RES/45/111.

Basic Principles on the Use of Force and Firearms by Law Enforcement Officials [*adopted by* Eighth United Nations Congress on the Prevention of Crime and the Treatment of Offenders, Havana, Cuba, 27 August-7 September 1990, U.N. Doc. A/Conf. 144/28/Rev.1, I.B.2.], U.N. Doc. E/AC.57/DEC/11/119.

Basic Principles on the Role of Lawyers [*adopted by* Eighth United Nations Congress on the Prevention of Crime and the Treatment of Offenders, Havana, Cuba, 27 August-7 September 1990, U.N. Doc. A/Conf. 144/28/Rev.1, I.B.3 (1990)], U.N. Doc. E/AC.57/DEC/11/109.

Basic Principles on the Independence of the Judiciary [*adopted by* Seventh Congress on the Prevention of Crime and the Treatment of Offenders, Milan, Italy, 26 August-6 September 1985, U.N. Doc. A/Conf./121/22/Rev.1, I.B.], G.A. Res. 40/146, 13 December 1985, 40 U.N. GAOR Supp. (No. 53) 254, U.N. Doc. A/40/1007.

Body of Principles for the Protection of All Persons under Any Form of Detention or Imprisonment, G.A. Res. 43/173, 9 December 1988, 43 U.N. GAOR Supp. (No. 49) 297, U.N. Doc. A/43/49.

Caracas Declaration [*adopted by* Sixth U.N. Congress on the Prevention of Crime and the Treatment of Offenders, Caracas, Venezuela, 25 August-5 September 1980, U.N. Doc. A/CONF.87/14/Rev.1, 2], G.A. Res. 35/171, 15 December 1980, 35 U.N. GAOR Supp. (No. 48) 193, U.N. Doc. A/35/742.

Code of Conduct for Law Enforcement Officials, [Fifth Congress on the Prevention of Crime and the Treatment of Offenders, Toronto, Canada, 8-12 September 1975, U.N. Doc. A/Conf./56/1 (1975)], G.A. Res. 34/169, 17 December 1979, 34 U.N. GAOR Supp. (No. 46) 185, U.N. Doc. A/34/46.

Communications Procedures, Centre for Human Rights, U.N. Office at Geneva, Fact Sheet No. 7 (May 1989).

Convention Relating to the Status of Refugees, *adopted* 28 July 1951, *entered into force* 22 April 1954, 189 U.N.T.S. 137 (1951).

Convention Against Torture and Other Cruel, Inhuman or Degrading Treatment or Punishment (Annex), G.A. Res. 39/46, 10 December 1984, 39 U.N. GAOR Supp. (No. 51) 197, U.N. Doc. E/CN.4/1984/72.

Convention on the Rights of the Child, G.A. Res. 44/25, 20 November 1989, 44 U.N. GAOR Supp. (No. 49) 166, U.N. Doc. A/44/736.

Convention Relating to the Status of Stateless Persons, *adopted* 28 September 1954, *entered into force* 28 March 1968, 21 U.N. ESCOR Supp. (No. 1) 12, 360 U.N.T.S. 117 (1954).

Convention on the Elimination of All Forms of Discrimination against Women, G.A. Res. 34/180 (XXXIV), 18 December 1979, 34 U.N. GAOR Supp. (No. 46) 194, U.N. Doc. A/34/830.

Declaration of Minimum Humanitarian Standards, *adopted* 2 December 1990 by U.N. Sub-Commission on the Prevention of Discrimination and the Protection of Minorities, U.N. Doc. E/CN.4/Sub.2/1991/55.

Declaration on the Protection of All Persons from Being Subjected to Torture and Other Cruel, Inhuman or Degrading Treatment or Punishment [*adopted by* Fifth Congress on the Prevention of Crime and the Treatment of Offenders, Toronto, Canada, 8-12 September 1975, U.N. Pub. Sales No. 76.IV.2], G.A. Res. 3452 (XXX), 9 December 1975, 30 U.N. GAOR Supp. (No. 34) 91, U.N. Doc. A/1034.

Declaration of Basic Principles of Justice for Victims of Crime and Abuse of Power [*adopted by* Seventh Congress on the Prevention of Crime and the Treatment of Offenders, Milan, Italy, 26 August-6 September 1985, U.N. Doc. A/Conf./121/22/Rev. 1, I.B.], G.A. Res. 40/34, 29 November 1985, 40 U.N. GAOR Supp. (No. 53) 213, U.N. Doc. A/40/881.

Declaration on the Human Rights of Individuals Who are not Nationals of the Country in which They Live, G.A. Res. 40/144, 13 December 1985, 40 U.N. GAOR Supp. (No. 53) 252-253, U.N. Doc. A/40/53.

Declaration on the Protection of All Persons from Enforced Disappearance, G.A. Res 47/133, 18 December 1992, 47 U.N. GAOR Supp. (No. 49) 207, U.N. Doc. A/RES/47/133.

Declaration on the rights of persons belonging to national or ethnic, religious and linguistic minorities, G.A. Res. 47/135, 18 December 1992, 47 U.N. GAOR Supp. (No. 49) 210, U.N. Doc. A/RES/47/135.

Draft Declaration on the Right to a Fair Trial and a Remedy, Sub-Commission on Prevention of Discrimination and Protection of Minorities, 25 June 1993, U.N. Doc. E/CN.4/Sub.2/1993/24/Add.1.

Draft Optional Protocol to the Convention Against Torture and Other Cruel, Inhuman or Degrading Treatment or Punishment, 22 January 1991, U.N. Doc. E/CN.4/1991/66.

Draft Third Optional Protocol to the International Covenant on Civil and Political Rights, aiming at guaranteeing under all circumstances the right to a fair trial and a remedy, 29 June 1993, Sub-Commission on Prevention of Discrimination and Protection of Minorities, U.N. Doc. E/CN.4/Sub.2/1993/24.

Enforced or Involuntary Disappearances, U.N. Centre for Human Rights, Fact Sheet No. 6, Rev. 1 (June 1993).

General Comment No. 15 of the Human Rights Committee on the position of aliens under the Covenant, Report of the Human Rights Committee, *adopted* 2 November 1986 by the Human Rights Committee, 42 U.N. GAOR Supp. (No. 40) Annex VI, U.N.Doc. A/42/40.

General Comment No. 4 of the Human Rights Committee on the International Covenant on Civil and Political Rights, Report of the Human Rights Committee, *adopted* Human Rights Committee, 36 U.N. GAOR (No. 40) Annex VII, U.N. Doc. A/36/40.

General Comment No. 13 of the Human Rights Committee on the International Covenant on Civil and Political Rights, Report of the Human Rights Committee, *adopted* 12 April 1984 by the Human Rights Committee, 40 U.N. GAOR Supp. (No. 40) Annex VI, U.N. Doc. A/40/40.

General Comments No. 6 and No. 8 of the Human Rights Committee on the International Covenant on Civil and Political Rights, Report of the Human Rights Committee, *adopted* 27 July 1982 by the Human Rights Committee, 38 U.N. GAOR Supp. (No. 40) Annex V, U.N. Doc. A/38/40.

General Comment No. 18 of the Human Rights Committee on the International Covenant on Civil and Political Rights, Report of the Human Rights Committee, *adopted* 28 July 1981 by the Human Rights Committee, 36 U.N

GAOR Supp. (No. 40) Annex VII, U.N. Doc. A/36/40; *adopted* 9 November 1989, 45 U.N. GAOR Supp. (No. 40) Annex VI A, U.N. Doc. A/45/40.

General Comments No. 20 and No. 21 of the Human Rights Committee on the International Covenant on Civil and Political Rights, Report of the Human Rights Committee, *adopted* 3 April 1992 by the Human Rights Committee, 47 U.N. GAOR Supp. (No. 40) Annexes VI A and VI B, U.N. Doc. A/47/40.

Guidelines on the Role of Prosecutors [*adopted by* Eighth United Nations Congress on the Prevention of Crime and the Treatment of Offenders, Havana, Cuba, 27 August-7 September 1990, U.N. Doc. A/Conf.144/28, I.C.26], U.N. Doc. E/AC.57/DEC/11/16.

Guiding Principles for Crime Prevention and Criminal Justice in the Context of Development and a New International Economic Order [Seventh United Nations Congress on the Prevention of Crime and the Treatment of Offenders, Milan, Italy, 26 August-6 September 1985, U.N. Doc. A/Conf./121/22/Rev.1, I.B.], G.A. Res. 40/32, 29 November 1985, 40 U.N. GAOR Supp. (No. 51) (A/40/51) 204-6, U.N. Doc. A/40/881.

International Covenant on Civil and Political Rights, *adopted* 16 December 1966, *entered into force* 23 March 1976, G.A. Res. 2200A (XXI), 21 U.N. GAOR Supp. (No. 16) 52, U.N. Doc. A/6316 (1967).

International Convention on the Elimination of All Forms of Racial Discrimination, G.A. Res. 2106A (XX), 21 December 1965, *entered into force* 4 January 1969, 660 U.N.T.S. 195 (1969).

*International Commission of Jurists, The Review, No. 47 (1991).

International Labour Conference Convention Concerning Indigenous and Tribal Peoples in Independent Countries, Draft Report of the Committee on Convention No. 107, *adopted* 27 June 1989 by Commission on Convention No. 107, U.N. Doc. 107/D.33, Appendix J.

Manual on Human Rights Reporting Under Six Major International Human Rights Instruments, April 1991, U.N. Doc. HR/PUB/91/1, U.N. Pub. Sales No. E. 91.XIV.I.

Model Questionnaire, Report of the Working Group on Arbitrary Detention to the Commission on Human Rights, *adopted by* Commission on Human Rights, 21 January 1992, U.N. Doc. E/CN.4/1992/20.

Model Treaty for the Prevention of Crimes that Infringe on the Cultural Heritage of Peoples in the Form of Movable Property [*adopted by* Eighth U.N. Congress on the Prevention of Crime and Treatment of Offenders, Havana, Cuba, 27 August-7 September 1990, U.N. Doc. A/Conf./144/28/Rev.1, I.B.1.], *adopted by* Committee on Crime Prevention and Control, 16 February 1990, U.N. Doc. E/AC.57/DEC/11/119.

Model Treaty on the Transfer of Proceedings in Criminal Matters [*adopted by* Eighth U.N. Congress on the Prevention of Crime and Treatment of Offenders, Havana, Cuba, 27 August-7 September 1990, U.N. Doc. A/Conf./144/28/Rev.1, I.A.12.], G.A. Res. 45/118, 14 December 1990, 45 U.N. GAOR Supp. (No. 49A) 219, U.N. Doc. A/RES/45/118.

Model Treaty on Mutual Assistance in Criminal Matters [*adopted by* Eighth U.N. Congress on the Prevention of Crime and Treatment of Offenders, Havana, Cuba, 27 August-7 September 1990, U.N. Doc. A/Conf. 144/28/Rev. 1, I.A.11], G.A. Res. 45/117 (1990), 14 December 1990, 45 U.N. GAOR Supp. (No. 49A) 215, U.N. Doc. A/RES/45/117.

Model Treaty on Extradition (Annex) [*adopted by* Eighth U.N. Congress on the Prevention of Crime and Treatment of Offenders, Havana, 27 August-7 September 1990, U.N. Doc. A/Conf. 144/28/Rev. 1, I.A.10], G.A. Res. 45/116, 14 December 1990, 45 U.N. GAOR Supp. (No. 49A) 211, U.N. Doc. A/RES/45/116.

Model Treaty on the Transfer of Supervision of Offenders Conditionally Sentenced or Conditionally Released [*adopted by* Eighth Congress on the Prevention of Crime and the Treatment of Offenders, Havana, Cuba, 27 August-7 September 1990, U.N. Doc. A/Conf./144/28/Rev.1, I.A.13.], G.A. Res. 45/119, 14 December 1990, 45 U.N. GAOR Supp. (No. 49A) 221, U.N. Doc. A/RES/45/119, U.N. Pub. Sales No. E.92.IV.1.

Optional Protocol to the International Covenant on Civil and Political Rights, *adopted* 16 December 1966, *entered into force* 23 March 1976, G.A. Res. 2200 (XXI), 21 U.N. GAOR Supp. (No. 16) 59, U.N. Doc. A/6316 (1967).

Prevention and Control of Organized Crime (Annex Guidelines) [*adopted by* Eighth United Nations Congress on the Prevention of Crime and the Treatment of Offenders, Havana, Cuba, 27 August-7 September 1990, U.N. Doc. A/Conf./144/28/Rev.1, I.C.24], *approved by* Committee on Crime Prevention and Control, 16 February 1990, U.N. Doc. E/AC.47/DEC/11/110.

Principles on the Effective Prevention and Investigation of Extra-legal, Arbitrary and Summary Executions (Annex), *adopted* 24 May 1987 by the

Committee on Crime Prevention and Control, E.S.C. Res. 1989/65, U.N. Pub. Sales No. E.92.IV.1.

Principles of Medical Ethics Relevant to the Role of Health Personnel, Particularly Physicians, in the Protection of Prisoners and Detainees Against Torture and Other Cruel, Inhuman or Degrading Treatment or Punishment, G.A. Res. 37/194 (1982), 18 December 1982, 37 U.N. GAOR Supp. (No. 51) 210, U.N. Doc. A/37/727.

*Proposed General Assembly Resolution on Measures for Implementation of the Declaration of Basic Principles of Justice for Victims of Crime and Abuse of Power, 7 Nouvelles Études Penales 28 (1988).

Question of Enforced or Involuntary Disappearances, Report of the Commission on Human Rights' Working Group on the Question of the Human Rights of All Persons Subjected to Any Form of Detention or Imprisonment, *presented* 31 January 1992 by the Human Rights Committee, U.N. Doc. E/CN.4/1992/19/Rev.1.

Question of the Human Rights of All Persons Subjected to Any Form of Detention or Imprisonment, Report of the Commission on Human Rights Working Group on Arbitrary Detention, *submitted* 21 January 1992 by the Working Group on Arbitrary Detention, U.N. Doc. E/CN.4/1992/20.

Report of the Commission on Human Rights Special Rapporteur on the Question of the Violation of Human Rights and Fundamental Freedoms in any Part of the World, with Particular Reference to Colonial and Other Dependent Countries and Territories; Summary or Arbitrary Executions, Report of the Human Rights Committee, *presented* 31 January 1992 by the Human Rights Committee, U.N. Doc. E/CN.4/1992/30.

The Right to a Fair Trial, Report to the U.N. Sub-Commission on the Prevention of Discrimination and the Protection of Minorities by Mr. S. Chernichenko and Mr. W. Treat on The Administration of Justice and the Human Rights of Detainees, *presented* 5 July 1991 by the Sub-Commission, U.N. Doc. E/CN.4/Sub. 2/1991/29.

Safeguards Guaranteeing Protection of the Rights of Those Facing the Death Penalty, *adopted* 25 May 1984 by Commission on Crime Prevention and Control, E.S.C. Res. 1984/50, 51 U.N. ESCOR Supp. (No. 1) 33, U.N. Doc. E/1984/92.

Second Optional Protocol to the International Covenant on Civil and Political Rights, Aiming at the Abolition of the Death Penalty, G.A. Res.

44/128, 15 December 1989, 44 U.N. GAOR Supp. (No.49) 206, U.N. Doc. A/44/824.

Standard Minimum Rules for the Treatment of Prisoners, E.S.C. Res. 663 C (XXIV), 31 July 1957, 24 U.N. ESCOR Supp. (No. 1) 11, U.N. Doc. E/3048 (1957) and 2076 (LXII) (1957).

Study Concerning the Right to Restitution, Compensation and Rehabilitation for Victims of Gross Violations of Human Rights and Fundamental Freedoms, Report of the Human Rights Committee, *submitted* 26 July 1990 by the Human Rights Committee, U.N. Doc. E/CN.4/Sub. 2/1990/10.

Terrorist Criminal Activities (Annex, Measures Against International Terrorism) [*adopted* by the Eighth United Nations Congress on the Prevention of Crime and the Treatment of Offenders, Havana, Cuba, 27 August-7 September 1990, U.N. Doc. A/Conf./144/28 (1990)], U.N. Doc. E/AC.57/DEC/11/112.

The Death Penalty. List of Abolitionist and Retentionist Countries, *submitted* by Amnesty International to the Sub-Commission on Prevention of Discrimination and Protection of Minorities, U.N. Doc. E/CN.4/Sub.2/1993/WG.1/CRP.2 (1993).

The Administration of Justice and the Human Rights of Detainees: Question of Human Rights and States of Emergency, Report of the Economic and Social Council, *presented* 21 November 1991 by the Economic and Social Council, U.N. Doc. E/CN.4/Sub.2/1991/28/Rev. 1.

United Nations Declaration on the Elimination of All Forms of Racial Discrimination, G.A. Res. 1904 (XVIII), 20 November 1963, 18 U.N. GAOR (No. 15) 35, U.N. Doc. A/5603.

United Nations Standard Minimum Rules for Non-custodial Measures (Annex) (The Tokyo Rules), G.A. Res. 45/110, 14 December 1990, 45 U.N. GAOR Supp. (No.49A) 195, U.N. Doc. A/RES/45/110.

United Nations Guidelines for the Prevention of Juvenile Delinquency (Annex) (The Riyadh Guidelines), G.A. Res. 45/112, 28 March 1991, 45 U.N. GAOR Supp. (No. 49A) 200, U.N. Doc. A/RES/45/112.

United Nations Resolution on International and Interregional Co-operation in Prison Management and Community-based Sanctions and Other Matters, Eighth Congress on the Prevention of Crime and the Treatment of Offenders, Havana, Cuba, 27 August-7 September 1990, U.N. Doc A/Conf.144/28, I.C.21.

United Nations Rules for the Protection of Juveniles Deprived of Their Liberty, G.A. Res. 45/113, 14 December 1990, 45 U.N. GAOR Supp. (No. 49A) 204, U.N. Doc. A/45/756.

United Nations Standard Minimum Rules for the Administration of Juvenile Justice (The Beijing Rules) [*adopted by* Seventh Congress on the Prevention of Crime and Treatment of Offenders, Milan, Italy, 26 August-6 September 1985, U.N. Doc. A/Conf./121/22/Rev.1 (1986)], G.A. Res. 40/33, 29 November 1985, 40 U.N. GAOR Supp. (No. 53) 206, U.N. Doc. A/40/881.

United Nations Resolution on Infection with Human Immunodeficiency Virus (HIV) and Acquired Immunodeficiency Syndrome (AIDS) in Prison, *adopted by* Eighth U.N. Congress on the Prevention of Crime and Treatment of Offenders, 27 August-7 September 1990, Havana, Cuba, U.N. Doc. A/Conf. 144/28/Rev. 1, I.C.18.

United Nations Resolution on Protection of the Human Rights of Victims of Crime and Abuse of Power, *adopted by* Eighth United Nations Congress on the Prevention of Crime and the Treatment of Offenders, Havana, Cuba, 27 August-7 September 1990, U.N. Doc. A/Conf. 144/28, I.C.27.

Universal Declaration of Human Rights, G.A. Res. 217A (III), 10 December 1948, 3 U.N. GAOR Supp. (No. 11A) 71, U.N. Doc. A/810, 7 (1948).

LIST OF ACRONYMS

A/	Document of the United Nations General Assembly
AI	Amnesty International
AIDS	Acquired Immune Deficiency Syndrome
AS	Anti-Slavery Society
CAT	Committee Against Torture
CEDAW	Committee on the Elimination of All Forms of Discrimination Against Woman
CERD	Convention on the Elimination of All Forms of Racial Discrimination; also Committee on the Elimination of Racial Discrimination
Conf.	Conference
DCI	Defence of Children International
Doc.	Document
E/	Document of the UN Economic and Social Council
E/CN.	Document symbol of the UN Commission on Human Rights
ECHR	European Commission on Human Rights
ESCOR	ECONOMIC AND SOCIAL COUNCIL OFFICIAL RECORDS
GA	General Assembly
GAOR	General Assembly Official Records
HIV	Human Immunodeficiency Virus
HRC	United Nations Human Rights Committee
HRI	Human Rights Instruments (a document series of the United Nations Centre for Human Rights)
IACHR	Inter-American Commission of Human Rights
IAPL	International Association of Penal Law
ICCPR	International Covenant on Civil and Political Rights
ICERD	International Covenant on the Elimination of Racial Discrimination
ICESCR	International Covenant on Economic, Social and Cultural Rights
ICJ	International Court of Justice; also International Commission of Jurists
ICRC	International Committee of the Red Cross
ILC	International Law Commission
ILM	International Legal Materials, published by the American Society of International Law
ILO	International Labour Organization
NGO	Non-governmental organization
Res.	Resolution
Rev.	Revised document, reissued for technical or other reasons
SPR	Special Rapporteur
SR	Summary records
Sub.	Subcommission on Prevention of Discrimination and Protection of Minorities

Supp.	Supplement
UN	United Nations
UNGA	United Nations General Assembly

Introduction

The United Nations Charter's formal recognition of individual human rights was the culmination of a long historic struggle. The Preamble of the Charter starts with these inspiring words:

> *We the peoples of the United Nations* determined to save succeeding generations from the scourge of war, which twice in our lifetime has brought untold sorrow to mankind, and to *reaffirm faith in fundamental human rights, in the dignity and worth of the human person, in the equal rights of men and women and of nations large and small, . . .*[1]

The United Nations' purposes also include significant references to human rights. As stated in Article I of the Charter they are:

1. To maintain international peace and security . . . ;

2. To develop friendly relations among nations based on respect for the *principle of equal rights and self- determination of peoples*, and to take other appropriate measures to strengthen universal peace;

3. To achieve international cooperation in solving international problems of an economic, social, cultural, or humanitarian character, and in *promoting and encouraging respect for human rights and for fundamental freedoms for all without distinction as to race, sex, language, or religion*; and

4. To be a center for harmonizing the actions of nations in the attainment of these common ends.[2]

The words of the Preamble and Article I concerning human rights are then given normative expression in Articles 55 and 56. Article 55 states:

> With a view to the creation of conditions of stability and well-being which are necessary for peaceful and friendly relations among nations based on *respect for the principle of equal rights and self-determination of peoples,* the United Nations shall promote:

---

[1]U.N. Charter, Preamble (emphasis added).

[2]*Id.* at Art. 1 (emphasis added).

a. higher standards of living, full employment, and conditions of economic and social progress and development;

b. solutions of international economic, social, health, and related problems; and international cultural and educational cooperation; and

c. *universal respect for, and observance of, human rights and fundamental freedoms for all without distinction as to race, sex, language, or religion.*[3]

Article 56 further states:

> All Members pledge themselves to take joint and separate action in cooperation with the Organization for the achievement of the purposes set forth in Article 55.[4]

These provisions unequivocally assert the existence, primacy and direct applicability of internationally protected human rights in those national legal systems that have ratified the Charter, irrespective of traditional claims of sovereignty. Thus, these provisions have put to rest the question of whether the individual is a subject of international law.

The San Francisco framers of the Charter in 1945 intended subsequent instruments to provide specific normative prescriptions concerning the meaning, content and application of the term "human rights." And the United Nations began the task of building a global framework with the adoption of the Universal Declaration of Human Rights in 1948 -- the "charter" of human rights.[5]

The Declaration, however, was adopted as a General Assembly Resolution and as such has no formal legally binding effect. However, the continued reiteration and reaffirmation of its principles in succeeding international instruments gave it an increasingly significant, though still questioned, legally enforceable status. Many scholars consider the Declaration to be legally binding because it constitutes part of the "general principles of international law," while more ardent human rights activists deem the Declaration to have reached the status of a *jus cogens.* At the other end of the spectrum, there are those who view it as a declaratory statement of principles without legally binding effect. This debate is largely academic and for a variety of reasons is beyond the scope

---

[3]*Id.* at Art. 55 (emphasis added).

[4]*Id.* at Art. 56 (emphasis added).

[5]Universal Declaration of Human Rights, G.A. Res. 217A (III), 10 December 1948, 3 GA Supp. (No. 11A) 71, U.N. Doc. A/810, 7 (1948).

of this Introduction. However, it is undeniable that the Declaration has inspired most of the subsequent normative prescriptions on the subject of human rights, particularly the International Covenant on Civil and Political Rights,[6] and the International Covenant on Economic, Social and Cultural Rights.[7]

The Declaration and the two Covenants are now commonly known as the "International Bill of Human Rights," making these instruments the constitutional framework of other international and regional human rights norms and standards. Indeed this international bill of rights has become the cornerstone for all subsequent norms and standards of individual human rights which provide content and specificity to a variety of more general human rights prescriptions.

This pattern of legal growth evidences an evolutionary process going from the more general to the more specific with each succeeding instrument building or relying on one or more of its predecessors. This process was neither systematic nor coherent. Instead it was the product of a variety of contingent factors. In retrospect, however, a certain pattern emerges, though it is much less the product of policy than the convergence of the world community's commonly shared values.

Nevertheless, this haphazard process can be somewhat systematized by examining the stages through which human rights principles, norms and standards have evolved. The stage of evolution of a given right reflects the significance that this right has attained in world community values. This pattern of emergence and development usually occurs in the following manner:

Stage 1 -- *The Enunciative Stage* -- The emergence and shaping of internationally perceived shared values through intellectual and social processes.

Stage 2 -- *The Declarative Stage* -- The declaration of certain identified human values, interests or rights expressed in broad generalities in an international instrument. This stage includes non-legally binding norms and standards, elaborated by international organs and bodies.

Stage 3 -- *The Prescriptive Stage* -- The articulation in prescriptive form of specific principles, norms and standards in an international instrument whether general or particular, developed by an international organ or body; or the elaboration of specific normative prescriptions in a binding international agreement.

Stage 4 -- *The Enforcement Stage* -- The development of enforcement modalities through general or particular conventions or other international instruments or procedural mechanisms, or a combination thereof.

Stage 5 -- *The Criminalization Stage* -- The development of international penal proscriptions as a means of criminalizing human rights violations of significant gravity.

---

[6]*See* G.A. Res. 2200A (XXI), 21 U.N. GAOR Supp. (No. 16) 52, U.N. Doc. A/6316 (1967).

[7]*See* G.A. Res. 2200 (XXI), 21 U.N. GAOR Supp. (No. 16) 49, U.N. Doc. 4/6316 (1966).

Rights in the declarative stage (Stage 2) are frequently framed in general terms. In the prescriptive stage (Stage 3), rights are more specifically articulated in general or particular international instruments, some of which have legally binding effect. In the final stage (international criminalization) rights are expressed in particular international conventions exclusively criminalizing the violation of protected rights.

A particular human rights principle, norm or standard may not necessarily evolve through each of these stages or in the order listed above. Nevertheless, there is sufficient similarity in the pattern of development and evaluation of many international human rights principles, norms and standards to validate this classification.

The positioning of a given right at one of these stages is a function of the significance of the protected interest and the degree of protection that it requires. This process of legal development and evaluation is analogous to development in the national legal context where the shaping of social values is followed by the development of general or particular legal prescriptions, with, in most cases, the civil controls preceding criminalization.

Since the Charter's adoption, the United Nations' concern for violations of individual human rights has focused on the fundamental or basic rights to life, liberty, personal security and physical integrity. The Charter is thus appropriately considered the "first generation" of human rights. Indeed, without these basic individual human rights, collective social, economic and cultural rights cannot be achieved. Surely without these fundamental human rights democracy cannot exist. Thus, an inexorable nexus exists between human rights and democracy. Experience also proves that a genuine link exists between peace on the one hand and democracy and human rights on the other. This pursuit and preservation of peace and the security of humankind, the first stated purpose of the United Nations, necessitate the protection and implementation of human rights and its corollary of pluralistic democracy without which human rights cannot be effectively achieved.

Infringement of the fundamental human rights to life, liberty, personal security and physical integrity affect not only individual rights, but also have a negative impact on the quality of life, curtail democracy and, when they rise to a certain level, affect the peace and security of humankind. These infringements are a product of both state practices and policies involving national criminal processes when carried out under the color of law by public officials. Because the protection of these rights is basic and fundamental to others, they became known as the "first generation" of human rights.

The United Nations responded by progressively developing procedural norms and standards for the protection of the individual against national policies and practices which infringe upon basic and fundamental human rights in criminal justice processes.

The evolution of these procedural norms and standards, however, emerged from separate United Nations organs and bodies, acting in a quasi-legislative capacity. This body of work was not based on a coherent policy or a specific program. Rather, it was the work of different organs and bodies, at different times and places with little or no enunciation of their activities and without any coordination effort.

These norms and standards have been developing since 1948. They are the result of work by the General Assembly, the Economic and Social Council, the Commission on Human Rights, the Sub-Commission on the Prevention of Discrimination and Protection of Minorities, the Crime Prevention and Criminal Justice Branch, the (quinquennial) Congresses on Crime Prevention and the Treatment of Offenders and the World Health Organization.

These procedural norms and standards are embodied in the resolutions adopted by these United Nations organs and bodies. Most of these norms and standards have also been embodied in General Assembly resolutions and some of these resolutions have ripened into multilateral Conventions.[8]

The resolutions adopted by the United Nations organs and bodies, particularly those of the General Assembly, "are variously referred to as: "principles," "declarations," or "guidelines." However, there are no criteria for the selection of such labels. Thus, it is difficult to distinguish between the resolutions on that basis alone.

The legal significance of the procedural norms and standards, however, does not rest on their label, but on their cumulative effect, their interlocking relationships, and their recognition and acceptance by a large number of states even without binding legal obligation.

The moral force of commonly shared values by the world's major cultures and legal systems supports these norms and standards in a far more meaningful way than the formal recognition of legal enforceability that a treaty or custom may confer upon them. That is why most scholars view these norms and standards as an expression of "general principles of international law," emanating

---

[8]The United Nations has also developed a number of substantive human rights protections in many conventions that are not included in this Compendium of procedural norms and standards such as: the Genocide Convention, the *Apartheid* Convention, the conventions against slavery and slave-related practices, the conventions concerning the safety of international civil aviation, the conventions on the law of the sea prohibiting piracy, slave trafficking and drug trafficking, the conventions for the protection of the safety of maritime operations, the conventions for the protection of internationally protected persons including diplomatic agents and against the taking of hostages, and the various postal union conventions prohibiting unlawful use of the mails likely to endanger or cause harm to persons. In addition, other international conventions also protect persons during the course of armed conflicts and regulate the conduct of armed conflicts and the use of weapons. Lastly, customary international law provides substantive international protection for persons under the law of piracy, the regulation of armed conflicts, and the concept of "crimes against humanity." For a listing of these conventions see Appendix A.

from both their international legal source and their existence in the world's major legal systems.

Thus, the protection of basic individual human rights and fundamental freedoms has been recognized and applied in a more effective manner than they would have been in a classical approach, as binding legal sources of international law would have attributed to them.

The far-reaching and lasting contribution of the United Nations in the development of international legal norms and standards for the procedural protection of basic individual human rights has not, however, been the sole product of governments. In fact, it has been achieved, for the most part, in spite of many governments and with the grudging acceptance of many other governments.

Surprising as it may seem, most of these norms and standards developed by the United Nations actually originated with non-governmental organizations with the support of a few committed states. These states and a number of leading NGO's like the International Commission of Jurists, Amnesty International, the International Association of Penal Law, Defense of Children International, and the Anti-Slavery Society deserve the highest credit and recognition for their important contributions to thickening the veneer of civilization. Even though these basic human rights are still all too frequently denied - some on a massive scale - at least the basic norms and standards are now set in specific terms.

This compilation brings together, for the first time, all the relevant procedural norms and standards applicable to criminal processes, whether national, regional, or international. The instruments are systematically arranged. The listing is in chronological order by category, irrespective of the legal source of the given instrument and the United Nations organ or body which produced it. Some of these instruments are embodied in multilateral conventions binding on their signatory states. Others are still at the stage of resolutions. But these enunciated human rights may also be binding on states by their reaching the level of customary international law or "general principles of international law," or both.

The procedural instruments contained in this compilation are exhaustive, and some additional commentary and explanatory material is added on a selective basis, thus providing the reader with a single comprehensive source for all these norms and standards.

As the world community's commonly shared values coalesce around a basic human interest sought to be protected, we witness its inclusion in a more specific instrument, and, as the need and opportunity arises, the right is embodied in a legally binding international instrument or it receives the same level of recognition as part of customary international law or "general principles of international law." This dynamic evolutionary process has been on the move since the Universal Declaration of Human Rights.[9] It is likely to continue in the years to come, probably with a greater focus on implementation, now that the ideological confrontation between East and West has ended. However, the challenge of enforcement is likely to be greater than that of enunciating norms and standards. This decade will therefore witness an unprecedented vitality and growth of enforcement mechanisms and procedures. They too, like the elaboration of norms and standards, will undergo an evolutionary stage which is likely to culminate in the establishment of an international criminal court which will adjudicate the more serious depredations.

---

[9]*Supra* note 5.

A. PREVENTION OF DISCRIMINATION

Central to the notion of human rights is that of equality and non-discrimination, both in law and in practice. Indeed, achieving equality of treatment in and before the law has been a paramount goal of human rights activists for hundreds of years, even before the English Bill of Rights (1689), the United States Declaration of Independence (1776) and the U.S. Bill of Rights (1791), and the French Revolution and Declaration of the Rights of Man and the Citizen (1789).

This does not mean that *any* distinction between individuals in the law constitutes prohibited discrimination. Distinctions that are based on reasonable and objective criteria are not necessarily incompatible with human rights standards.

The United Nations has devoted much attention to codifying and further elaborating the principle of non-discrimination. Beginning with the Universal Declaration of Human Rights, drafted by the UN Commission on Human Rights and adopted by the General Assembly on 10 December 1948, the commitment to achieving non-discrimination through standard-setting and establishment of implementation machinery has been constant.

1. Universal Declaration of Human Rights (excerpts)

Article 1

All human beings are born free and equal in dignity and rights. They are endowed with reason and conscience and should act towards one another in a spirit of brotherhood.

Article 2

Everyone is entitled to all the rights and freedoms set forth in this Declaration, without distinction of any kind, such as race, colour, sex, language, religiòn, political or other opinion, national or social origin, property, birth or other status.

Furthermore, no distinction shall be made on the basis of the political, jurisdictional or international status of the country or territory to which a person belongs, whether it be independent, trust, non-selfgoverning or under any other limitation of sovereignty.

Article 7

All are equal before the law and are entitled without any discrimination to equal protection of the law. All are entitled to equal protection against any discrimination in violation of this Declaration and against any incitement to such discrimination.

Article 10

Everyone is entitled in full equality to a fair and public hearing by an independent and impartial tribunal, in the determination of his rights and obligations and of any criminal charge against him.

* * *

2. United Nations Declaration on the Elimination of All Forms of Racial Discrimination (excerpts)

Article 7

1. Everyone has the right to equality before the law and to equal justice under the law. Everyone, without distinction as to race, colour or ethnic origin has the right to security of person and protection by the State against violence or bodily harm, whether inflicted by government officials or by any individual, group or institution.

2. Everyone shall have the right to an effective remedy and protection against any discrimination he may suffer on the ground of race, colour or ethnic origin with respect to his fundamental rights and freedoms through independent national tribunals competent to deal with such matters.

* * *

3. International Convention on the Elimination of All Forms of Racial Discrimination (excerpts)

Article 5

In compliance with the fundamental obligations laid down in article 2 of this Convention, States Parties undertake to prohibit and to eliminate racial discrimination in all its forms and to guarantee the right of everyone, without distinction as to race, colour, or national or ethnic origin, to equality before the law, notably in the enjoyment of the following rights:

(a) The right to equal treatment before the tribunals and all other organs administering justice;

* * *

4. The International Covenant on Civil and Political Rights

Article 3

The States Parties to the present Covenant undertake to ensure the equal right of men and women to the enjoyment of all civil and political rights set forth in the present Covenant.

Article 26

All persons are equal before the law and are entitled without any discrimination to the equal protection of the law. In this respect, the law shall prohibit any discrimination and guarantee to all persons equal and effective protection against discrimination on any ground such as race, colour, sex, language, religion, political or other opinion, national or social origin, property, birth or other status.

* * *

5. Convention on the Elimination of All Forms of Discrimination against Women

Article 15

1. States Parties shall accord to women equality with men before the law.

2. States Parties shall accord to women, in civil matters, a legal capacity identical to that of men and the same opportunities to exercise that capacity. In particular, they shall give women equal rights to conclude contracts and to administer property and shall treat them equally in all stages of procedure in courts and tribunals.

3. States Parties agree that all contracts and all other private instruments of any kind with a legal effect which is directed at restricting the legal capacity of women shall be deemed null and void.

4. States Parties shall accord to men and women the same rights with regard to the law relating to the movement of persons and the freedom to choose their residence and domicile.

* * *

6. International Labour Conference Convention (No. 169) Concerning Indigenous and Tribal Peoples in Independent Countries

Part I. General Policy

Article 1

1. This Convention applies to:

(a) tribal peoples in independent countries whose social, cultural and economic conditions distinguish them from other sections of the national community, and whose status is regulated wholly or partially by their own customs or traditions or by special laws or regulations;

(b) peoples in independent countries who are regarded as indigenous on account of their descent from the populations which inhabited the country, or a geographical region to which the country belongs, at the time of conquest or colonization or the establishment of present state boundaries and who, irrespective of their legal status, retain some or all of their own social, economic, cultural and political institutions.

2. Self-identification as indigenous or tribal shall be regarded as a fundamental criterion for determining the groups to which the provisions of this Convention apply.

3. The use of the term "peoples" in this Convention shall not be construed as having any implications as regards the rights which may attach to the term under international law.

Article 3

1. Indigenous and tribal peoples shall enjoy the full measure of human rights and fundamental freedoms without hindrance or discrimination. The provisions

of the Convention shall be applied without discrimination to male and female members of these peoples.

2. No form of force or coercion shall be used in violation of the human rights and fundamental freedoms of the peoples concerned, including the rights contained in this Convention.

Article 9

1. To the extent compatible with the national legal system and internationally recognized human rights, the methods customarily practised by the peoples concerned for dealing with offences committed by their members shall be rejected.

2. The customs of these peoples in regard to penal matters shall be taken into consideration by the authorities and courts dealing with such cases.

Article 10

1. In imposing penalties laid down by general law on members of these peoples account shall be taken on their economic, social and cultural characteristics.

2. Preference shall be given to methods of punishment other than confinement in prison.

Article 12

The peoples concerned shall be safeguarded against the abuse of their rights and shall be able to take legal proceedings, either individually or through their representative bodies, for the effective protection of these rights. Measures shall be taken to ensure that members of these peoples can understand and be understood in legal proceedings, where necessary through the provision of interpretation or by other effective means.

* * *

7. Declaration on the Rights of Persons Belonging to National or Ethnic, Religious or Linguistic Minorities

Article 1

1. States shall protect the existence and the national or ethnic, cultural, religious and linguistic identity of minorities within their respective territories, and shall encourage conditions for the promotion of that identity.

2. States shall adopt appropriate legislative and other measures to achieve those ends.

Article 2

1. Persons belonging to national or ethnic, religious and linguistic minorities (hereinafter referred to as persons belonging to minorities) have the right to enjoy their own culture, to profess and practice their own religion, and to use their own language, in private and in public, freely and without interference or any form of discrimination.

2. Persons belonging to minorities have the right to participate effectively in cultural, religious, social, economic and public life.

3. Persons belonging to minorities have the right to participate effectively in decisions on the national and, where appropriate, regional level concerning the minority to which they belong or the regions in which they live, in a manner not incompatible with national legislation.

4. Persons belonging to minorities have the right to establish and maintain their own associations.

5. Persons belonging to minorities have the right to establish and maintain, without any discrimination, free and peaceful contacts with other members of their group, with persons belonging to other minorities, as well as contacts across frontiers with citizens of other States to whom they are related by national or ethnic, religious or linguistic ties.

Article 3

1. Persons belonging to minorities may exercise their rights including those as set forth in this Declaration individually as well as in community with other members of their group, without any discrimination.

2. No disadvantage shall result for any person belonging to a minority as the consequence of the exercise or non-exercise of the rights as set forth in this Declaration.

Article 4

1. States shall take measures where required to ensure that persons belonging to minorities may exercise fully and effectively all their human rights and fundamental freedoms without any discrimination and in full equality before the law.

2. States shall take measures to create favourable conditions to enable persons belonging to minorities to express characteristics and to develop their culture, language, religion, traditions and customs, except where specific practices are in violation of national law and contrary to international standards.

3. States should take appropriate measures so that, wherever possible, persons belonging to minorities have adequate opportunities to learn their mother tongue or to have instruction in their mother tongue.

4. States should, where appropriate, take measures in the field of education, in order to encourage knowledge of the history, traditions, language and culture of the minorities existing within their territory. Persons belonging to minorities should have adequate opportunities to gain knowledge of the society as a whole.

5. States should consider appropriate measures so that persons belonging to minorities may participate fully in the economic progress and development in their country.

Article 5

1. National policies and programmes shall be planned and implemented with due regard for the legitimate interests of persons belonging to minorities.

2. Programmes of cooperation and assistance among States should be planned and implemented with due regard for the legitimate interests of persons belonging to minorities.

Article 6

States should cooperate on questions relating to persons belonging to minorities, including exchange of information and experiences, in order to promote mutual understanding and confidence.

Article 7

States should cooperate in order to promote respect for the rights as set forth in this Declaration.

Article 8

1. Nothing in this Declaration shall prevent the fulfillment of international obligations of States in relation to persons belonging to minorities. In particular, States shall fulfil in good faith the obligations and commitments they have assumed under international treaties and agreements to which they are parties.

2. The exercise of the rights as set forth in this Declaration shall not prejudice the enjoyment by all persons of universally recognized human rights and fundamental freedoms.

3. Measures taken by States in order to ensure the effective enjoyment of the rights as set forth in this Declaration shall not *prima facie* be considered contrary to the principle of equality contained in the Universal Declaration of Human Rights.

4. Nothing in this Declaration may be construed as permitting any activity contrary to the purposes and principles of the United Nations, including sovereign equality, territorial integrity and political independence of States.

Article 9

The organs and specialized agencies of the United Nations system shall contribute to the full realization of the rights and principles as set forth in this Declaration, within their respective fields of competence.

* * *

8. General Comments Adopted by the Human Rights Committee

GENERAL COMMENT 4 *Article 3 (Thirteenth session, 1981)*

1. Article 3 of the Covenant requiring, as it does, States parties to ensure the equal rights of men and women to the enjoyment of all civil and political rights provided for in the Covenant, has been insufficiently dealt with in a considerable number of States reports and has raised a number of concerns, two of which may be highlighted.

2. Firstly, article 3, as articles 2 (1) and 26 in so far as those articles primarily deal with the prevention of discrimination on a number of grounds, among which sex is one, requires not only measures of protection but also affirmative action designed to ensure the positive enjoyment of rights. This cannot be done simply by enacting laws. Hence, more information has generally been required regarding the role of women in practice with a view to ascertaining what measures, in addition to purely legislative measures of protection, have been or are being taken to give effect to the precise and positive obligation under article 3 and to ascertain what progress is being made or what factors or difficulties are being met in this regard.

3. Secondly, the positive obligation undertaken by States parties under that article may itself have an inevitable impact on legislation or administrative measures specifically designed to regulate matters other than those dealt with in the Covenant but which may adversely affect rights recognized in the Covenant. One example, among others, is the degree to which immigration laws which distinguish between a male and a female citizen may or may not adversely affect the scope of the right of the woman to marriage to non-citizens or to hold public office.

4. The Committee, therefore, considers that it might assist States parties if special attention were given to a review by specially appointed bodies or institutions of laws or measures which inherently draw a distinction between men and women in so far as those laws or measures adversely affect the rights provided for in the Covenant and, secondly, that States parties should give specific information in their reports about all measures, legislative or otherwise, designed to implement their undertaking under this article.

5. The Committee considers that it might help the States parties in implementing this obligation, if more use could be made of existing means of international cooperation with a view to exchanging experience and organizing assistance in solving the practical problems connected with the ensurance of equal rights for men and women.

GENERAL COMMENT 18 *Non-discrimination (Thirty-seventh session, 1989)*

1. Non-discrimination, together with equality before the law and equal protection of the law without any discrimination, constitute a basic and general principle relating to the protection of human rights. Thus, article 2, paragraph 1, of the International Covenant on Civil and Political Rights obligates each State party to respect and ensure to all persons within its territory and subject to its jurisdiction the right recognized in the Covenant without distinction of any kind, such as race, colour, sex, language, religion, political or other opinion, national or social origin, property, birth or other status. Article 26 not only entitles all persons to equality before the law as well as equal protection of the law but also prohibits equal and effective protection against discrimination on any ground such as race, colour, sex, language, religion, political or other opinion, national or social origin, property, birth or other status.

2. Indeed, the principle of non-discrimination is so basic that article 3 obligates each State party to ensure the equal right of men and women to the enjoyment of the rights set forth in the Covenant. While article 4, paragraph 1, allows States parties to take measures derogating from certain obligations under the Covenant in time of public emergency, the same article requires, *inter alia*, that those

measures should not involve discrimination solely on the ground of race, colour, sex, language, religion or social origin. Furthermore, article 20, paragraph 2, obligates States parties to prohibit, by law, any advocacy of national, racial or religious hatred which constitutes incitement to discrimination.

3. Because of their basic and general character, the principle of non-discrimination as well as that of equality before the law and equal protection of the law are sometimes expressly referred to in articles relating to particular categories of human rights. Article 14, paragraph 1, provides that all persons shall be equal before the courts and tribunals, and paragraph 3 of the same article provides that, in the determination of any criminal charge against him, everyone shall be entitled, in full equality, to the minimum guarantees enumerated in subparagraphs (a) to (g) of paragraph 3. Similarly, article 25 provides for the equal participation in public life of all citizens, without any of the distinctions mentioned in article 2.

4. It is for the States parties to determine appropriate measures to implement the relevant provision. However, the Committee is to be informed about the nature of such measures and their conformity with the principles of non-discrimination and equality before the law and equal protection of the law.

5. The Committee wishes to draw the attention of States parties to the fact that the Covenant sometimes expressly requires them to take measures to guarantee the equality of rights of the persons concerned. For example, article 23, paragraph 4, stipulates that States parties shall take appropriate steps to ensure equality of rights as well as responsibilities of spouses as to marriage, during marriage and at its dissolution. Such steps may take the form of legislative, administrative or other measures, but it is a positive duty of States parties to make certain that spouses have equal rights as required by the Covenant. In relation to children, article 24 provides that all children, without any discrimination as to race, colour, sex, language, religion, national or social origin, property or birth, have the right to such measures of protection as are required by their status as minors, on the part of their family, society and the State.

6. The Committee notes that the Covenant neither defines the term "discrimination" nor indicates what constitutes discrimination. However, article 1 of the International Convention on the Elimination of All Forms of Racial Discrimination provides that the term "racial discrimination" shall mean any distinction, exclusion, restriction or preference based on race, colour, descent, or national or ethnic origin which has the purpose or effect of nullifying or impairing the recognition, enjoyment or exercise, on an equal footing, of human rights and fundamental freedoms in the political, economic, social, cultural or any other field of public life. Similarly, article 1 of the Convention on the Elimination of All Forms of Discrimination against Women provides that "discrimination against

women" shall mean any distinction, exclusion or restriction made on the basis of sex which has the effect or purpose of impairing or nullifying the recognition, enjoyment or exercise by women, irrespective of their marital status, on a basis of equality of men and women, of human rights and fundamental freedoms in the political, economic, social, cultural, civil or any other field.

7. While these conventions deal only with cases of discrimination on specific grounds, the Committee believes that the term "discrimination" as used in the Covenant should be understood to imply any distinction, exclusion, restriction or preference which is based on any ground such as race, colour, sex, language, religion, political or other opinion, national or social origin, property, birth or other status, and which has the purpose or effect of nullifying or impairing the recognition, enjoyment or exercise by all persons, on an equal footing, of all rights and freedoms.

8. The enjoyment of rights and freedoms on an equal footing, however, does not mean identical treatment in every instance. In this connection, the provisions of the Covenant are explicit. For example, article 6, paragraph 5, prohibits the death sentence from being imposed on persons below 18 years of age. The same paragraph prohibits that sentence from being carried out on pregnant women. Similarly, article 10, paragraph 3, requires the segregation of juvenile offenders from adults. Furthermore, article 25 guarantees certain political rights, differentiating on grounds of citizenship.

9. Reports of many States parties contain information regarding legislative as well as administrative measures and court decisions which relate to protection against discrimination in law, but they very often lack information which would reveal discrimination in act. When reporting on articles 2 (1), 3 and 26 of the Covenant, States parties usually cite provisions of their constitution or equal opportunity laws with respect to equality of persons. While such information is of course useful, the Committee wishes to know if there remain any problems of discrimination in fact, which may be practised either by public authorities, by the community, or by private persons or bodies. The Committee wishes to be informed about legal provisions and administrative measures directed at diminishing or eliminating such discrimination.

10. The Committee also wishes to point out that the principle of equality sometimes requires States parties to take affirmative action in order to diminish or eliminate conditions which cause or help to perpetuate discrimination prohibited by the Covenant. For example, in a State where the general conditions of a certain part of the population prevent or impair their enjoyment of human rights, the State should take specific action to correct these conditions. Such action may involve granting for a time to the part of the population concerned certain preferential treatment in specific matters as compared with the rest of the

population. However, as long as such action is needed to correct discrimination in fact, it is a case of legitimate differentiation under the Covenant.

11. Both article 2, paragraph 1, and article 26 enumerate grounds of discrimination such as race, colour, sex, language, religion, political or other opinion, national or social origin, property, birth or other status. The Committee has observed that in a number of constitutions and laws not all the grounds on which discrimination is prohibited, as cited in article 2, paragraph 1, are enumerated. The Committee would therefore like to receive information from States parties as to the significance of such omissions.

12. While article 2 limits the scope of the rights to be protected against discrimination to these provided for in the covenant, article 26 does not specify such limitations. That is to say, article 26 provides that all persons are equal before the law and are entitled to equal protection of the law without discrimination, and that the law shall guarantee to all person equal and effective protection against discrimination on any of the enumerated grounds. In the view of the Committee, article 26 does not merely duplicate the guarantee already provided for in article 2 but provides in itself any autonomous right. It prohibits discrimination in law or in fact in any field regulated and protected by public authorities. Article 26 is therefore concerned with the obligations imposed on States parties in regard to their legislation and the application thereof. Thus, when legislation is adopted by a State party, it must comply with the requirement of article 26 that its content should not be discriminatory. In other words, the application of the principles of non-discrimination contained in article 26 is not limited to those rights which are provided for in the Covenant.

13. Finally, the Committee observes that not every differentiation of treatment will constitute discrimination, if the criteria for such differentiation are reasonable and objective and if the aim is to achieve a purpose which is legitimate under the Covenant.

* * *

B. STATELESSNESS AND REFUGEES

The Universal Declaration of Human Rights already signals the concern of the international community over the rights of the homeless. Articles 14 and 15 represent a goal that, unfortunately, is still far from being achieved.

Indeed, when the drafters of the International Covenant on Civil and Political Rights started discussing the issues of refugees and asylum, no consensus could be found and no article on the right to asylum was adopted.

The most important guarantees of the rights of refugees and stateless persons are to be found in two specific Conventions that have achieved considerable universality.

The Declaration on the Human Rights of Individuals Who are not Nationals of the Country in which They Live, adopted by the General Assembly in 1985, provides yet another expression of the goal to grant aliens equal rights in the administration of justice.

1. Universal Declaration of Human Rights

Article 14

1. Everyone has the right to seek and to enjoy in other countries asylum from persecution.

2. This right may not be invoked in the case of prosecutions genuinely arising from non-political crimes or from acts contrary to the purposes and principles of the United Nations.

Article 15

1. Everyone has the right to a nationality.

2. No one shall be arbitrarily deprived of his nationality nor denied the right to change his nationality.

2. International Convention on Civil and Political Rights

Article 13

An alien lawfully in the territory of a State Party to the present Covenant may be expelled therefrom only in pursuance of a decision reached in accordance with law and shall, except where compelling reasons of national security otherwise require, be allowed to submit the reasons against his expulsion and to have his case reviewed by, and be represented for the purpose before, the competent authority or a person or persons especially designated by the competent authority.

3. Convention Relating to the Status of Refugees

Article 16 - Access to courts

1. A refugee shall have free access to the courts of law on the territory of all Contracting States.

2. A refugee shall enjoy in the Contracting State in which he has his habitual residence the same treatment as a national in matters pertaining to access to the courts, including legal assistance and exemption from *cautio judicatum solvi.*

3. A refugee shall be accorded in the matters referred to in paragraph 2 in countries other than that in which he has his habitual residence the treatment granted to a national of the country of his habitual residence.

4. Convention Relating to the Status of Stateless Persons

Article 16 - Access to courts

1. A stateless person shall have free access to the courts of law on the territory of all Contracting States.

2. A stateless person shall enjoy in the Contracting State in which he has his habitual residence the same treatment as a national in matters pertaining to access to the courts, including legal assistance and exemption from [*cautio judicatum solvi*].

3. A stateless person shall be accorded in the matters referred to in paragraph 2 in countries other than that in which he has his habitual residence the treatment granted to a national of the country of his habitual residence.

5. General Comments of the Human Rights Committee

General Comment 15 *(Twenty-seventh session, 1986)*
The position of aliens under the Covenant

1. Reports from States parties have often failed to take into account that each State party must ensure the rights in the Covenant to "all individuals within its territory and subject to its jurisdiction" (art. 2, para. 1). In general, the rights set forth in the Covenant apply to everyone, irrespective of reciprocity, and irrespective of his or her nationality or statelessness.

2. Thus, the general rule is that each one of the rights of the Covenant must be guaranteed without discrimination between citizens and aliens. Aliens receive the benefit of the general requirement of non-discrimination in respect of the rights guaranteed in the Covenant, as provided for in article 2 thereof. This guarantee applies to aliens and citizens alike. Exceptionally, some of the rights recognized in the Covenant are expressly applicable only to citizens (art. 25), while article 13 applies only to aliens. However, the Committee's experience in examining reports show that in a number of countries other rights that aliens should enjoy under the Covenant are denied to them or are subject to limitations that cannot always be justified under the Covenant.

3. A few constitutions provide for equality of aliens with citizens. Some constitutions adopted more recently carefully distinguish fundamental rights that apply to all and those granted to citizens only, and deal with each in detail. In many States, however, the constitutions are drafted in terms of citizens only when granting relevant rights. Legislation and case law may also play an important part in providing for the rights of aliens. The Committee has been informed that in some States fundamental rights, though not guaranteed to aliens by the Constitution or other legislation, will also be extended to them as required by the Covenant. In certain cases, however, there has clearly been a failure to implement Covenant rights without discrimination in respect of aliens.

4. The Committee considers that in their reports States parties should give attention to the position of aliens, both under their law and in actual practice. The Covenant gives aliens all the protection regarding rights guaranteed therein, and its requirements should be observed by States parties in their legislation and in practice as appropriate. The position of aliens would thus be considerably

improved. States parties should ensure that the provisions of the Covenant and the rights under it are made known to aliens within their jurisdiction.

5. The Covenant does not recognize the right of aliens to enter or reside in the territory of a State party. It is in principle a matter for the State to decide who it will admit to its territory. However, in certain circumstances an alien may enjoy the protection of the Covenant even in relation to entry or residence, for example, when considerations of non-discrimination, prohibition of inhuman treatment and respect for family life arise.

6. Consent for entry may be given subject to conditions relating, for example, to movement, residence and employment. A State may also impose general conditions upon an alien who is in transit. However, once aliens are allowed to enter the territory of a State party they are entitled to the rights set out in the Covenant.

7. Aliens thus have an inherent right to life, protected by law, and may not be arbitrarily deprived of life. They must not be subjected to torture or to cruel, inhuman or degrading treatment or punishment; nor may they be held in slavery or servitude. Aliens have the full right to liberty and security of the person. If lawfully deprived of their liberty, they shall be treated with humanity and with respect for the inherent dignity of their person. Aliens may not be imprisoned for failure to fulfil a contractual obligation. They have the right to liberty of movement and free choice of residence; they shall be free to leave the country. Aliens shall be equal before the courts and tribunals, and shall be entitled to a fair and public hearing by a competent, independent and impartial tribunal established by law in the determination of any criminal charge or of rights and obligations in a suit at law. Aliens shall not be subjected to retrospective penal legislation, and are entitled to recognition before the law. They may not be subjected to arbitrary or unlawful interference with their privacy, family, home or correspondence. They have the right to freedom of thought, conscience and religion, and the right to hold opinions and to express them. Aliens receive the benefit of the right of peaceful assembly and of freedom of association. They may marry when at marriageable age. Their children are entitled to those measures of protection required by their status as minors. In those cases where aliens constitute a minority within the meaning of article 27, they shall not be denied the right, in community with other members of their group, to enjoy their own culture, to profess and practice their own religion and to use their own language. Aliens are entitled to equal protection by the law. There shall be no discrimination between aliens and citizens in the application of these rights. These rights of aliens may be qualified only by such limitations as may be lawfully imposed under the Covenant.

8. Once an alien is lawfully within a territory, his freedom of movement within the territory and his right to leave that territory may only be restricted in accordance with article 12, paragraph 3. Differences in treatment in this regard between aliens and nationals, or between different categories of aliens, need to be justified under article 12, paragraph 3. Since such restrictions must, *inter alia*, be consistent with the other rights recognized in the Covenant, a State party cannot, by restraining an alien or deporting him to a third country arbitrarily prevent his return to his own country (art. 12, para. 4).

9. Many reports have given insufficient information on matters relevant to article 13. That article is applicable to all procedures aimed at the obligatory departure of an alien, whether described in national law as expulsion or otherwise. If such procedures entail arrest, the safeguards of the Covenant relating to deprivation of liberty (arts. 9 and 10) may also be applicable. If the arrest is for the particular purpose of extradition, other provisions of national and international law may apply. Normally an alien who is expelled must be allowed to leave for any country that agrees to take him. The particular rights of article 13 only protect those aliens who are lawfully in the territory of a State party. This means that national law concerning the requirements for entry and stay must be taken into account in determining the scope of that protection, and that illegal entrants and aliens who have stayed longer than the law or their permits allow, in particular, are not covered by its provisions. However, if the legality of an alien's entry or stay is in dispute, any decision on this point leading to his expulsion or deportation ought to be taken in accordance with article 13.

It is for the competent authorities of the State party, in good faith and in the exercise of their powers, to apply and interpret the domestic law, observing, however, such requirements under the Covenant as equality before the law (art. 26).

10. Article 13 directly regulates only the procedure and not the substantive grounds for expulsion. However, by allowing only those carried out "in pursuance of a decision reached in accordance with law," its purpose is clearly to prevent arbitrary expulsions. On the other hand, it entitles each alien to a decision in his own case and, hence, article 13 would not be satisfied with laws or decisions providing for collective or mass expulsions. This understanding, in the opinion of the Committee, is confirmed by further provisions concerning the right to submit reasons against expulsion and to have the decision reviewed by and to be represented before the competent authority or someone designated by it. An alien must be given full facilities for pursuing his remedy against expulsion so that this right will in all the circumstances of his case be an effective one. The principles of article 13 relating to appeal against expulsion and the entitlement to review by a competent authority may only be departed from when compelling reasons of national security" so require. Discrimination

may not be made between different categories of aliens in the application of article 13.

* * *

6. Declaration on the Human Rights of Individuals Who are not Nationals of the Country in which They Live

Article 5

1. Aliens shall enjoy, in accordance with domestic law and subject to the relevant international obligation of the State in which they are present, in particular the following rights:

(a) The right to life and security of person; no alien shall be subjected to arbitrary arrest or detention; no alien shall be deprived of his or her liberty except on such grounds and in accordance with such procedures as are established by law;

. . .

(c) The right to be equal before the courts, tribunals and all other organs and authorities administering justice and, when necessary, to free assistance of an interpreter in criminal proceedings and, when prescribed by law, other proceedings.

* * *

C. PRINCIPLES OF LEGALITY

Fundamental principles of legality are laid down both in the Universal Declaration and in the International Covenant on Civil and Political Rights, in articles 6 and 16 respectively: "Everyone has the right to recognition everywhere as a person before the law". Another crucial principle of legality, well known and cited since the days of Roman Law, concerns the non-retroactivity of criminal legislation, in other words, the prohibition of *ex post facto* criminal statutes (*nullum crimen sine lege, nulla poena sine lege*).

Other principles of legality, such as the presumption of innocence and the prohibition of double jeopardy (*ne bis in idem*) are similarly anchored in these instruments. They are dealt with in Section F below, "Right to a Fair Trial".

1. Universal Declaration of Human Rights

Article 11

2. No one shall be held guilty of any penal offence on account of any act or omission which did not constitute a penal offence, under national or international law, at the time when it was committed. Nor shall a heavier penalty be imposed than the one that was applicable at the time the penal offence was committed.

2. International Covenant On Civil and Political Rights

Article 15

1. No one shall be held guilty of any criminal offence on account of any act or omission which did not constitute a criminal offence, under national or international law, at the time when it was committed. Nor shall a heavier penalty be imposed than the one that was applicable at the time when the criminal offence was committed. If, subsequent to the commission of the offence, provision is made by law for the imposition of the lighter penalty, the offender shall benefit thereby.

2. Nothing in this article shall prejudice the trial and punishment of any person for any act or omission which, at the time when it was committed, was criminal according to the general principles of law recognized by the community of nations.

* * *

D. RIGHT TO LIFE AND FREEDOM FROM CRUEL AND UNUSUAL PUNISHMENT

The supreme human right is indubitably the right to life, and all other rights are subordinate to it. This right is enunciated in the Universal Declaration of Human Rights and in the International Covenant on Civil and Political Rights.

Moreover, deprivation of life is the ultimate denial of human dignity. This is why article 6, paragraph 2, of the Covenant provides that in those countries which have not abolished the death penalty, a "sentence of death may be imposed only for the most serious crimes in accordance with the law in force at the time of the commission of the crime and not contrary to the provisions of the present Covenant and to the Convention on the Prevention and Punishment of the Crime of Genocide."

A general trend toward the abolition of the death penalty is reflected in the adoption of the Second Optional Protocol to the International Covenant on Civil and Political Rights[1] by the United Nations General Assembly. This Protocol entered into force in 1991 and 18 States have become parties as of August 1993.

Unfortunately, this trend is being implemented only very slowly. In a paper dated 28 June 1993 and submitted to the United Nations Sub-Commission on Prevention of Discrimination and Protection of Minorities,[2] Amnesty International lists 103 countries which retain and use the death penalty for ordinary crimes. In a separate annex, it lists 16 countries which provide for the death penalty only for exceptional crimes such as crimes under military law or crimes committed in exceptional circumstances such as wartime.[3] In the report of the United Nations Secretary-General on Capital Punishment, presented to the Second - regular session of ECOSOC in 1990, 91 countries are listed as retaining and using the death penalty for ordinary crimes.[4]

---

[1]G.A. Res. No. 44/128, 15 December 1989.

[2]E/CN.4/Sub.2/1993/WG.1/CRP 2.

[3]*See* the recent Amnesty International publication: When the State kills... the death penalt v. human rights, London, 1989.

[4]E/1990/38/Rev.1/Corr.1. The United Nations Crime Prevention Branch in Vienna, howeve indicates that this list only includes those States that responded to UN inquiries, and that th number of States retaining capital punishment may be higher.

Torture is a scourge of humanity, the prohibition of which constitutes a high priority for all civilized men and women. Although lawyers affirm that the prohibition of torture has become *jus cogens*, as indeed torture is prohibited in numerous international instruments as well as in the municipal law of most countries, it still continues to be practised.

Summary executions have led the UN Commission on Human Rights to appoint a Special Rapporteur to investigate this practice and periodically report to the Commission. Also, the *Nacht und Nebel* practice of enforced or involuntary disappearances have led the Commission on Human Rights to establish a Working Group on Enforced or Involuntary Disappearances. Recent reports are included in this Compendium.

1. Universal Declaration of Human Rights

Article 3

Everyone has the right to life, liberty and security of person.

Article 5

No one shall be subjected to torture or to cruel, inhuman or degrading treatment or punishment.

* * *

2. International Covenant on Civil and Political Rights

Article 6

1. Every human being has the inherent right to life. This right shall be protected by law. No one shall be arbitrarily deprived of his life.

2. In countries which have not abolished the death penalty, sentence of death may be imposed only for the most serious crimes in accordance with the law in force at the time of the commission of the crime and not contrary to the provisions of the present Covenant and to the Convention on the Prevention and Punishment of the Crime of Genocide. This penalty can only be carried out pursuant to a final judgment rendered by a competent court.

3. When deprivation of life constitutes the crime of genocide, it is understood that nothing in this article shall authorize any State Party to the present Covenant to derogate in any way from any obligation assumed under the provisions of the Convention on the Prevention and Punishment of the Crime of Genocide.

4. Anyone sentenced to death shall have the right to seek pardon or commutation of the sentence. Amnesty, pardon or commutation of the sentence of death may be granted in all cases.

5. Sentence of death shall not be imposed for crimes committed by persons below 18 years of age and shall not be carried out on pregnant women.

6. Nothing in this article shall be invoked to delay or to prevent the abolition of capital punishment by any State Party to the present Covenant.

Article 7

No one shall be subjected to torture or to cruel, inhuman or degrading treatment or punishment. In particular, no one shall be subjected without his free consent to medical or scientific experimentation.

Article 10

1. All persons deprived of their liberty shall be treated with humanity and with respect for the inherent dignity of the human person.

2. (a) Accused persons shall, save in exceptional circumstances, be segregated from convicted persons and shall be subject to separate treatment appropriate to their status as unconvicted persons;

   (b) Accused juvenile persons shall be separated from adults and brought as speedily as possible for adjudication.

3. The penitentiary system shall comprise treatment of prisoners the essential aim of which shall be their reformation and social rehabilitation. Juvenile offenders shall be segregated from adults and be accorded treatment appropriate to their age and legal status.

* * *

3. General Comments of the Human Rights Committee of the International Covenant on Civil and Political Rights

GENERAL COMMENT 6 *Article 6 (Sixteenth session, 1982)*

1.The right to life enunciated in article 6 of the Covenant has been dealt with in all State reports. It is the supreme right from which no derogation is permitted even in time of public emergency which threatens the life of the nation (art. 4). However, the Committee has noted that quite often the information given concerning article 6 was limited to only one or other aspect of this right. It is a right which should not be interpreted narrowly.

2.The Committee observes that war and other acts of mass violence continue to be a scourge of humanity and take the lives of thousands of innocent human beings every year. Under the Charter of the United Nations the threat or use of force by any State against another State, except in exercise of the inherent right of self-defence, is already prohibited. The Committee considers that States have the supreme duty to prevent wars, acts of genocide and other acts of mass violence causing arbitrary loss of life. Every effort they make to avert the danger of war, especially thermonuclear war, and to strengthen international peace and security would constitute the most important condition and guarantee for the safeguarding of the right to life. In this respect, the Committee notes, in particular, a connection between article 6 and article 20, which states that the law shall prohibit any propaganda for war (para. 1) or incitement to violence (para. 2) as therein described.

3.The protection against arbitrary deprivation of life, which is explicitly required by the third sentence of article 6 (1), is of paramount importance. The Committee considers that States parties should take measures not only to prevent and punish deprivation of lifc by criminal acts, but also to prevent arbitrary killing by their own security forces. The deprivation of life by the authorities of the State is a matter of the utmost gravity. Therefore, the law must strictly control and limit the circumstances in which a person may be deprived of his life by such authorities.

4.States parties should also take specific and effective measures to prevent the disappearance of individuals, something which unfortunately has become all too frequent and leads too often to arbitrary deprivation of life. Furthermore, States should establish effective facilities and procedures to investigate thoroughly cases of missing and disappeared persons in circumstances which may involve a violation of the right to life.

5.Moreover, the Committee has noted that the right to life has been too often narrowly interpreted. The expression "inherent right to life" cannot properly be understood in a restrictive manner, and the protection of this right requires that States adopt positive measures. In this connection, the Committee considers that it would be desirable for States parties to take all possible measures to reduce infant mortality and to increase life expectancy, especially in adopting measures to eliminate malnutrition and epidemics.

6. While it follows from article 6 (2) to (6) that States parties are not obliged to abolish the death penalty totally they are obliged to limit its use and, in particular, to abolish it for other than the "most serious crimes." Accordingly, they ought to consider reviewing their criminal laws in this light and, in any event, are obliged to restrict the application of the death penalty to the "most serious crimes". The article also refers generally to abolition in terms which strongly suggest (paras. 2 (2) and (6)) that abolition is desirable. The Committee concludes that all measures of abolition should be considered as progress in the enjoyment of the right to life within the meaning of article 40, and should as such be reported to the Committee. The Committee notes that a number of States have already abolished the death penalty or suspended its application. Nevertheless, States' reports show that progress made towards abolishing or limiting the application of the death penalty is quite inadequate.

7. The Committee is of the opinion that the expression "most serious crimes" must be read restrictively to mean that the death penalty should be a quite exceptional measure. It also follows from the express terms of article 6 that it can only be imposed in accordance with the law in force at the time of the commission of the crime and not contrary to the Covenant. The procedural guarantees therein prescribed must be observed, including the right to a fair hearing by an independent tribunal, the presumption of innocence, the minimum guarantees for the defence, and the right to review by a higher tribunal. These rights are applicable in addition to the particular right to seek pardon or commutation of the sentence.

GENERAL COMMENT 20 *Article 7 (Forty-fourth session, 1992)*

1. This general comment replaces general comment 7 (sixteenth session, 1982) reflecting and further developing it.

2. The aim of the provisions of article 7 of the International Covenant on Civil and Political Rights is to protect both the dignity and the physical and mental integrity of the individual. It is the duty of the State party to afford everyone protection through legislative and other measures as may be necessary against the acts prohibited by article 7, whether inflicted by people acting in their official capacity, outside their official capacity or in a private capacity. The prohibition in article 7 is complemented by the positive requirements of article 10, paragraph

1, of the Covenant, which stipulates that "All persons deprived of their liberty shall be treated with humanity and with respect for the inherent dignity of the human person."

3. The text of article 7 allows of no limitation. The Committee also reaffirms that, even in situations of public emergency such as those referred to in article 4 of the Covenant, no derogation from the provision of article 7 is allowed and its provisions must remain in force. The Committee likewise observes that no justification or extenuating circumstances may be invoked to excuse a violation of article 7 for any reasons, including those based on an order from a superior officer or public authority.

4. The Covenant does not contain any definition of the concepts covered by article 7, nor does the Committee consider it necessary to draw up a list of prohibited acts or to establish sharp distinctions between the different kinds of punishment or treatment; the distinctions depend on the nature, purpose and severity of the treatment applied.

5. The prohibition in article 7 relates not only to acts that cause physical pain but also to acts that cause mental suffering to the victim. In the Committee's view, moreover, the prohibition must extend to corporal punishment, including excessive chastisement ordered as punishment for a crime or as an educative or disciplinary measure. It is appropriate to emphasize in this regard that article 7 protects, in particular, children, pupils and patients in teaching and medical institutions.

6. The Committee notes that prolonged solitary confinement of the detained or imprisoned person may amount to acts prohibited by article 7. As the Committee has stated in its general comment No. 6 (16), article 6 of the Covenant refers generally to abolition of the death penalty in terms that strongly suggest that abolition is desirable. Moreover, when the death penalty is applied by a State party for the most serious crimes, it must not only be strictly limited in accordance with article 6 but it must be carried out in such a way as to cause the least possible physical and mental suffering.

7. Article 7 expressly prohibits medical or scientific experimentation without the free consent of the person concerned. The Committee also observes that special protection in regard to such experiments is necessary in the case of persons not capable of giving valid consent, and in particular those under any form of detention or imprisonment. Such persons should not be subjected to any medical or scientific experimentation that may be detrimental to their health.

8. The Committee notes that it is not sufficient for the implementation of article 7 to prohibit such treatment or punishment or to make it a crime. States parties should inform the Committee of the legislative, administrative, judicial

and other measures they take to prevent and punish acts of torture and cruel, inhuman and degrading treatment in any territory under their jurisdiction.

9. In the view of the Committee, States parties must not expose individuals to the danger of torture or cruel, inhuman or degrading treatment or punishment upon return to another country by way of their extradition, expulsion or refoulement. States parties should indicate in their reports what measures they have adopted to that end.

10. The Committee should be informed how States parties disseminate, to the population at large, relevant information concerning the ban on torture and the treatment prohibited by article 7. Enforcement personnel, medical personnel, police officers and any other persons involved in the custody or treatment of any individual subjected to any form of arrest, detention or imprisonment must receive appropriate instruction and training. States parties should inform the Committee of the instruction and training given and the way in which the prohibition of article 7 forms an integral part of the operational rules and ethical standards to be followed by such persons.

11. In addition to describing steps to provide the general protection against acts prohibited under article 7 to which anyone is entitled, the State party should provide detailed information on safeguards for the special protection of particularly vulnerable persons. It should be noted that keeping under systematic review interrogation rules, instructions, methods and practices as well as arrangements for the custody and treatment of persons subjected to any form of arrest, detention or imprisonment is an effective means of preventing cases of torture and ill-treatment. To guarantee the effective protection of detained persons, provisions should be made for detainees to be held in places officially recognized as places of detention and for their names and places of detention, as well as for the names of persons responsible for their detention, to be kept in registers readily available and accessible to those concerned, including relatives and friends. To the same effect, the time and place of all interrogations should be recorded, together with the names of all those present and this information should also be available for purposes of judicial or administrative proceedings. Provisions should also be made against incommunicado detention. In that connection, States parties should ensure that any places of detention be free from any equipment liable to be used for inflicting torture or ill-treatment. The protection of the detainee also requires that prompt and regular access be given to doctors and lawyers and, under appropriate supervision when the investigation so requires, to family members.

12. It is important for the discouragement of violations under article 7 that the law must prohibit the use of admissibility in judicial proceedings of statements or confessions obtained through torture or other prohibited treatment.

13. States parties should indicate when presenting their reports the provisions of their criminal law which penalize torture and cruel, inhuman and degrading treatment or punishment, specifying the penalties applicable to such acts, whether committed by public officials or other persons acting on behalf of the State, or by private persons. Those who violate article 7, whether by encouraging, ordering, tolerating or perpetrating prohibited acts, must be held responsible. Consequently, those who have refused to obey orders must not be punished or subjected to any adverse treatment.

14. Article 7 should be read in conjunction with article 2, paragraph 3, of the Covenant. In their reports, States parties should indicate how their legal system effectively guarantees the immediate termination of all the acts prohibited by article 7 as well as appropriate redress. The right to lodge complaints against maltreatment prohibited by article 7 must be recognized in the domestic law. Complaints must be investigated promptly and impartially by competent authorities so as to make the remedy effective. The reports of States parties should provide specific information on the remedies available to victims of maltreatment and the procedure that complainants must follow, and statistics on the number of complaints and how they have been dealt with.

15. The Committee has noted that some States have granted amnesty in respect of acts of torture. Amnesties are generally incompatible with the duty of States to investigate such acts; to guarantee freedom from such acts within their jurisdiction; and to ensure that they do not occur in the future. States may not deprive individuals of the right to an effective remedy, including compensation and such full rehabilitation as may be possible.

GENERAL COMMENT 21 *Article 10 (Forty-fourth session, 1992)*

1. Article 10, paragraph 1 of the Covenant provides that all persons deprived of their liberty shall be treated with humanity and with respect for the inherent dignity of the human person. However, by no means all the reports submitted by States parties have contained information on the way in which this paragraph of the article is being implemented. The Committee is of the opinion that it would be desirable for the reports of States parties to contain specific information on the legal measures designed to protect that right. The Committee also considers that reports should indicate the concrete measures being taken by the competent State organs to monitor the mandatory implementation of national legislation concerning the humane treatment and respect for the human dignity of all person deprived of their liberty that paragraph 1 requires.

The Committee notes, in particular, that paragraph 1 of this article is generally applicable to persons deprived of their liberty, whereas paragraph 2 deals with accused as distinct from convicted persons, and paragraph 3 with convicted persons only. This structure quite often is not reflected in the reports, which mainly have related to accused and convicted persons. The wording of paragraph 1, its context - especially its proximity to article 9, paragraph 1, which also deals with all deprivations of liberty - and its purpose support a broad application of the principles expressed in that provision. Moreover, the Committee recalls that this article supplements article 7 as regards the treatment of all persons deprived of their liberty.

The humane treatment and the respect for the dignity of all persons deprived of their liberty is a basic standard of universal application which cannot depend entirely on material resources. While the Committee is aware that in other respects the modalities and conditions of detention may vary with the available resources, they must always be applied without discrimination, as required by article 2 (1).

Ultimate responsibility for the observance of this principle rests with the State as regards all institutions where persons are lawfully held against their will, not only in prisons but also, for example, hospitals, detention camps or correctional institutions.

2. Subparagraph 2 (a) of the article provides that, save in exceptional circumstances, accused persons shall be segregated from convicted persons and shall receive separate treatment appropriate to their status as unconvicted persons. Some reports have failed to pay proper attention to this direct requirement of the Covenant and, as a result, to provide adequate information on the way in which the treatment of accused persons differs from that of convicted persons. Such information should be included in future reports.

Subparagraph 2 (b) of the article calls, *inter alia*, for accused juvenile persons to be separated from adults. The information in reports shows that a number of states are not taking sufficient account of the fact that this is an unconditional requirement of the Covenant. It is the Committee's opinion that, as is clear from the text of the Covenant, deviation from States parties' obligations under subparagraph 2 (b) cannot be justified by any consideration whatsoever.

3. In a number of cases, the information appearing in reports with respect to paragraph 3 of the article has contained no concrete mention either of legislative or administrative measures or of practical steps to promote the reformation and social rehabilitation of prisoners, by, for example, education, vocational training and useful work. Allowing visits, in particular by family members, is normally also such a measure which is required for reasons of humanity. There are also similar lacunae in the reports of certain States with respect to information

concerning juvenile offenders, who must be segregated from adults and given treatment appropriate to their age and legal status.

4. The Committee further notes that the principles of humane treatment and respect for human dignity set out in paragraph 1 are the basis for the more specific and limited obligation of States in the field of criminal justice set out in paragraphs 2 and 3 of article 10. The segregation of accused persons from convicted ones is required in order to emphasize their status as unconvicted persons who are at the same time protected by the presumption of innocence stated in article 14, paragraph 2. The aim of these provisions is to protect the groups mentioned, and the requirements contained therein should be seen in that light. Thus, for example, the segregation and treatment of juvenile offenders should be provided for in such a way that it promotes their reformation and social rehabilitation.

* * *

4. Declaration on the Protection of All Persons from Being Subjected to Torture and Other Cruel, Inhuman or Degrading Treatment or Punishment

Article 1

1. For the purpose of this Declaration, torture means any act by which severe pain or suffering, whether physical or mental, is intentionally inflicted by or at the instigation of a public official on a person for such purposes as obtaining from him or a third person information or confession, punishing him for an act he has committed or is suspected of having committed, or intimidating him or other persons. It does not include pain or suffering arising only from, inherent in or incidental to, lawful sanctions to the extent consistent with the Standard Minimum Rules for the Treatment of Prisoners.

2. Torture constitutes an aggravated and deliberate form of cruel, inhuman or degrading treatment or punishment.

Article 2

Any act of torture or other cruel, inhuman or degrading treatment or punishment is an offence to human dignity and shall be condemned as a denial of the purposes of the Charter of the United Nations and as a violation of the human rights and fundamental freedoms proclaimed in the Universal Declaration of Human Rights.

Article 3

No state may permit or tolerate torture or other cruel, inhuman or degrading treatment or punishment. Exceptional circumstances such as a state of war or a threat of war, internal political instability or any other public emergency may not be invoked as a justification of torture or other cruel, inhuman or degrading treatment or punishment.

Article 4

Each State shall, in accordance with the provisions of this Declaration, take effective measures to prevent torture and other cruel, inhuman or degrading treatment or punishment from being practised within its jurisdiction.

Article 5

The training of law enforcement personnel and of other public officials who may be responsible for persons deprived of their liberty shall ensure that full account is taken of the prohibition against torture and other cruel, inhuman or degrading treatment or punishment. This prohibition shall also, where appropriate, be included in such general rules or instructions as are issued in regard to the duties and functions of anyone who may be involved in the custody or treatment of such persons.

Article 6

Each State shall keep under systematic review interrogation methods and practices as well as arrangements for the custody and treatment of persons deprived of their liberty in its territory, with a view to preventing any cases of torture or other cruel, inhuman or degrading treatment or punishment.

Article 7

Each State shall ensure that all acts of torture as defined in Article 1 are offences under its criminal law. The same shall apply in regard to acts which constitute participation in, complicity in, incitement to or an attempt to commit torture.

Article 8

Any person who alleges that he has been subjected to torture or other cruel, inhuman or degrading treatment or punishment by or at the instigation of a public official shall have the right to complain to, and to have his case impartially examined by, the competent authorities of the State concerned.

Article 9

Wherever there is reasonable ground to believe that an act of torture as defined in Article 1 has been committed, the competent authorities of the State concerned shall promptly proceed to an impartial investigation even if there has been no formal complaint.

Article 10

If an investigation under Article 8 or Article 9 establishes that an act of torture as defined in article 1 appears to have been committed, criminal proceedings shall be instituted against the alleged offender or offenders in accordance with national law. If an allegation of other forms of cruel, inhuman or degrading treatment or punishment is considered to be well founded, the alleged offender or offenders shall be subject to criminal, disciplinary or other appropriate proceedings.

Article 11

Where it is proved that an act of torture or other cruel, inhuman or degrading treatment or punishment has been committed by or at the instigation of a public official, the victim shall be afforded redress and compensation in accordance with national law.

5. Convention against Torture and Other Cruel Inhuman or Degrading Treatment or Punishment

PART I

Article 1

1. For the purposes of this Convention, the term "torture" means any act by which severe pain or suffering, whether physical or mental, is intentionally inflicted on a person for such purposes as obtaining from him or a third person information or a confession, punishing him for an act he or a third person has committed or is suspected of having committed, or intimidating or coercing him or a third person, or for any reason based on discrimination of any kind, when such pain or suffering is inflicted by or at the instigation of or with the consent or acquiescence of a public official or other person acting in an official capacity. It does not include pain or suffering arising only from, inherent in or incidental to lawful sanctions.

2. This article is without prejudice to any international instrument or national legislation which does or may contain provisions of wider applications.

Article 2

1. Each State Party shall take effective legislative, administrative, judicial or other measures to prevent acts of torture in any territory under its jurisdiction.

2. No exceptional circumstances whatsoever, whether a state of war or a threat of war, internal political instability or any other public emergency, may be invoked as a justification of torture.

3. An order from a superior officer or a public authority may not be invoked as a justification of torture.

Article 3

1. No State Party shall expel, return ("*refouler*") or extradite a person to another State where there are substantial grounds for believing the he would be in danger of being subject to torture.

2. For the purpose of determining whether there are such grounds, the competent authorities shall take into account all relevant considerations including, where applicable, the existence in the State concerned of a consistent pattern of gross, flagrant or mass violations of human rights.

Article 4

1. Each State Party shall ensure that all acts of torture are offences under its criminal law. The same shall apply to an attempt to commit torture and to an act by any persons which constitutes complicity or participation in torture.

2. Each State Party shall make these offences punishable by appropriate penalties which take into account their grave nature.

Article 5

1. Each State Party shall take such measures as may be necessary to establish its jurisdiction over the offences referred to in article 4 in the following cases:

   (a) When the offences are committed in any territory under its jurisdiction or on board a ship or aircraft registered in that State;

   (b) When the alleged offender is a national of that State;

(c) When the victim is a national of that State if that State considers it appropriate.

2. Each State Party shall likewise take such measures as may be necessary to establish its jurisdiction over such offences in cases where the alleged offender is present in any territory under its jurisdiction and it does not extradite him pursuant to article 8 to any of the States mentioned in paragraph 1 of this article.

3. This Convention does not exclude any criminal jurisdiction exercised in accordance with internal law.

Article 6

1. Upon being satisfied, after an examination of information available to it, that the circumstances so warrant, any State Party in whose territory a person alleged to have committed any offence referred to in article 4 is present shall take him into custody or take other legal measures to ensure his presence. The custody and other legal measures shall be as provided in the law of that State but may be continued only for such time as necessary to enable any criminal or extraditing proceedings to be instituted.

2. Such State shall immediately make a preliminary inquiry into the facts.

3. Any person in custody pursuant to paragraph 1 of this article shall be assisted in communicating immediately with the nearest appropriate representative of the State of which he is a national, or, if he is a stateless person, with the representative of the State where he usually resides.

4. When a State, pursuant to this article, has taken a person into custody, it shall immediately notify the States referred to in article 5, paragraph 1, of the fact that such person is in custody and of the circumstances which warrant his detention. The State which makes the preliminary inquiry contemplated in paragraph 2 of this article shall promptly report its findings to the said States and shall indicate whether it intends to exercise jurisdiction.

Article 7

1. The State Party in the territory under whose jurisdiction a person alleged to have committed any offence referred to in article 4 is found shall, in the cases contemplated in article 5, if it does not extradite him, submit the case to its competent authorities for the purpose of prosecution.

2. These authorities shall take their decision in the same manner as in the case of any ordinary offence of a serious nature under the law of that State. In the

cases referred to in article 5, paragraph 2, the standards of evidence required for prosecution and conviction shall in no way be less stringent than those which apply in the cases referred to in article 5, paragraph 1.

3. Any person regarding whom proceedings are brought in connection with any of the offences referred to in article 4 shall be guaranteed fair treatment at all stages of the proceedings.

Article 10

1. Each State Party shall ensure that education and information regarding the prohibition against torture are fully included in the training of law enforcement personnel, civil or military, medical personnel, public officials and other persons who may be involved in the custody, interrogation or treatment of any individual subjected to any form of arrest, detention or imprisonment.

2. Each State Party shall include this prohibition in the rules or instructions issued in regard to the duties and functions of any such persons.

Article 11

Each State Party shall keep under systematic review interrogation rules, instructions, methods and practices as well as arrangements for the custody and treatment of persons subjected to any form of arrest, detention or imprisonment in any territory under its jurisdiction, with a view to preventing any cases of torture.

Article 12

Each State Party shall ensure that its competent authorities proceed to a prompt and impartial investigation, wherever there is reasonable ground to believe that an act of torture has been committed in any territory under its jurisdiction.

Article 13

Each State Party shall ensure that any individual who alleges he has been subjected to torture in any territory under its jurisdiction has the right to complain to, and to have his case promptly and impartially examined by, its competent authorities. Steps shall be taken to ensure that the complainant and witnesses are protected against all ill-treatment or intimidation as a consequence of his complaint or any evidence given.

Article 14

1. Each State Party shall ensure in its legal system that the victim of an act of torture obtains redress and has an enforceable right to fair and adequate compensation, including the means for as full rehabilitation as possible. In the event of the death of the victim as a result of an act of torture, his dependents shall be entitled to compensation.

2. Nothing in this article shall affect any right of the victim or other persons compensation which may exist under national law.

Article 15

Each State Party shall ensure that any statement which is established to have been made as a result of torture shall not be invoked as evidence in any proceedings, except against a person accused of torture as evidence that the statement was made.

Article 16

1. Each State Party shall undertake to prevent in any territory under its jurisdiction other acts of cruel, inhuman or degrading treatment or punishment which do not amount to torture as defined in article 1, when such acts are committed by or at the instigation of or with the consent or acquiescence of a public official or other person acting in an official capacity. In particular, the obligations contained in articles 10, 11, 12, and 13 shall apply with the substitution for references to torture of references to other forms of cruel, inhuman or degrading treatment or punishments.

2. The provisions of this Convention are without prejudicc to the provisions of any other international instrument or national law which prohibits cruel, inhuman or degrading treatment or punishment or which relates to extradition or expulsion.

PART II

Article 17

1. There shall be established a Committee against Torture (hereinafter referred to as the Committee) which shall carry out the functions hereinafter provided. The Committee shall consist of ten experts of high moral standing and recognized competence in the field of human rights,who shall serve in their personal capacity. The experts shall be elected by the States Parties, consider-

ations being given to equitable geographical distribution and to the usefulness of the participation of some persons having legal experience.

Article 20

1. If the Committee receives reliable information which appears to it to contain well-founded indications that torture is being systematically practised in the territory of a State Party, the Committee shall invite that State Party to co-operate in the examination of the information and to this end to submit observations with regard to the information concerned.

2. Taking into account any observations which may have been submitted by the State Party concerned, as well as any other relevant information available to it, the Committee may, if it decides that this is warranted, designate one or more of its members to make a confidential inquiry and to report to the Committee urgently.

3. If an inquiry is made in accordance with paragraph 2 of this article, the Committee shall seek the co-operation of the State Party concerned. In agreement with that State Party, such an inquiry may include a visit to its territory.

4. After examining the findings of its member or members submitted in accordance with paragraph 2 of this article, the Committee shall transmit these findings to the State Party concerned together with any comments or suggestions which seem appropriate in view of the situation.

5. All the proceedings of the Committee referred to in paragraphs 1 to 4 of this article shall be confidential, and at all stages of the proceedings the co-operation of the State Party shall be sought. After such proceedings have been completed with regard to an inquiry made in accordance with paragraph 2, the Committee may, after consultations with the State Party concerned, decide to include a summary account of the results of the proceedings in its annual report made in accordance with article 24.

6. Safeguards Guaranteeing Protection of the Rights of Those Facing the Death Penalty

1. In countries which have not abolished the death penalty, capital punishment may be imposed only for the most serious crimes, it being understood that their scope should not go beyond intentional crimes with lethal or other extremely grave consequences.

2. Capital punishment may be imposed only for a crime for which the death penalty is prescribed by law at the time of its commission, it being understood that if, subsequent to the commission of the crime, provision is made by law for the imposition of a lighter penalty, the offender shall benefit thereby.

3. Persons below 18 years of age at the time of the commission of the crime shall not be sentenced to death, nor shall the death sentence be carried out on pregnant women, or on new mothers, or on persons who have become insane.

4. Capital punishment may be imposed only when the guilt of the person charged is based upon clear and convincing evidence leaving no room for an alternative explanation of the facts.

5. Capital punishment may only be carried out pursuant to a final judgment rendered by a competent court after legal process which gives all possible safeguards to ensure a fair trial, at least equal to those contained in article 14 of the International Covenant on Civil and Political Rights, including the right of anyone suspected of or charged with a crime for which capital punishment may be imposed to adequate legal assistance at all stages of the proceedings.

6. Anyone sentenced to death shall have the right to appeal to a court of higher jurisdiction, and steps should be taken to ensure that such appeals shall become mandatory.

7. Anyone sentenced to death shall have the right to seek pardon, or commutation of sentence; pardon or commutation of sentence may be granted in all cases of capital punishment.

8. Capital punishment shall not be carried out pending any appeal or other recourse procedure or other proceeding relating to pardon or commutation of the sentence.

9. Where capital punishment occurs, it shall be carried out so as to inflict the minimum possible suffering.

* * *

7. Principles on the Effective Prevention and Investigation of Extra-legal, Arbitrary and Summary Excutions (excerpts)

1. Governments shall prohibit by law all extra-legal, arbitrary and summary executions and shall ensure that any such executions are recognized as offences under their criminal laws, and are punishable by appropriate penalties which take

into account the seriousness of such offences. Exceptional circumstances including a state of war or threat of war, internal political instability or any other public emergency may not be invoked as a justification of such executions. Such exceptions shall not be carried out under any circumstances including, but not limited to, situations of internal armed conflict, excessive or illegal use of force by a public official or other person acting in an official capacity or by a person acting at the instigation, or with the consent or acquiescence of such person, and situations in which deaths occur in custody. This prohibition shall prevail over decrees issued by governmental authority.

2. In order to prevent extra-legal, arbitrary and summary executions, Governments shall ensure strict control, including a clear chain of command over all officials responsible for apprehension, arrest, detention, custody and imprisonment, as well as those officials authorized by law to use force and firearms.

3. Governments shall prohibit orders from superior officers or public authorities authorizing or inciting other persons to carry out any such extra-legal, arbitrary or summary executions. All persons shall have the right and the duty to defy such orders. Training of law enforcement officials shall emphasize the above provisions.

4. Effective protection through judicial or other means shall be guaranteed to individuals and groups who are in danger of extra-legal, arbitrary or summary executions, including those who receive death threats.

5. No one shall be involuntarily returned or extradited to a country where there are substantial grounds for believing that he or she may become a victim of extra-legal, arbitrary or summary execution in that country.

6. Governments shall ensure that persons deprived of their liberty are held in officially recognized places of custody, and that accurate information on their custody and whereabouts, including transfers, is made promptly available to their relatives and lawyer or other persons of confidence.

7. Qualified inspectors, including medical personnel, or an equivalent independent authority, shall conduct inspections in places of custody on a regular basis, and be empowered to undertake unannounced inspections on their own initiative, with full guarantees of independence in the exercise of this function. The inspectors shall have unrestricted access to all persons in such places of custody, as well as to all their records.

8. Governments shall make every effort to prevent extra-legal, arbitrary and summary executions through measures such as diplomatic intercession, improved access of complainants to intergovernmental and judicial bodies, and public

denunciation. Intergovernmental mechanisms shall be used to investigate reports of any such executions and to take effective action against such practices. Governments, including those of countries where extra-legal, arbitrary and summary executions are reasonably suspected to occur, shall co-operate fully in international investigations on the subject.

LEGAL PROCEEDINGS

18. Governments shall ensure that persons identified by the investigation as having participated in extra-legal, arbitrary or summary executions in any territory under their jurisdiction are brought to justice. Governments shall either bring such persons to justice or co-operate to extradite any such persons to other countries wishing to exercise jurisdiction. This principle shall apply irrespective of who and where the perpetrators or the victims are, their nationalities or where the offence was committed.

19. Without prejudice to principle 3 above, an order from a superior officer or a public authority may not be invoked as a justification for extra-legal, arbitrary or summary executions. Superiors, officers or other public officials may be held responsible for acts committed by officials under their authority if they had a reasonable opportunity to prevent such acts. In no circumstances, including a state of war, siege or other public emergency, shall blanket immunity from prosecution be granted to any person allegedly involved in extra-legal, arbitrary or summary executions.

20. The families and dependents of victims of extra-legal, arbitrary or summary executions shall be entitled to fair and adequate compensation within a reasonable period of time.

8. Second Optional Protocol to the International Covenant on Civil and Political Rights, Aiming at the Abolition of the Death Penalty (excerpts)

Article 1

1. No one within the jurisdiction of a State Party to the present Protocol shall be executed.

2. Each State Party shall take all necessary measures to abolish the death penalty within its jurisdiction.

9. Question of the Violation of Human Rights and Fundamental Freedoms in Any Part of the World, with Particular Reference to Colonial and Other Dependent Countries and Territories

Summary or Arbitrary Executions

Report by the Special Rapporteur, Mr. S. Amos Wako, pursuant to Commission on Human Rights Resolution 1991/71 (excerpts)

B. Recommendations

648. On the basis of the experience in monitoring summary and arbitrary executions throughout the world for 10 years, the Special Rapporteur would like to make the following recommendations addressed to governments in general, to governments which have received his communications, to the international community and finally to the Centre for Human Rights.

1. General recommendations to governments

649. The Special Rapporteur would like to recommend to Governments in general:

(a) To ratify international human rights treaties relevant to the protection of the right to life, and to make such treaties and other relevant human rights instruments widely available, in particular those mentioned in Chapter II of this report;

(b) To review national law and practice with a view to ensuring full compatibility with such international human rights standards, and to provide appropriate training concerning the meaning and implementation of such standards to law enforcement, judicial, correctional and military personnel;

(c) To investigate rigorously any allegations concerning summary or arbitrary execution which may be presented, regardless of the status, position or office of those responsible, and to ensure that the responsible parties are prosecuted without delay, by an independent and impartial tribunal with full respect for the rights of the victims;

(d) To take all necessary measures to ensure the rapid and complete elimination of unnatural deaths in custody, whether due to torture, excessive use of force in controlling prisoners or lack of minimally adequate nutrition, sanitation and health care;

(e) To consider establishing an independent governmental body for the promotion, defence and protection of human rights with competence, *inter alia*, to monitor alleged human rights violations and to facilitate cooperation between the Government and the United Nations human rights bodies, as well as other relevant international, regional and national bodies;

(f) Where situations of internal armed conflict, disturbances or tensions exist, to cooperate fully with the International Committee of the Red Cross and to seek reconciliation, in appropriate cases, through the mediation of the United Nations or competent regional bodies;

(g) To make concerted, long-term efforts to eliminate the root causes of violence and intolerance, in particular economic injustice, totalitarian political ideologies, and racial, national, ethnic and religious prejudice.

3. Recommendations to the international community

651. The Special Rapporteur wishes to recommend to the international community:

(a) To ensure that governments requiring technical or material assistance in order to eliminate the causes of summary and arbitrary executions and strengthen national mechanisms for the protection of human rights are provided with effective and appropriate assistance, either through United Nations programmes and bodies or bilaterally, in particular in improving the capacity for forensic investigation, increasing the efficiency, professionalism and independence of the administration of justice and in the modernization of correctional systems;

(b) To make every possible effort to respond rapidly and effectively to situations of internal armed conflict and civil strife, which remain the major cause of summary and arbitrary executions, in particular by offering to mediate a peaceful solution to such conflicts and by strongly encouraging the concerned parties to accept such solutions.

(c) To promote information and awareness campaigns, in particular campaigns at the national and regional level in regions particularly affected by summary and arbitrary executions, designed to eliminate the root causes of violence by promoting tolerance, social solidarity and concern for human rights and the inherent dignity of every person.

10. The Death Penalty. List of Abolitionist and Retentionist Countries (June 1993). Paper Submitted by Amnesty International to the Sub-Commission on Prevention of Discrimination and Protection of Minorities. (excerpts)

THE ADMINISTRATION OF JUSTICE AND THE HUMAN RIGHTS OF DETAINEES

THE DEATH PENALTY LIST OF ABOLITIONIST AND RETENTIONIST COUNTRIES (JUNE 1993)

Paper submitted by Amnesty International

Amnesty International's latest information shows that 52 countries have abolished the death penalty for all offences, while 16 have done so for all but exceptional crimes such as wartime crimes. Nineteen countries can be considered abolitionist *de facto*: they retain the death penalty in law but have not carried out any executions for the past 10 years or more. One hundred and three countries retain and use the death penalty.

Following is a list of countries, indicating whether or not their laws provide for the death penalty. For abolitionist countries, information is also given, where available, on the date of abolition and the date of the last execution carried out; and for countries which have abolished the death penalty for all crimes, the date when it was abolished for ordinary offences if this was done before. (The date given for abolition is normally the date when the decision to abolish the death penalty was taken, but if that decision only came into effect several years later, the latter date is given.)

Also attached is a list of countries which have abolished the death penalty in law since 1976. It shows that in recent years, an average of two countries a year has abolished the death penalty in law or, having done so for ordinary offences, has gone on to abolish it for all offences.

The lists have been compiled on the basis of information available to Amnesty International as of June 1993.

1. ABOLITIONIST FOR ALL CRIMES

(Countries whose laws do not provide for the death penalty for any crime)

Country	Date of Abolition
ANDORRA	1990
ANGOLA	1992
AUSTRALIA	1985
AUSTRIA	1968
CAMBODIA	1989
CAPE VERDE	1981
COLOMBIA	1910
COSTA RICA	1877
CROATIA	1990
CZECH REPUBLIC	1990
DENMARK	1978
DOMINICAN REPUBLIC	1966
ECUADOR	1906
FEDERAL REPUBLIC OF GERMANY	1949/1987
FINLAND	1972
FRANCE	1981
GAMBIA	1993
GUINEA-BISSAU	1993
HAITI	1987
HONDURAS	1956
HONG KONG	1993
HUNGARY	1990
ICELAND	1928
IRELAND	1990
KIRIBATI	
LIECHTENSTEIN	1987
LUXEMBOURG	1979
MARSHALL ISLANDS	
MICRONESIA (Federated States)	
MONACO	1962
MOZAMBIQUE	1990
NAMIBIA	1990
NETHERLANDS	1982
NEW ZEALAND	1989
NICARAGUA	1979
NORWAY	1979
PANAMA	
PHILIPPINES	1987

PORTUGAL	1976
ROMANIA	1989
SAN MARINO	1865
SAO TOME AND PRINCIPE	1990
SLOVAK REPUBLIC	1990
SLOVENIA	1989
SOLOMON ISLANDS	
SWEDEN	1972
SWITZERLAND	1992
TUVALU	
URUGUAY	1907
VANUATU	
VATICAN CITY STATE	1969
VENEZUELA	1863

TOTAL: 52 countries

2. ABOLITIONIST FOR ORDINARY CRIMES ONLY

(Countries whose laws provide for the death penalty only for exceptional crimes such as crimes under military law or crimes committed in exceptional circumstances such as wartime)

Country	Date of Abolition
ARGENTINA	1984
BRAZIL	1979
CANADA	1976
CYPRUS	1983
EL SALVADOR	1983
FIJI	1979
ISRAEL	1954
ITALY	1947
MALTA	1971
MEXICO	
NEPAL	1990
PARAGUAY	1992
PERU	1979
SEYCHELLES	
SPAIN	1978
UNITED KINGDOM	1973

TOTAL: 16 countries

3. LIST OF COUNTRIES WHICH HAVE ABOLISHED THE DEATH PENALTY SINCE 1976

1976: PORTUGAL abolished the death penalty for all offences.
CANADA abolished the death penalty for ordinary offences.

1978: DENMARK abolished the death penalty for all offences.
SPAIN abolished the death penalty for ordinary offences.

1979: LUXEMBOURG, NICARAGUA and NORWAY abolished the death penalty for all offences.
BRAZIL, FIJI and PERU abolished the death penalty for ordinary offences. (1)

1981: FRANCE and CAPE VERDE abolished the death penalty for all offences.

1982: The NETHERLANDS abolished the death penalty for all offences.

1983: CYPRUS and EL SALVADOR abolished the death penalty for ordinary offences.

1984: ARGENTINA and AUSTRALIA abolished the death penalty for ordinary offences. (2) (3)

1985: AUSTRALIA abolished the death penalty for all offences. (3)

1987: The PHILIPPINES, HAITI, LIECHTENSTEIN and the GERMAN DEMOCRATIC REPUBLIC (4) abolished the death penalty for all offences.

1989: CAMBODIA, NEW ZEALAND, ROMANIA and SLOVENIA (5) abolished the death penalty for all offences.

1990: ANDORRA, CROATIA (5), the CZECH AND SLOVAK FEDERAL REPUBLIC (6), HUNGARY, IRELAND, MOZAMBIQUE, NAMIBIA and SAO TOME AND PRINCIPE abolished the death penalty for all offences.
NEPAL abolished the death penalty for ordinary offences. (7)

1992: ANGOLA and SWITZERLAND abolished the death penalty for all offences.
PARAGUAY abolished the death penalty for ordinary offences.

1993: GAMBIA, GUINEA-BISSAU and HONG KONG abolished the death penalty for all offences.

Notes:

1. Brazil had abolished the death penalty in 1882 but reintroduced it in 1969 while under military rule.

2. Argentina had abolished the death penalty for all offences in 1921 and again in 1972 but reintroduced it in 1976 following a military coup.

3. In 1984 the death penalty was abolished in Western Australia, the last Australian state to retain the death penalty for ordinary offences. In 1985 it was abolished entirely in Australia when the state of New South Wales abolished it for piracy, treason and arson at military and naval establishments -- the only remaining capital offences.

4. In 1990 the German Democratic Republic became unified with the Federal Republic of Germany, where the death penalty had been abolished in 1949.

5. Slovenia and Croatia abolished the death penalty while they were still republics of the Socialist Federal Republic of Yugoslavia. The two republics became independent in 1991.

6. In 1993 the Czech and Slovak Federal Republic divided into two states, the Czech Republic and the Slovak Republic.

7. Nepal had abolished the death penalty for murder in 1946 but reintroduced it in 1985 after bomb explosions in which several people were killed.

4. RETENTIONIST

(Countries and territories which retain and use the death penalty for ordinary crimes)*

Country

AFGHANISTAN
ALBANIA
ALGERIA
ANTIGUA AND BARBUDA
ARMENIA
AZERBAYDZHAN

BAHAMAS
BANGLADESH
BARBADOS
BELARUS
BELIZE
BENIN
BOTSWANA
BULGARIA
BURKINA FASO
BURUNDI
CAMEROON
CENTRAL AFRICAN REPUBLIC
CHAD
CHILE
CHINA (People's Republic)
CONGO
CUBA
DOMINICA
EGYPT
EQUATORIAL GUINEA
ESTONIA
ETHIOPIA
GABON
GEORGIA
GHANA
GRENADA
GUATEMALA
GUINEA
GUYANA
INDIA
INDONESIA
IRAN
IRAQ
JAMAICA
JAPAN
JORDAN
KAZAKHSTAN
KENYA
KOREA (Democratic People's Republic) [North Korea]
KOREA (Republic) [South Korea]
KUWAIT
KYRGYZSTAN
LAOS
LATVIA

LEBANON
LESOTHO
LIBERIA
LIBYA
LITHUANIA
MALAWI
MALAYSIA
MALI
MAURITANIA
MAURITIUS
MOLDOVA
MONGOLIA
MOROCCO
MYANMAR
NIGERIA
OMAN
PAKISTAN
POLAND
QATAR
RUSSIA
RWANDA
SAINT CHRISTOPHER AND NEVIS
SAINT LUCIA
SAINT VINCENT AND THE GRENADINES
SAUDI ARABIA
SIERRA LEONE
SINGAPORE
SOMALIA
SOUTH AFRICA
SUDAN
SURINAME
SWAZILAND
SYRIA
TADZHIKISTAN
TAIWAN (Republic of China)
TANZANIA
THAILAND
TONGA
TRINIDAD AND TOBAGO
TUNISIA
TURKEY
TURKMENISTAN
UGANDA
UKRAINE

UNITED ARAB EMIRATES
UNITED STATES OF AMERICA
UZBEKISTAN
VIETNAM
YEMEN
YUGOSLAVIA
ZAIRE
ZAMBIA
ZIMBABWE

TOTAL: 103 countries and territories

* Most of these countries and territories are known to have carried out executions during the past 10 years. On some countries Amnesty International has no record of executions but is unable to ascertain whether or not executions have in fact been carried out. Several countries have carried out executions in the past 10 years but have since instituted moratoria on executions.

* * *

11. Declaration on the Protection of All Persons from Enforced Disappearance (without preambular paragraphs)

Article 1

1. Any act of enforced disappearance is an offence to human dignity. It is condemned as a denial of the purposes of the Charter of the United Nations and as a grave and flagrant violation of the human rights and fundamental freedoms proclaimed in the Universal Declaration of Human Rights and reaffirmed and developed in international instruments in this field.

2. Any act of enforced disappearance places the persons subjected thereto outside the protection of the law and inflicts severe suffering on them and their families. It constitutes a violation of the rules of international law guaranteeing, *inter alia*, the right to recognition as a person before the law, the right to liberty and security of the person and the right not to be subjected to torture and other cruel, inhuman or degrading treatment or punishment. It also violates or constitutes a grave threat to the right to life.

Article 2

1. No State shall practice, permit or tolerate enforced disappearances.

2. States shall act at the national and regional levels and in cooperation with the United Nations to contribute by all means to the prevention and eradication of enforced disappearance.

Article 3

Each State shall take effective legislative, administrative, judicial or other measures to prevent and terminate acts of enforced disappearance in any territory under its jurisdiction.

Article 4

1. All acts of enforced disappearance shall be offences under criminal law punishable by appropriate penalties which shall take into account their extreme seriousness.

2. Mitigating circumstances may be established in national legislation for persons who, having participated in enforced disappearances, are instrumental in bringing the victims forward alive or in providing voluntarily information which would contribute to clarifying cases of enforced disappearance.

Article 5

In addition to such criminal penalties as are applicable, enforced disappearances render their perpetrators and the State or State authorities which organize, acquiesce in or tolerate such disappearances liable under civil law, without prejudice to the international responsibility of the State concerned in accordance with the principles of international law.

Article 6

1. No order or instruction of any public authority, civilian, military or other, may be invoked to justify an enforced disappearance. Any person receiving such an order or instruction shall have the right and duty not to obey it.

2. Each State shall ensure that orders or instructions directing, authorizing or encouraging any enforced disappearance are prohibited.

3. Training of law enforcement officials shall emphasize the provisions in paragraphs 1 and 2 of the present article.

Article 7

No circumstances whatsoever, whether a threat of war, a state of war, internal political instability or any other public emergency, may be invoked to justify enforced disappearances.

Article 8

1. No State shall expel, return (*refouler*) or extradite a person to another State where there are substantial grounds to believe that he would be in danger of enforced disappearance.

2. For the purpose of determining whether there are such grounds, the competent authorities shall take into account all relevant considerations including, where applicable, the existence in the State concerned of a consistent pattern of gross, flagrant or mass violations of human rights.

Article 9

1. The right to a prompt and effective judicial remedy as a means of determining the whereabouts or state of health of persons deprived of their liberty and/or identifying the authority ordering or carrying out the deprivation of liberty is required to prevent enforced disappearances under all circumstances, including those referred to in article 7 above.

2. In such proceedings, competent national authorities shall have access to all places where persons deprived of their liberty are being held and to each part of those places, as well as to any place in which there are grounds to believe that such persons may be found.

3. Any other competent authority entitled under the law of the State or by any international legal instrument to which the State is a party may also have access to such places.

Article 10

1. Any person deprived of liberty shall be held in an officially recognized place of detention and, in conformity with national law, be brought before a judicial authority promptly after detention.

2. Accurate information on the detention of such persons and their place or places of detention, including transfers, shall be made promptly available to their family members, their counsel or to any other persons having a legitimate

interest in the information unless a wish to the contrary has been manifested by the persons concerned.

3. An official up-to-date register of all persons deprived of their liberty shall be maintained in every place of detention. Additionally, each State shall take steps to maintain similar centralized registers. The information contained in these registers shall be made available to the persons mentioned in the preceding paragraph, to any judicial or other competent and independent national authority and to any other competent authority entitled under the law of the State concerned or any international legal instrument to which a State concerned is a party, seeking to trace the whereabouts of a detained person.

Article 11

All persons deprived of liberty must be released in a manner permitting reliable verification that they have actually been released and, further, have been released in conditions in which their physical integrity and ability fully to exercise their rights are assured.

Article 12

1. Each State shall establish rules under its national law indicating those officials authorized to order deprivation of liberty, establishing the conditions under which such orders may be given, and stipulating penalties for officials who, without legal justification, refuse to provide information on any detention.

2. Each State shall likewise ensure strict supervision, including a clear chain of command, of all law enforcement officials responsible for apprehensions, arrests, detentions, custody, transfers and imprisonment, and of other officials authorized by law to use force and firearms.

Article 13

1. Each State shall ensure that any person having knowledge or a legitimate interest who alleges that a person has been subjected to enforced disappearance has the right to complain to a competent and independent State authority and to have that complaint promptly, thoroughly and impartially investigated by that authority. Whenever there are reasonable grounds to believe that an enforced disappearance has been committed, the State shall promptly refer the matter to that authority for such an investigation, even if there has been no formal complaint. No measure shall be taken to curtail or impede the investigation.

2. Each State shall ensure that the competent authority shall have the necessary powers and resources to conduct the investigation effectively, including powers

to compel attendance of witnesses and production of relevant documents and to make immediate on-site visits.

3. Steps shall be taken to ensure that all involved in the investigation, including the complainant, counsel, witnesses and those conducting the investigation, are protected against ill-treatment, intimidation or reprisal.

4. The findings of such an investigation shall be made available upon request to all persons concerned, unless doing so would jeopardize an ongoing criminal investigation.

5. Steps shall be taken to ensure that any ill-treatment, intimidation or reprisal or any other form of interference on the occasion of the lodging of a complaint or during the investigation procedure is appropriately punished.

6. An investigation, in accordance with the procedures described above, should be able to be conducted for as long as the fate of the victim of enforced disappearance remains unclarified.

Article 14

Any persons alleged to have perpetrated an act of enforced disappearance in a particular State shall, when the facts disclosed by an official investigation so warrant, be brought before the competent civil authorities of that State for the purpose of prosecution and trial unless he has been extradited to another State wishing to exercise jurisdiction in accordance with the relevant international agreements in force. All States should take any lawful and appropriate action available to them to bring to justice all persons presumed responsible for an act of enforced disappearance, who are found to be within their jurisdiction or under their control.

Article 15

The fact that there are grounds to believe that a person has participated in acts of an extremely serious nature such as those referred to in article 4, paragraph 1, above, regardless of the motives, shall be taken into account when the competent authorities of the State decide whether or not to grant asylum.

Article 16

1. Persons alleged to have committed any of the acts referred to in article 4, paragraph 1, above, shall be suspended from any official duties during the investigation referred to in article 13 above.

2. They shall be tried only by the competent ordinary courts in each State, and not by any other special tribunal, in particular military courts.

3. No privileges, immunities or special exemptions shall be admitted in such trials, without prejudice to the provisions contained in the Vienna Convention on Diplomatic Relations.[5]

4. The persons presumed responsible for such acts shall be guaranteed fair treatment in accordance with the relevant provisions of the Universal Declaration of Human Rights and other relevant international agreements in force at all stages of the investigation and eventual prosecution and trial.

Article 17

1. Acts constituting enforced disappearance shall be considered a continuing offence as long as the perpetrators continue to conceal the fate and the whereabouts of persons who have disappeared and these facts remain unclarified.

2. When the remedies provided for in article 2 of the International Covenant on Civil and Political Rights are no longer effective, the statute of limitations relating to acts of enforced disappearance shall be suspended until these remedies are re-established.

3. Statutes of limitations, where they exist, relating to acts of enforced disappearance shall be substantial and commensurate with the extreme seriousness of the offence.

Article 18

1. Persons who have or are alleged to have committed offences referred to in article 4, paragraph 1, above, shall not benefit from any special amnesty law or similar measures that might have the effect of exempting them from any criminal proceedings or sanction.

2. In the exercise of the right of pardon, the extreme seriousness of acts of enforced disappearance shall be taken into account.

Article 19

The victims of acts of enforced disappearance and their family shall obtain redress and shall have the right to adequate compensation, including the means

---

[5] 500 U.N.T.S. 96.

for as complete a rehabilitation as possible. In the event of the death of the victim as a result of an act of enforced disappearance, their dependents shall also be entitled to compensation.

Article 20

1. States shall prevent and suppress the abduction of children of parents subjected to enforced disappearance and of children born during their mother's enforced disappearance, and shall devote their efforts to the search for and identification of such children and to the restitution of the children to their families of origin.

2. Considering the need to protect the best interests of children referred to in the preceding paragraph, there shall be an opportunity, in States which recognize a system of adoption, for a review of the adoption of such children and, in particular, for annulment of any adoption which originated in enforced disappearance. Such adoption should, however, continue to be in force if consent is given, at the time of the review, by the child's closest relatives.

3. The abduction of children of parents subjected to enforced disappearance or of children born during their mother's enforced disappearance, and the act of altering of suppressing documents attesting to their true identity, shall constitute an extremely serious offence, which shall be punished as such.

4. For these purposes, States shall, where appropriate, conclude bilateral and multilateral agreements.

Article 21

The provisions of the present Declaration are without prejudice to the provisions enunciated in the Universal Declaration of Human Rights or in any other international instrument, and shall not be construed as restricting or derogating from any of those provisions.

* * *

12. Question of the Human Rights of All Persons Subjected to Any Form of Detention or Imprisonment; Question of Enforced or Involuntary Disappearances

ANNEX

DECLARATION ON THE PROTECTION OF ALL PERSONS FROM ENFORCED DISAPPEARANCE (excerpts)

The General Assembly,

Deeply concerned that in many countries, often in a persistent manner, enforced disappearances occur, in the sense that persons are arrested, detained or abducted against their will or otherwise deprived of their liberty by officials of different branches or levels of Government, or by organized groups or private individuals acting on behalf of, or with the support, direct or indirect, consent or acquiescence of the Government, followed by a refusal to disclose the fate or whereabouts of the persons concerned or a refusal to acknowledge the deprivation of their liberty, thereby placing such persons outside the protection of the law,

Considering that enforced disappearance undermines the deepest values of any society committed to respect for the rule of law, human rights and fundamental freedoms, and that the systematic practice of such acts is of the nature of a crime against humanity,

Bearing in mind that, while the acts which comprise enforced disappearances constitute a violation of the prohibitions found in the aforementioned international instruments, it is none-the-less important to devise an instrument which characterizes all acts of enforced disappearance of persons as very serious offences setting forth standards designed to punish and prevent their commission,

Proclaims the present Declaration on the Protection of All Persons from Enforced Disappearance, as a body of principles for all States,

Urges that all efforts be made so that this Declaration becomes generally known and respected.

Article 1

1. Any act of enforced disappearance is an offence to human dignity. It is condemned as a denial of the purposes of the Charter of the United Nations and as a grave and flagrant violation of the human rights and fundamental freedoms

proclaimed in the Universal Declaration of Human Rights and reaffirmed and developed in international instruments in this field.

2. Such act of enforced disappearance places the persons subjected thereto outside the protection of the law and inflicts severe suffering on them and their families. It constitutes a violation of the rules of international law guaranteeing, *inter alia*, the right to recognition as a person before the law, the right to liberty and security of the person and the right not to be subjected to torture and other cruel, inhuman or degrading treatment or punishment. It also violates or constitutes a grave threat to the right to life.

Article 2

1. No State shall practice, permit or tolerate enforced disappearances.

2. States shall act at the national and regional levels and in cooperation with the United Nations to contribute by all means to the prevention and eradication of enforced disappearance.

Article 3

Each State shall take effective legislative, administrative, judicial or other measures to prevent and terminate acts of enforced disappearance in any territory under its jurisdiction.

Article 4

1. All acts of enforced disappearance shall be offences under the criminal law punishable by appropriate penalties which shall take into account their extreme seriousness.

2. Mitigating circumstances may be established in national legislation for persons who, having participated in enforced disappearances, are instrumental in bringing the victims forward alive or in providing voluntarily information which would contribute to clarify cases of enforced disappearance.

Article 5

In addition to such criminal penalties as are applicable, enforced disappearances render their perpetrators and the State or State authorities which organize, acquiesce in or tolerate such disappearances liable at civil law, without prejudice to the international responsibility of the State concerned in accordance with the principles of international law.

Article 6

1. No order or instruction of any public authority, civilian, military or other, may be invoked to justify an enforced disappearance. Any person receiving such an order or instruction shall have the right and duty not to obey it.

2. Each State shall ensure that orders or instructions directing, authorizing or encouraging any enforced disappearance are prohibited.

3. Training of law enforcement officials shall emphasize the above provisions.

Article 7

No circumstances whatsoever, whether a threat of war, a state of war, internal political instability or any other public emergency, may be invoked to justify enforced disappearances.

Article 9

1. The right to a prompt and effective judicial remedy as a means of determining the whereabouts or state of health of persons deprived of their liberty and/or identifying the authority ordering or carrying out the deprivation of liberty, is required to prevent enforced disappearances under all circumstances, including those referred to in Article 7.

2. In such proceedings, competent national authorities shall have access to all places holding persons deprived of their liberty and to each part thereof, as well as to any place in which there are grounds to believe that such persons may be found.

3. Any other competent authority entitled under law of the State or by any international legal instruments to which a State is a party may also have access to such places.

Article 10

1. Any person deprived of liberty shall be held in an officially recognized place of detention and, in conformity with national law, be brought before a judicial authority promptly after detention.

2. Accurate information on the detention of such persons and their place or places of detention, including transfers, shall be made promptly available to their family members, their counsel or to any other persons having a legitimate

interest in the information unless a wish to the contrary has been manifested by the persons concerned.

3. An official up-to-date register of all persons deprived of their liberty shall be maintained in every place of detention. Additionally, each State shall take steps to maintain similar centralized registers. The information contained in these registers shall be made available to the persons mentioned in the paragraph above, to any judicial or other competent and independent national authority as well as to any other competent authority entitled under the law of the State concerned or any international legal instrument to which a State concerned is a party, seeking to trace the whereabouts of a detained person.

Article 13

1. Each State shall ensure that any person having knowledge or a legitimate interest who alleges that a person has been subjected to enforced disappearance has the right to complain to a competent and independent State authority and to have that complaint promptly, thoroughly and impartially investigated by that authority. Whenever there are reasonable grounds to believe that an enforced disappearance has been committed, the State shall promptly refer the matter to that authority for such an investigation, even if there has been no formal complaint. No measure shall be taken to curtail or impede the investigation.

2. Each State shall ensure that the competent authority shall have the necessary powers and resources to conduct the investigation effectively, including powers to compel attendance of witnesses and production of relevant documents and to make immediate on-site visits.

3. Steps shall be taken to ensure that all involved in the investigation, including the complainant, counsel, witnesses and those conducting the investigation, are protected against ill-treatment, intimidation or reprisal.

4. The findings of such an investigation shall be made available upon request to all persons concerned, unless doing so would jeopardize an ongoing criminal investigation.

5. Steps shall be taken to ensure that any ill-treatment, intimidation or reprisal or any other form of interference on the occasion of the lodging of a complaint or the investigation procedure is appropriately punished.

6. An investigation, in accordance with the procedures described above, should be able to be conducted for as long as the fate of the victim of enforced disappearance remains unclarified.

Article 19

The victims of acts of enforced disappearance and their family shall obtain redress and shall have the right to adequate compensation, including the means for as complete a rehabilitation as possible. In the event of the death of the victim as a result of an act of enforced disappearance, their dependents shall also be entitled to compensation.

E. RIGHT TO LIBERTY AND PRISONERS' RIGHTS

Arbitrary arrest and detention are grave violations of human dignity, which continue to victimize hundreds of thousands of persons in the world.

The United Nations has focused its attention not only on the arrest and detention of members of the political opposition of a given country, but also on the arbitrary arrest of other persons, and on their treatment in prisons. As human beings, they are entitled to treatment consistent with article 10, paragraph 1, of the International Covenant on Civil and Political Rights, which requires that detainees be treated "with respect for the inherent dignity of the human person."

Many United Nations organs have been involved in this struggle for human dignity. Important new standards have been drafted in connection with the United Nations Crime Prevention and Justice Branch by the United Nations Congresses on the Prevention of Crime and the Treatment of Offenders. Thus emerged the 1957 Standard Minimum Rules for the Treatment of Prisoners, the 1988 Body of Principles for the Protection of All Persons under Any Form of Detention or Imprisonment, the 1990 Basic Principles for the Treatment of Prisoners, the 1990 Standard Minimum Rules for Non-custodial Measures (the Tokyo rules), and the United Nations Resolution on Infection with Human Immunodeficiency Virus (HIV) and Acquired Immunodeficiency Syndrome (AIDS) in Prison.

But the declarative and prescriptive stages of evolution, as important as they are, would be of little use unless they are followed by the enforcement stage. This stage includes monitoring by specialized bodies such as the United Nations Commission on Human Rights and Sub-Commission on Prevention of Discrimination and Protection of Minorities, as well as the reporting practice and individual complaints procedures of the United Nations Human Rights Committee and Committee Against Torture.

In order to enhance the prospects of implementation, a draft Optional Protocol to the Convention Against Torture has been proposed, which would allow visits to places of detention with a view to strengthening the protection of such persons from torture and from other cruel, inhuman or degrading treatment or punishment.

1. Universal Declaration of Human Rights

Article 3

Everyone has the right to life, liberty and security of person.

Article 9

No one shall be subjected to arbitrary arrest, detention or exile.

2. International Covenant on Civil and Political Rights

Article 9

1. Everyone has the right to liberty and security of person. No one shall be subjected to arbitrary arrest or detention. No one shall be deprived of his liberty except on such grounds and in accordance with such procedure as are established by law.

2. Anyone who is arrested shall be informed, at the time of arrest, of the reasons for his arrest and shall be promptly informed of any charges against him.

3. Anyone arrested or detained on a criminal charge shall be brought promptly before a judge or other officer authorized by law to exercise judicial power and shall be entitled to trial within a reasonable time or to release. It shall not be the general rule that persons awaiting trial shall be detained in custody, but release may be subject to guarantees to appear for trial, at any other stage of the judicial proceedings, and, should occasion arise, for execution of the judgement.

4. Anyone who is deprived of his liberty by arrest or detention shall be entitled to take proceedings before a court, in order that court may decide without delay on the lawfulness of his detention and order his release if the detention is not lawful.

5. Anyone who has been victim of unlawful arrest or detention shall have an enforceable right to compensation.

Article 11

No one shall be imprisoned merely on the ground of inability to fulfil a contractual obligation.

3. General Comments of the Human Rights Committee on the International Covenant on Civil and Political Rights

GENERAL COMMENT 8 *Article 9 (Sixteenth session, 1982)*

1. Article 9 which deals with the right to liberty and security of persons has often been somewhat narrowly understood in reports by States parties, and they have therefore given incomplete information. The Committee points out that paragraph 1 is applicable to all deprivation of liberty, whether in criminal cases or in other cases such as, for example, mental illness, vagrancy, drug addiction, educational purposes, immigration control, etc. It is true that some of the provisions of article 9 (part of para. 2 and the whole of para. 3) are only applicable to persons against whom criminal charges are brought. But the rest, and in particular the important guarantee laid down in paragraph 4, i.e., the right to control by a court of the legality of the detention, applies to all persons deprived of their liberty by arrest or detention. Furthermore, States parties have in accordance with article 2 (3) also to ensure that an effective remedy is provided in other cases in which an individual claims to be deprived of his liberty in violation of the Covenant.

2. Paragraph 3 of article 9 requires that in criminal cases any person arrested or detained has to be brought "promptly" before a judge or other officer authorized by law to exercise judicial power. More precise time-limits are fixed by law in most States parties and, in the view of the Committee, delays must not exceed a few days. Many States have given insufficient information about the actual practices in this respect.

3. Another matter is the total length of detention pending trial. In certain categories of criminal cases in some countries this matter has caused some concern within the Committee, and members have questioned whether their practices have been in conformity with the entitlement "to trial within a reasonable time or to release" under paragraph 3. Pre-trial detention should be an exception and as short as possible. The Committee would welcome information concerning mechanisms existing and measures taken with a view to reducing the duration of such detention.

4. Also if so-called preventive detention is used, for reasons of public security, it must be controlled by these same provisions, i.e., it must not be arbitrary, and must be based on grounds and procedures established by law (para. 1), information of the reasons must be given (para. 2) and court control of the detention must be available (para. 4) as well as compensation in the case of a breach (para. 5). And if, in addition, criminal charges are brought in such cases, the full protection of article 9 (2) and (3), as well as article 14, must also be granted.

* * *

4. Standard Minimum Rules for the Treatment of Prisoners

PRELIMINARY OBSERVATIONS

1. The following rules are not intended to describe in detail a model system of penal institutions. They seek only, on the basis of the general consensus of contemporary thought and the essential elements of the most adequate systems of today, to set out what is generally accepted as being good principle and practice in the treatment of prisoners and the management of institutions.

2. In view of the great variety of legal, social, economic and geographical conditions of the world, it is evident that not all of the rules are capable of application in all places and at all times. They should, however, serve to stimulate a constant endeavour to overcome practical difficulties in the way of their application, in the knowledge that they represent, as a whole, the minimum conditions which are accepted as suitable by the United Nations.

3. On the other hand, the rules cover a field in which thought is constantly developing. They are not intended to preclude experiment and practices, provided these are in harmony with the principles and seek to further the purposes which derive from the text of the rules as a whole. It will always be justifiable for the central prison administration to authorize departures from the rules in this spirit.

4. (1) Part I of the rules covers the general management of institutions, and is applicable to all categories of prisoners, criminal or civil, untried or convicted, including prisoners subject to "security measures" or corrective measures ordered by the judge.

   (2) Part II contains rules applicable only to the special categories dealt with in each section. Nevertheless, the rules under section A, applicable to prisoners under sentence, shall be equally applicable to categories of prisoners dealt with in sections B, C and D, provided they do not conflict with the rules governing those categories and are for their benefit.

5. (1) The rules do not seek to regulate the management of institutions set aside for young persons such as Borstal institutions or correctional schools, but in general part I would be equally applicable in such institutions.

   (2) The category of young prisoners should include at least all young persons who come within the jurisdiction of juvenile courts. As a rule, such young persons should not be sentenced to imprisonment.

Part I

RULES OF GENERAL APPLICATION

Basic Principle

6. (1) The following rules shall be applied impartially. There shall be no discrimination on grounds of race, colour, sex, language, religion, political or other opinion, national or social origin, property, birth or other status.

(2) On the other hand, it is necessary to respect the religious beliefs and moral precepts of the group to which a prisoner belongs.

Register

7. (1) In every place where persons are imprisoned there shall be kept a bound registration book with numbered pages in which shall be entered in respect of each prisoner received:

(a) Information concerning his identity;

(b) The reasons for his commitment and the authority therefore;

(c) The day and hour of his admission and release.

(2) No person shall be received in an institution without a valid commitment order of which the details shall have been previously entered in the register.

Separation of Categories

8. The different categories of prisoners shall be kept in separate institutions or parts of Institutions taking account of their sex, age, criminal record, the legal reason for their detention and the necessities of their treatment. Thus,

(a) Men and women shall so far as possible be detained in separate institutions; in an institution which receives both men and women the whole of the premises allocated to women shall be entirely separate;

(b) Untried prisoners shall be kept separate from convicted prisoners;

(c) Persons imprisoned for debt and other civil prisoners shall be kept separate from persons imprisoned by reason of a criminal offence;

(d) Young prisoners shall be kept separate from adults.

Accommodation

9. (1) Where sleeping accommodation is in individual cells or rooms, each prisoner shall occupy by night a cell or room by himself. If for special reasons, such as temporary overcrowding, it becomes necessary for the central prison administration to make an exception to this rule, it is not desirable to have two prisoners in a cell or room.

(2) Where dormitories are used, they shall be occupied by prisoners carefully selected as being suitable to associate with one another in those conditions. There shall be regular supervision by night, in keeping with the nature of the institution.

10. All accommodation provided for the use of prisoners and in particular all sleeping accommodation shall meet all requirements of health, due regard being paid to climatic conditions and particularly to cubic content of air, minimum floor space, lighting, heating and ventilation.

11. In all places where prisoners are required to live or work,

(a) The windows shall be large enough to enable the prisoners to read or work by natural light, and shall be so constructed that they can allow the entrance of fresh air whether or not there is artificial ventilation;

(b) Artificial light shall be provided sufficient for the prisoners to read or work without injury to eyesight.

12. The sanitary installations shall be adequate to enable every prisoner to comply with the needs of nature when necessary and in a clean and decent manner.

13. Adequate bathing and shower installations shall be provided so that every prisoner may be enabled and required to have a bath or shower, at a temperature suitable to the climate, as frequently as necessary for general hygiene according to season and geographical region, but at least once a week in a temperate climate.

14. All parts of an institution regularly used by prisoners shall be properly maintained and kept scrupulously clean at all times.

Personal Hygiene

15. Prisoners shall be required to keep their persons clean, and to this end they shall be provided with water and with such toilet articles as are necessary for health and cleanliness.

16. In order that prisoners may maintain a good appearance compatible with their self-respect, facilities shall be provided for the proper care of the hair and beard, and men shall be enabled to shave regularly.

Clothing and Bedding

17. (1) Every prisoner who is not allowed to wear his own clothing shall be provided with an outfit of clothing suitable for the climate and adequate to keep him in good health. Such clothing shall in no manner be degrading or humiliating.

(2) All clothing shall be clean and kept in proper condition. Underclothing shall be changed and washed as often as necessary for the maintenance of hygiene.

(3) In exceptional circumstances, whenever a prisoner is removed outside the institution for an authorized purpose, he shall be allowed to wear his own clothing or other inconspicuous clothing.

18. If prisoners are allowed to wear their own clothing, arrangements shall be made on their admission to the institution to ensure that it shall be clean and fit for use.

19. Every prisoner shall, in accordance with local or national standards, be provided with a separate bed, and with separate and sufficient bedding which shall be clean when issued, kept in good order and changed often enough to ensure its cleanliness.

Food

20. (1) Every prisoner shall be provided by the administration at the usual hours with food of nutritional value adequate for health and strength, of wholesome quality and well prepared and served.

(2) Drinking water shall be available to every prisoner whenever he needs it.

Exercise and Sport

21. (1) Every prisoner who is not employed in outdoor work shall have at least one hour of suitable exercise in the open air daily if the weather permits.

(2) Young prisoners, and others of suitable age and physique, shall receive physical and recreational training during the period of exercise. To this end space, installations and equipment should be provided.

Medical Services

22. (1) At every institution there shall be available the services of at least one qualified medical officer who should have some knowledge of psychiatry. The medical services should be organized in close relationship to the general health administration of the community or nation. They shall include a psychiatric service for the diagnosis and, in proper cases, the treatment of states of mental abnormality.

(2) Sick prisoners who require specialist treatment shall be transferred to specialized institutions or to civil hospitals. Where hospital facilities are provided in an institution, their equipment, furnishings and pharmaceutical supplies shall be proper for the medical care and treatment of sick prisoners, and there shall be a staff of suitable trained officers.

(3) The services of a qualified dental officer shall be available to every prisoner.

23. (1) In women's institutions there shall be special accommodation for all necessary prenatal and post-natal care and treatment. Arrangements shall be made wherever practicable for children to be born in a hospital outside the institution. If a child is born in prison, this fact shall not be mentioned in the birth certificate.

(2) Where nursing infants are allowed to remain in the institution with their mothers, provision shall be made for a nursery staffed by qualified persons, where the infants shall be placed when they are not in the care of their mothers.

24. The medical officer shall see and examine every prisoner as soon as possible after his admission and thereafter as necessary, with a view particularly to the discovery of physical or mental illness and the taking of all necessary measures; the segregation of prisoners suspected of infectious or contagious conditions; the noting of physical or mental defects which might hamper rehabilitation, and the determination of the physical capacity of every prisoner for work.

25. (1) The medical officer shall have the care of the physical and mental health of the prisoners and should daily see all sick prisoners, all who complain of illness, and any prisoner to whom his attention is specially directed.

(2) The medical officer shall report to the director whenever he considers that a prisoner's physical or mental health has been or will be injuriously affected by continued imprisonment or by any condition of imprisonment.

26. (1) The medical officer shall regularly inspect and advise the director upon:

(a) The quantity, quality, preparation and service of food;

(b) The hygiene and cleanliness of the institution and the prisoners;

(c) The sanitation, heating, lighting and ventilation of the institution;

(d) The suitability and cleanliness of the prisoners' clothing and bedding;

(e) The observance of the rules concerning physical education and sports, in cases where there is no technical personnel in charge of these activities.

(2) The director shall take into consideration the reports and advice that the medical officer submits according to rules 25 (2) and 26 and, in case he concurs with the recommendations made, shall take immediate steps to give effect to those recommendations; if they are not within his competence or if he does not concur with them, he shall immediately submit his own report and the advice of the medical officer to higher authority.

Discipline and Punishment

27. Discipline and order shall be maintained with firmness, but with no more restriction than is necessary for safe custody and well-ordered community life.

28. (1) No prisoner shall be employed, in the service of the institution, in any disciplinary capacity.

(2) This rule shall not, however, impede the proper functioning of systems based on self-government, under which specified social, educational or sports activities or responsibilities are entrusted, under supervision, to prisoners who are formed into groups for the purposes of treatment.

29. The following shall always be determined by the law or by the regulation of the competent administrative authority:

(a) Conduct constituting a disciplinary offence;

(b) The types and duration of punishment which may be inflicted;

(c) The authority competent to impose such punishment.

30. (1) No prisoner shall be punished except in accordance with the terms of such law or regulation, and never twice for the same offence.

(2) No prisoner shall be punished unless he has been informed of the offence alleged against him and given a proper opportunity of presenting his defence. The competent authority shall conduct a thorough examination of the case.

(3) Where necessary and practicable the prisoner shall be allowed to make his defence through an interpreter.

31. Corporal punishment, punishment by placing in a dark cell, and all cruel, inhuman or degrading punishments shall be completely prohibited as punishments for disciplinary offences.

32. (1) Punishment by close confinement or reduction of diet shall never be inflicted unless the medical officer has examined the prisoner and certified in writing that he is fit to sustain it.

(2) The same shall apply to any other punishment that may be prejudicial to the physical or mental health of a prisoner. In no case may such punishment be contrary to or depart from the principle stated in rule 31.

(3) The medical officer shall visit daily prisoners undergoing such punishments and shall advise the director if he considers the termination or alteration of the punishment necessary on grounds of physical or mental health.

Instruments of Restraint

33. Instruments of restraint, such as handcuffs, chains, irons and straitjackets, shall never be applied as a punishment. Furthermore, chains or irons shall not be used as restraints. Other instruments of restraint shall not be used except in the following circumstances:

(a) As a precaution against escape during a transfer, provided that they shall be removed when the prisoner appears before a judicial or administrative authority;

(b) On medical grounds by direction of the medical officer;

(c) By order of the director, if other methods of control fail, in order to prevent a prisoner from injuring himself or others or from damaging property; in such instances the director shall at once consult the medical officer and report to the higher administrative authority.

34. The patterns and manner of use of instruments of restraint shall be decided by the central prison administration. Such instruments must not be applied for any longer time than is strictly necessary.

Information to and Complaints by Prisoners

35. (1) Every prisoner on admission shall be provided with written information about the regulations governing the treatment of prisoners of his category, the disciplinary requirements of the institution, the authorized methods of seeking information and making complaints, and all such other matters as are necessary to enable him to understand both his rights and his obligations and to adapt himself to the life of the institution.

(2) If a prisoner is illiterate, the aforesaid information shall be conveyed to him orally.

36. (1) Every prisoner shall have the opportunity each week day of making requests or complaints to the director of the institution or the officer authorized to represent him.

(2) It shall be possible to make requests or complaints to the inspector of prisons during his inspection. The prisoner shall have the opportunity to talk to the inspector or to any other inspecting officer without the director or other members of the staff being present.

(3) Every prisoner shall be allowed to make a request or complaint, without censorship as to substance but in proper form, to the central prison administration, the judicial authority or other proper authorities through approved channels.

(4) Unless it is evidently frivolous or groundless, every request or complaint shall be promptly dealt with and replied to without undue delay.

Contact with the Outside World

37. Prisoners shall be allowed under necessary supervision to communicate with their family and reputable friends at regular intervals both by correspondence and by receiving visits.

38. (1) Prisoners who are foreign nationals shall be allowed reasonable facilities to communicate with the diplomatic and consular representatives of the State to which they belong.

(2) Prisoners who are nationals of States without diplomatic or consular representation in the country and refugees or stateless persons shall be allowed similar facilities to communicate with the diplomatic representative of the State which takes charge of their interests or any national or international authority whose task it is to protect such persons.

39. Prisoners shall be kept informed regularly of the more important items of news by the reading of newspapers, periodicals or special institutional publications, by hearing wireless transmissions, by lectures or by any similar means as authorized or controlled by the administration.

Books

40. Every institution shall have a library for the use of all categories of prisoners adequately stocked with both recreational and instructional books, and prisoners shall be encouraged to make full use of it.

Religion

41. (1) If the institution contains a sufficient number of prisoners of the same religion, a qualified representative of that religion shall be appointed or approved. If the number of prisoners justifies it and conditions permit, the arrangement should be on a full-time basis.

(2) A qualified representative appointed or approved under paragraph (1) shall be allowed to hold regular services and to pay pastoral visits in private to prisoners of his religion at proper times.

(3) Access to a qualified representative of any religion shall not be refused to any prisoner. On the other hand, if any prisoner should object to a visit of any religious representative, his attitude shall be fully respected.

42. So far as practicable, every prisoner shall be allowed to satisfy the needs of his religious life by attending the services provided in the institution and having

in his possession the books of religious observance and instruction of his denomination.

Retention of Prisoners' Property

43. (1) All money, valuables, clothing and other effects belonging to a prisoner which under the regulations of the institution he is not allowed to retain shall on his admission to the institution be placed in safe custody. An inventory thereof shall be signed by the prisoner. Steps shall be taken to keep them in good condition.

(2) On the release of the prisoner all such articles and money shall be returned to him except in so far as he has been authorized to spend money or send any such property out of the institution, or it has been found necessary on hygienic grounds to destroy any article of clothing. The prisoner shall sign a receipt for the articles and money returned to him.

(3) Any money or effects received for a prisoner from outside shall be treated in the same way.

(4) If a prisoner brings in any drugs or medicine, the medical officer shall decide what use shall be made of them.

Notification of Death, Illness, Transfer, etc.

44. (1) Upon the death or serious illness of, or serious injury to a prisoner, or his removal to an institution for the treatment of mental affections, the director shall at once inform the spouse, if the prisoner is married, or the nearest relative and shall in any event inform any other person previously designated by the prisoncr.

(2) A prisoner shall be informed at once of the death or serious illness of any near relative. In case of the critical illness of a near relative, the prisoner should be authorized, whenever circumstances allow, to go to his bedside either under escort or alone.

(3) Every prisoner shall have the right to inform at once his family of his imprisonment or his transfer to another institution.

Removal of Prisoners

45. (1) When the prisoners are being removed to or from an institution, they shall be exposed to public view as little as possible, and proper safeguards shall be adopted to protect them from insult, curiosity and publicity in any form.

(2) The transport of prisoners in conveyances with inadequate ventilation or light, or in any way which would subject them to unnecessary physical hardship, shall be prohibited.

(3) The transport of prisoners shall be carried out at the expense of the administration and equal conditions shall obtain for all of them.

Institutional Personnel

46. (1) The prison administration shall provide for the careful selection of every grade of the personnel, since it is on their integrity, humanity, professional capacity and personal suitability for the work that the proper administration of the institutions depends.

(2) The prison administration shall constantly seek to awaken and maintain in the minds both of the personnel and of the public the conviction that this work is a social service of great importance, and to this end all appropriate means of informing the public should be used.

(3) To secure the foregoing ends, personnel shall be appointed on a full-time basis as professional prison officers and have civil service status with security of tenure subject only to good conduct, efficiency and physical fitness. Salaries shall be adequate to attract and retain suitable men and women; employment benefits and conditions of service shall be favourable in view of the exacting nature of the work.

47. (1) The personnel shall possess an adequate standard of education and intelligence.

(2) Before entering on duty, the personnel shall be given a course of training in their general and specific duties and be required to pass theoretical and practical tests.

(3) After entering on duty and during their career; the personnel shall maintain and improve their knowledge and professional capacity by attending courses of in-service training to be organized at suitable intervals.

48. All members of the personnel shall at all times so conduct themselves and perform their duties as to influence the prisoners for good by their example and to command their respect.

49. (1) So far as possible, the personnel shall include a sufficient number of specialists such as psychiatrists, psychologists, social workers, teachers and trade instructors.

(2) The services of social workers, teachers and trade instructors shall be secured on a permanent basis, without thereby excluding part-time or voluntary workers.

50. (1) The director of an institution should be adequately qualified for his task by character, administrative ability, suitable training and experience.

(2) He shall devote his entire time to his official duties and shall not be appointed on a part-time basis.

(3) He shall reside on the premises of the institution or in its immediate vicinity.

(4) When two or more institutions are under the authority of one director, he shall visit each of them at frequent intervals. A responsible resident official shall be in charge of each of these institutions.

51. (1) The director, his deputy, and the majority of the other personnel of the institution shall be able to speak the language of the greatest number of prisoners, or a language understood by the greatest number of them.

(2) Whenever necessary, the services of an interpreter shall be used.

52. (1) In institutions which are large enough to require the services of one or more full-time medical officers, at least one of them shall reside on the premises of the institution or in its immediate vicinity.

(2) In other institutions the medical officer shall visit daily and shall reside near enough to be able to attend without delay in cases of urgency.

53. (1) In an institution for both men and women, the part of the institution set aside for women shall be under the authority of a responsible woman officer who shall have the custody of the keys of all that part of the institution.

(2) No male member of the staff shall enter the part of the institution set aside for women unless accompanied by a woman officer.

(3) Women prisoners shall be attended and supervised only by women officers. This does not, however, preclude male members of the staff, particularly doctors and teachers, from carrying out their professional duties in institutions or parts of institutions set aside for women.

54. (1) Officers of the institutions shall not, in their relations with the prisoners, use force except in self-defence or in cases of attempted escape, or active or

passive physical resistance to an order based on law or regulations. Officers who have recourse to force must use no more than is strictly necessary and must report the incident immediately to the director of the institution.

(2) Prison officers shall be given special physical training to enable them to restrain aggressive prisoners.

(3) Except in special circumstances, staff performing duties which bring them into direct contact with prisoners should not be armed. Furthermore, staff should in no circumstances be provided with arms unless they have been trained in their use.

Inspection

55. There shall be a regular inspection of penal institutions and services by qualified and experienced inspectors appointed by a competent authority. Their task shall be in particular to ensure that these institutions are administered in accordance with existing laws and regulations and with a view to bringing about the objectives of penal and correctional services.

Part II

RULES APPLICABLE TO SPECIAL CATEGORIES

A. PRISONERS UNDER SENTENCE

Guiding Principles

56. The guiding principles hereafter are intended to show the spirit in which penal institutions should be administered and the purposes at which they should aim, in accordance with the declaration made under Preliminary Observation 1 of the present text.

57. Imprisonment and other measures which result in cutting off an offender from the outside world are afflictive by the very fact of taking from the person the right of self-determination by depriving him of his liberty. Therefore the prison system shall not, except as incidental to justifiable segregation or the maintenance of discipline, aggravate the suffering inherent in such a situation.

58. The purpose and justification of a sentence of imprisonment or a similar measure deprivative of liberty is ultimately to protect society against crime. This end can only be achieved if the period of imprisonment is used to ensure, so far as possible, that upon his return to society the offender is not only willing but able to lead a law-abiding and self-supporting life.

59. To this end, the institution should utilize all the remedial, educational, moral, spiritual and other forces and forms of assistance which are appropriate and available, and should seek to apply them according to the individual treatment needs of the prisoners.

60. (1) The regime of the institution should seek to minimize any differences between prison life and life at liberty which tend to lessen the responsibility of the prisoners or the respect due to their dignity as human beings.

(2) Before the completion of the sentence, it is desirable that the necessary steps be taken to ensure for the prisoner a gradual return to life in society. This aim may be achieved, depending on the case, by a pre-release regime organized in the same institution or in another appropriate institution, or by release on trial under some kind of supervision which must not be entrusted to the police but should be combined with effective social aid.

61. The treatment of prisoners should emphasize not their exclusion from the community, but their continuing part in it. Community agencies should, therefore, be enlisted wherever possible to assist the staff of the institution in the task of social rehabilitation of the prisoners. There should be in connection with every institution social workers charged with the duty of maintaining and improving all desirable relations of a prisoner with his family and with valuable social agencies. Steps should be taken to safeguard, to the maximum extent compatible with the law and the sentence, the rights relating to civil interests, social security rights and other social benefits of prisoners.

62. The medical services of the institution shall seek to detect and shall treat any physical or mental illnesses or defects which may hamper a prisoner's rehabilitation. All necessary medical, surgical and psychiatric services shall be provided to that end.

63. (1) The fulfillment of these principles requires individualization of treatment and for this purpose a flexible system of classifying prisoners in groups; it is therefore desirable that such groups should be distributed in separate institutions suitable for the treatment of each group.

(2) These institutions need not provide the same degree of security for every group. It is desirable to provide varying degrees of security according to the needs of different groups. Open institutions, by the very fact that they provide no physical security against escape but rely on the self-discipline of the inmates, provide the conditions most favourable to rehabilitation for carefully selected prisoners.

(3) It is desirable that the number of prisoners in closed institutions should not be so large that the individualization of treatment is hindered. In some countries it is considered that the population of such institutions should not exceed five hundred. In open institutions the population should be as small as possible.

(4) On the other hand, it is undesirable to maintain prisons which are so small that proper facilities cannot be provided.

64. The duty of society does not end with a prisoner's release. There should, therefore, be governmental or private agencies capable of lending the released prisoner efficient after-care directed towards the lessening of prejudice against him and towards his social rehabilitation.

Treatment

65. The treatment of persons sentenced to imprisonment or a similar measure shall have as its purpose, so far as the length of the sentence permits, to establish in them the will to lead law-abiding and self-supporting lives after their release and to fit them to do so. The treatment shall be such as will encourage their self-respect and develop their sense of responsibility.

66. (1) To these ends, all appropriate means shall be used, including religious care in the countries where this is possible, education, vocational guidance and training, social casework, employment counselling, physical development and strengthening of moral character, in accordance with the individual needs of each prisoner, taking account of his social and criminal history, his physical and mental capacities and aptitudes, his personal temperament, the length of his sentence and his prospects after release.

(2) For every prisoner with a sentence of suitable length, the director shall receive, as soon as possible after his admission, full reports on all the matters referred to in the foregoing paragraph. Such reports shall always include a report by a medical officer, wherever possible qualified in psychiatry, on the physical and mental condition of the prisoner.

(3) The reports and other relevant documents shall be placed in an individual file. This file shall be kept up to date and classified in such a way that it can be consulted by the responsible personnel whenever the need arises.

Classification and Individualization

67. The purposes of classification shall be:

(a) To separate from others those prisoners who, by reason of their criminal records or bad characters, are likely to exercise a bad influence;

(b) To divide the prisoners into classes in order to facilitate their treatment with a view to their social rehabilitation.

68. So far as possible separate institutions or separate sections of an institution shall be used for the treatment of the different classes of prisoners.

69. As soon as possible after admission and after a study of the personality of each prisoner with a sentence of suitable length, a programme of treatment shall be prepared for him in the light of the knowledge obtained about his individual needs, his capacities and dispositions.

Privileges

70. Systems of privileges appropriate for the different classes of prisoners and the different methods of treatment shall be established at every institution, in order to encourage good conduct, develop a sense of responsibility and secure the interest and cooperation of the prisoners in their treatment.

Work

71. (1) Prison labour must not be of an afflictive nature.

(2) All prisoners under sentence shall be required to work, subject to their physical and mental fitness as determined by the medical officer.

(3) Sufficient work of a useful nature shall be provided to keep prisoners actively employed for a normal working day.

(4) So far as possible the work provided shall be such as will maintain or increase the prisoners' ability to earn an honest living after release.

(5) Vocational training in useful trades shall be provided for prisoners able to profit thereby and especially for young prisoners.

(6) Within the limits compatible with proper vocational selection and with the requirements of institutional administration and discipline, the prisoners shall be able to choose the type of work they wish to perform.

72. (1) The organization and methods of work in the institutions shall resemble as closely as possible those of similar work outside institutions, so as to prepare prisoners for the conditions of normal occupational life.

(2) The interests of the prisoners and of their vocational training, however, must not be subordinated to the purpose of making a financial profit from an industry in the institution.

73. (1) Preferably institutional industries and farms should be operated directly by the administration and not by private contractors.

(2) Where prisoners are employed in work not controlled by the administration, they shall always be under the supervision of the institution's personnel. Unless the work is for other departments of the government the full normal wages for such work shall be paid to the administration by the persons to whom the labour is supplied, account being taken of the output of the prisoners.

74. (1) The precautions laid down to protect the safety and health of free workmen shall be equally observed in institutions.

(2) Provision shall be made to indemnify prisoners against industrial injury, including occupational disease, on terms not less favourable than those extended by law to free workmen.

75. (1) The maximum daily and weekly working hours of the prisoners shall be fixed by law or by administrative regulation, taking into account local rules or custom in regard to the employment of free workmen.

(2) The hours so fixed shall leave one rest day a week and sufficient time for education and other activities required as part of the treatment and rehabilitation of the prisoners.

76. (1) There shall be a system of equitable remuneration of the work of prisoners.

(2) Under the system prisoners shall be allowed to spend at least a part of their earnings on approved articles for their own use and to send a part of their earnings to their family.

(3) The system should also provide that a part of the earnings should be set aside by the administration so as to constitute a savings fund to be handed over to the prisoner on his release.

Education and Recreation

77. (1) Provision shall be made for the further education of all prisoners capable of profiting thereby, including religious instruction in the countries where

this is possible. The education of illiterates and young prisoners shall be compulsory and special attention shall be paid to it by the administration.

(2) So far as practicable, the education of prisoners shall be integrated with the educational system of the country so that after their release they may continue their education without difficulty.

78. Recreational and cultural activities shall be provided in all institutions for the benefit of the mental and physical health of prisoners.

Social Relations and After-care

79. Special attention shall be paid to the maintenance and improvement of such relations between a prisoner and his family as are desirable in the best interests of both.

80. From the beginning of a prisoner's sentence consideration shall be given to his future after release and he shall be encouraged and assisted to maintain or establish such relations with persons or agencies outside the institution as may promote the best interests of his family and his own social rehabilitation.

81. (1) Services and agencies, governmental or otherwise, which assist released prisoners to reestablish themselves in society shall ensure, so far as is possible and necessary, that released prisoners be provided with appropriate documents and identification papers, have suitable homes and work to go to, are suitably and adequately clothed having regard to the climate and season, and have sufficient means to reach their destination and maintain themselves in the period immediately following their release.

(2) The approved representatives of such agencies shall have all necessary access to the institution and to prisoners and shall be taken into consultation as to the future of a prisoner from the beginning of his sentence.

(3) It is desirable that the activities of such agencies shall be centralized or coordinated as far as possible in order to secure the best use of their efforts.

B. INSANE AND MENTALLY ABNORMAL PRISONERS

82. (1) Persons who are found to be insane shall not be detained in prisons and arrangements shall be made to remove them to mental institutions as soon as possible.

(2) Prisoners who suffer from other mental diseases or abnormalities shall be observed and treated in specialized institutions under medical management.

(3) During their stay in a prison, such prisoners shall be placed under the special supervision of a medical officer.

(4) The medical or psychiatric service of the penal institutions shall provide for the psychiatric treatment of all other prisoners who are in need of such treatment.

83. It is desirable that steps should be taken, by arrangement with the appropriate agencies, to ensure if necessary the continuation of psychiatric treatment after release and the provision of social-psychiatric after-care.

C. PRISONERS UNDER ARREST OR AWAITING TRIAL

84. (1) Persons arrested or imprisoned by reason of a criminal charge against them, who are detained either in police custody or in prison custody (jail) but have not yet been tried and sentenced, will be referred to as "untried prisoners" hereinafter in these rules.

(2) Untried prisoners are presumed to be innocent and shall be treated as such.

(3) Without prejudice to legal rules for the protection of individual liberty or prescribing the procedure to be observed in respect of untried prisoners, these prisoners shall benefit by a special regime which is described in the following rules in its essential requirements only.

85. (1) Untried prisoners shall be kept separate from convicted prisoners.

(2) Young untried prisoners shall be kept separate from adults and shall in principle be detained in separate institutions.

86. Untried prisoners shall sleep singly in separate rooms, with the reservation of different local custom in respect of the climate.

87. Within the limits compatible with the good order of the institution, untried prisoners may, if they so desire, have their food procured at their own expense from the outside, either through the administration or through their family or friends. Otherwise, the administration shall provide their food.

88. (1) An untried prisoner shall be allowed to wear his own clothing if it is clean and suitable.

(2) If he wears prison dress, it shall be different from that supplied to convicted prisoners.

89. An untried prisoner shall always be offered opportunity to work, but shall not be required to work. If he chooses to work, he shall be paid for it.

90. An untried prisoner shall be allowed to procure at his own expense or at the expense of a third party such books, newspapers, writing materials and other means of occupation as are compatible with the interests of the administration of justice and the security and good order of the institution.

91. An untried prisoner shall be allowed to be visited and treated by his own doctor or dentist if there is reasonable ground for his application and he is able to pay any expenses incurred.

92. An untried prisoner shall be allowed to inform immediately his family of his detention and shall be given all reasonable facilities for communicating with his family and friends, and for receiving visits from them, subject only to restrictions and supervision as are necessary in the interests of the administration of justice and of the security and good order of the institution.

93. For the purposes of his defence, an untried prisoner shall be allowed to apply for free legal aid where such aid is available, and to receive visits from his legal adviser with a view to his defence and to prepare and hand to him confidential instructions. For these purposes, he shall if he so desires be supplied with writing material. Interviews between the prisoner and his legal adviser may be within sight but not within the hearing of a police or institution official.

D. CIVIL PRISONERS

94. In countries where the law permits imprisonment for debt, or by order of a court under any other non-criminal process, persons so imprisoned shall not be subjected to any greater restriction or severity than is necessary to ensure safe custody and good order. Their treatment shall be not less favourable than that of untried prisoners, with the reservation, however, that they may possibly be required to work.

E. PERSONS ARRESTED OR DETAINED WITHOUT CHARGE

95. Without prejudice to the provisions of article 9 of the International Covenant on Civil and Political Rights, persons arrested or imprisoned without charge shall be accorded the same protection as that accorded under part I and part II, section C. Relevant provisions of part II, section A, shall likewise be applicable where their application may be conducive to the benefit of this special group of persons in custody, provided that no measures shall be taken implying that re-education or rehabilitation is in anyway appropriate to persons not convicted of any criminal offence.

* * *

5. Body of Principles for the Protection of All Persons under Any Form of Detention or Imprisonment

ANNEX

Body of Principles for the Protection of All Persons under Any Form of Detention or Imprisonment

SCOPE OF THE BODY OF PRINCIPLES

These principles apply for the protection of all persons under any form of detention or imprisonment.

USE OF TERMS

For the purposes of the Body of Principles:

(a) "Arrest" means the act of apprehending a person for the alleged commission of an offence or by the action of an authority;

(b) "Detained person" means any person deprived of personal liberty except as a result of conviction for an offence;

(c) "Imprisoned person" means any person deprived of personal liberty as a result of conviction for an offence;

(d) "Detention" means the condition of detained persons as defined above;

(e) "Imprisonment" means the condition of imprisoned persons as defined above;

(f) The words "a judicial or other authority" mean a judicial or other authority under the law whose status and tenure should afford the strongest possible guarantees of competence, impartiality and independence,

Principle 1

All persons under any form of detention or imprisonment shall be treated in a humane manner and with respect for the inherent dignity of the human person.

Principle 2

Arrest, detention or imprisonment shall only be carried out strictly in accordance with the provisions of the law and by competent officials or persons authorized for that purpose.

Principle 3

There shall be no restriction upon or derogation from any of the human rights of persons under any form of detention or imprisonment recognized or existing in any State pursuant to law, conventions, regulations or custom on the pretext that this Body of Principles does not recognize such rights or that it recognizes them to a lesser extent.

Principle 4

Any form of detention or imprisonment and all measures affecting the human rights of a person under any form of detention or imprisonment shall be ordered by, or be subject to the effective control of, a judicial or other authority.

Principle 5

1. These principles shall be applied to all persons within the territory of any given State, without distinction of any kind, such as race, colour, sex, language, religion or religious belief, political or other opinion, national, ethnic or social origin, property, birth or other status.

2. Measures applied under the law and designed solely to protect the rights and special status of women, especially pregnant women and nursing mothers, children and juveniles, aged, sick or handicapped persons shall not be deemed to be discriminatory. The need for, and the application of, such measures shall always be subject to review by a judicial or other authority.

Principle 6

No person under any form of detention or imprisonment shall be subjected to torture or to cruel, inhuman or degrading treatment or punishment.[1] No

---

[1]The term "cruel, inhuman or degrading treatment or punishment" should be interpreted so as to extend the widest possible protection against abuses, whether physical or mental, including the holding of a detained or imprisoned person in conditions which deprive him, temporarily or permanently, of the use of any of his natural senses, such as sight or hearing, or of his awareness of place and the passing of time.

circumstance whatever may be invoked as a justification for torture or other cruel, inhuman or degrading treatment or punishment.

Principle 7

1. States should prohibit by law any act contrary to the rights and duties contained in these principles, make any such act subject to appropriate sanctions and conduct impartial investigations upon complaints.

2. Officials who have reason to believe that a violation of this Body of Principles has occurred or is about to occur shall report the matter to their superior authorities and, where necessary, to other appropriate authorities or organs vested with reviewing or remedial powers.

3. Any other person who has ground to believe that a violation of this Body of Principles has occurred or is about to occur shall have the right to report the matter to the superiors of the officials involved as well as to other appropriate authorities or organs vested with reviewing or remedial powers.

Principle 8

Persons in detention shall be subject to treatment appropriate to their unconvicted status. Accordingly, they shall, whenever possible, be kept separate from imprisoned persons.

Principle 9

The authorities which arrest a person, keep him under detention or investigate the case shall exercise only the powers granted to them under the law and the exercise of these powers shall be subject to recourse to a judicial or other authority.

Principle 10

Anyone who is arrested shall be informed at the time of his arrest of the reason for his arrest and shall be promptly informed of any charges against him.

Principle 11

1. A person shall not be kept in detention without being given an effective opportunity to be heard promptly by a judicial or other authority. A detained person shall have the right to defend himself or to be assisted by counsel as prescribed by law.

2. A detained person and his counsel, if any, shall receive prompt and full communication of any order of detention, together with the reasons therefor.

3. A judicial or other authority shall be empowered to review as appropriate the continuance of detention.

Principle 12

1. There shall be duly recorded:

   (a) The reasons for the arrest;

   (b) The time of the arrest and the taking of the arrested person to a place of custody as well as that of his first appearance before a judicial or other authority;

   (c) The identity of the law enforcement officials concerned;

   (d) Precise information concerning the place of custody.

2. Such records shall be communicated to the detained person, or his counsel, if any, in the form prescribed by law.

Principle 13

Any person shall, at the moment of arrest and at the commencement of detention or imprisonment, or promptly thereafter, be provided by the authority responsible for his arrest, detention or imprisonment, respectively, with information on and an explanation of his rights and how to avail himself of such rights.

Principle 14

A person who does not adequately understand or speak the language used by the authorities responsible for his arrest, detention or imprisonment is entitled to receive promptly in a language which he understands the information referred to in principle 10, principle 11, paragraph 2, principle 12, paragraph 1, and principle 13 and to have the assistance, free of charge, if necessary, of an interpreter in connection with legal proceedings subsequent to his arrest.

Principle 15

Notwithstanding the exceptions contained in principle 16, paragraph 4, and principle 18, paragraph 3, communication of the detained or imprisoned person with the outside world, and in particular his family or counsel, shall not be denied for more than a matter of days.

Principle 16

1. Promptly after arrest and after each transfer from one place of detention or imprisonment to another, a detained or imprisoned person shall be entitled to notify or to require the competent authority to notify members of his family or other appropriate persons of his choice of his arrest, detention or imprisonment or of the transfer and of the place where he is kept in custody.

2. If a detained or imprisoned person is a foreigner, he shall also be promptly informed of his right to communicate by appropriate means with a consular post or the diplomatic mission of the State of which he is a national or which is otherwise entitled to receive such communication in accordance with international law or with the representative of the competent international organization, if he is a refugee or is otherwise under the protection of an intergovernmental organization.

3. If a detained or imprisoned person is a juvenile or is incapable of understanding his entitlement, the competent authority shall on its own initiative undertake the notification referred to in the present principle. Special attention shall be given to notifying parents or guardians.

4. Any notification referred to in the present principle shall be made or permitted to be made without delay. The competent authority may however delay a notification for a reasonable period where exceptional needs of the investigation so require.

Principle 17

1. A detained person shall be entitled to have the assistance of legal counsel. He shall be informed of his right by the competent authority promptly after arrest and shall be provided with reasonable facilities for exercising it.

2. If a detained person does not have legal counsel of his own choice, he shall be entitled to have legal counsel assigned to him by a judicial or other authority in all cases where the interests of justice so require and without payment by him if he does not have sufficient means to pay.

Principle 18

1. A detained or imprisoned person shall be entitled to communicate and consult with his legal counsel.

2. A detained or imprisoned person shall be allowed adequate time and facilities for consultation with his legal counsel.

3. The right of a detained or imprisoned person to be visited by and to consult and communicate, without delay or censorship and in full confidentiality, with his legal counsel may not be suspended or restricted save in exceptional circumstances, to be specified by law or lawful regulations, when it is considered indispensable by a judicial or other authority in order to maintain security and good order.

4. Interviews between a detained or imprisoned person and his legal counsel may be within sight, but not within the hearing, of a law enforcement official.

5. Communications between a detained or imprisoned person and his legal counsel mentioned in the present principle shall be inadmissible as evidence against the detained or imprisoned person unless they are connected with a continuing or contemplated crime.

Principle 19

A detained or imprisoned person shall have the right to be visited by and to correspond with, in particular, members of his family and shall be given adequate opportunity to communicate with the outside world, subject to reasonable conditions and restrictions as specified by law or lawful regulations.

Principle 20

If a detained or imprisoned person so requests, he shall if possible be kept in a place of detention or imprisonment reasonably near his usual place of residence.

Principle 21

1. It shall be prohibited to take undue advantage of the situation of a detained or imprisoned person for the purpose of compelling him to confess, to incriminate himself otherwise or to testify against any other person.

2. No detained person while being interrogated shall be subject to violence, threats or methods of interrogation which impair his capacity of decision or his judgment.

Principle 22

No detained or imprisoned person shall, even with his consent, be subjected to any medical or scientific experimentation which may be detrimental to his health.

Principle 23

1. The duration of any interrogation of a detained or imprisoned person and of the intervals between interrogations as well as the identity of the officials who conducted the interrogations and other persons present shall be recorded and certified in such form as may be prescribed by law.

2. A detained or imprisoned person, or his counsel when provided by law, shall have access to the information described in paragraph 1 of the present principle.

Principle 24

A proper medical examination shall be offered to a detained or imprisoned person as promptly as possible after his admission to the place of detention or imprisonment, and thereafter medical care and treatment shall be provided whenever necessary. This care and treatment shall be provided free of charge.

Principle 25

A detained or imprisoned person or his counsel shall, subject only to reasonable conditions to ensure security and good order in the place of detention or imprisonment, have the right to request or petition a judicial or other authority for a second medical examination or opinion.

Principle 26

The fact that a detained or imprisoned person underwent a medical examination, the name of the physician and the results of such an examination shall be duly recorded. Access to such records shall be ensured. Modalities therefore shall be in accordance with relevant rules of domestic law.

Principle 27

Non-compliance with these principles in obtaining evidence shall be taken into account in determining the admissibility of such evidence against a detained or imprisoned person.

Principle 28

A detained or imprisoned person shall have the right to obtain within the limits of available resources, if from public sources, reasonable quantities of educational, cultural and informational material, subject to reasonable conditions to ensure security and good order in the place of detention or imprisonment.

Principle 29

1. In order to supervise the strict observance of relevant laws and regulations, places of detention shall be visited regularly by qualified and experienced persons appointed by, and responsible to, a competent authority distinct from the authority directly in charge of the administration of the place of detention or imprisonment.

2. A detained or imprisoned person shall have the right to communicate freely and in full confidentiality with the persons who visit the places of detention or imprisonment in accordance with paragraph 1 of the present principle, subject to reasonable conditions to ensure security and good order in such places.

Principle 30

1. The types of conduct of the detained or imprisoned person that constitute disciplinary offences during detention or imprisonment, the description and duration of disciplinary punishment that may be inflicted and the authorities competent to impose such punishment shall be specified by law or lawful regulations and duly published.

2. A detained or imprisoned person shall have the right to be heard before disciplinary action is taken. He shall have the right to bring such action to higher authorities for review.

Principle 31

The appropriate authorities shall endeavour to ensure, according to domestic law, assistance when needed to dependent and, in particular, minor members of the families of detained or imprisoned persons and shall devote a particular measure of care to the appropriate custody of children left without supervision.

Principle 32

1. A detained person or his counsel shall be entitled at any time to take proceedings according to domestic law before a judicial or other authority to

challenge the lawfulness of his detention in order to obtain his release without delay, if it is unlawful.

2. The proceedings referred to in paragraph 1 of the present principle shall be simple and expeditious and at no cost for detained persons without adequate means. The detaining authority shall produce without unreasonable delay the detained person before the reviewing authority.

Principle 33

1. A detained or imprisoned person or his counsel shall have the right to make a request or complaint regarding his treatment, in particular in case of torture or other cruel, inhuman or degrading treatment, to the authorities responsible for the administration of the place of detention and to higher authorities and, when necessary, to appropriate authorities vested with reviewing or remedial powers.

2. In those cases where neither the detained or imprisoned person nor his counsel has the possibility to exercise his rights under paragraph 1 of the present principle, a member of the family of the detained or imprisoned person or any other person who has knowledge of the case may exercise such rights.

3. Confidentiality concerning the request or complaint shall be maintained if so requested by the complainant.

4. Every request or complaint shall be promptly dealt with and replied to without undue delay. If the request or complaint is rejected or, in case of inordinate delay, the complainant shall be entitled to bring it before a judicial or other authority. Neither the detained or imprisoned person nor any complainant under paragraph 1 of the present principle shall suffer prejudice for making a request or complaint.

Principle 34

Whenever the death or disappearance of a detained or imprisoned person occurs during his detention or imprisonment, an inquiry into the cause of death or disappearance shall be held by a judicial or other authority, either on its own motion or at the instance of a member of the family of such a person or any person who has knowledge of the case. When circumstances so warrant, such an inquiry shall be held on the same procedural basis whenever the death or disappearance occurs shortly after the termination of the detention or imprisonment. The findings of such inquiry or a report thereon shall be made available upon request, unless doing so would jeopardize an ongoing criminal investigation.

Principle 35

1. Damage incurred because of acts or omissions by a public official contrary to the rights contained in these principles shall be compensated according to the applicable rules or liability provided by domestic law.

2. Information required to be recorded under these principles shall be available in accordance with procedures provided by domestic law for use in claiming compensation under the present principle.

Principle 36

1. A detained person suspected of or charged with a criminal offence shall be presumed innocent and shall be treated as such until proved guilty according to law in a public trial at which he has had all the guarantees necessary for his defence.

2. The arrest or detention of such a person pending investigation and trial shall be carried out only for the purposes of the administration of justice on grounds and under conditions and procedures specified by law. The imposition of restrictions upon such a person which are not strictly required for the purpose of the detention or to prevent hindrance to the process of investigation or the administration of justice, or for the maintenance of security and good order in the place of detention shall be forbidden.

Principle 37

A person detained on a criminal charge shall be brought before a judicial or other authority provided by law promptly after his arrest. Such authority shall decide without delay upon the lawfulness and necessity of detention. No person may be kept under detention pending investigation or trial except upon the written order of such an authority. A detained person shall, when brought before such an authority, have the right to make a statement on the treatment received by him while in custody.

Principle 38

A person detained on a criminal charge shall be entitled to trial within a reasonable time or to release pending trial.

Principle 39

Except in special cases provided for by law, a person detained on a criminal charge shall be entitled, unless a judicial or other authority decides otherwise in the interest of the administration of justice, to release pending trial subject to the conditions that may be imposed in accordance with the law. Such authority shall keep the necessity of detention under review.

* * *

6. Draft Optional Protocol to the Convention Against Torture and Other Cruel, Inhuman or Degrading Treatment or Punishment

PART I

Article 1

1. A State Party to the present Protocol agrees to permit visits, in accordance with this Protocol, to any place within its jurisdiction where persons deprived of their liberty by a public authority or at its instigation or with its consent or acquiescence are held or may be held.

2. The object of the visits shall be to examine the treatment of persons deprived of their liberty with a view to strengthening, if necessary, the protection of such persons from torture and from other cruel, inhuman or degrading treatment or punishment in accordance with international standards.

Article 2

The Committee against Torture shall establish a Sub-Committee for the Prevention of Torture and other Cruel, Inhuman or Degrading Treatment or Punishment (hereinafter referred to as the Sub-Committee); the Sub-Committee shall be responsible for organizing missions to the States Parties to the present Protocol for the purposes stated in article 1.

Article 3

In the application of this Protocol, the Subcommittee and the competent national authorities of the State Party concerned shall cooperate with each other.

PART II

Article 4

1. The Sub-Committee shall consist of a minimum of 25 members. While there are less than 25 States Parties to the present Protocol, the number of members of the Sub-Committee shall be equal to that of the States Parties.

2. The members of the Sub-Committee shall be chosen from among persons of high moral character, having proven professional experience in the field of prison or police administration or in the various medical fields relevant to the treatment of persons deprived of their liberty or in the field of the international protection of human rights.

3. No two members of the Sub-Committee may be nationals of the same State.

4. The members of the Sub-Committee shall serve in their individual capacity, shall be independent and impartial and shall be available to serve the Sub-Committee effectively.

Article 5

1. The members of the Sub-Committee shall be elected by the Committee against Torture by an absolute majority of votes from a list of persons possessing the qualifications prescribed in article 4 and nominated by the States Parties to the present Protocol.

2. Within three months of the entry into force of the present Protocol, the accession of a new member or a vacancy, each State Party shall nominate three persons, at least two of whom shall possess its nationality. They shall be indicated in alphabetical order.

3. Subject to article 4, paragraph 1, the Committee against Torture shall hold elections whenever there is an accession to the present Protocol or a vacancy in the Sub-Committee.

4. A member shall be eligible for re-election if renominated.

Article 6

1. The members of the Sub-Committee shall be elected for a period of four years. However, among the members elected at the first election, the terms of five members, to be chosen by lot, shall expire at the end of two years.

2. In the election of the members of the Sub-Committee, consideration shall be given to equitable geographical distribution of membership, to a proper balance among the various fields of competence referred to in article 4, paragraph 2, and to the representation of different traditions and legal systems.

Article 7

1. The Sub-Committee shall meet for a regular session at least twice a year; for special sessions at the initiative of its Chairman or at the request of not less than one third of its members.

2. The Sub-Committee shall meet *in camera*. Half of the members shall constitute a quorum. The decisions of the Sub-Committee shall be taken by a majority of the members present, subject to article 14, paragraph 2.

3. The Sub-Committee shall draw up its own rules of procedure.

4. The Secretary-General of the United Nations shall provide the necessary staff and facilities for the effective performance of the functions of the Committee against Torture and the Sub-Committee under this Protocol.

PART III

Article 8

1. The Sub-Committee shall establish a programme of regular missions to each of the States Parties. Apart from regular missions, it shall also undertake such other missions as appear to it to be required in the circumstances.

2. The Sub-Committee shall postpone any such mission if the State Party concerned has agreed to a visit to its territory by the Committee against Torture pursuant to article 20, paragraph 3, of the Convention.

Article 9

1. If, on the basis of a regional convention, a system of visits to places of detention similar to the one of the present Protocol is in force for a State Party, the Sub-Committee shall only in exceptional cases, when required by important circumstances, send its own mission to such a State Party. It may, however, consult with the organs established under such regional conventions with a view to coordinating activities including the possibility of having one of its members participate in missions carried out under the regional conventions as an observer.

Such an observer shall report to the Sub-Committee. This report shall be strictly confidential and shall not be made public.

2. The present Protocol does not affect the provisions of the Geneva Conventions of 12 August 1949 for the protection of victims of war and their Additional Protocols of 8 June 1977 by which the Protecting Powers and the International Committee of the Red Cross visit places of detention, or the right of any State Party to authorize the International Committee to visit places of detention in situations not covered by international humanitarian law.

Article 10

1. As a general rule, the missions shall be carried out by at least two members of the Sub-Committee, assisted by experts and interpreters if necessary.

2. No member of a delegation shall be a national of the State to be visited.

Article 11

1. Experts shall act on the instructions and under the authority of the Sub-Committee. They shall have particular knowledge and experience in the areas covered by this Protocol and shall be bound by the same duties of independence, impartiality and availability as the members of the Sub-Committee.

2. A State Party may exceptionally and for reasons given confidentially declare that an expert or other person assisting the Sub-Committee may not take part in a mission to its territory.

Article 12

1. The Sub-Committee shall notify the Government of the State Party concerned of its intention to organize admission. After such notification, it may at any time visit any place referred to in article 1, paragraph 1.

2. The State Party within whose jurisdiction a mission is to take place or is being carried out shall provide the delegation with all the facilities necessary for the proper fulfillment of their tasks and shall not obstruct by any means or measures the programme of visits or any other activities which the delegation is carrying out specifically for or in relation to the visits. In particular, the State Party shall provide the delegation with the following facilities:

(a) access to its territory and the right to travel without restriction,

(b) full information on the places referred to in article 1, paragraph 1, including information requested about specific persons;

(c) unlimited access to any place referred to in article 1, paragraph 1, including the right to move inside such places without restriction;

(d) assistance in gaining access to places where the delegation has reason to believe that persons may be deprived of their liberty;

(e) producing any person deprived of his liberty whom the delegation wishes to interview, at the request of the delegation and at a convenient location;

(f) other information available to the State Party which is necessary for the delegation to carry out its task.

3. Members of the delegation may interview in private, inside or outside place of detention, without witnesses, and for the time they deem necessary, any person deprived of his liberty under the terms of article 1. They may also communicate without restriction with relatives, friends, lawyers and doctors of persons who are or have been deprived of their liberty, and with any other person or organization that they think may be able to provide them with relevant information for their mission. In seeking such information, the delegation shall have regard to applicable rules of national law relating to data protection and principles of medical ethics.

4. No authority or official shall order, apply, permit or tolerate any sanction against any person or organization for having communicated to the Sub-Committee or to the delegates any information, whether true or false, and no such person or organization shall be otherwise prejudiced in any way.

5. In urgent cases the delegation shall at once submit observations and recommendations either of general or specific nature to the competent authorities of the State Party concerned.

Article 13

1. In the context of a mission, the competent authorities of the State Party concerned may make representations to the Sub-committee or its delegation against a particular visit if urgent and compelling reasons relating to serious disorder in the particular place to be visited temporarily prevent the carrying out of the visit.

2. Following any such representation, the Sub-Committee and the State Party shall immediately enter into consultations in order to clarify the situation and seek agreement on arrangements to enable the Sub-Committee to exercise its functions expeditiously. Such arrangements may include the transfer to another place of any person whom the Sub-Committee proposed to visit. Until the visit takes place, the State Party shall provide information to the Sub-Committee about any person concerned.

Article 14

1. After each mission, the Sub-Committee shall draw up a report on the facts found during the mission, taking account of any observations which may have been submitted by the State Party concerned. It shall transmit to the latter its report containing any recommendations it considers necessary and may consult with the State Party with a view to suggesting, if necessary, improvements in the protection of persons deprived of their liberty.

2. If the State Party fails to co-operate or refuses to improve the situation in the light of the Sub-Committee's recommendations, the Committee against Torture may at the request of the Sub-Committee decide by a majority of its members, after the State Party has had an opportunity to make known its views, to make a public statement on the matter or to publish the Sub-Committee's report.

3. The Sub-Committee shall publish its report, together with any comments of the State Party concerned, whenever requested to do so by that State Party. If the State Party makes part of the report public, the Sub-Committee may publish the report in whole or in part. However, no personal data shall be published without the express consent of the person concerned.

4. In all other respects, the information gathered by the Sub-Committee and its delegation in relation to a mission, its report and its consultation with the State Party concerned shall remain confidential. Members of the Committee against Torture, the Sub-Committee, its delegations and their staff are required to maintain confidentiality during and after their terms of office.

Article 15

1. The Committee against Torture shall examine the reports and recommendations which may be submitted to it by the Sub-Committee. It shall keep them confidential as long as no public statement in accordance with article 14, paragraph 2, has been made or as long as they have not become public in accordance with article 14, paragraph 3, of this Protocol.

2. Subject to the rules of confidentiality, the Sub-Committee shall every year submit a general annual report on its activities to the Committee against Torture, which shall include information on the activities under this Protocol in its annual report to the General Assembly of the United Nations in accordance with article 24 of the Convention.

PART IV

Article 16

The expenditures incurred by the implementation of the present Protocol, including all its missions, shall be borne by the United Nations.

1. States Parties shall contribute to the expenditure incurred in the implementation of the present Protocol on the basis of the scale used by the United Nations.

2. There may be established a Special Fund based on voluntary contributions of States, intergovernmental organizations, non-governmental organizations, private institutions and individuals.

3. The Special Fund shall supplement the financing by the States Parties of all the activities provided for in this Protocol. It shall be managed by the Sub-Committee, which shall report to a Board of Trustees appointed by the States Parties.

4. Any expenses, such as the cost of staff, interpreters and facilities, incurred by the United Nations pursuant to article 7, paragraph 4, shall be reimbursed by contributions of the States Parties and the Special Fund.

Article 17

1. The present Protocol is open for signature by any State which has signed the Convention.

2. The present Protocol is subject to ratification or open to accession by any State which has ratified or acceded to the Convention. Instruments of ratification or accession shall be deposited with the Secretary-General of the United Nations.

3. The Secretary-General of the United Nations shall inform all States which have signed the present Protocol or acceded to it of the deposit of each instrument of ratification or accession.

Article 18

1. The present Protocol shall enter into force three months after the deposit of the tenth instrument of ratification or accession.

2. For each State ratifying the present Protocol or acceding to it after the deposit of the tenth instrument of ratification or instrument of accession, the present Protocol shall enter into force three months after the date of the deposit of its own instrument of ratification or accession.

3. No reservations may be made in respect of the provisions of this Protocol.

Article 19

Any State Party may denounce the present Protocol at any time by written notification addressed to the Secretary-General of the United Nations, who shall thereafter inform the other States Parties, the Committee against Torture and the Sub-Committee. Denunciation shall take effect one year after the date of receipt of the notification by the Secretary-General.

Article 20

The members of the Sub-Committee and of its delegations shall be entitled to the facilities, privileges and immunities referred to in article 23 of the Convention.

Article 21

1. The present Protocol, of which the Arabic, Chinese, English, French, Russian and Spanish texts are equally authentic, shall be deposited in the archives of the United Nations.

2. The Secretary-General of the United Nations shall transmit certified copies of this Protocol to all States.

* * *

7. United Nations Resolution on Infection with Human Immunodeficiency Virus (HIV) and Acquired Immunodeficiency Syndrome (AIDS) in Prison

The Eighth United Nations Congress on the Prevention of Crime and the Treatment of Offenders,

Recognizing the seriousness and urgency of problems relating to the human immunodeficiency virus (HIV) and the acquired immunodeficiency syndrome (AIDS) in prisons world wide,

Stressing the need to address these problems at the national, regional and international levels,

Aware of the fact that the phenomenon of HIV/AIDS in prison raises difficult questions in respect of the protection of prisoners, prison staff and the general community,

Aware also of the fact that the management of prisoners who are HIV-infected and those with AIDS has created a new set of problems for the prison authorities,

1. *Acknowledges* with appreciation the report on HIV/AIDS in prison, prepared by the World Health Organization in collaboration with the Crime Prevention and Criminal Justice Branch of the United Nations Secretariat, and the activities already undertaken by the United Nations and the World Health Organization in this field;

2. *Recommends* that Member States consider the preliminary findings and conclusions in the report and take steps towards the development of a policy on AIDS prevention and control in prisons based on the World Health Organization Global AIDS Strategy, as a part of their national AIDS prevention and control strategy;

3. *Requests* the Secretary-General, in collaboration with regional institutes for crime prevention and control and with the World Health Organization:

(a) To assist prison administrations, at the request of the Member States concerned, in the development of national AIDS prevention and control programmes for the prison population, and to promote international exchanges of information in this area;

(b) To encourage, as an integral part of the increased emphasis on prison education programmes, international co-operation in the elaboration and exchange of education materials designed to prevent further spread of HIV infection in prison;

(c) To undertake the elaboration of guidelines for the institutional and clinical management of HIV-infected prisoners and those with AIDS.

* * *

8. United Nations Resolution on International and Interregional Co-operation in Prison Management and Community-based Sanctions and Other Matters

A

Custodial and non-custodial treatment of offenders

The Eighth United Nations Congress on the Prevention of Crime and the Treatment of Offenders,

Emphasizing the importance of the Standard Minimum Rules for the Treatment of Prisoners and other international instruments in relation to the treatment of prisoners and prison management,

Conscious of the heavy demands made by the criminal justice system on the human and material resources of Member States,

Taking account of the high economic and social costs of imprisonment as a penal sanction,

Bearing in mind the effects of imprisonment on the psychological, emotional and social aspects of the personality of the individual offender,

Bearing in mind also the potentially damaging consequences of imprisonment for the family and for the social relationships of the offender,

Taking into account the lower economic and social cost of non-custodial sanctions,

Cognizant of the need to intensify the search for credible non-custodial sanctions and to expand their application,

Reaffirming that crime prevention, criminal justice and the treatment of offenders are important elements of the overall social defence and socio-economic development of States that embody respect for human rights and fundamental freedoms,

Invites Member States:

(a) To consider the extent to which the use of imprisonment might be replaced by non-custodial sanctions consistent with public safety;

(b) To emphasize that non-custodial sanctions constitute sentences in their own right and should not be seen as merely substitutes for sentences for imprisonment;

(c) To create the necessary infrastructure and resources and to foster favourable attitudes on the part of the community at large, especially legislators, judges, prosecutors and administrators to their use;

(d) To broaden the availability of non-custodial sanctions as judicial sanctions;

(e) To take into consideration, in the framework of non-custodial sanctions, the availability of alternatives to pre-trial custody which could be adopted more extensively;

(f) To avoid, reduce or eliminate overcrowding in prisons by considering the use of a combination of factors; a reduction in the length of prison sentences available; the substitution of non-custodial sanctions or measures; and the reduction of pre-trial detention by facilitating pre-trial release or the use of bail and recognizances;

(g) To limit the use of pre-trial detention to those cases where there are reasonable grounds to believe that the persons concerned have been involved in the commission of the alleged offences and there is a danger of their absconding or committing further serious offences or a danger that the course of justice will be seriously interfered with, if they are left free;

(h) To examine methods of ensuring that the access of persons in pre-trial detention to legal or other advice and assistance is not impeded and the conditions of detention are no more restrictive than is necessary to ensure the secure containment of such persons;

(i) To work towards the more complete implementation of the Standard Minimum Rules for the Treatment of Prisoners;

(j) To acknowledge that penal institutions are an integral part of the society they serve and that, in consequence, staff should be encouraged and enabled to play an active part in community affairs, as should prisoners, so far as is consistent with public safety;

(k) To develop the closest possible links between penal institutions and other national and local statutory and voluntary agencies and their local communities to limit the inherently deleterious effects of social isolation and to foster and maintain a sense of citizenship;

(l) To develop the organizational and social structure of prisons so that they more nearly reflect the arrangements prevailing in society, of which the prisoners remain members and to which they will return based on their individual needs in so far as these are consistent with the requirements of security and the maintenance of a safe and orderly environment;

(m) To consider the scope for establishing a system that achieves a proper balance between the rights and responsibilities of members of society, with special regard to the victims of crimes, those of the management and staff of penal institutions and those of the prisoners that takes account of the requirements of due process and need to limit the range of discretion exercised by management and staff so as to prevent the arbitrary use of authority, through appropriate organizational structures and effective management procedures, the provision of effective complaints and grievance procedures, access to the courts, and regulatory and inspectorial arrangements;

(n) To examine ways in which reconciliation between offenders and their victims might be facilitated by the development of programmes designed to provide opportunities for mediation and reparation;

(o) To consider also the need to review the managerial arrangements and working practices and their legal framework so as to reflect the implications of such an approach for the deployment of staff, their roles and responsibilities, and the relationship between prison officers and specialists and between prison officers and prisoners;

(p) To pursue, in view of the above, new managerial arrangements and training programmes to establish and maintain the central role of prison officers, thereby contributing to the enhancement of their status and professional identity;

(q) To establish and maintain a better understanding of the issues relating to penal systems through public education programmes and contact with the media and other interested organizations and institutions, so as to create a more positive image of all staff, whether they work in penal institutions or in the community, with responsibility for the maintenance of public safety and the reintegration of offenders into the community;

(r) To consider how the status and public image of prison officers might be enhanced by the introduction of a new designation that more accurately reflects their expanded role, together with a suitably styled uniform and appropriate conditions of service, pay and pension arrangements;

(s) To establish appropriate training programmes to prepare and enable both management and staff to exercise their responsibilities within a legal and police framework that determines their authority and accountability at all levels to make decisions and use discretion in relation to the individual treatment and personal development of prisoners, their security, care and control;

(t) To consider using increasingly the provision for the transfer of foreign prisoners to their country of normal residence to serve their sentence.

B

Work, education, leisure and family visits

The Eighth United Nations Congress on the Prevention of Crime and the Treatment of Offenders,

Acknowledging the contribution of prison labour to the process of the rehabilitation and the reintegration of inmates into society,

Emphasizing the need for further research, exchange of information and provision of technical assistance through the United Nations human rights and criminal justices programmes,

Considering the universal right to education as a means of fully developing the human personality, as set out in article 26 of the Universal Declaration of Human Rights and in article 13 of the International Covenant on Economic, Social and Cultural Rights,

Bearing in mind article 16 of the Universal Declaration of Human Rights and article 23 of the International Covenant on Civil and Political Rights. Both of which proclaim, *inter alia*, that the family is the natural and fundamental group unit of society and is entitled to protection by society and the State,

Recalling rule 37 of the Standard Minimum Rules for the Treatment of Prisoners, which provides that prisoners shall be allowed under the necessary supervision to communicate with their family and reputable friends at regular intervals, both by correspondence and by receiving visits,

Invites Member States:

(a) To develop education in prisons, including the provision of adequate library services, and the availability of trained teachers and volunteers from the community, with a view to facilitating the resocialization of prisoners;

(b) To permit prisoners to receive frequent and prolonged visits from family and friends in the most favourable conditions possible.

C

Drugs

The Eighth United Nations Congress on the Prevention of Crime and the Treatment of Offenders,

Acknowledging that drug-related issues deserve particular attention in view of their impact on the functioning of society and also the need to develop greater knowledge concerning the medical and social treatment of drug users,

Considering that the abuse of drugs is a global problem of great complexity requiring social policies on preventive measures and treatment,

Recognizing its adverse effects on the administration of the criminal justice system,

Invites Member States to consider the extent to which they may wish:

(a) To differentiate in the application of the criminal law and in the nature and type of treatment provided to occasional users from those physically and/or psychologically dependent; to the user from the dealers; and to those whose offences are directly related to their drug dependence from those whose offences are not so related;

(b) To give preference to the use of non-custodial measures in relation to the personal use of drugs;

(c) To provide medical, psychological and social treatment programmes for drug-dependent offenders, to be applied in appropriate cases;

(d) To initiate or develop research programmes on the relationship between drug dependence and crime.

D

Health care

The Eighth United Nations Congress on the Prevention of Crimes and the Treatment of Offenders,

Recalling that in accordance with rule 22(2) of the Standard Minimum Rules for the Treatment of Prisoners sick prisoners in need of specialist treatment shall be transferred to specialized institutions or to civil hospitals,

Aware of the need to provide resocialization opportunities for mentally disturbed and physically disabled prisoners,

Invites Member States:

(a) To arrange for the treatment of sick prisoners to be conducted in a multidisciplinary context and to employ the services of specialized professional personnel;

(b) To consider the human immunodeficiency virus, the acquired immunodeficiency syndrome, hepatitis and similar transmittable diseases as a growing public health issue concerning not only the wider community but also the prison population and, in consequence, to provide information and encouragement to prisoners and staff to take the necessary measures to avoid the transmission of these diseases and, in the event of infection, to take the necessary measures to ensure their proper treatment, including counselling;

(c) To ensure that there is no discrimination on the grounds of infection.

* * *

9. Basic Principles for the Treatment of Prisoners

The General Assembly,

Bearing in mind the long-standing concern of the United Nations for the humanization of criminal justice and the protection of human rights,

Bearing in mind also that sound policies of crime prevention and control are essential to viable planning for economic and social development,

Recognizing that the Standard Minimum Rules for the Treatment of Prisoners, adopted by the First United Nations Congress on the Prevention of Crime and the Treatment of Offenders, are of great value and influence in the development of penal policy and practice,

Considering the concern of previous United Nations congresses on the prevention of crime and the treatment of offenders, regarding the obstacles of various kinds that prevent the full implementation of the Standard Minimum Rules,

Believing that the full implementation of the Standard Minimum Rules would be facilitated by the articulation of the basic principles underlying them,

Recalling resolution 10 on the status of prisoners and resolution 17 on the human rights of prisoners, adopted by the Seventh United Nations Congress on the Prevention of Crime and the Treatment of Offenders,

Recalling also the statement submitted at the tenth session of the Committee on Crime Prevention and Control by Caritas Internationalis, the Commission of the Churches on International Affairs of the World Council of Churches, the International Association of Educators for World Peace, the International Council for Adult Education, the International Federation of Human Rights, the International Prisoners' Aid Association, the International Union of Students, the World Alliance of Young Men's Christian Associations and the World Council of Indigenous Peoples, which are non-governmental organizations in consultative status with the Economic and Social Council, category II,

Recalling further the relevant recommendations contained in the report of the Interregional Preparatory Meeting for the Eighth United Nations Congress on the Prevention of Crime and the Treatment of Offenders on topic II, "Criminal Justice Policies in Relation to Problems of Imprisonment, Other Penal Sanctions and Alternative Measures,"

Aware that the Eighth Congress coincided with International Literacy Year, proclaimed by the General Assembly in its resolution 42/104 of 7 December 1987,

Desiring to reflect the perspective noted by the Seventh Congress, namely, that the function of the criminal justice system is to contribute to safeguarding the basic values and norms of society,

Recognizing the usefulness of drafting a declaration on the human rights of prisoners,

Affirms the Basic Principles for the Treatment of Prisoners, annexed to the present resolution, and requests the Secretary-General to bring it to the attention of Member States.

ANNEX

Basic Principles for the Treatment of Prisoners

1. All prisoners shall be treated with the respect due to their inherent dignity and value as human beings.

2. There shall be no discrimination on the grounds of race, colour, sex, language, religion, political or other opinion, national or social origin, property, birth or other status.

3. It is, however, desirable to respect the religious beliefs and cultural precepts of the group to which prisoners belong, whenever local conditions so require.

4. The responsibility of prisons for the custody of prisoners and for the protection of society against crime shall be discharged in keeping with a State's other social objectives and its fundamental responsibilities for promoting the well-being and development of all members of society.

5. Except for those limitations that are demonstrably necessitated by the fact of incarceration, all prisoners shall retain the human rights and fundamental freedoms set out in the Universal Declaration of Human Rights, and, where the State concerned is a party, the International Covenant on Economic, Social and Cultural Rights, and the International Covenant on Civil and Political Rights and Optional Protocol thereto, as well as such other rights as are set out in other United Nations covenants.

6. All prisoners shall have the right to take part in cultural activities and education aimed at the full development of the human personality.

7. Efforts addressed to the abolition of solitary confinement as a punishment, or to the restriction of its use, should be undertaken and encouraged.

8. Conditions shall be created enabling prisoners to undertake meaningful remunerated employment which will facilitate their reintegration into the country' s labour market and permit them to contribute to their own financial support and to that of their families.

9. Prisoners shall have access to the health services available in the country without discrimination on the grounds of their legal situation.

10. With the participation and help of the community and social institution, and with due regard to the interests of victims, favourable conditions shall be created

for the reintegration of the ex-prisoner into society under the best possible conditions.

11. The above principles shall be applied impartially.

10. United Nations Standard Minimum Rules for Non-custodial Measures (The Tokyo Rules)

ANNEX

United Nations Standard Minimum Rules for Non-custodial Measures (The Tokyo Rules)

I. GENERAL PRINCIPLES

1. *Fundamental aims*

1.1 The present Standard Minimum Rules provide a set of basic principles to promote the use of non-custodial measures, as well as minimum safeguards for persons subject to alternatives to imprisonment.

1.2 The Rules are intended to promote greater community involvement in the management of criminal justice, specifically in the treatment of offenders, as well as to promote among offenders a sense of responsibility towards society.

1.3 The Rules shall be implemented taking into account the political, economic, social and cultural conditions of each country and the aims and objectives of its criminal justice system.

1.4 When implementing the Rules, Member States shall endeavour to ensure a proper balance between the rights of individual offenders, the rights of victims, and the concern of society for public safety and crime prevention.

1.5 Member States shall develop non-custodial measures within their legal systems to provide other options, thus reducing the use of imprisonment, and to rationalize criminal justice policies, taking into account the observance of human rights, the requirements of social justice and the rehabilitation needs of the offender.

2. *The scope of non-custodial measures*

2.1 The relevant provisions of the present Rules shall be applied to all persons subject to prosecution, trial or the execution of a sentence, at all stages of the administration of criminal justice. For the purposes of the Rules, these persons are referred to as "offenders," irrespective of whether they are suspected, accused or sentenced.

2.2 The Rules shall be applied without any discrimination on the grounds of race, colour, sex, age, language, religion, political or other opinion, national or social origin, property, birth or other status.

2.3 In order to provide greater flexibility consistent with the nature and gravity of the offence, with the personality and background of the offender and with the protection of society and to avoid unnecessary use of imprisonment, the criminal justice system should provide a wide range of non-custodial measures, from pretrial to post-sentencing dispositions. The number and types of non-custodial measures available should be determined in such a way so that consistent sentencing remains possible.

2.4 The development of new non-custodial measures should be encouraged and closely monitored and their use systematically evaluated.

2.5 Consideration shall be given to dealing with offenders in the community avoiding as far as possible resort to formal proceedings or trial by a court, in accordance with legal safeguards and the rule of law.

2.6 Non-custodial measures should be used in accordance with the principle of minimum intervention.

2.7 The use of non-custodial measures should be part of the movement towards depenalization and decriminalization instead of interfering with or delaying efforts in that direction.

3. *Legal safeguards*

3.1 The introduction, definition and application of non-custodial measures shall be prescribed by law.

3.2 The selection of a non-custodial measure shall be based on an assessment of established criteria in respect of both the nature and gravity of the offence and the personality, background of the offender, the purposes of sentencing and the rights of victims.

3.3 Discretion by the judicial or other competent independent authority shall be exercised at all stages of the proceedings by ensuring full accountability and only in accordance with the rule of law.

3.4 Non-custodial measures imposing an obligation on the offender, applied before or instead of formal proceedings or trial, shall require the offender's consent.

3.5 Decisions on the imposition of non-custodial measures shall be subject to review by a judicial or other competent independent authority, upon application by the offender.

3.6 The offender shall be entitled to make a request or complaint to a judicial or other competent independent authority on matters affecting his or her individual rights in the implementation of non-custodial measures.

3.7 Appropriate machinery shall be provided for the recourse and, if possible, redress of any grievance related to non-compliance with internationally recognized human rights.

3.8 Non-custodial measures shall not involve medical or psychological experimentation on, or undue risk of physical or mental injury to, the offender.

3.9 The dignity of the offender subject to non-custodial measures shall be protected at all times.

3.10 In the implementation of non-custodial measures, the offender's rights shall not be restricted further than was authorized by the competent authority that rendered the original decision.

3.11 In the application of non-custodial measures, the offender's right to privacy shall be respected, as shall be the right to privacy of the offender's family.

3.12 The offender's personal records shall be kept strictly confidential and closed to third parties. Access to such records shall be limited to persons directly concerned with the disposition of the offender's case or to other duly authorized persons.

4. *Saving clause*

4.1 Nothing in these Rules shall be interpreted as precluding the application of the Standard Minimum Rules for the Treatment of Prisoners, the United Nations Standard Minimum Rules for the Administration of Juvenile Justice, the

Body of Principles for the Protection of All Persons under Any Form of Detention or Imprisonment or any other human rights instruments and standards recognized by the international community and relating to the treatment of offenders and the protection of their basic human rights.

II. PRETRIAL STAGE

5. *Pretrial dispositions*

5.1 Where appropriate and compatible with the legal system, the police, the prosecution service or other agencies dealing with criminal cases should be empowered to discharge the offender if they consider that it is not necessary to proceed with the case for the protection of society, crime prevention or the promotion of respect for the law and the rights of victims. For the purpose of deciding upon the appropriateness of discharge or determination of proceedings, a set of established criteria shall be developed within each legal system. For minor cases the prosecutor may impose suitable non-custodial measures, as appropriate.

6. *Avoidance of pretrial detention*

6.1 Pretrial detention shall be used as a means of last resort in criminal proceedings, with due regard for the investigation of the alleged offence and for the protection of society and the victim.

6.2 Alternatives to pretrial detention shall be employed at as early a stage as possible. Pre-trial detention shall last no longer than necessary to achieve the objectives stated under rule 5.1 and shall be administered humanely and with respect for the inherent dignity of human beings.

6.3 The offender shall have the right to appeal to a judicial or other competent independent authority in cases where pretrial detention is employed.

III. TRIAL AND SENTENCING STAGE

7. *Social inquiry reports*

7.1 If the possibility of social inquiry reports exists, the judicial authority may avail itself of a report prepared by a competent, authorized official or agency. The report should contain social information on the offender that is relevant to the person's pattern of offending and current offences. It should also contain information and recommendations that are relevant to the sentencing procedure.

The report shall be factual, objective and unbiased, with any expression of opinion clearly identified.

8. *Sentencing dispositions*

8.1 The judicial authority, having at its disposal a range of non-custodial measures, should take into consideration in making its decision the rehabilitative needs of the offender, the protection of society and the interests of the victim, who should be consulted whenever appropriate.

8.2 Sentencing authorities may dispose of cases in the following ways:

(a) Verbal sanctions, such as admonition, reprimand and warning;

(b) Conditional discharge;

(c) Status penalties;

(d) Economic sanctions and monetary penalties, such as fines and day-fines;

(e) Confiscation or an expropriation order;

(f) Restitution to the victim or a compensation order;

(g) Suspended or deferred sentence;

(h) Probation and judicial supervision;

(i) A community service order;

(j) Referral to an attendance centre;

(k) House arrest;

(l) Any other mode of non-institutional treatment;

(m) Some combination of the measures listed above.

IV. POST-SENTENCING STAGE

9. *Post-sentencing dispositions*

9.1 The competent authority shall have at its disposal a wide range of post-sentencing alternatives in order to avoid institutionalization and to assist offenders in their early reintegration into society.

9.2 Post-sentencing dispositions may include:

(a) Furlough and half-way houses;

(b) Work or education release;

(c) Various forms of parole;

(d) Remission;

(e) Pardon.

9.3 The decision on post-sentencing dispositions, except in the case of pardon, shall be subject to review by a judicial or other competent independent authority, upon application of the offender.

9.4 Any form of release from an institution to a non-custodial programme shall be considered at the earliest possible stage.

V. IMPLEMENTATION OF NON-CUSTODIAL MEASURES

10. *Supervision*

10.1 The purpose of supervision is to reduce reoffending and to assist the offender's integration into society in a way which minimizes the likelihood of a return to crime.

10.2 If a non-custodial measure entails supervision, the latter shall be carried out by a competent authority under the specific conditions prescribed by law.

10.3 Within the framework of a given non-custodial measure, the most suitable type of supervision and treatment should be determined for each individual case aimed at assisting the offender to work on his or her offending. Supervision and treatment should be periodically reviewed and adjusted as necessary.

10.4 Offenders should, when needed, be provided with psychological, social and material assistance and with opportunities to strengthen links with the community and facilitate their reintegration into society.

11. *Duration*

11.1 The duration of a non-custodial measure shall not exceed the period established by the competent authority in accordance with the law.

11.2 Provision may be made for early termination of the measure if the offender has responded favourably to it.

12. *Conditions*

12.1 If the competent authority shall determine the conditions to be observed by the offender, it should take into account both the needs of society and the needs and rights of the offender and the victim.

12.2 The conditions to be observed shall be practically precise and as few as possible, and be aimed at reducing the likelihood of an offender relapsing into criminal behaviour and of increasing the offender's chances of social integration, taking into account the needs of the victim.

12.3 At the beginning of the application of a non-custodial measure, the offender shall receive an explanation, orally and in writing, of the conditions governing the application of the measure, including the offender's obligations and rights.

12.4 The conditions may be modified by the competent authority under the established statutory provisions, in accordance with the progress made by the offender.

13. *Treatment process*

13.1 Within the framework of a given non-custodial measure, in appropriate cases, various schemes, such as case-work, group therapy, residential programmes and the specialized treatment of various categories of offenders, should be developed to meet the needs of offenders more effectively.

13.2 Treatment should be conducted by professionals who have suitable training and practical experience.

13.3 When it is decided that treatment is necessary, efforts should be made to understand the offender's background, personality, aptitude, intelligence, values and, especially the circumstances leading to the commission of the offence.

13.4 The competent authority may involve the community and social support systems in the application of non-custodial measures.

13.5 Case-load assignments shall be maintained as far as practicable at a manageable level to ensure the effective implementation of treatment programmes.

13.6 For each offender, a case record shall be established and maintained by the competent authority.

14. *Discipline and breach of conditions*

14.1 A breach of the conditions to be observed by the offender may result in a modification or revocation of the non-custodial measure.

14.2 The modification or revocation of the non-custodial measure shall be made by the competent authority; this shall be done only after a careful examination of the facts adduced by both the supervising officer and the offender.

14.3 The failure of a non-custodial measure should not automatically lead to the imposition of a custodial measure.

14.4 In the event of a modification or revocation of the non-custodial measure, the competent authority shall attempt to establish a suitable alternative non-custodial measure. A sentence of imprisonment may be imposed only in the absence of other suitable alternatives.

14.5 The power to arrest and detain the offender under supervision in cases where there is a breach of the conditions shall be prescribed by law.

14.6 Upon modification or revocation of the non-custodial measure, the offender shall have the right to appeal to a judicial or other competent independent authority.

VI. STAFF

15. *Recruitment*

15.1 There shall be no discrimination in the recruitment of staff on the grounds of race, colour, sex, age, language, religion, political or other opinion, national or social origin, property, birth or other status. The policy regarding staff recruitment should take into consideration national policies of affirmative action and reflect the diversity of the offenders to be supervised.

15.2 Persons appointed to apply non-custodial measures should be personally suitable and, whenever possible, have appropriate professional training and practical experience. Such qualifications shall be clearly specified.

15.3 To secure and retain qualified professional staff, appropriate service status, adequate salary and benefits commensurate with the nature of the work should be ensured and ample opportunities should be provided for professional growth and career development.

16. *Staff training*

16.1 The objective of training shall be to make clear to staff their responsibilities with regard to rehabilitating the offender, ensuring the offender's rights and protecting society. Training should also give staff an understanding of the need to cooperate in and coordinate activities with the agencies concerned.

16.2 Before entering duty, staff shall be given training that includes instruction on the nature of non-custodial measures, the purposes of supervision and the various modalities of the application of non-custodial measures.

16.3 After entering duty, staff shall maintain and improve their knowledge and professional capacity by attending in-service training and refresher courses. Adequate facilities shall be made available for that purpose.

VII. VOLUNTEERS AND OTHER COMMUNITY RESOURCES

17. *Public participation*

17.1 Public participation should be encouraged as it is a major resource and one of the most important factors in improving ties between offenders undergoing non-custodial measures and the family and community. It should complement the efforts of the criminal justice administration.

17.2 Public participation should be regarded as an opportunity for members of the community to contribute to the protection of their society.

18. *Public understanding and cooperation*

18.1 Government agencies, the private sector and the general public should be encouraged to support voluntary organizations that promote non-custodial measures.

18.2 Conferences, seminars, symposia and other activities should be regularly organized to stimulate awareness of the need for public participation in the application of non-custodial measures.

18.3 All forms of the mass media should be utilized to help to create a constructive public attitude, leading to activities conducive to a broader application of non-custodial treatment and the social integration of offenders.

18.4 Every effort should be made to inform the public of the importance of its role in the implementation of non-custodial measures.

19. *Volunteers*

19.1 Volunteers shall be carefully screened and recruited on the basis of their aptitude for and interest in the work involved. They shall be properly trained for the specific responsibilities to be discharged by them and shall have access to support and counselling from, and the opportunity to consult with, the competent authority.

19.2 Volunteers should encourage offenders and their families to develop meaningful ties with the community and a broader sphere of contact by providing counselling and other appropriate forms of assistance according to their capacity and the offenders needs.

19.3 Volunteers shall be insured against accident, injury and public liability when carrying out their duties. They shall be reimbursed for authorized expenditures incurred in the course of their work. Public recognition should be extended to them for the services they render for the well-being of the community.

VIII. RESEARCH, PLANNING, POLICY FORMULATION AND EVALUATION

20. *Research and planning*

20.1 As an essential aspect of the planning process, efforts should be made to involve both public and private bodies in the organization and promotion of research on the non-custodial treatment of offenders.

20.2 Research on the problems that confront clients, practitioners, the community and policy-makers should be carried out on a regular basis.

20.3 Research and information mechanisms should be built into the criminal justice system for the collection and analysis of data and statistics on the implementation of non-custodial treatment for offenders.

21. *Policy formulation and programme development*

21.1 Programmes for non-custodial measures should be systematically planned and implemented as an integral part of the criminal justice system within the national development process.

21.2 Regular evaluations should be carried out with a view to implementing non-custodial measures more effectively.

21.3 Periodic reviews should be conducted to assess the objectives, functioning and effectiveness of non-custodial measures.

22. *Linkages with relevant agencies and activities*

22.1 Suitable mechanisms should be evolved at various levels to facilitate the establishment of linkages between services responsible for non-custodial measures, other branches of the criminal justice system, social development and welfare agencies, both governmental and non-governmental, in such fields as health, housing, education and labour, and the mass media.

23. *International cooperation*

23.1 Efforts shall be made to promote scientific cooperation between countries in the field of non-institutional treatment. Research, training, technical assistance and the exchange of information among Member States on non-custodial measures should be strengthened, through the United Nations Institutes for the Prevention of Crime and the Treatment of Offenders, in close collaboration with the Crime Prevention and Criminal Justice Branch of the Centre for Social Development and Humanitarian Affairs of the United Nations Secretariat.

23.2 Comparative studies and the harmonization of legislative provisions should be furthered to expand the range of non-institutional options and facilitate their application across national frontiers, in accordance with the Model Treaty on the Transfer of Supervision of Offenders Conditionally Sentenced or Conditionally Released.

11. The Administration of Justice and the Human Rights of Detainees: Question of Human Rights and States of Emergency

Guidelines for the Development of Legislation on States of Emergency (excerpts)*

* These initial draft guidelines and commentaries thereto are submitted solely for information of the Sub-Commission and the Commission on Human Rights.

Part One

1. General Principle

No state of emergency should be declared or renewed except in conformity with the Constitution, obligations arising under international law and legislation concerning states of emergency and their consequences. Legislation concerning states of emergencies should be adopted, incorporating the relevant international standards into the national law and carefully defining the extent to which the constitutional order may be altered during an emergency situation. It should govern any type of emergency or state of exception which might arise or be declared.

2. Proclamation of a state of emergency

(a) The legislation should authorize the competent authority to declare a state of emergency only in the event of a grave disruption of organized life of the community endangering the vital interests of the population which the measures normally compatible with the Constitution and laws in force are plainly inadequate to redress, or a present or imminent threat of such disruption, and only in order to safeguard the rights and security of the population and the functioning of public institutions within the rule of law.

(b) The declaration of a state of emergency should be required to state clearly the circumstances which motivate it, the emergency measures which are authorized, any provisions of the Constitution, law and obligations arising under international law which may be affected by such measures, and the area and the period for which the declaration shall have effect, unless rescinded earlier.

3. Duration of the state of emergency

(a) The legislation should indicate that no state of emergency is valid for more than the period which is strictly necessary.

(b) The legislation should require the competent authorities to terminate the state of emergency immediately if the circumstances which motivated the declaration of emergency cease to exist, or if the resulting threat is reduced to such proportions that measures normally compatible with the law and Constitution are sufficient to control it.

Part Two

6. Measures taken pursuant to a state of emergency

(a) The legislation concerning states of emergency should allow the competent authority to authorize, pursuant to a declaration of emergency, only such specific measures as are strictly required by the exigencies of the circumstances which have led to the declaration, subject to the other limitations indicated in these guidelines.

(b) In determining which measures shall be taken pursuant to a declaration of emergency, the competent authorities should be required to evaluate the foreseeable consequences of such measures on the enjoyment of fundamental rights and liberties recognized by the Constitution, laws and international law of human rights, in order to identify and implement those measures which will enable the authorities to respond efficiently to the danger motivating the declaration of emergency while having the least possible impact on fundamental rights. The results of such evaluation shall be made public.

(c) When an emergency affects the enjoyment of fundamental rights recognized by the Constitution or international law in force, administrative or legal measures designed to compensate or minimize the adverse consequences of the state of emergency on the enjoyment of such rights should be taken whenever possible.

7. Rights and liberties which may not be affected by emergency measures

The legislation should indicate that nothing done pursuant to a state of emergency may be incompatible with enjoyment of the following:

(a) the right of peoples to self-determination, including the right to determine the system of government and to elect public officials in free and periodic elections and the right not to be subject to practices constituting genocide under international law;

(b) the right to life, personal integrity and the right of every person deprived of liberty to humane treatment and not to be subject to forced labour;

(c) freedom of thought, conscience and religion, the right to legal personality and nationality and the right to the equal protection of the law against discrimination on grounds of race, colour, sex, language, religion, opinion, social origin or other status;

(d) the right of persons accused of an offence not to be subject to retroactive application of criminal law, except for law more favourable to the accused or convicted person, and to a fair trial before a competent, independent and impartial court, including:

(i) the right to be presumed innocent and the right not to be obliged to testify or give evidence against oneself or to confess guilt;

(ii) the right to be informed of the charges promptly and in detail, in a language which he or she understands;

(iii) the right to defend oneself in person or through counsel of his or her choice, including the right of indigent defendants to free legal assistance;

(iv) the right to have adequate time and facilities for the preparation of a defence, including the right to communicate with counsel in confidence and the right to an interpreter, if needed;

(v) the right to be present at trial, to examine or have examined prosecution witnesses, to give evidence and to present witnesses for the defence;

(vi) the right to appeal, if convicted, and the right not to be charged more than once for the same offence;

(vii) in no case shall a sentence of death be carried out during a state of emergency with regard to any person convicted of an offence on the basis of charges related to the emergency, or whose sentence has been imposed or reviewed by proceedings in which constitutional or legal safeguards have not been fully applied due to the exigencies of the emergency.

(e) the right of the child and the family to special protection, including the right of children to be among the first to receive protection and relief, the right of the family to privacy and unit, and the right of juveniles accused of an offence to be tried under procedures especially intended for persons of their age;

(f) rights recognized by international humanitarian law.

8. The rights of persons deprived of liberty

Without prejudice to the principles set forth in other guidelines, in particular 7 and 9, the legislation should provide that nothing done pursuant to a state of emergency may affect the following rights:

(a) No person deprived of liberty for whatever reason shall be denied the following:

(i) the right to be informed of the reasons for detention promptly and in writing, in a language which he or she understands;

(ii) the right to have his or her family informed of the detention without delay, and to receive visits;

(iii) the right of prompt and regular access to a lawyer of his or her choice;

(iv) the right to challenge the legality of the deprivation of liberty before a court of law by *habeas corpus* or other prompt and effective remedy.

(b) If the exigencies of the emergency are such that the detention of persons not accused of an offence is strictly necessary:

(i) deprivation of liberty may only be authorized by a special authority established for this purpose, which shall be impartial and independent from any other public authority;

(ii) no person shall be detained without charge for longer than strictly necessary;

(iii) persons detained without charge pursuant to measures authorized by the declaration of emergency shall be detained separately from prisoners charged or convicted of an offence, in circumstances which take fully into account their status, and shall not be obliged to perform work nor to participate in rehabilitation programmes;

(iv) all possible measures shall be taken to protect the family of the detainee from the adverse consequences of detention.

9. Effects of a state of emergency on the judiciary

(a) The legislation should provide that nothing done pursuant to a state of emergency should diminish the jurisdiction of the courts:

(i) to review the compatibility of a declaration of emergency with the law, the Constitution and obligations arising under international law, and to declare the declaration illegal or unconstitutional in the event of incompatibility;

(ii) to review the compatibility of any action taken by a public authority with the terms of a declaration of emergency;

(iii) over legal actions to enforce or protect any rights recognized by the Constitution, national and international law whose effectiveness is not affected by the declaration of emergency;

(iv) over criminal matters, including offences related to the emergency.

(b) The legislation should provide that nothing done pursuant to a state of emergency should diminish the provisions of the Constitution and laws concerning the appointment, terms of office or privileges and immunities of members of the judiciary, nor the independence and impartiality of the judicial branch.

Part Three

11. Restoration of rights and compensation

The legislation should provide that, when a state of emergency has terminated, all possible efforts should be made to restore those whose rights have been adversely affected by measures taken pursuant to the emergency to full enjoyment of their rights and, when appropriate, to compensate them for injuries suffered and to provide such rehabilitation as may be necessary. In particular:

(a) that all persons detained without charge be released without delay, and provided with any necessary assistance in reintegration into their homes, employment and community.

(b) that any sentence imposed by judicial proceedings in which constitutional or legal safeguards were not fully applied due to the exigencies of the emergency be reviewed promptly with a view to determining whether the interests of fairness might require reopening of the judgment, pardon or retrial.

12. Prohibition of discrimination

The legislation should provide that no person should be subject to any form of discrimination by reason of his or her participation, or participation of relatives, in any event related to the state of emergency.

13. Right to a remedy

The legislation should provide that nothing done pursuant to the declaration of emergency should restrict the right of a person who considers that he or she has suffered a violation of a legally recognized right during the state of emergency to seek redress before the courts once the emergency has ceased, and the right to a prompt decision on his or her claim.

* * *

12. Question of the Human Rights of All Persons Subjected to Any Form of Detention or Imprisonment

Report of the Commission on Human Rights Working Group on Arbitrary Detention (excerpts)

ANNEX

PRINCIPLES APPLICABLE IN THE CONSIDERATION OF CASES SUBMITTED TO THE WORKING GROUP

With a view to taking a decision, the Working Group proposes to proceed as follows for the consideration of cases submitted to it. The Working Group will consider such cases if they fall into one, or more, of the following three categories:

I. Cases in which the deprivation of freedom is arbitrary, as it manifestly cannot be linked to any legal basis (such as continued detention beyond the execution of the sentence or dispute an amnesty act, etc.); or

II. Cases of deprivation of freedom when the facts giving rise to the prosecution or conviction concern the exercise of the rights and freedoms protected by articles 7, 13, 14, 19, 20 and 21 of the Universal Declaration of Human Rights and articles 12, 18, 19, 21, 22, 25, 26 and 27 of the International Covenant on Civil and Political Rights; or

III. Cases in which non-observance of all or part of the international provisions relating to the right to a fair trial is such that it confers on the deprivation of freedom, of whatever kind, an arbitrary character. In order to assess the arbitrary character or otherwise of the deprivation of freedom, the following elements, in particular are deemed relevant:

A. *Pre-trial situations* (applicable to both judicial and administrative detention)[2]

1. Cases in which arrest, detention or imprisonment is not carried out strictly in accordance with the provisions of the law and by competent officials or persons authorized for that purpose (Principles 2 and 4 of the Body of Principles; article 9 (1) of the International Covenant on Civil and Political Rights);

2. Cases of detention in which the authorities exceed the powers granted to them under the law and where the exercise of those powers is not subject to recourse to a judicial or other authority (Principle 9 of the Body of Principles);

3. Cases in which a person arrested is not informed, in a language which he understands, of the reasons for his arrest, and the charges against him and is not given information or an explanation concerning his rights. (Principles 10, 13 and 14 of the Body of Principles; article 9 (2) of the International Covenant on Civil and Political Rights.

4. Cases in which a person arrested is denied the opportunity to be heard promptly by a judicial or other authority (Principles 11 (1) of the Body of Principles);

5. Cases in which a detained person is denied his right to defend himself or to be assisted by a legal counsel, or the right to have such counsel assigned to him (Principles 11, para. 1, and 17 of the Body of Principles);

6. Cases in which a detained person and his counsel do not receive prompt and full communication of any order of detention, and the reasons therefore (Principle 11, para. 2, of the Body of Principles);

---

[2]As regards administrative detention, the various categories of such detention are described in detail in the report submitted by Mr. Joinet to the forty-second session of the Sub-Commission on Prevention of Discrimination and Protection of Minorities (E/CN.4/Sub.2/1990/29, paras. 28-46).

7. Cases in which the continuance of detention is not subject to a review by a judicial or other authority (Principle 11, para. 3, of the Body of Principles);

8. Cases in which information concerning the detention is not duly recorded (Principles 12 of the Body of Principles);

9. Cases of unduly prolonged incommunicado detention (Principle 15 of the Body of Principles);

10. Cases in which the detainee is not entitled to promptly notify his family of his arrest, detention, or transfer to another place of detention or to communicate with a consular post, a diplomatic mission or a representative of a competent international organization (Principle 16 of the Body of Principles);

11. Cases in which a detained person is denied his right to communicate and consult, without delay or censorship and privately, with his legal counsel when there are no "exceptional circumstances" to justify such a denial (Principles 18 of the Body of Principles);

12. Cases where undue advantage is taken of a detainee's situation to compel him to confess, to incriminate himself otherwise or to testify against any other person (Principle 21 of the Body of Principles);

13. Cases in which a detained person, or his counsel, is denied his right to institute proceedings, at any time, before a judicial or other authority to challenge the lawfulness of his detention (Principles 32, para. 1, of the Body of Principles);

14. Cases in which a person suffers administrative detention for an obviously abusive period of time.

B. *Pre-trial situations applicable only to judicial detention*

1. Cases in which a detained person suspected of or charged with a criminal offence is denied his right to be presumed innocent and to be treated as such pending his trial, and is subjected to undue restrictions (Principle 36 of the Body of Principles);

2. Cases in which a person suspected of a criminal offence is detained pending investigation or trial without a written order by a judicial or other legal authority.

3. Cases of unduly prolonged pre-trial detention (Principle 38 of the Body of Principles, arts. 9 (3) and 14, para. 3 (c), of the International Covenant on Civil and Political Rights);

4. Cases in which a person arrested or detained on a criminal charge is denied the right to be brought promptly before a judge or other officer authorized by law to exercise judicial power (art. 9, para. 3, of the International Covenant on Civil and Political Rights).

C. *Post-trial imprisonment*

1. Cases of imprisonment following conviction resulting from trials of whatever nature held in violation of internationally accepted norms, in particular the following:

(a) Trial which is not held by a competent, independent and impartial tribunal established by law (art. 14, para. 1, of the International Covenant on Civil and Political Rights.

(b) Trial in which the defendant was not informed promptly and in detail, in a language which he understands, of the nature and cause of the charge against him (art. 14, para. 3 (a), of the International Covenant on Civil and Political Rights);

(c) Trial in which the defendant did not have the adequate time and facilities for the preparation of his defence and to communicate with his counsel (art. 14, para. 3 (b), of the International Covenant on Civil and Political Rights);

(d) Trial in which the defendant is not tried in his presence and is denied the right to defend himself in person or through legal assistant of his own choosing (art. 14, para. 3 (d), of the International Covenant on Civil and Political Rights);

(e) Trial in which the defendant is denied the right to examine, or have examined, the witnesses against him and to obtain the attendance and examination of witnesses on his behalf under the same conditions as witnesses against him (art. 14, para. 3 (e), of the International Covenant on Civil and Political Rights);

(f) Trial in which the defendant is denied the right to the free assistance of an interpreter, if he cannot understand or speak the language used in court (art. 14, para. 3 (f), of the International Covenant on Civil and Political Rights);

(g) Trial in which the defendant is compelled to testify against himself or to confess guilt (art. 14, para. 3 (g), of the International Covenant on Civil and Political Rights);

(h) Trial in which the defendant is presumed to be guilty until he proves his innocence during the course of such trial (art. 14, para. 2, of the International Covenant on Civil and Political Rights);

2. Cases of denial of the convicted person's right to have his conviction and sentence reviewed by a higher tribunal (art. 14, para. 5, of the International Covenant on Civil and Political Rights);

3. Cases of imprisonment following conviction for acts for which the same person has already been tried and convicted and served the sentence, or acquitted, by a national or foreign court (art. 14, para. 7, of the International Covenant on Civil and Political Rights);

4. Cases of imprisonment following conviction in violation of the principles that no one shall be held guilty of any act or omission which did not constitute a criminal offence at the time when it was committed (art. 15 of the International Covenant on Civil and Political Rights);

5. Cases of sentencing to prison terms longer than the term provided by law.

* * *

F. RIGHT TO A FAIR TRIAL

Indispensable to a democratic system of government is an independent judiciary that guarantees a fair trial to all persons accused of offences.

The Universal Declaration of Human Rights and the International Covenant on Civil and Political Rights set the standards, which the Human Rights Committee has further elaborated in a general comment on Article 14 of the Covenant.

These guarantees have been concretely tested by individuals who claimed to have been denied a fair trial and who denounced the alleged violations by invoking the Optional Protocol to the International Covenant on Civil and Political Rights.

In 1991, two expert members of the Sub-Commission on Prevention of Discrimination and Protection of Minorities presented a study on the right to a fair trial, which reviewed the jurisprudence of the United Nations Human Rights Committee on numerous cases concerning the administration of justice.

1. Universal Declaration of Human Rights

Article 10

Everyone is entitled in full equality to a fair and public hearing by an independent and impartial tribunal, in

the determination of his rights and obligations and of any criminal charge against him.

Article 11

1. Everyone charged with a penal offence has the right to be presumed innocent until proved guilty according to law in a public trial at which he has had all the guarantees necessary for his defence.

* * *

2. International Covenant on Civil and Political Rights

Article 14

1. All persons shall be equal before the courts and tribunals. In the determination of any criminal charge against him, or of his rights and obligations in a suit at law, everyone shall be entitled to a fair and public hearing by a competent, independent and impartial tribunal established by law. The Press and the public may be excluded from all or part of a trial for reasons of morals, public order (*ordre public*) or national security in a democratic society, or when the interest of the private lives of the parties so requires, or to the extent strictly necessary in the opinion of the court in special circumstances where publicity would prejudice the interests of justice; but any judgment rendered in a criminal case or in a suit at law shall be made public except where the interest of juvenile persons otherwise requires or the proceedings concern matrimonial disputes of the guardianship of children.

2. Everyone charged with a criminal offence shall have the right to be presumed innocent until proved guilty according to law.

3. In the determination of any criminal charge against him, everyone shall be entitled to the following minimum guarantees, in full equality:

(a) To be informed promptly and in detail in a language which he understands of the nature and cause of the charge against him;

(b) To have adequate time and facilities for the preparation of his defence and to communicate with counsel of his own choosing;

(c) To be tried without undue delay;

(d) To be tried in his presence and to defend himself in person or through legal assistance of his own choosing; to be informed, if he does not have legal assistance, of this right; and to have legal assistance assigned to him, in any case where the interests of justice so require, and without payment by him in any such case if he does not have sufficient means to pay for it;

(e) To examine, or have examined, the witnesses against him and to obtain the attendance and examination of witnesses on his behalf under the same conditions as witnesses against him;

(f) To have the free assistance of an interpreter if he cannot understand or speak the language used in court;

(g) Not to be compelled to testify against himself or to confess guilt.

4. In the case of juvenile persons, the procedure shall be such as will take account of their age and the desirability of promoting their rehabilitation.

5. Everyone convicted of a crime shall have the right to his conviction and sentence being reviewed by a higher tribunal according to law.

6. When a person has by a final decision been convicted of a criminal offence and when subsequently his conviction has been reversed or he has been pardoned on the ground that a new or newly discovered fact shows conclusively that there has been a miscarriage of justice, the person who has suffered punishment as a result of such conviction shall be compensated according to law, unless it is proved that the non-disclosure of the unknown fact in time is wholly or partly attributable to him.

7. No one shall be liable to be tried or punished again for an offence for which he has already been finally convicted or acquitted in accordance with the law and penal procedure of each country.

Article 15

1. No one shall be held guilty of any criminal offence on account of any act or omission which did not constitute criminal offence, under national or international law, at the time when it was committed. Nor shall a heavier penalty be imposed than the one that was applicable at the time when the criminal offence was committed. If, subsequent to the commission of the offence, provision is made by law for the imposition of the lighter penalty, the offender shall benefit thereby.

2. Nothing in this article shall prejudice the trial and punishment of any person for any act or omission which, at the time when it was committed, was criminal according to the general principles of law recognized by the community of nations.

* * *

3. General Comments of the Human Rights Committee of the International Covenant on Civil and Political Rights

GENERAL COMMENT 13 *Article 14 (Twenty-first session, 1984)*

1. The Committee notes that article 14 of the Covenant is of a complex nature and that different aspects of its provisions will need specific comments. All of these provisions are aimed at ensuring the proper administration of justice, and to this end uphold a series of individual rights such as equality before the courts and tribunals and the right to a fair and public hearing by a competent, independent and impartial tribunal established by law. Not all reports provided details on the legislative or other measures adopted specifically to implement each of the provisions of article 14.

2. In general, the reports of States parties fail to recognize that article 14 applies not only to procedures for the determination of criminal charges against individuals but also to procedures to determine their rights and obligations in a suit at law. Laws and practices dealing with these matters vary widely from State to State. This diversity makes it all the more necessary for States parties to provide all relevant information and to explain in greater detail how the concepts of "criminal charge" and "rights and obligations in a suit at law" are interpreted in relation to their respective legal systems.

3. The Committee would find it useful if, in their future reports, States parties could provide more detailed information on the steps taken to ensure that equality before the courts, including equal access to courts, fair and public hearings and competence, impartiality and independence of the judiciary are established by law and guaranteed in practice. In particular, States parties should specify the relevant constitutional and legislative texts which provide for the establishment of the courts and ensure that they are independent, impartial and competent, in particular with regard to the manner in which judges are appointed, the qualifications for appointment, and the duration of their terms of office; the condition governing promotion, transfer and cessation of their functions and the actual independence of the judiciary from the executive branch and the legislative.

4. The provisions of article 14 apply to all courts and tribunals within the scope of that article whether ordinary or specialized. The Committee notes the existence, in many countries, of military or special courts which try civilians. This could present serious problems as far as the equitable, impartial and independent administration of justice is concerned. Quite often the reason for the establishment of such courts is to enable the exceptional procedures to be applied which do not comply with normal standards of justice. While the Covenant does not prohibit such categories of courts, nevertheless the conditions which it lays

down clearly indicate that the trying of civilians by such courts should be very exceptional and take place under conditions which genuinely afford the full guarantees stipulated in article 14. The Committee has noted a serious lack of information in this regard in the reports of some States parties whose judicial institutions include such courts for the trying of civilians. In some countries such military and special courts do not afford the strict guarantees of the proper administration of justice in accordance with the requirements of article 14 which are essential for the effective protection of human rights. If States parties decide in circumstances of a public emergency as contemplated by article 4 to derogate from normal procedures required under article 14, they should ensure that such derogations do not exceed those strictly required by the exigencies of the actual situation, and respect the other conditions in paragraph 1 of article 14.

5. The second sentence of article 14, paragraph 1, provides that "everyone shall be entitled to a fair and public hearing". Paragraph 3 of the article elaborates on the requirements of a "fair hearing" in regard to the determination of criminal charges. However, the requirements of paragraph 3 are minimum guarantees, the observance of which is not always sufficient to ensure the fairness of a hearing as required by paragraph 1.

6. The publicity of hearings is an important safeguard in the interest of the individual and of society at large. At the same time article 14, paragraph 1, acknowledges that courts have the power to exclude all or part of the public for reasons spelled out in that paragraph. It should be noted that apart from such exceptional circumstances, the Committee considers that a hearing must be open to the public in general, including members of the press, and must not, for instance, be limited only to a particular category of persons. It should be noted that, even in cases in which the public is excluded from the trial, the judgement must, with certain strictly defined exceptions, be made public.

7. The Committee has noted a lack of information regarding article 14, paragraph 2 and, in some cases, has even observed that the presumption of innocence, which is fundamental to the protection of human rights, is expressed in very ambiguous terms or entails conditions which render it ineffective. By reason of the presumption of innocence. The burden of proof of the charge is on the prosecution and the accused has the benefit of the doubt. No guilt can be presumed until the charge has been proved beyond a reasonable doubt. Further, the presumption of innocence implies a right to be treated in accordance with this principle. It is, therefore, a duty for all public authorities to refrain from prejudging the outcome of a trial.

8. Among the minimum guarantees in criminal proceedings prescribed by paragraph 3, the first concerns the right of everyone to be informed in a language which he understands of the charge against him (subpara. (a)). The Committee

notes that State reports often do not explain how this right is respected and ensured. Article 14 (3) (a) applies to all cases of criminal charges including those of persons not in detention. The Committee notes further that the right to be informed of the charge "promptly" requires that information is given in the manner described as soon as the charge is first made by a competent authority. In the opinion of the Committee this right must arise when in the course of an investigation a court or an authority of the prosecution decides to take procedural steps against a person suspected of a crime or publicly names him as such. The specific requirements of subparagraph 3 (a) may be met by stating the charge either orally or in writing, provided that the information indicates both the law and the alleged facts on which it is based.

9. Subparagraph 3 (b) provides that the accused must have adequate time and facilities for the preparation of his defence and to communicate with counsel of his own choosing. What is "adequate time" depends on the circumstances of each case, but the facilities must include access to documents and other evidence which the accused requires to prepare his case, as well as the opportunity to engage and communicate with counsel. When the accused does not want to defend himself in person or request a person or an association of his choice, he should be able to have recourse to a lawyer. Furthermore, this subparagraph requires counsel to communicate with the accused in conditions given full respect for the confidentiality of their communications. Lawyers should be able to counsel and to represent their clients in accordance with their established professional standards and judgement without any restrictions, influences, pressures or undue interference from any quarter.

10. Subparagraph 3 (c) provides that the accused shall be tried without undue delay. This guarantee relates not only to the time by which it should end and judgement be rendered; all stages must take place "without undue delay". To make this right effective, a procedure must be available in order to ensure that their trial will proceed "without undue delay", both in first instance and on appeal.

11. Not all reports have dealt with all aspects of the right of defence as defined in subparagraph 3 (d). The Committee has not always received sufficient information concerning the protection of the right of the accused to be present during the determination of any charge against him nor how the legal system assures his right either to defend himself in person or to be assisted by counsel of is own choosing, or what arrangements are made if a person does not have sufficient means to pay for legal assistance. The accused or his lawyer must be the right to act diligently and fearlessly in pursuing all available defences and the right to challenge the conduct of the case if they believe it to be unfair. When for exceptionally justified reasons trials *in absentia* are held, strict observance of the rights of the defence is all the more necessary.

12. Subparagraph 3 (e) states that the accused shall be entitled to examine or have examined the witnesses against him and to obtain the attendance and examination of witnesses against him. This provision is designed to guarantee to the accused the same legal powers of compelling the attendance of witnesses and of examining or cross-examining any witnesses as are available to the prosecution.

13. Subparagraph 3 (f) provides that if the accused cannot understand or speak the language used in court he is entitled to the assistance of an interpreter free of any charge. This right is independent of the outcome of the proceedings and applies to aliens as well as to nationals. It is of basic importance in cases in which ignorance of the language used by a court or difficulty in understanding may constitute a major obstacle to the right of defence.

14. Subparagraph 3 (g) provides that the accused may not be compelled to testify against himself or to confess guilt. In considering this safeguard the provisions of article 7 and article 10, paragraph 1, should be borne in mind. In order to compel the accused to confess or to testify against himself, frequently methods which violate these provisions are used. The law should require that evidence provided by means of such methods or any other form of compulsion is wholly unacceptable.

15. In order to safeguard the rights of the accused under paragraphs 1 and 3 of article 14, judges should have authority to consider any allegations made of violations of the rights of the accused during any stage of the prosecution.

16. Article 14, paragraph 4, provides that in the case of juvenile persons, the procedure shall be such as will take account of their age and the desirability of promoting their rehabilitation. Not many reports have furnished sufficient information concerning such relevant matters as the minimum age at which a juvenile may be charged with a criminal offence, the maximum age at which a person is still considered to be a juvenile, the existence of special courts and procedures, the laws governing procedures against juveniles and how all these special arrangements for juveniles take account of "the desirability of promoting their rehabilitation". Juveniles are to enjoy at least the same guarantees and protection as are accorded to adults under article 14.

17. Article 14, paragraph 5, provides that everyone convicted of a crime shall have the right to his conviction and sentence being reviewed by a higher tribunal according to law. Particular attention is drawn to the other language versions of the word "crime" ("*infraction*", "*delito*", "*prestuplenie*") which show that the guarantee is not confined only to the most serious offences. In this connection, not enough information has been provided concerning the procedures of appeal, in particular the access to and the powers of reviewing tribunals, what require-

ments must be satisfied to appeal against a judgement, and the way in which the procedures before review tribunals take account of the fair and public hearing requirements of paragraph 1 of article 14.

18. Article 14, paragraph 6, provides for compensation according to law in certain cases of a miscarriage of justice as described therein. It seems from many State reports that this right is often not observed or insufficiently guaranteed by domestic legislation. States should, where necessary, supplement their legislation in this area in order to bring it into line with the provisions of the Covenant.

19. In considering State reports differing views have often been expressed as to the scope of paragraph 7 of article 14. Some States parties have even felt the need to make reservations in relation to procedures for the resumption of criminal cases. It seems to the Committee that most States parties make a clear distinction between a resumption of a trial justified by exceptional circumstances and a re-trial prohibited pursuant to the principle of *ne bis in idem* as contained in paragraph 7. This understanding of the meaning of *ne bis in idem* may encourage States parties to reconsider their reservation to article 14, paragraph 7.

* * *

4. The Administration of Justice and the Human Rights of Detainees

The right to a fair trial; current recognition and measures necessary for its strengthening

Introduction

1. By its resolution 1989/27, the Sub-Commission on Prevention of Discrimination and Protection of Minorities appointed two of its members, Mr. Stanislav Chernichenko and Mr. William Treat, as rapporteurs to prepare a brief report on existing international standards pertaining to the right to a fair trial. The Sub-Commission also requested that the rapporteurs recommend "which provisions guaranteeing the right to a fair trial should be made non-derogable."

2. On 7 March 1990, the Commission on Human Rights by its decision 1990/108, welcomed the Sub-Commission's decision to appoint Mr. Stanislav Chernichenko and Mr. William Treat to prepare a report on the right to a fair trial and requested the Sub-Commission to consider that report directly under agenda item 10 (d) at its forty-second session.

3. The two rapporteurs prepared their first brief report (E/CN.4/Sub.2/1990/34) to provide an overview of the subject and to indicate the areas concerning which further study was needed. The brief report also made some general observations and set forth the principle treaties and other international human rights standards that are the most protective of each attribute of a fair trial. Further, the first brief report discussed considerations relevant to making non-derogable at least some aspects of the right to a fair trial. In addition, its report recommended a more comprehensive study on the right to a fair trial and how that right might be strengthened.

4. Resolution 1990/18 of the Sub-Commission requested that the Commission and the Economic and Social Council endorse the decision to entrust Mr. Chernichenko and Mr. Treat, as Special Rapporteurs, to prepare a study entitled "The right to a fair trial: current recognition and measures necessary for its strengthening."

5. Resolution 1991/43 of the Commission and resolution 1991/28 of the Economic and Social Council endorsed the decision of the Sub-Commission and requested the Special Rapporteurs to draft a questionnaire on the right to a fair trial.

6. Chapter I of this second report summarizes the discussion of the first brief report and indicates several revisions in that report which will be made in the final report. Chapter II identifies new sources of international fair trial norms that have been issued since the first brief report of June 1990. Chapter III summarizes the interpretations of fair trial standards by the Human Rights Committee under the international Covenant on Civil and Political Rights. Chapter IV indicates the replies received thus far in response to the questionnaire which was distributed in April 1991. Chapter V suggests further work that needs to be accomplished in order to prepare a more comprehensive report on the right to a fair trial and to recommend ways to strengthen that report on the right to a fair trial and to recommend ways to strengthen that right, for example, by drafting an international standard or model code. Annex I contains a supplemental bibliography of relevant material identified since the first brief report. Annex II contains a slightly revised version of the preliminary questionnaire prepared by the two Special Rapporteurs and on which they would be pleased to receive comments by members of the Sub-Commission, observers, and others who receive this preliminary report.

I. First Brief Report, Comments and Revisions

7. The first brief report (E/CN.4/Sub.2/1990/34) looked at the treaties and other instruments defining the attributes of the right to a fair trial that are the most protective of the right. For example, the first brief report identified the principal

treaties containing provisions on the right to a fair trial, including the International Covenant on Civil and Political Rights; the Convention against Torture and Other Cruel, Inhuman and Degrading Treatment or Punishment; the African Charter on Human and Peoples' Rights; the American Convention on Human Rights; the European Convention on Human Rights; the four Geneva Conventions for the Protection of Victims of War of 1949; and the two Additional Protocols of 1977 to the Geneva Conventions of 1949.

8. The first brief report also discusses other instruments with provisions on the right to a fair trial: the Universal Declaration of Human Rights; the American Declaration of the Rights and Duties of Man; the Basic Principles on the Independence of the Judiciary; the Principles on the Effective Prevention and Investigation of Extra-Legal, Arbitrary and Summary Executions; the Standard Minimum Rules for the Treatment of Prisoners; the Code of Conduct for Law Enforcement; the Body of Principles for the Protection of All Persons under Any Form of Detention or Imprisonment; the Standard Minimum Rules for the Administration of Juvenile Justice ("The Beijing Rules"); Conclusion No. 44 of the Executive Committee of the United Nations High Commissioner for Refugees on the Detention of Refugees and Asylum-seekers; and the Concluding Document of the Vienna Follow-up Meeting of the Conference on Security and Cooperation in Europe.

9. Further, the first report excerpts the General Comments of the Human Rights Committee on articles of the International Covenant on Civil and Political Rights relevant to the right to a fair trial.

10. The first report was discussed at the forty-second session of the Sub-Commission and several useful comments were received. Sub-Commission members suggested that certain aspects of the right to a fair trial, for example, the right to petition for *habeas corpus*, should be made non-derogable even during periods of emergency. Other members noted the need for fair trial standards to apply to military courts, emergency courts, other special tribunals, administrative procedures, and similar proceedings. One member questioned whether there could ever be a fair trial *in absentia*. Another member drew attention to the importance of the requirement of a "public hearing" and queried whether it was desirable to allow television, radio, and photographic coverage in courtrooms. It was suggested that the two rapporteurs should consider not only which attributes of the right to a fair trial ought to be made non-derogable, but also whether a model code for the right to a fair trial could be developed. Those comments should be reflected in the present second report, the questionnaire prepared by the rapporteurs, and/or the final report.

11. The comments at the forty-second session gave rise to a few specific corrections to the first brief report and which will eventually be reflected in the

final report. In paragraph 37 of the first report (E/CN.4/Sub.2/1990/34), the fourth sentence should read, "Impartiality also indicates the appropriate attitude of the court to the case being tried and that there will be an unbiased assessment of the evidence."

12. One member of the Sub-Commission questioned whether the Nuremberg and Tokyo Tribunals should have been cited in paragraph 30 of the first report as examples of "international courts dealing with cases related to human rights." The rapporteurs agree that the principles related to a fair trial should be applied to such post-war military tribunals.

13. A member of the Sub-Commission correctly suggested that paragraphs 56 and 94 should be made consistent in referring to evidence obtained by illegal means.

14. One member of the Sub-Commission suggested that the rapporteurs should in future reports include the provisions of national legislation and practices in regard to the right to a fair trial. The rapporteurs drafted a questionnaire to seek information on national legislation, decisions and practices, so that they can eventually be incorporated in the study. It was also suggested in the Working Group on Detention that the rapporteurs should develop model national legislation or principles for such legislation as part of their study on the right to a fair trial. (*See, e.g.*, document E/CN/.4/Sub.2-/1990/32, para. 25). The rapporteurs intend to pursue those suggestions after they have amassed adequate information on national legislation and practice.

15. In other respects, the discussion at the Sub-Commission was either reflected in the resolution adopted by the Sub-Commission recommending that a comprehensive study should be undertaken by the two Special Rapporteurs, or will be reflected in this preliminary report and/or in later reports as information becomes available.

II. New Sources of the Right to a Fair Trial, Norms and Tendencies of Their Development

16. On 2 September 1990 the Convention on the Rights of the Child came into force; the Convention contains several provisions relevant to the right to a fair trial for children.

17. In September 1990 the Eighth United Nations Congress on the Prevention of Crime and Treatment of Offenders adopted Basic Principles on the Roles of Lawyers, Guidelines on the Role of Prosecutors, Principles [on] Pre-trial Detention, and Rules for the Protection of Juveniles Deprived of their Liberty.

(See document A/CONF.144/28), by its resolution 45/166 of 18 December 1990, the General Assembly, *inter alia*, welcomed those standards which were relevant to the right to a fair trial.

18. On 5 March 1991 the Commission on Human Rights adopted resolution 1991/42 recommending to the Economic and Social Council the establishment of a "working group composed of five independent experts, with the task of investigating cases of detention imposed arbitrarily or otherwise inconsistently with relevant international standards . . .". The working group's investigations may help interpret fair trial standards in cases in which persons are arbitrarily detained.

19. On 5 March 1991 the Commission on Human Rights also adopted resolution 1991/39 endorsing the decision of the Sub-Commission to entrust Mr. Louis Joinet with the preparation of a report on strengthening the independence of the judiciary and the protection of practicing lawyers. There may be some overlap between the present study on the right to a fair trial and the report on the independence of the judiciary. Further, the Working Group on Detention at its 1990 session agreed to ask Mr. John Carey and Mr. Edwardo Suescún Monroy to prepare a working paper on *habeas corpus* and *amparo* as non-derogable rights. The respective members of the Sub-Commission will need to coordinate their efforts.

20. In June 1990 the Copenhagen Meeting of the Conference on the Human Dimension of the Conference on Security and Cooperation in Europe adopted a document containing several provisions relating to the right to a fair trial. The Charter of Paris for a New Europe issued in November 1990 pursuant to a meeting of the Conference on Security and Cooperation and Europe states that everyone has the right "to know and act upon his rights [and] to fair and public trial if charged with an offence. . .". The Charter also provides, "We will ensure that everyone will enjoy recourse to effective remedies, national or international, against any violation of his rights."

III. Interpretations of International Fair Trial Norms

21. The right to a fair trial has been a norm of international human rights law for over 40 years and a substantial body of interpretation has developed elaborating and construing this right, but relatively little research has been undertaken to analyze the developing content of the right. The three principal sources of interpretation of the right to a fair trial have been the Human Rights Committee, the European Commission and Court of Human Rights, and the Inter-American Commission on the Court of Human Rights. This part of the present second report provides an initial summary of the interpretation of the right to a fair trial in the decisions of the Human Rights Committee. The two rapporteurs expect to

prepare summaries of the European and Inter-American materials for their next report.

22. The International Covenant on Civil and Political Rights grants basic fair trial rights individuals in both civil and criminal proceedings. The rights guaranteed at the various stages of the pre-trial and trial process vary in civil and criminal proceedings. The preliminary report prepared for the forty-second session of the Sub-Commission (E/CN.4/Sub.2/1990/34) discusses the provisions of the International Covenant on Civil and Political Rights and the general comments on the right to a fair trial issued by the Human Rights Committee. This part of the present report recounts the interpretations which the Human Rights Committee has given in its decisions on individual cases concerning provisions on the right to fair trial in the International Covenant.

23. The first section of this part of the present report discusses the rights extended to persons who have been arrested and those who have been detained in criminal and non-criminal proceedings. The second section covers the rights protecting any person held in detention. The third section focuses on the right to notice for any person arrested or detained on a criminal charge. The fourth section deals with the right to release pending trial. The fifth section examines the right to counsel. The sixth section describes the rights protecting an accused during the hearing or trial. The seventh section discusses rights which ensure a fair decision and includes the rights of persons in civil proceedings. The eighth section considers the right to appeal. The ninth section covers the right to a remedy.

A. Arrest and detention

24. Article 9 (1) of the International Covenant on Civil and Political Rights prohibits arbitrary detention and declares that detention must be in accordance with procedures established by law.

1. Prompt review of detention required

25. Article 9 (3) provides that anyone arrested or detained on a criminal charge has the right to be brought promptly before a judge or authorized judicial officer. The Committee considered the case of several Bolivians arrested and detained on suspicion of being *guerrilleros*. Military authorities held the group incommunicado for 44 days before their first hearing in a military court. The Committee

found the 44-day detention violated their right under article 9 (3) to be brought promptly before a judge.[1]

2. The court must have legal authority over detainees

26. It is implicit in article 9 (3) that the judge or officer exercising judicial control has legal authority over the detainee. In case of the Bolivian civilians detained for 44 days before being heard by a military court, the Committee found that the military lacked jurisdiction over the civilians and that the detainees should have been brought promptly before a civilian judge.[2]

3. Right to *habeas corpus*

27. Under article 9 (4) any individual arrested or put in detention has the right to an immediate determination of the lawfulness of his/her detention. Article 9 (4) protects individuals detained in non-criminal cases. The Committee examined the case of a Finnish serviceman sanctioned with 10 days of detention in a military disciplinary proceeding. The Committee held that article 9 (4) applies to all cases of detention, including decisions of an administrative body or authority and that the serviceman was entitled to review in a court of a law.[3]

4. No suspension of the right to *habeas corpus*

28. The Committee disfavours any suspension of the right to *habeas corpus*. The Committee found that detention of a Uruguayan union official during a time of "prompt security measures" when *habeas corpus* was inoperative, violated article 9 (4) because the detainee had no recourse to habeas corpus.[4]

---

[1]Lafuente Peñarrieta et al. v. Bolivia, SELECTED DECISIONS OF THE HUMAN RIGHTS COMMITTEE UNDER THE OPTIONAL PROTOCOL. Volume 2, communication No. 176/1984 (CCPR/C/OP/2), 1990.

[2]Lafuente Peñarrieta et al. v. Bolivia, REPORT OF THE HUMAN RIGHTS COMMITTEE. *Official Records of the General Assembly, Forty-third session, Supplement No. 40* (A/43/40), annex VII.C (hereinafter *Report*).

[3]Vuolanne v. Finland, *Report*. Op. cit., Forty-fourth session (A/44/40), annex X.J; "Although administrative detention may not be objectionable in [certain] circumstances . . . the guarantees enshrined in . . . article 9 fully apply in such instance." (Cámpora Schweizer v. Uruguay, *Report*. Op. Cit., Thirty-eighth session (A/38/40), annex VIII).

[4]Drescher Caldas v. Uruguay, *Report*. *Id.*, annex XVIII.

B. Treatment during pre-trial detention and imprisonment

29. Article 7 prohibits torture and cruel, inhuman, or degrading treatment or punishment, and applies to the pre-trial period as well as other periods of detention. Article 10 provides that all persons deprived of their liberty shall be treated with humanity and respect.

1. Prohibited treatment

30. Prolonged judicial proceedings could constitute cruel, inhuman, or degrading treatment or punishment. The Committee found that although excessive delays in judicial proceedings are not *per se* cruel, inhuman, or degrading treatment, the situation in each case must be considered. In capital cases prolonged judicial proceedings may constitute cruel, inhuman, or degrading treatment or punishment.

31. A warrant of execution causes intense anguish to the individual concerned and a delay in proceedings regarding the warrant may constitute cruel, inhuman, or degrading treatment. Two men under a death warrant were granted a stay of execution 45 minutes before the scheduled time of execution. Authorities kept the men in their death cell for 20 hours after the stay was granted. The Committee held that the delay in removing the men constituted cruel and inhuman treatment within the meaning of article 7.[5]

32. A detainee's rights under article 10 include the right to adequate medical care during the detention and extend to persons under a sentence of death. The Committee considered allegations of a prisoner on deathrow that he was denied necessary ophthalmologic and dental treatment. The Committee found insufficient facts to decide the issue but affirmed that a person imprisoned under a death sentence cannot be denied medical treatment.[6]

33. No prisoner can be subjected to compulsory experimentation while in detention or prison. A Uruguayan journalist was sentenced to seven years imprisonment for subversive association with an opposition political party. While in prison, the author was subjected to psychiatric experiments. For three years he was injected against his will with tranquilizers every two weeks. When he refused, he was forcibly subdued, injected with the drug, and subsequently held

---

[5]Pratt and Morgan v. Jamaica, *Report*, Op. cit., Forty-fourth session (A/44/40), annex X.F.

[6]Pinto v. Trinidad and Tobago, *Report*, Op. cit., Forty-fifth session (A/45/40), vol. II, annex IX.H.

incommunicado in a punishment cell for 45 days. The Committee found that the treatment constituted inhuman treatment and violated articles 7 and 10 (1).[7]

2. Prolonged incommunicado detention prohibited

34. Holding an individual incommunicado for a substantial period is a form of ill-treatment and violates article 10. The Committee examined the case of a Uruguayan student detained 14 months for subversive association.[8] She was kept incommunicado for 15 days and was subjected to beatings and other acts of torture during her detention. The Committee found the detention violated two provisions. The torture and cruel and degrading treatment she received while being kept incommunicado constituted a violation of article 7. The 15 days of incommunicado detention violated her right to humane treatment under article 10.[9] In another case where a man was detained incommunicado for six weeks, the Committee again found two violations. First, it found that the incommunicado detention was "incompatible with the standard of humane treatment required by article 10 (1)."[10] In addition, it found the detention deprived him of his right to counsel.[11]

3. Right to correspond with and to see family

35. The standard of humane treatment requires that prisoners be allowed to communicate with family and friends by correspondence as well as by receiving visits. In *Estrella v. Uruguay*,[12] the Committee determined that the restrictions on correspondence and visits by prison authorities constituted inhumane prison conditions in violation of article 10 (1). Prison authorities can exercise measures of control and censorship over prisoners' correspondence. The restrictions, however, are subject to article 17 which prohibits arbitrary or unlawful

---

[7]Acosta v. Uruguay, *Report*, Op. Cit., Thirty-ninth session (A/39/40), annex XI.

[8]Gilboa v. Uruguay, *Report*. Op. cit., Forty-first session (A/41/40), annex VIII.B.

[9]*Id.*

[10]Caldas v. Uruguay, *Report*. Op. cit.

[11]*See* note 36 *infra* and accompanying text. See also Muteba v. Zaire, *Report*. Op. cit., Thirty-ninth session (A/39/40), annex XIII. (Holding a detainee for several months incommunicado violates his right to humane treatment under article 10 (1).)

[12]Estrella v. Uruguay, *Report*. Op. cit., Thirty-eighth session (A/38/40), annex XII.

interference with a person's correspondence. In addition, restrictions must be consistent with the standard of humane treatment of detained persons.

36. A prisoner or detainee has the right to write and receive correspondence. In *Estrella* a prisoner in a Uruguayan prison was denied mail for a seven-month period. Prison authorities also subjected his correspondence to several restrictions. Authorities censored and arbitrarily deleted sentences in his correspondence, prohibited letters to lawyers or international organizations, and refused to dispatch letters. The Committee found that authorities had no reasonable basis to deny a prisoner the right to correspond. The Committee held that prisoners and detainees have the right to correspond with their family and reputable friends at regular intervals.

37. Arbitrary restrictions on visits also violate the right to humane treatment. In *Estrella*, prison officials allowed only two 45-minute visits per month, taped all conversations, restricted topics of conversation, and could arbitrarily end any visit. The committee found that a detainee has the right to receive visits at regular intervals under necessary supervision and that the conditions of Estrella's detention violated article 10 (1).

C. Notice

38. Article 14 (3) (a) provides that everyone charged with a criminal offence has the right to be informed promptly, in detail, and in a language she/he understands, of the nature and cause of the charge.

1. Notice of charges must be timely

39. The notice must allow sufficient time to prepare a defence. The Committee found that a summons issued three days before the start of trial did not provide sufficient notice.[13] The Committee stated that the purpose of notice was to inform the accused in a manner which would allow him/her to prepare a defence. Three days prevented any effective preparation of a defence. In addition, the notice must comply with all the requirements of article 14 (3) (a). Notice must be provided in time to allow the accused sufficient opportunity to examine or have examined the witnesses against him/her and obtain the attendance and examination of witnesses on his/her behalf.

40. Article 9 (2) provides that anyone arrested shall be informed at the time of the arrest of the reasons and any charges. The Committee insists upon strict compliance with the promptness requirement in article 9 (2). The Committee

---

[13] Mbenge v. Zaire, *Report*. Op. cit.

found that detaining a lawyer for a Dominican Republic human rights organization for 50 hours without informing the lawyer of the reasons for his arrest violated article 9(2).[14] Not surprisingly, the Committee found that a Uruguayan trade union official detained by Uruguayan authorities for over two years without being informed of the charges against him was also in violation of article 9 (2).[15]

2. Detailed notice of charges required

41. The Committee found that the function of the notice requirement was to enable a person to take immediate steps to secure release if she/he believes the reasons are invalid. The Committee held that this purpose requires that the notice include details of the charges.[16] Where an individual was arrested and told the arrest came under "prompt security measures", the Committee determined that he was not given sufficient detail to indicate the substance of the complaint against him.[17]

42. In addition to detailed notice of the charges or applicable law, the Committee found that there must be sufficient evidence to show that the detention falls within the law. A Malagasy political opposition leader was placed under house arrest on the basis of a law relating to the dissolution of certain associations. The detainee claimed that he was being held for his political beliefs and for having charged the Government with election fraud. The Committee found that government authorities failed to show that his arrest came within the law cited for his arrest. Furthermore, the arrest appeared to be on account of his political opinions, and violated article 9 (1).[18]

D. Right to release pending trial

43. Article 9 (3) provides that those detained or arrested on a criminal charge have the right to trial within a reasonable time or release. Detention of a person in custody must not only be lawful but reasonable and necessary in the

---

[14]Portorreal v. Dominican Republic, *Report*. Op. cit., Forty-third session, annex VII.D.

[15]Conteris v. Uruguay, *Report*. Op. cit., Fortieth session (A/40/40), annex X.

[16]Caldas v. Uruguay, *Report*. Op. cit.

[17]*Id.*, para. 13.2.

[18]Jaona v. Madagascar, *Report*. Op. cit., Fortieth session (A/40/40), annex IX.

circumstances.[19] The Committee examined the court-ordered detention of a lawyer who refused to co-operate in an investigation of his clients on the basis of lawyer-client privilege. The Netherlands argued that his nine-week detention was lawful and therefore did not violate article 9. The Committee found that detention "must be interpreted more broadly to include elements of inappropriateness, injustice and lack of predictability."[20] The lawyer was being held in custody to ensure his accessibility for authorities carrying out a criminal investigation. The Committee found that the lawyer was not obliged to provide such cooperation; hence, the detention was neither necessary nor reasonable and violated article 9 (4).

44. The Committee narrowly interprets the "necessity" requirement which justifies continued pre-trial custody. Custody may be necessary "to prevent flight, interference with evidence or the recurrence of crime."[21] The accused may be detained "where the person concerned constitutes a clear and serious threat to society which cannot be contained by any other manner."[22]

45. The Committee held that suspicion of murder alone did not demonstrate a sufficient interest to justify pre-trial detention. An individual arrested in Ecuador for murder was detained for five years before indictment.[23] The Committee recognized that article 9 (3) allows legal authorities to hold a person in custody if it is necessary to assure that the accused appears at trial. The Ecuadorian authorities expressed no concerns about the reappearance of the suspect. Absent an explanation for detaining the suspect without bail, the Committee found that the suspect must be granted a prompt trial or released.

46. An incomplete criminal investigation does not justify keeping an individual in detention. Ecuadorian authorities argued that the detention was not prolonged because the pre-trial investigation was completed just prior to indictment.[24] The Committee held that the entire trial must be complete to satisfy the prompt trial

---

[19]Van Alphen v. the Netherlands, *Report*. Op cit., Forty-fifth session (A/45/40), vol. II, annex IX.M.

[20]*Id.*

[21]*Id.*

[22]Càmpora Schweizer v. Uruguay, *Report*. Op. cit.

[23]Bolaños v. Ecuador, *Report*. Op. cit., Forty-fourth session (A/44/40), annex XIX.

[24]*Id.*

requirement. A completed trial produces a final judgment; because an indictment is not a final judgment, the detainee is entitled to release.

E. Counsel

47. Article 14 (3) (d) provides that an accused has the right to defend him/herself in person or through legal assistance of his/her own choosing.

1. Right to select counsel

48. The accused's right to choose his/her own counsel requires that she/he have an opportunity to choose freely. Concert pianist Estrella was arrested and brought before a military court in Uruguay; he was forced to choose his defence from two lawyers officially appointed by the military.[25] The Committee found that Estrella did not, in effect, have a choice when forced to pick from two lawyers pre-selected by the military. In the case of another Uruguayan accused who was forced to choose a lawyer from a list of military lawyers, the Committee held that the accused's right under article 14 (3) (d) was violated. [26]

49. A court cannot assign a lawyer for an accused when counsel of his own choosing is available. A journalist in Uruguay charged with subversive association was sentenced by a military tribunal to seven years' imprisonment. The following year he was brought before the Supreme Military Tribunal on charges of conspiracy, possession of arms, and use of false papers. The two lawyers who defended him during his previous trial had to renounce his defence and later left the country. Although he had found another civilian lawyer who would defend him, he was forced to accept a military *ex officio* counsel. The Committee held that the court could not prevent a qualified lawyer selected by the accused from representing him.[27]

2. Right to appointed counsel in capital cases

50. Article 14 (3) (d) provides that a person charged with a criminal offence has the right "to have legal assistance assigned to him, in any case where the interests of justice so require." The Committee found that a Norwegian driver charged with speeding and tried at the same time for an unrelated offence concerning the failure to provide information to an official register about a

---

[25]Estrella v. Uruguay, *Report*. Op. cit.

[26]Burgos v. Uruguay, *Report*. Op. cit., Thirty-sixth session (A/36/40), annex X.I.

[27]Acosta v. Uruguay, *Report*. Op. cit.

business firm did not demonstrate that the interests of justice required the assistance of a lawyer. It held that the State did not violate article 14 (3) (d) by failing to provide him with free legal assistance.[28]

51. The Committee has observed that cases involving a death sentence clearly require counsel in the interests of justice. In *Robinson v. Jamaica*,[29] a man arrested and charged with murder arranged for two lawyers to undertake his defence. The first day of trial the lawyers did not appear, but the judge allowed the trial to proceed. On the following day one of the lawyers appeared and requested permission for both lawyers to withdraw from the case. The judge denied permission and asked the two lawyers to represent the accused through legal aid. When counsel refused the request, the judge continued the trial with the accused unrepresented. The Committee found that the accused's right to counsel in a capital case was violated. It held that even where the unavailability of counsel was partially attributable to the accused, the court must accommodate the right to counsel and, if necessary, adjourn the proceedings. The assistance of a trial judge does not eliminate the accused's right to counsel.

52. An accused in a capital case has the right to legal representation and to choose his own legal representation at the trial and appellate levels.[30] Legal representation appointed to defend a man on trial for murder in Trinidad and Tobago displayed no interest in the case, remained passive throughout the trial, and failed to challenge evidence presented by the prosecution. After the accused was convicted and sentenced to death, he initiated an appeal. The accused did not want the attorney to represent him on appeal. Although he arranged for different representation and informed the court of his new defence attorney, the court of appeals reappointed his old lawyer. The Committee found that under the circumstances and especially because the case involved the death penalty, the State should have accepted the appellant's choice even if it required an adjournment of the proceedings. The Committee maintained that in capital cases legal assistance must be provided in ways that adequately and effectively ensure justice and that the appellant's right under article 14 (3) (d) was violated because he was denied effective representation during appeal.

---

[28]O.F. v. Norway, *Report*. Op. cit., Fortieth session (A/40/40), annex XII.

[29]Robinson v. Jamaica, *Report*. Op. Cit., Forty-fourth session (A/44/40), annex X.H.

[30]Pinto v. Trinidad and Tobago, *Report*. Op. cit.

53. The accused in a capital case may contest the choice of his court-appointed lawyer. A Jamaican convicted of murder appealed his case.[31] The court-appointed attorney assigned to him for the appeal, the same one who represented him in the trial court, informed the accused that there was no merit to the appeal. The accused requested a new attorney and requested to be present in person at the appeal. The court did not assign a new lawyer and did not allow him to be present since legal aid counsel had been assigned to him. The attorney did not advance arguments in favour of the appeal being granted and it was dismissed. The Committee found that the accused was effectively without legal representation in violation of article 14 (3) (d) and should have had another lawyer appointed for his defence or been allowed to represent himself at the appeal processing.

3. Right to adequate counsel

54. Where legal representation is provided, the person must be qualified to represent and defend the accused. A medical student detained in Uruguay was charged with being a member of a clandestine opposition group and was brought before a military court. The military court appointed a colonel as her defence counsel even though he was not a lawyer. The Committee found that the accused did not have adequate legal assistance and the appointment of unqualified counsel violated her rights under article 14 (3) (b) and (d).[32]

55. If legal representation is provided, the lawyer must actually advocate in favour of the accused. The officially appointed lawyer representing the accused pianist, Estrella, questioned his innocence, stressing confessions from friends.[33] The lawyer failed to arrange an examination of Estrella's accusers. The Committee held that Estrella's lawyer did not provide an adequate defence in violation of article 14 (3) (d).[34]

56. A lawyer's exercise of professional judgement in preparing his/her client's defence does not violate the accused's right to adequate representation even if the advice turns out to be incorrect. In a murder trial in Jamaica the court closed the case before the defence presented one of its witnesses. The accused claimed that the witness could have provided him with an alibi and that his lawyer, provided

---

[31]Reid v. Jamaica, *Report*, *Id.*, annex IX.J.

[32]Vasilskis v. Uruguay, *Report*. Op. cit., Thirty-eighth session (A/38/40), annex XV.

[33]Estrella v. Uruguay, *Report*. Op. cit.

[34]*Id.*

by the State, failed to afford an adequate defence by not calling the witness. The Committee noted that it is not unusual for the accused to believe that he would have been better represented by counsel of his own choosing, than by counsel provided by the State; but where the accused avails himself of legal representation provided by the State, he cannot claim inadequate representation simply because other counsel might have conducted the trial differently.[35]

57. Where an accused has legal representation, authorities may not try a person without notifying his/her attorney of the proceedings in time to allow adequate preparation for the defence. A military court tried a Uruguayan on charges of subversive association without notifying his attorney. After he was convicted the court informed the attorney of the results. The Committee held that failing to notify defence counsel barred the lawyer from participating in the defence and violated article 14 (3) (b) and (d).[36]

4. Opportunity to prepare a defence

58. The accused has the right under article 14 (3) (b) to communicate with counsel and have adequate facilities for the preparation of his/her defence. Actions taken by government authorities which deny an attorney the opportunity and adequate time to communicate with the accused violate article 14 (b) and (d) of the Covenant.

59. Marais, a South African national, and Wright, a United States citizen, made an emergency landing in Madagascar and were arrested. They were convicted of overflying Madagascar without authority and were sentenced to five years in prison. Marais escaped, was rearrested, and was charged with escaping from prison. Malagasy authorities created circumstance which made it difficult or impossible for Marais to speak with his attorney. After Marais' attorney left Madagascar, he was refused re-entry upon return. Marais retained a new attorney but during the 18 months Marais spent in detention awaiting trial, he was allowed to meet with his attorney only twice. After an initial hearing, authorities moved Marais to a political prison where all communication was forbidden. Malagasy political police eventually arrested Marais' attorney, detained him, and expelled him from Madagascar. The Committee found that Marais was not provided with conditions that allowed him to exercise his right

---

[35]Pratt and Morgan v. Jamaica, *Report*. Op. cit.

[36]Nieto v. Uruguay, *Report*. Op. cit., Thirty-eighth session (A/38/40), annex XX.

to counsel effectively and that the Malagasy authorities' interference violated articles 14 (3) (b) and (d).[37]

60. Incommunicado pre-trial detention for a prolonged period violates the accused's right to prepare his/her defence and is prohibited. The Committee found that holding a detainee incommunicado for six weeks after his arrest deprived him of the possibility of communicating with counsel at a critical pre-trial stage and was prohibited.[38]

61. An accused held in detention may not be prevented from seeing his/her attorney for an extended period. A Uruguayan indicted by a military tribunal in January 1973 was not allowed to see his defence lawyer for two years from March 1975 to mid-1977. He was sentenced in 1979. The Committee found that denying the accused the right to see his attorney for two years violated the accused's right under articles 14 (3) (b).[39] The Committee's decision suggests that the accused had a right to see an attorney at all times during the pre-trial period.

62. The accused must be given sufficient minimum time to prepare a defence. A Jamaican accused of murder was provided with a legal-aid attorney but was not able to communicate with the attorney until the opening day of trial.[40] The lawyer had not discussed the case with the accused nor had time to prepare questions to ask the witnesses, and requested a postponement which the judge denied. The Committee found that the court's failure to grant the defence sufficient minimum time to prepare his examination of witnesses constituted a violation of article 14 (3) (b).

63. The right to prepare a defence includes the right to private communication with counsel. A Uruguayan awaiting trial on charges of subversive association was permitted to speak with her defence lawyer through a glass wall only over the prison's telephone and while guards stood at their side. Although the Committee found that the accused's rights appeared to be violated, it was

---

[37]Marais v. Madagascar, *Report. Id.*, annex XI.

[38]Caldas v. Uruguay, *Report.* Op. Cit. *See also* Portorreal v. Dominican Republic, *Report.* Op. cit., (where accused held 44 days without access to legal counsel violates article 14 (3) (b).

[39]Lluberas v. Uruguay, *Report.* Op. cit., Thirty-ninth session (A/39/40), annex XII.

[40]Reid v. Jamaica, *Report.* Op. cit.

procedurally barred from ruling on the issue because the facts were disputed by the State party.[41]

F. Hearing

1. Right to prompt trial

64. Article 9 (4) provides that anyone deprived of his/her liberty by arrest or detention is entitled to have a court decide without undue delay on the lawfulness of the detention. The Committee recognized that it is not useful to set precise deadlines for issuing a judgement.[42] Instead, the Committee has assessed the timeliness of decisions on a case-by-case basis. The Committee held that a seven-day detention which did not provide the detainee with an opportunity to bring his detention before a court violated article 9 (4). A Spanish citizen in Finland requested asylum and was placed in detention under the Finnish Aliens Act. The law provided him with a right to request review of his detention by the Minister of Interior after seven days. The Committee found that the detention violated his rights under article 9 (4) because he was not allowed to take proceedings and obtain a court decision promptly.

65. In the same case the Committee found that a three-month delay between the filing of the detainee's appeal and the decision on the appeal was "in principle too extended."[43] The Committee, however, noted that it lacked facts necessary to evaluate the reason for the delay and could not make any findings on the issue.

66. Article 14 (3) (c) guarantees an individual charged with a criminal offence the right to a trial without undue delay. The cases under this provision indicate that the right to trial without undue delay must be understood as the right to a trial which produces a final judgement and sentence without undue delay.[44] The

---

[41]Gómez de Voituret v. Uruguay, *Report*. Op. cit., Thirty-ninth session (A/39/40), annex X. The Committee bases its views on facts which appear uncontested or facts contested only by general denials. Lluberas v. Uruguay, *Report*. Op. cit.

[42]Torres v. Finland, *Report*. Op. cit., Forty-fifth session (A/45/40), vol. II, annex IX.K.

[43]*Id.*

[44]*See* Caldas v. Uruguay, *Report*. Op. cit. The Committee found that absent information about the outcome of the criminal proceedings or copies of the court decisions, it could not find that the individual had been tried or tried without undue delay and concluded that article 14 (3) (c) had been violated.

founder of an alleged guerilla group in Uruguay was indicted on charges of subversion, storage of explosives, and manslaughter. It was not until six years later that a military tribunal sentenced him to 30 years' imprisonment. The Committee held that he was tried with undue delay.[45]

67. The right to be tried without undue delay includes the right to a review of conviction and sentence without undue delay. Two Jamaican men took an appeal of a murder conviction and death sentence which was rejected by the appellate court. The court's opinion stating the reasons for rejecting the appeal was not issued until nearly four years later. The two could not petition for special leave to appeal to a higher tribunal until they received the opinion of the appellate court. The Committee noted that articles 14 (3) (c) and 14 (5) must be read together so that the right to review of conviction and sentence is made available without undue delay.[46] In another case an appeal was delayed for 34 months because of an administrative failure to produce the trial transcripts. The State argued that the accused should have requested an order to produce the transcripts. The Committee rejected the State's argument and found that the undue delay in the appeal violated the accused's rights under article 14 (3) (c).[47]

68. The State has the responsibility to see that the entire process completed without delay. The State in *Pratt and Morgan v. Jamaica* argued that the delay in proceedings was due to an oversight by the judge and that there was no violation of the right to trial without undue delay because the accused had a responsibility to assert his right to the judgement which he failed to exercise. The Committee found that the right to a prompt trial does not depend upon the accused's request that the right be observed.

69. Article 9 (3) provides that anyone arrested or detained on a criminal charge must be tried within a reasonable time or released. The Committee considered the case of a Venezuelan detained on suspicion of participating in an armed rebellion and indicted 10 months later by a military court. Two years after the indictment the proceedings were interrupted, but the detainee remained in detention. He was released five years later. The Committee found that absent a final judgement in the case the detention violated article 9 (3).[48]

---

[45]Lluberas v. Uruguay, *Report*. Op. cit.

[46]Pratt and Morgan v. Jamaica, *Report*. Op. cit.

[47]*Pinkney v. Canada, Report*. Op. cit., Thirty-seventh session (A/37/40), annex VII.

[48]*Solórzano v. Venezuela, Report*. Op. cit., Forty-first session (A/41/40), annex VIII.C.

2. Equality of arms

70. Article 14 (1) declares that all persons shall be equal before the courts and tribunals. Although this provision applies equally to individuals in civil and criminal proceedings, the Committee has not had an opportunity to apply it to a civil proceeding.

71. The right of all persons to be equal before the courts requires that the prosecution and defence be treated equally in a criminal trial. The court cannot act in a way which gives the prosecution an advantage over the defence. The Committee considered a case where the accused's request for adjournment in a murder trial was denied by the trial court. Prior to the accused man's request for adjournment, the court had postponed the trial on seven occasions because the prosecution could not find the address to subpoena its chief witness. On the day the trial commenced, the two lawyers for the accused did not appear and on the following day they withdrew from the case. The accused requested adjournment to arrange legal representation and the trial judge refused. The Committee found that the refusal raised issues of fairness and violated article 14 (1) because of the "inequality of arms" between the parties.[49]

3. Right to interpretation

72. Article 14 (3) (f) provides the accused with the right to have the free assistance of an interpreter if he/she cannot understand or speak the language used in court. The Committee found that this provision does not imply that the accused has the right to express him/herself in the language which he/she normally speaks or speaks with most ease if the accused is sufficiently proficient in the court's language.[50] A French citizen whose mother tongue was Breton was charged with defacing road signs in French and tried in a French court. The accused requested that the court allow him and his witnesses to give their testimony in Breton. The court noted that the accused was able to express himself in French and that his witnesses understood and spoke French, although they preferred to speak in Breton. The court denied the accused's request for an interpreter and to speak in Breton and conducted the trial in French. The accused alleged that denying him the right to express himself in his mother tongue violated his right to a fair trial. The Committee noted that article 14 (1) ensures procedural equality and the equality of arms in criminal proceedings. The Committee found that this provision, however, does not prevent a State from

---

[49]Robinson v. Jamaica, *Report*. Op. cit.

[50]Guesdon v. France, *Report*. Op. cit., para. 1.5.

using one official court language. Under this provision a State is not obligated to provide an interpreter for a citizen whose mother tongue differs from the official court language. The State is obligated to provide an interpreter under article 14 (3) (f) if the accused or the defence witnesses have difficulty understanding or expressing themselves in the court language.[51] The Committee concluded that denying the accused the right to speak in Breton, when he understood and spoke French, did not violate his right to a fair trial or his rights under article 14 (3) (f).

4. Right to be present at trial

73. Article 14 (3) (d) provides the accused with a right to be tried in his/her presence. A Uruguayan professor, Hiber Conteris, charged with subverting the constitution, "criminal and political association," illegal entry, and kidnapping, was denied any opportunity to appear in person before a judge. He was convicted by a military tribunal *in absentia.* On appeal, he was not brought before members of the military tribunal reviewing his case but instead "a junior functionary confined himself to reading the sentence and asking for my signature."[52] The Committee found that both trial and appeal denied his right to a public trial in violation of article 14 (1).

74. Another Uruguayan tried by military courts challenged the fairness of a military procedure which permitted the accused to submit only written statements taken by a court clerk and did not allow her to be brought before the judge in person. Although the Committee could not rule on the issue, it supported the accused's right to appear in person before the court.[53]

75. The Committee held that the right to a public trial does not forbid all proceedings *in absentia.* The Committee stated that proceedings *in absentia* may be permissible in the proper administration of justice, for example, when the accused person has been informed of the proceedings sufficiently in advance and declines to exercise the right to be present.[54] According to the Committee, a

---

[51]*Id.*

[52]Conteris v. Uruguay, *Report.* Op. cit., para. 1.5.

[53]The Committee requested that the State provide information on whether it allowed the accused to appear in person. When it received the State's routine assurance, the facts were placed in dispute. The Committee will not decide on an issue when the facts are disputed. Gómez de Voituret v. Uruguay, *Report.* Op. cit.

[54]Mbenge v. Zaire, *Report.* Op. cit.

valid judgement *in absentia* requires that steps be taken to inform the accused beforehand about the proceedings against him/her, especially the requirements of article 14 (3) (a). The Committee found that the purpose of the notice was to allow the accused an opportunity to exercise his/her rights under article 14 effectively. To satisfy this purpose, the notice must inform the accused of the date and place of trial and request his/her attendance.[55]

76. The Committee considered the case of a Zairian citizen living in Belgium as a political refugee who was sentenced to death for murder in two separate trials made known to him only through the press. The Committee acknowledged that although there are certain limits on the efforts authorities may be expected to make in contacting the accused, the State had not reached those limits in the case of the Zairian citizen.[56] Judicial authorities had issued summonses but did not attempt to send them to the accused even though his address was known. The Committee held that the trial violated his right under article 14 (3) (d).

5. Right not to be compelled to confess guilt

77. The Committee held that a confession obtained after ill-treatment violated the accused's right not to be compelled to confess guilt under article 14 (3) (g). Professor Conteris was arrested by security police for crimes associated with subverting the constitution and spent three months in incommunicado detention; he was subjected to various forms of torture, and eventually signed a confession.[57] The Committee held that he did not voluntarily sign the confession and that a forced confession violated article 14 (3) (g).[58]

6. Right to call and examine witnesses

78. The accused's right to obtain the attendance and examination of witnesses on his/her behalf under article 14 (3) (e) may be waived by counsel. In *Pratt and Morgan v. Jamaica* two men convicted for murder and sentenced to be executed argued that the judge improperly closed the case before an important defence witness was allowed to provide an alibi for one of the accused. The Committee found that the defence attorney did not call the witness because of

---

[55] *Id.*

[56] *Id.*

[57] Conteris v. Uruguay, *Report.* Op. cit.

[58] *See also* Cariboni v. Uruguay, *Selected Decisions of the Human Rights Committee Under the Optional Protocol.* Op. cit., communication no. 159/1983.

tactical considerations. The accused argued that his counsel should have insisted upon calling the witness, and failing to do so constituted a violation of article 14 (3) (e). The Committee held that counsel's decision not to call the witness was within the professional judgement of the attorney and not a denial of the accused's right to call and examine witnesses.

7. Civil suits entitled to protection

79. Under article 14 (1) any individual in a suit at law is entitled to a fair hearing. The Committee found an action is a suit at law in two circumstances: if the forum where the particular question is adjudicated is one where courts normally exercise control over the proceedings; or where the right in question is subject to judicial control or judicial review. The Committee held that a Canadian denied a disability pension by the Canadian Pension Commission had the right to a fair hearing under article 14 (1).[59] The Committee found that because Canadian law allowed the individual to appeal the decision to the federal court, even though the individual did not appeal it, the decision was subject to judicial supervision and control; therefore, he was engaged in a suit at law under article 14 (1).

80. Immigration hearings and deportation proceedings may be suits at law. The Committee considered a Salvadorian's claim that Canada violated his right to a fair hearing in deportation proceedings. Canada argued that deportation proceedings were not suits at law and thus not subject to article 14 (1). The Committee did not accept Canada's argument and stated explicitly that such proceedings were suits at law. It held that even if immigration and deportation proceedings were within the meaning of article 14 (1), however, the Salvadorian failed to establish any violation.[60]

8. Limitation on derogability of rights in the trial process

81. The Committee held that a State cannot derogate from due process guarantees by invoking "prompt security measures" without explaining the national emergency situation and the specific derogations required by the situation.[61]

---

[59]Y.L. v. Canada, *Report.* Op. cit., Forty-first session (A/41/40), annex IX.A.

[60]V.M.R.B. v. Canada, *Report.* Op. cit., Forty-third session (A/43/40), annex VIII. F.

[61]Lanza de Netto v. Uruguay, *Report.* Op. cit., Thirty-fifth session (A/43/40), annex VI.

82. The Committee considered violations of articles 14 (1), 14 (2), and 14 (3) in the case of two Uruguayan nationals who were detained, tried by a military judge, and sentenced under "prompt security measures." The Government argued that the two received all guarantees of due process and that the derogations were justified under the country's "prompt security measures." Article 4 allows States in times of public emergency which threaten the life of the nation to derogate from their obligations under the Covenant. The derogations, however, can only be made to the extent strictly necessary by the exigencies of the situation. The Committee found that a legislative enactment of emergency laws was not sufficient to permit derogation. Article 4 allows derogation only in "strictly defined circumstances" and "prompt securities measures" did not justify derogation. In conclusion, the Committee held that the trial violated articles 14 (1), 14 (2), and 14 (3) because they were tried in circumstances in which "irrespective of legislative provisions" they could not effectively enjoy the safeguards of fair trial.[62]

83. In another case security forces arrested a Uruguayan without a warrant. The Committee found that arresting and detaining him without a warrant could not be excused by the "prompt security measures" and that his detention violated article 9 (1).[63] The Committee held that charges brought after arrest and detention did not make the detention lawful.[64]

84. A Columbian law enacted under a state of siege allowed members of the police to escape prosecution for crimes intended to prevent or curb extortion, kidnapping, or drug trafficking.[65] Police raided a house looking for alleged kidnappers, waited in hiding for the suspects, and subsequently shot and killed seven individuals who entered. The police involved were charged and then acquitted under the special Colombia law. The Committee found that even if an effective derogation under article 4 was assumed, the Columbian law could not come within the derogation to exonerate the police action. The Committee noted that the individuals killed were only suspects in a kidnapping and held that their killing had deprived them of due process. In addition, article 6 (1) provides that the right to life shall be protected by law and that this article cannot be the subject of derogation under any circumstances. The Committee's opinion suggests

---

[62]*Id.*, para. 16.

[63]Conteris v. Uruguay, *Report*. Op. cit.

[64]*Id.*

[65]Camargo v. Colombia, *Report*. Op. cit., Thirty-seventh session (A/37/40), annex XI.

that a State cannot derogate from its right to guarantee due process protection especially when the life of the individual is at stake.

G. Decision

85. Article 14 (1) provides all persons in criminal trials and civil suits the right to a fair and public hearing by a competent, independent, and impartial tribunal established by law.

1. Right to an independent judiciary

86. Several communications have challenged the competency, independence, and authority of a military court under article 14 (1), however, the Committee has not ruled on the issue. In each case the person alleging the violation was still in detention controlled by the military.[66]

87. Article 9 (4) provides that any person deprived of his liberty by arrest or detention has the right to bring proceedings before a court.

88. The Committee holds that an authority is not a "court" simply because it reviews detention according to established legal procedures. The body conducting the review must be a court of law. The Committee found that a military disciplinary proceeding and a military appeal process did not constitute a court within the meaning of article 9 (4). The Committee examined the case of a Finnish serviceman sanctioned with 10 days of detention in military proceeding. The serviceman was allowed to request a review by a superior military officer.[67] Finland argued that since military disciplinary detention was regulated by law, it did not require the legal or procedureal safeguards stipulated in article 9 (4). The Committee disagreed. The purpose of article 9 (4) is not to ensure that detention is reviewed in a judicial or quasi-judicial manner or that judicial scrutiny is provided on appeal. Its purpose is to ensure that a court reviews the detention. The Committee held that a supervisory military officer is not a "court" within the meaning of article 9 (4).[68]

---

[66]A Uruguayan arrested and tried by a military court under "prompt security measures" alleged that his trial violated article 14 because the court was a military court, lacking in procedureal guarantees and impartiality. The Committee did not reject the allegation but failed to resolve the issue raised. Procedureal v. Uruguay, 24 *Report* Op. cit., Thirty-eighth session (A/38/40), annex IX.

[67]Vuolanne v. Finland, *Report*. Op. cit.

[68]*Id.*

89. The court reviewing the legality of detention must be objective and independent. The Committee considered a Spanish citizen's claim that he had no recourse to a court to challenge his detention in Finland. The Spanish citizen had requested asylum in Finland and was detained under the Finnish Aliens Act. Under the Act a detained alien may appeal his/her detention to the Minister of Interior. Finland argued that the law and appeal process protected aliens against unlawful detention thus satisfying the purpose of article 9 (4). The Committee declared that the purpose of requiring review by a court is to ensure "a higher degree of objectivity and independence" in exercising control over detention.[69] The Committee held that the Minister of Interior could not review the detention with the necessary objectivity.

2. Right to a public trial

90. Article 14 (1) provides that the public may be excluded from a trial only for reasons of morals, public order, or national security in a democratic society, or where required by the private lives of the parties. A Uruguayan tried by a military court for conspiracy to subvert the Constitution was sentenced to four and a half years of imprisonment at a trial held *in camera*. The Committee found that a trial *in camera* violates article 14 (1) if the State fails to provide a reason for not providing a public trial,[70]

91. Where a party is entitled to a public trial, the court must make information about time and venue of the proceedings available to the public and must provide adequate facilities for the attendance of interested members of the public.[71]

3. Right to have judgment made public

92. Article 14 (1) provides that any judgment rendered in a criminal case or in a suit at law shall be made public except in juvenile proceedings or matrimonial disputes about the guardianship of children. The right to a public judgment requires that any judgment be in writing. The Committee examined the trial of a Uruguayan who was charged with subversive association and sentenced to 14 years' imprisonment but who never received the texts of any court decisions. The Committee found that where the judgment was not in writing, it could not hold

---

[69]Torres v. Finland, *Report*. Op. cit.

[70]Estralla v. Uruguay, *Report*. Op. cit.

[71]Van Meurs v. the Netherlands, *Report*. Op. cit., Forty-fifth session (A/45/40), vol. II, annex IX.F.

that the proceedings or the severity of the sentence complied with the Covenant.[72] It held that the trial violated article 14 (1) because the judgment rendered against him was not made public.

4. Right to benefit from lighter penalty

93. Article 15 (1) states that if subsequent to the commission of an offence a provision is made for the imposition of a lighter penalty, the lighter penalty shall benefit the offender. The article applies to penalties imposed by civil and administrative bodies as well as those imposed for criminal offences. A Canadian on parole from an eight-year sentence for armed robbery committed an offence and was convicted for that offence.[73] Under Canadian law, a person convicted of a criminal offence while on parole automatically forfeits the time spent on parole and must re-serve the time in prison. During his imprisonment the criminal law was amended making the revocation of parole a discretionary rather than mandatory sanction. The imprisoned man claimed that Canada, in not making the law retroactive, denied his right to a lighter penalty under article 15.

94. Canada argued that article 15 refers to criminal penalties and that the grant of parole is an administrative sanction which is not included in article 15. The Committee rejected that argument, interpreting "penalty" to include sanctions imposed in administrative and disciplinary proceedings.[74] The Committee held, however, that he had not been denied the benefit of a lighter sentence and that the judge considered the time he had served when imposing the sentence for the second crime. The Committee questioned whether article 15 (1) requires that a lighter penalty be created prior to the time of sentencing, or at any time before the sentence is fully served. The Committee disliked the narrow construction which would eliminate the benefit of a lighter penalty for persons in the process of serving a sentence but did not decide the issue.

5. Second trial for same offence prohibited

95. A Uruguayan serving the last year of a 10-year sentence for charges of subversion was brought before a military court and charged on the basis of the same facts used in the first trial. The authorities claimed that there was fresh evidence against the accused and that the new charges were not brought in the first trial. The committee found that absent a judgment in the second trial, it

---

[72]Tourón v. Uruguay, *Report*. Op. cit., Thirty-sixth session (A/36/40), annex X.

[73]MacIsaac v. Canada. *Report*, Op. Cit., Thirty-eighth session (A/38/40), annex VII.

[74]*Id.*

could not hold that article 14 (7) was violated. It did note that more detail was required to establish that the facts and evidence were, in fact, new and not part of the old trial.[75]

96. An individual may be tried in two separate States for the same offence. A man convicted and sentenced in Switzerland for exchanging money received as ransom for a kidnapping in Italy was later tried and convicted in Italy. The accused argued that article 14 (7) prohibits a second trial for the same offence and should be interpreted broadly to apply to judicial decisions of different States. The Committee rejected this argument, holding that article 14 (7) prohibits only double jeopardy for an offence adjudicated in a given State.[76]

H. Right to appeal

97. Article 14 (5) provides that everyone convicted of a crime shall have the right to review his/her conviction and sentence by a higher tribunal. The Committee held that a charge which involved a one-year sentence was serious enough to come within article 14 (5) and required review by a higher tribunal regardless of whether domestic law viewed it as a "criminal" charge.[77] A Colombian woman charged with selling a gun was sentenced to one year imprisonment by a military judge. On appeal her sentence was confirmed by the same judge. Colombia argued that a state of siege was in effect in the country which made it necessary to adopt extraordinary legal procedures. The Committee found that the State could not evade its obligations under the Covenant by invoking a state of siege. Although article 4 allows a State to derogate from certain obligations in a time of public emergency, the Committee held that the State must demonstrate that an emergency situation does exist in the country and that the derogation is one permitted by article 4 (1) as strictly required by the situation. The Committee found that the State did not show derogation from article 14 (5) in accordance with article 4 and Colombia violated article 14 (5) by failing to provide an appeal to a higher tribunal.

98. The Committee considered an Italian law removing the right of the President and government ministers to appeal in cases involving certain charges brought before the constitutional court. Italy had submitted a limited reservation under article 4 to give effect to the law. The question arose as to whether an air force general brought before the constitutional court on charges of bribery was denied

---

[75]Nieto v. Uruguay. *Report*, Op. cit.

[76]A.P. v. Italy, *Report*. Op. cit. Forty-third session (A/43/40), annex VIII.A.

[77]Montejo v. Colombia, *Report*. Op. cit., Thirty-seventh session (A/37/40), annex XV.

his right under the Covenant, since his position was not expressly included in the reservation for the President and his ministers.[78] The Committee noted that Italian law established a rule permitting an ordinary trial for persons accused of the same crime. The general argued that reading the two provisions together was an expansive interpretation of the reservation and contrary to the generally accepted legal principle of "restrictive" interpretation of reservations. The general claimed that he was a "layman" within the meaning of the provision and his right to appeal should not be limited by the reservation. The Committee disagreed and found that a narrow reading of the restriction, excluding the general, would be contrary to the working and purpose of the reservation, which was to safeguard provisions in Italian law.

I. Remedies

99. Article 14 (6) provides that a person is entitled to compensation for punishment after a conviction which is reversed or pardoned on the basis of new or newly discovered facts which conclusively show there has been a miscarriage of justice. Muhonen, a Finnish citizen, claimed conscientious objector status and submitted an application to the Military Service Examining Board which was denied.[79] When he refused military service, criminal court proceedings were initiated and he was sentenced to 11 months' imprisonment. After he had served nearly eight months of his sentence, the Examining Board found that he was entitled to conscientious objector status. He was subsequently pardoned and released from prison. Muhonen claimed that he was entitled to compensation under article 14 (6) because his conviction had been pardoned. The Committee rejected the compensation claim because Muhonen's pardon was not on the basis of new or newly discovered evidence but a resubmitted application for conscientious objector status.

100. Article 2 (3) (a) provides that any person whose rights under the Covenant have been violated shall have an effective remedy. The Committee considered the application of article 2 to the case of a Zairian citizen detained without warrant of arrest for over nine months without leave to test the lawfulness of his detention before a court. While in detention he appealed to an administrateur general and by letter to the head of State, but claimed that no other remedy was available to him under Zairian law. The Committee found a violation of article

---

[78]Fanali v. Italy, *Report.* Op. cit., Thirty-eighth session (A/38/40), annex XIII.

[79]Muhonen v. Finland, *Report.* Op. cit., Fortieth session (A/40/40), annex VII.

2 (3) because there was no effective remedy under the domestic law of Zaire for violations of an individual's rights under the articles 9 and 10.[80]

101. The Committee found that a reservation to one of the provisions of the Covenant effectively bars the accused's right to a remedy under article 2 (3) even when the State has not expressly excluded one by reservation. As discussed above, an Italian air force general who lacked the right to appeal his conviction because of Italy's reservation to article 14 (5), maintained that he was entitled to a remedy under article 2 (3) of the Covenant which declares that a person whose rights or freedoms are violated shall have an effective remedy. The Committee held that the right to a remedy is linked to the right violated and cannot be invoked when the purported right is excluded by reservation.[81]

* * *

V. CONCLUSIONS AND RECOMMENDATIONS

108.Resolution 1991/43 entitled "Right to a fair trial," adopted by the Commission on Human Rights on 5 March 1991, welcomed the brief report (E/CN.4/Sub.2/1990/34) prepared by the two Special Rapporteurs, Mr. Stanislav Chernichenko and Mr. William Treat, and requested them to undertake a more complete study of the right to a fair trial, including the preparation of a questionnaire to Governments and other sources of information.

109.The two Special Rapporteurs have begun their study with a review of the fair trial standards in international instruments and in the interpretations of international bodies, such as the Human Rights Committee.

110.The next, that is, third report of the two Special Rapporteurs will largely be devoted to a review of the interpretations of fair trial standards by the European Commission and Court of Human Rights as well as the Inter-American Commission on the Court of Human Rights.

111.In addition, the two Special Rapporteurs have prepared an initial questionnaire on the right to a fair trial, which they have revised for reproduction in Annex II of this report and concerning which they would be very grateful for comments. The two Special Rapporteurs will revise the questionnaire further in the light of the comments received, so that the questionnaire can be sent to Member States again soon after the forty-third session of the Sub-Commission.

---

[80]Luyeye v. Zaire, *Report*. Op. cit., Thirty-eighth session (A/38/40), annex XIX.

[81]Fanali v. Italy, *Report*. Op. cit.

112. Furthermore, the questionnaire will be revised for transmittal to interested specialized agencies and non-governmental organizations after the forty-third session of the Sub-Commission.

113. It is hoped that responses to the questionnaires will be received in time for the two Special Rapporteurs to provide the Sub-Commission at its forty-fourth session with an initial summary of the material received and other relevant information on national practises related to the right to a fair trial. Since a review of national practises will be a very time-consuming, difficult, and complex task, however, it is unlikely that the Special Rapporteurs will be able to produce an analysis of national practises until their fourth report for the forty-fifth session of the Sub-Commission.

114. In light of the views of Governments, it would be desirable to consider the preparation of a model code or declaration on the right to a fair trial.

115. In light of the view of Governments, it would also be desirable to consider ways by which the right to a fair trial might be strengthened, for example, by making the right to a fair trial or certain aspects of the right non-derogable. In that regard the study would consider the elaboration of a Third Optional Protocol to the International Covenant on Civil and Political Rights which would add article 14 (the right to a fair trial provision) to the list of provisions which cannot be derogated from in article 4 of the Covenant.

116. Also in light of the view of Governments, it would be desirable to consider other means of strengthening the implementation of the right to a fair trial, as discussed in the first brief report.

117. The two Special Rapporteurs note the tasks they have undertaken covers a vast and complex subject. The two Special Repporteurs wish to express their appreciation for the cooperation and assistance they have received in taking the initial steps of the study.

* * *

5. Draft Declaration on the Right to a Fair Trial and a Remedy

Provisions applicable to all adjudicative proceedings

1. In the determination of any criminal charge against a person, or of the person's rights and obligations in a suit at law, everyone shall be entitled to a fair and public hearing by a competent, independent, and impartial tribunal established by law. Any judgment rendered in a criminal case or in a suit at law shall be made public, except where the interests of juvenile persons otherwise

require or the proceedings concern matrimonial disputes or the guardianship of children.

Fair hearing

2. A "fair ... hearing" requires respect for the principle of equality of arms between parties to the proceedings, whether they be civil, criminal, administrative, or military.

3. All persons shall be equal before the courts and tribunals. The right of every individual to a fair trial is recognized without any distinction whatsoever as regards race, colour, sex, language, religion, political or other convictions, national or social origin, means or other circumstance.

4. If a person's rights and obligations may be adversely affected in a suit at law or by particularized actions or inactions taken or proposed by a public authority, the court or the public authority shall give the person adequate notice of the nature and purpose of the proceedings and shall give the person a fair and public hearing by a competent, independent and impartial tribunal established by law.

5. A fair hearing requires that a person entitled to adequate notice of the nature and purpose of proceedings shall have the right:

(a) To adequate opportunity to prepare a case;

(b) To present arguments and evidence, and to meet opposing arguments and evidence, either in writing, orally or by both means;

(c) To consult and be represented by counsel or other qualified persons of the person's choice during all stages of the proceedings;

(d) To consult an interpreter during all stages of the proceedings, if he or she cannot understand or speak the language used in the court or tribunal;

(e) To have their rights and obligations affected only by a decision based solely on evidence known to parties to public proceedings;

(f) To have their rights and obligations affected only by a decision rendered without undue delay and as to which the parties are provided adequate notice thereof and the reasons therefor:

(i) Factors relevant to what constitutes undue delay include, *inter alia*, the complexity of the case, the conduct of the parties, the conduct of other relevant participants, whether an individual is detained pending proceedings, and the interest of the persons at stake in the proceeding;

(g) To appeal decisions to a higher administrative authority, a judicial tribunal, or both.

Public hearing

6. In order to hold a "public hearing", the court or tribunal shall make information about the time and venue of the public hearing available, and provide adequate facilities for attendance by interested members of the public.

7. In a public hearing, the court or tribunal may not limit attendance to only a particular category of people and should allow local, national and international observers to attend, so as to verify that justice is done and seen to be done. Representatives of the press and of other media may be present at a public hearing.

8. Exceptions to a public hearing shall be narrowly construed. In regard to each exception, the tribunal shall determine whether the strong public and individual interest in seeing that justice is done would be substantially outweighed by the rationale for the exception which is proposed for closure from public attendance. If an exception to the right to a public hearing is found to justify at least some degree of closure, the tribunal should also consider closing only portions of the proceedings or should consider taking evidence *in camera* so as to implement to the greatest extent possible the right to a public hearing.

9. The press and the public may be excluded from all or part of a trial for reasons of morals, public order, or national security in a democratic society, when the interest of the private lives of the parties so requires, or to the extent strictly necessary in the opinion of the court or tribunal in special circumstances where publicity would prejudice the interests of justice.

10. In further defining these exceptions to the right to a public hearing, the public may be excluded from hearings on the grounds of morals, where the testimony will have such a corrupting or intimidating influence on the observers or participants as to outweigh the strong public and individual interest in a public hearing. Moral grounds for excluding the public may be asserted primarily in the trial of cases involving sexual offences. The public may be excluded from hearings on the grounds of a grave threat to public order; such a threat might outweigh the strong public and individual interest in a public hearing for cases of disciplinary proceedings in prisons. The public may be excluded from hearings because of national security concerns when hearings involve State

defence secrets in a democratic society. Privacy interests may merit excluding the public from hearings relating to family issues, such as divorce and guardianship, and from juvenile proceedings involving sexual offences, in so far as public proceedings would constitute a clearly unwarranted invasion of personal privacy outweighing the strong public and individual interest in a public hearing.

11. A public hearing shall occur where the merits of the case are being examined - either at the trial or appellate level - but not necessarily at both levels.

12. An individual party may waive his or her right to a public hearing if consent is given of one's own free will, is made in an unequivocal manner and preferably in writing, and does not infringe any important public interest in seeing that justice is done.

Independent tribunal

13. Every person has the right to a fair hearing of his or her case by a legally constituted competent, independent and impartial court or tribunal.

14. In order to be "independent", a tribunal shall be established by law to have adjudicative functions to determine matters within its competence on the basis of rules of law and in accordance with proceedings conducted in a prescribed manner. A tribunal may be established by legislative, executive or judicial power.

15. The judiciary shall have jurisdiction over all issues of a judicial nature and shall have exclusive authority to decide whether an issue submitted for decision is within the tribunal's competence as defined by law.

16. A tribunal's jurisdiction may be determined, *inter alia*, by considering where the events involved in the dispute or offence took place, where the property in dispute is located, the place of residence or domicile of the parties and the consent of the parties.

17. Tribunals that do not use the duly established procedures of the legal process shall not be created to displace the jurisdiction belonging to the ordinary courts or judicial tribunals.

18. There shall not be any inappropriate or unwarranted interference with the judicial process, nor shall judicial decisions by the courts be subject to revision. This provision is without prejudice to judicial review or to mitigation or commutation by competent authorities of sentences by the judiciary, in accordance with the law.

19. A court shall be independent from the executive branch. The executive branch in a State shall not be able to interfere in a court's proceedings and a court shall not act as an agent for the executive against an individual citizen.

20. The term of office of judges and members of a tribunal, their independence, security, adequate remuneration, conditions of service, pensions and the age of retirement shall be adequately secured by law.

21. Judges or members of a tribunal, whether appointed or elected, shall have guaranteed tenure until a mandatory retirement age or the expiry of their term of office, where such exists.

22. Promotion of judges and members of tribunals, where such a system exists, should be based on objective factors, in particular ability, integrity and experience.

23. It is essential that a judge or member of a tribunal should not be subject to any authority in the performance of his or her duties, aside from duly registered appeals after judgement has been announced.

24. A tribunal shall be independent from the parties in the case.

Impartial tribunal

25. A tribunal shall be "impartial"; it shall base its opinion only on objective arguments and evidence presented. The judiciary shall decide matters before them without any restrictions, improper influences, inducements, pressures, threats or interferences, direct or indirect, from any quarter or for any reason.

26. The impartiality of a tribunal may be subject to challenge if the public is entitled to question, on the basis of ascertainable facts, that the fairness of the judge or tribunal was capable of appearing open to doubt. Three relevant factors should be considered in determining impartiality: whether the trial judge's position allows him or her to play a crucial role in the proceedings; whether the judge may have a pre-formed opinion which would weigh heavily on the decision-making; and whether a judge would have to rule on an action taken in a prior capacity.

27. A tribunal lacks impartiality if, *inter alia*, a former public prosecutor or attorney sits as a judge on a case in which he or she prosecuted or served as counsel to a party; a trial judge actively participated in the secret, preparatory investigation of a case; or a judge has some connection with the case which might bias the decision.

28. In the circumstances identified in the preceding paragraphs and in other cases where impartiality appears open to doubt, judges and members of a tribunal have the obligation to recuse themselves.

29. A judge may not consult a higher authority before rendering a decision in order to ensure that his or her decision will be upheld.

Right to a remedy

30. Everyone has the right to an effective remedy by the competent national tribunals for acts violating the rights granted by the constitution, by law, or by the present Declaration, notwithstanding that the acts had been committed by persons acting in an official capacity.

31. Any person claiming such a remedy shall have such a right determined by competent judicial, administrative, or legislative authorities, or by any other competent authority provided for by the legal system of the State, which may include judicial remedy.

32. Any person claiming such a remedy shall have the right to have the remedy enforced by competent authorities.

Provisions applicable to arrest and detention

33. Everyone has the right to liberty and security of the person. No one shall be subjected to arbitrary arrest or detention. No one shall be deprived of his or her liberty except on such grounds and in accordance with such procedures as are established by law.

34. A person may be detained only for probable cause or pursuant to a warrant from a competent authority.

35. Anyone who is arrested shall be informed, at the time of arrest, of the reasons for his or her arrest and shall be promptly informed of any charges against him or her.

36. Anyone who is arrested or detained on a criminal charge shall be brought promptly before a judge or other officer authorized by law to exercise judicial power and shall be entitled to trial within a reasonable time or to release. It shall not be general rule that persons awaiting trial shall be detained in custody, but release may be subject to guarantees to appear for trial, at any other stage of the judicial proceedings, and, should occasion arise, for execution of the judgement.

37. Anyone who is deprived of his or her liberty by arrest or detention shall be entitled to take proceedings before a court, in order that that court may decide without delay on the lawfulness of his or her detention and order release if the detention is not lawful:

(a) Any person arrested or detained has the right to be brought within 24 hours before a judge or authorized judicial officer who shall review the lawfulness of his or her detention and shall order release if the detention is not lawful. The judge or judicial officer shall be authorized by law to exercise judicial power;

(b) Any person arrested or detained shall have prompt access to a lawyer, and in any case not later than 24 hours from the time of arrest or detention. Access to a lawyer includes the attributes of the right to counsel prescribed in the paragraphs below relating to that subject.

38. States shall ensure the right to habeas corpus, *amparo* or similar procedures. The courts shall at all times hear and act upon petitions for habeas corpus, *amparo*, or similar procedures. No circumstances whatever may be invoked as a justification for denying the right to habeas corpus, *amparo*, or similar procedures.

39. Detention shall be administered by competent authorities established by law and duly identified.

40. Detainees shall be housed in places established by law for that purpose and duly identified.

41. The court with judicial control over the detainee shall be promptly informed that a person has been detained and shall have authority over the officials detaining an individual.

42. The authorities which arrest a person, keep him or her under detention, or investigate the case shall exercise only the powers granted to them under the law, and the exercise of these powers shall be subject to a judicial or other authority.

43. The judiciary shall at all times have authority over executive action resulting in detention.

44. Military courts do not have legal authority over civilians except in narrowly defined circumstances, for example, when the civilian has committed an offence in a military facility.

Right to humane treatment

45. All persons under any form of detention or imprisonment shall be treated in a humane manner and with respect for the inherent dignity of the human person. Persons under any form of detention or imprisonment shall not be subjected to torture or cruel, inhuman or degrading treatment or punishment. In particular, such persons shall not be subjected to the following cruel, inhuman or degrading treatment:

(a) No detainee shall be subjected to incommunicado detention. Communication of the detained or imprisoned person with the outside world shall not be denied for more than a matter of days;

(b) No detainee shall be denied prompt and adequate medical care including necessary medication. No detainee shall be subjected to compulsory medical experimentation;

(c) Accused persons shall be segregated from convicted persons and have the right to separate treatment appropriate to their status as unconvicted persons;

(d) Accused juvenile persons shall be segregated from adults and from juvenile persons whose guilt has been adjudicated. States shall set a minimum age below which a juvenile may not be deprived of his or her liberty;

(e) All detainees have the right to write, send, and receive correspondence. Restrictions on correspondence shall not constitute an arbitrary or unlawful interference with the detainee's correspondence;

(f) All detainees have the right to receive visits from attorneys, family, friends, and others at regular intervals under necessary supervision.

46. All detainees have the right to trial within a reasonable time or release. Pre-trial detention is justified only to prevent flight, interference with evidence or the recurrence of crime.

47. Pre-trial release may be made subject to guarantees, such as bail, to assure appearance at trial.

Provisions applicable to proceedings relating to criminal charges

Notice

48. Any person charged with a criminal offence shall be informed promptly, in detail, and in a language which he or she understands, of the nature and cause of the charge against him or her:

(a) The accused has the right to be informed as soon as a charge is first made by a competent authority. A person suspected of a crime shall be notified as soon as a court or the prosecution decides to take procedural steps against him or her, or publicly names him or her as a suspect;

(b) The purpose of the notice is to inform the accused in a manner that would allow him or her to prepare a defence. The notice shall be provided in time to allow the accused a fair opportunity to examine or have examined the witnesses against him or her and to secure the attendance of witnesses on his or her behalf. The notice shall be provided before the accused is required to make any statement;

(c) The purpose of the notice is also to enable a person to take immediate steps to secure his or her release; hence, the notice shall include details of the charges or applicable law and the alleged facts on which the charge is based sufficient to indicate the substance of the complaint against the accused. The arresting authorities shall have sufficient evidence to show that the detention falls within the law on which the charge is based;

(d) The accused has the right to translation of the notice of the charges into a language which he or she understands. The notice of charges shall actually be communicated to the accused and not only to a representative or agent; notice in a language understood only by the defence counsel is insufficient.

Right to counsel

49. The accused has the right to defend himself or herself in person or through legal assistance of his or her own choosing. Legal representation is regarded as the best means of legal defence against infringements of human rights and fundamental freedoms:

(a) The accused has the right to be informed, if he or she does not have legal assistance, of the right to defend himself or herself through legal assistance of his or her own choosing;

(b) This right applies during all stages of any criminal prosecution, including, *inter alia*, preliminary investigations in which evidence is taken, periods of administrative detention, trial and appeal proceedings;

(c) The accused has the right to choose his or her own counsel freely. This right begins when the accused is first detained or charged. A court may not assign counsel for the accused if a qualified lawyer of the accused's own choosing is available.

Right to free legal assistance

50. The accused has the right to have legal assistance assigned to him or her, in any case where the interests of justice so require, and without payment by the accused in any such case if he or she does not have sufficient means to pay for it:

(a) The interests of justice in a particular case should be determined by consideration of the seriousness of the offence of which the defendant is accused and the severity of the sentence which he or she risks;

(b) The interests of justice always require counsel for an accused in any capital case. An accused in a capital case has the right to choose his or her own legal representative at all stages of the case. An accused in a capital case may contest the choice of his or her court-appointed lawyer. A prisoner sentenced to death shall have the right to appointed counsel for petition for pardon or clemency;

(c) An accused may not be denied counsel on the ground that he or she has or has had the opportunity to defend himself or herself, but does not wish to defend himself or herself.

51. An accused has a right to an effective defence. Attorneys appointed by the court shall provide effective defence counsel:

(a) When legal assistance is provided by the court, the lawyer appointed shall be qualified to represent and defend the accused;

(b) A lawyer appointed by the court shall have the training and experience necessary to represent and defend the accused in cases of the nature and seriousness involved in the matter;

(c) When legal assistance is provided by the court, the lawyer shall be free to exercise his or her professional judgment in an independent manner, free of influence from the State or the court;

(d) When legal assistance is provided by the court, the lawyer shall actually advocate in favour of the accused. The lawyer representing the accused may exercise professional judgment in choosing the strategy of the defence;

(e) Lawyers appointed to defend the accused shall be sufficiently compensated to provide an incentive to accord the accused adequate and effective representation.

Right to adequate time and facilities for the preparation of a defence

52. The accused has the right to communicate with counsel and have adequate time and facilities for the preparation of his or her defence:

(a) The accused has a right to see an attorney during all stages of any criminal proceeding, including any preliminary investigation in which evidence is taken, any period of administrative detention, trial and any appeal;

(b) The accused may not be tried without notifying his or her counsel of the trial date and of the charges in time to allow adequate preparation of a defence;

(c) The accused has a right to adequate time for the preparation of a defence appropriate to the nature of the proceedings and the factual circumstances of the case. Factors which may affect the adequacy of time for preparation of a defence include, *inter alia*, the complexity of the case, the defendant's access to evidence, the length of time provided by rules of procedure prior to particular proceedings, and prejudice to the defence;

(d) The accused has a right to facilities which assist or may assist the accused in the preparation of his or her defence. The essential elements of the right to adequate facilities are the right to communicate with defence counsel and the right to materials necessary to the preparation of a defence:

- (i) All arrested, detained or imprisoned persons shall be provided with adequate opportunities, time and facilities to be visited by and to communicate with a lawyer, without delay, interception or censorship and in full confidentiality;

- (ii) The right to confer privately with one's lawyer and exchange confidential information or instructions is a fundamental part of the preparation of a defence. Facilities shall be provided such that communications with counsel shall be made under circumstances in which the confidentiality of the communications is preserved;

(iii) Governments shall recognize and respect that all communications and consultations between lawyers and their clients within their professional relationship are confidential;

(iv) The accused or the accused's defence counsel has a right to all relevant information held by the prosecution that could help the accused exonerate himself or herself;

(v) It is the duty of the competent authorities to ensure lawyers access to appropriate information, files and documents in their possession or control in sufficient time to enable lawyers to provide effective legal assistance to their clients. Such access should be provided at the earliest appropriate time;

(vi) The accused has a right to consult legal materials reasonably necessary for the preparation of his or her defence;

(vii) Before judgment or sentence is rendered, the accused and his or her defence counsel shall have the right to know all the evidence which may be used to support the decision. All evidence submitted must be considered by the court;

(viii) Following a trial and before any appellate proceeding, the accused or the defence counsel has a right to access to (or to consult) the evidence which the court considered in making a decision and the court's reasoning in arriving at the judgment.

The right to an interpreter

53. The accused has the right to the free assistance of an interpreter if he or she cannot understand or speak the language used in court:

(a) The right to an interpreter applies when the accused or a defence witness has difficulty understanding or expressing himself or herself in the court's language;

(b) The right to an interpreter does not extend to the right to express oneself in the language of one's choice if the accused or the defence witness is sufficiently proficient in the language of the court;

(c) The right to an interpreter applies to both nationals and aliens;

(d) The right to an interpreter applies at all stages of the proceedings, including pre-trial proceedings;

(e) The right to an interpreter applies to written as well as oral proceedings. The right extends to translation or interpretation of all documents or statements necessary for the defendant to understand the proceedings or assist in the preparation of a defence;

(f) The interpretation or translation provided shall be adequate to permit the accused to understand the proceedings and for the tribunal to understand the testimony of the accused or defence witnesses;

(g) The right to interpretation or translation cannot be qualified by a requirement that the accused pay for the costs of an interpreter or translator. Even if the accused is convicted, he or she cannot be required to pay for the costs of interpretation or translation.

Right to trial without undue delay

54. Every person charged with a criminal offence has the right to a trial without undue delay:

(a) The right to a trial without undue delay means the right to a trial which produces a final judgment and a sentence without undue delay;

(b) In assessing whether there has been undue delay, the period of review of any conviction or sentence shall be included in the assessment;

(c) The right to a trial without undue delay does not depend upon assertion of that right by the accused. The accused is not required to demand a trial without undue delay in order to preserve his or her right in this regard;

(d) Factors relevant to what constitutes undue delay include, *inter alia*, the complexity of the case, the conduct of the parties, the conduct of other relevant authorities, whether an accused is detained pending proceedings, and the interest of the person at stake in the proceeding.

Rights during a trial

55. In criminal proceedings, the principle of equality of arms imposes procedural equality between the accused and the public prosecutor:

(a) The prosecution and defence shall be allowed equal time to present evidence;

(b) Prosecution and defence witnesses shall be given equal treatment in all procedural matters;

(c) Evidence unlawfully obtained shall not be used as evidence against the accused or against any other person in any proceeding.

56. The accused is entitled to a hearing in which an individualized consideration of culpability is afforded. Group trials in which many persons are involved may violate the person's right to a fair hearing.

57. The accused has the right to be tried in his or her presence:

(a) The accused has the right to appear in person before the court;

(b) If the accused is personally served with adequate notice of the date, time and place of the trial (in a timely matter, in sufficient detail, and in a language he or she understands) and the accused fails to appear for trial, the accused may be tried *in absentia*;

(c) If an accused is tried *in absentia*, the accused shall have the right to petition for a reopening of the proceedings upon a showing that inadequate notice was given, that the notice was not personally served on the accused, or that his or her failure to appear was for exigent reasons beyond his or her control. If the petition is granted, the accused is entitled to a fresh determination of the merits of the charge;

(d) The accused may voluntarily waive the right to appear at a hearing, but such a waiver shall be established in an unequivocal manner and preferably in writing.

58. The accused has the right not to be compelled to testify against himself or herself or to confess guilt:

(a) Any confession or other evidence obtained by any form of coercion or force may not be admitted into evidence or considered as probative of any fact at trial or in sentencing. Any confession or admission obtained during incommunicado detention shall be considered to have been obtained by coercion;

(b) Silence by the accused may not be used as evidence to prove guilt.

59. Everyone charged with a criminal offence shall have the right to be presumed innocent until proven guilty according to the law:

(a) The presumption of innocence places the burden of proof during trial in any criminal case on the prosecution. The criminal charge shall be proved to the intimate conviction of the trier of fact or beyond a reasonable doubt, whichever standard of proof provides the greatest protection for the presumption of innocence under national law;

(b) Public officials shall maintain a presumption of innocence. This provision applies to the judge presiding over the trial and to any other public official who deals with the case in any way. The accused is entitled to the benefit of the doubt during the trial. Public officials, including prosecutors, may inform the public about criminal investigations or charges, but shall not express a view as to the guilt of any suspect;

(c) Legal presumptions of fact or law are permissible in a criminal case only if they are rebuttable, allowing a defendant to prove his or her innocence;

(d) In applying the presumption of innocence, a State is not required to reimburse a person who has been found not guilty for the cost of his or her defence;

(e) In applying the presumption of innocence, the State may not require a person, who has been found not guilty of a criminal offence, to pay any portion of the costs of prosecution.

60. The accused has a right to examine or have examined, witnesses against him or her and to obtain the attendance and examination of witnesses on his or her behalf under the same conditions as witnesses against him or her:

(a) The contentious nature of a trial is regarded as one effective means of ensuring its fairness;

(b) The accused's right to obtain the attendance and examination of witnesses on his or her behalf may be waived by counsel if such a waiver is properly within the professional judgment of the attorney;

(c) The prosecution shall provide the defence with the names of the witnesses it intends to call at trial within a reasonable time prior to trial which allows the defendant sufficient time to prepare his or her defence;

(d) The accused's right to examine witnesses may be limited to those witnesses whose testimony is relevant and likely to assist in ascertaining the truth;

(e) The accused has the right to be present during the testimony of a witness. This right may be limited only for exceptional circumstances such as when a witness reasonably fears reprisal by the defendant, when the accused engages in a course of conduct seriously disruptive of the proceedings, or when the accused repeatedly fails to appear for trivial reasons and after having been duly notified;

(f) A trial may also be conducted in the absence of an individual accused of any offences against the peace and security of humanity, if that individual is a fugitive from justice or has died before the commencement of such a trial, but when the consequences of the offences of which the person stands accused are still extant and the court examination is necessary for the protection of human rights and fundamental freedoms and to prevent perpetration of such offences in the future;

(g) If the defendant is excluded or if the presence of the defendant cannot be ensured, the defendant's counsel shall always have the right to be present to preserve the defendant's right to examine the witness;

(h) If the presence of the defendant or any party cannot be ensured when the sentence or decision is announced, measures shall be taken to ensure that the defendant or any other party is informed as quickly as possible concerning the substance of the verdict or decision and the possibility of appeal against it;

(i) If national law does not permit the accused to examine witnesses during pre-trial investigations, the defendant shall have the opportunity to cross-examine the witness at trial;

(j) The use of testimony of anonymous witnesses during a trial is a violation of the defendant's right to examine witnesses against him or her.

Right to benefit from a lighter sentence or administrative sanction

61. No one shall be held guilty of any criminal offence on account of any act or omission which did not constitute a criminal offence, under national or international law, at the time when it was committed. Nor shall a heavier penalty be imposed than the one that was applicable at the time when the criminal offence was committed. If, subsequent to the commission of the offence, provision is made by law for the imposition of a lighter penalty, the offender shall benefit thereby.

62. A lighter penalty created any time before an accused's sentence has been fully served should be applied to any offender serving a sentence under the previous penalty.

63. Administrative tribunals conducting disciplinary proceedings shall not impose a heavier penalty than the one that was applicable at the time when the offending conduct occurred. If, subsequent to the conduct, provision is made by law for the imposition of a lighter penalty, the person disciplined shall benefit thereby.

Second trial for same offence prohibited

64. No one shall be liable to be tried or punished again for an offence for which he or she has already been finally convicted or acquitted in accordance with the law and penal procedure of each country.

Sentencing and punishment

65. Punishments constituting a deprivation of liberty shall have as an essential aim the reform and social re-adaptation of the prisoners.

Appeal

66. Everyone convicted in a criminal proceeding shall have the right to review of his or her sentence by a higher tribunal:

(a) The right to appeal shall provide a genuine and timely review of the case. If exculpatory evidence is discovered after a person is tried and convicted, the right to appeal or some other post-conviction procedure shall permit the possibility of correcting the verdict if the new evidence would have been likely to change the verdict, unless it is proved that the non-disclosure of the unknown fact in time is wholly or partly attributable to the accused;

(b) A court shall stay execution of any sentence while the case is on appeal to a higher tribunal, unless the accused voluntarily accepts the earlier implementation of sentence.

67. Anyone sentenced to death shall have the right to appeal to a court of higher jurisdiction, and steps should be taken to ensure that such appeals shall become mandatory.

68. When a person has by a final decision been convicted of a criminal offence and when subsequently his or her conviction has been reversed or he or she has been pardoned on the ground that a new or newly discovered fact shows conclusively that there has been a miscarriage of justice, the person who has suffered punishment as a result of such conviction shall be compensated according to law, unless it is proved that the non-disclosure of the unknown fact in time is wholly or partly attributable to him or her.

69. Every person convicted of a crime has a right to seek pardon, amnesty or commutation of sentence. Pardon or commutation of sentence may be granted in all cases of capital punishment.

General clauses

70. There shall be no restriction upon or derogation from any element of the right to a fair trial and a remedy recognized or existing in any State pursuant to law, conventions, regulations or custom on the pretext that the present Declaration does not recognize such rights or that it recognizes them to a lesser extent.

71. Nothing in the present declaration shall be construed as restricting or derogating from any right defined in the International Covenant on Civil and Political Rights or any other relevant treaty or international instrument.

72. While the present Declaration is not principally intended to apply to proceedings for juvenile offenders, there are certain protections that relate specifically to juvenile offenders. Juvenile offenders should be entitled to procedures no less protective of their rights than the rights provided in the present Declaration and other international instruments, including, *inter alia*, the Convention on the Rights of the Child, General Assembly resolution 44/25 of 20 November 1989; the Minimum Rules for the Administration of Juvenile Justice, General Assembly resolution 40/33 of 29 November 1985; and the United Nations Rules for the Protection of Juveniles Deprived of their Liberty, General Assembly resolution 45/113 of 14 December 1990.

73. No circumstances whatsoever, whether a threat of war, a state of international or non-international armed conflict, internal political instability or any other public emergency may be invoked to justify derogations from the right to a fair trial or a remedy.

Use of terms

74. For the purposes of the present Declaration:

(a) A "criminal charge" is defined by the nature of the offence and the nature and degree of severity of the penalty incurred. An accusation may constitute a criminal charge although the offence is not classified as criminal under national law:

(i) Criminal charges relate to all offences with penalties involving a serious deprivation of liberty. Imprisonment is always a serious deprivation of liberty. Expulsion from one's country by administrative decree is also a serious deprivation of liberty which requires the guarantees of a fair criminal trial;

(ii) Criminal charges do not constitute actions by disciplinary bodies when the penalty imposed is only a reprimand or warning;

(b) The "determination of rights and obligations in a suit at law" is defined by the character of the rights at issue. Civil rights and obligations include all proceedings that are decisive for private rights and obligations, including proceedings before administrative tribunals:

(i) Civil rights and obligations may be determined in proceedings involving such matters as bankruptcy, commitment to a mental institution, compensation claims against domestic authorities, contractual rights and obligations, drivers' licenses, family-related issues, health insurance benefits, labour disputes, land consolidation issues, libel, personal injury claims, professional employment qualifications and rights, property rights, and scope and ownership of patents, as well as other proceedings in which a person has the right to appear and present evidence;

(ii) Proceedings as to civil rights and obligations do not require that both parties to the proceedings be private persons; hence, such proceedings encompass hearings before administrative tribunals where one of the parties is a public authority and the other is a private person;

(c) "Arrest" means the act of apprehending a person for the alleged commission of an offence or by the action of an authority;

(d) "Detained person" means any individual deprived of personal liberty except as a result of conviction for an offence;

(e) "Imprisoned person" means any individual deprived of personal liberty as a result of conviction for an offence;

(f) "Detention" means the condition of detained persons as defined above;

(g) "Imprisonment" means the condition of imprisoned persons as defined above.

* * *

6. Draft Third Optional Protocol to the International Covenant on Civil and Political Rights, Aiming at Guaranteeing Under All Circumstances the Right to a Fair Trial and a Remedy

The States Parties to the present Protocol,

Guided by articles 8, 10 and 11 of the Universal Declaration of Human Rights which affirm the right of every individual to a fair and public hearing by an impartial tribunal and an effective remedy,

Recalling articles 9.3, 9.4 and 14 of the International Covenant on Civil and Political Rights,

Concerned that the right to a fair trial and a remedy may be most threatened during a time of public emergency,

Desiring to undertake an international commitment to protect in all circumstances the right to a fair trial and a remedy by adding the rights referred to in articles 9.3 and 9.4 and 14 to the rights which are non-derogable under article 4 of the International Covenant on Civil and Political Rights,

Have agreed as follows:

Article 1

No derogation from article 9(3), article 9(4) or article 14 of the International Covenant on Civil and Political Rights may be made under the provisions of article 4 of the Covenant.

Article 2

No reservation is admissible to the present Protocol.

Article 3

The States Parties to the present Protocol shall include in the reports they submit to the Human Rights Committee, in accordance with article 40 of the Covenant, information on the measures that they have adopted to give effect to the present Protocol.

Article 4

With respect to the States Parties to the Covenant that have made a declaration under article 41, the competence of the Human Rights Committee to receive and consider communications when a State Party claims that another State Party is not fulfilling its obligations shall extend to the provisions of the present Protocol, unless the State Party concerned has made a statement to the contrary at the moment of ratification or accession.

Article 5

With respect to the States Parties to the first Optional Protocol to the International Covenant on Civil and Political Rights adopted on 16 December 1966, the competence of the Human Rights Committee to receive and consider communications from individuals subject to its jurisdiction shall extend to the provisions of the present Protocol, unless the State Party concerned has made a statement to the contrary at the moment of ratification or accession.

Article 6

The provisions of the present Protocol shall apply as additional provisions to the Covenant.

Article 7

1. The present Protocol is open for signature by any State that has signed the Covenant.

2. The present Protocol is subject to ratification by any State that has ratified the Covenant or acceded to it. Instruments of ratification shall be deposited with the Secretary-General of the United Nations.

3. The present Protocol shall be open to accession by any State that has ratified the Covenant or acceded to it.

4. Accession shall be effected by the deposit of an instrument of accession with the Secretary-General of the United Nations.

5. The Secretary-General of the United Nations shall inform all States that have signed the present Protocol or acceded to it of the deposit of each instrument of ratification or accession.

Article 8

1. The present Protocol shall enter into force three months after the date of the deposit with the Secretary-General of the United Nations of the tenth instrument of ratification or accession.

2. For each State ratifying the present Protocol or acceding to it after the deposit of the tenth instrument of ratification or accession, the present Protocol shall enter into force three months after the date of the deposit of its own instrument of ratification or accession.

Article 9

The provisions of the present Protocol shall extend to all parts of federal States without any limitations or exceptions.

Article 10

The Secretary-General of the United Nations shall inform all States referred to in article 48, paragraph 1, of the Covenant of the following particulars:

(a) Statements made under articles 4 or 5 of the present Protocol;

(b) Signatures, ratifications and accessions under article 7 of the present Protocol;

(c) The date of entry into force of the present Protocol under article 8 thereof.

Article 11

1. The present Protocol, of which the Arabic, Chinese, English, French, Russian and Spanish texts are equally authentic, shall be deposited in the archives of the United Nations.

2. The Secretary-General of the United Nations shall transmit certified copies of the present Protocol to all States referred to in article 48 of the Covenant.

* * *

G. ADMINISTRATION OF JUVENILE JUSTICE

The attention of the world community has been directed increasingly to the special problems raised by the apprehension, trial and detention of juveniles.

Of course, the provisions of the Universal Declaration of Human Rights and of the International Covenant on Civil and Political Rights apply to juveniles. However, it has been considered important to draft special rules aimed at protecting juveniles, such as those set forth in the Convention on the Rights of the Child.

There is also important "soft law" concerning juveniles, notably the United Nations Standard Minimum Rules for the Administration of Juvenile Justice (the Beijing Rules) which were proclaimed by the General Assembly in 1985, following the Interregional Preparatory Meeting held at Beijing, which recommended the rules for adoption by the Seventh United Nations Congress on the Prevention of Crime and the Treatment of Offenders, held at Milan in 1985. Also important are the Guidelines for the Prevention of Juvenile Delinquency (the Riyadh Guidelines), which were proclaimed by the General Assembly in 1990, following adoption by an International Meeting of Experts hosted by the Arab Security Studies and Training Centre at Riyadh, held from 28 February to 1 March 1988 in cooperation with the United Nations Crime Prevention Branch in Vienna.

1. Convention on the Rights of the Child (excerpts)

PART I

Article 1

For the purposes of the present Convention, a child means every human being below the age of eighteen years unless, under the law applicable to the child, majority is attained earlier.

Article 22

1. States Parties shall take appropriate measures to ensure that a child who is seeking refugee status or who is considered a refugee in accordance with applicable international or domestic law and procedures shall, whether unaccompanied or accompanied by his or her parents or by any other person, receive appropriate protection and humanitarian assistance in the enjoyment of applicable

rights set forth in the present Convention and in other international human rights or humanitarian instruments to which the said States are Parties.

2. For this purpose, States Parties shall provide, as they consider appropriate, co-operation in any efforts by the United Nations and other competent inter-governmental organizations or non-governmental organizations co-operating with the United Nations to protect and assist such a child and to trace the parents or other members of the family of any refugee child in order to obtain information necessary for reunification with his or her family. In cases where no parents or other members of the family can be found, the child shall be accorded the same protection as any other child permanently or temporarily deprived of his or her family environment for any reason, as set forth in the present Convention.

Article 37

States Parties shall ensure that:

(a) No child shall be subjected to torture or other cruel, inhuman or degrading treatment or punishment. Neither capital punishment nor life imprisonment without possibility of release shall be imposed for offences committed by persons below eighteen years of age;

(b) No child shall be deprived of his or her liberty unlawfully or arbitrarily. The arrest, detention or imprisonment of a child shall be in conformity with the law and shall be used only as a measure of last resort and for the shortest appropriate period of time;

(c) Every child deprived of liberty shall be treated with humanity and respect for the inherent dignity of the human person, and in a manner which takes into account the needs of persons of his or her age. In particular, every child deprived of liberty shall be separated from adults unless it is considered in the child's best interest not to do so and shall have the right to maintain contact with his or her family through correspondence and visits, save in exceptional circumstances;

(d) Every child deprived of his or her liberty shall have the right to prompt access to legal and other appropriate assistance, as well as the right to challenge the legality of the deprivation of his or her liberty before a court or other competent, independent and impartial authority, and to a prompt decision on any such action.

Article 39

States Parties shall take all appropriate measures to promote physical and psychological recovery and social reintegration of a child victim of: any form of neglect, exploitation, or abuse; torture or any other form of cruel, inhuman or degrading treatment or punishment; or armed conflicts. Such recovery and reintegration shall take place in an environment which fosters the health, self-respect and dignity of the child.

Article 40

1. States Parties recognize the right of every child alleged as, accused of, or recognized as having infringed the penal law to be treated in a manner consistent with the promotion of the child's sense of dignity and worth, which reinforces the child's respect for the human rights and fundamental freedoms of others and which takes into account the child's age and the desirability of promoting the child's reintegration and the child's assuming a constructive role in society.

2. To this end, and having regard to the relevant provisions of international instruments, States Parties shall, in particular, ensure that:

(a) No child shall be alleged as, be accused of, or recognized as having infringed the penal law by reason of acts or omissions that were not prohibited by national or international law at the time they were committed;

(b) Every child alleged as or accused of having infringed the penal law has at least the following guarantees:

(i) To be presumed innocent until proven guilty according to law;

(ii) To be informed promptly and directly of the charges against him or her, and if appropriate, through his or her parents or legal guardians, and to have legal or other appropriate assistance in the preparation and presentation of his or her defence;

(iii) To have the matter determined without delay by a competent, independent and impartial authority or judicial body in a fair hearing according to law, in the presence of legal or other appropriate assistance and, unless it is considered not to be in the best interest of the child, in particular, taking into account his or her age or situation, his or her parents or legal guardians;

(iv) Not to be compelled to give testimony or to confess guilt; to examine or have examined adverse witnesses and to obtain the participation and examination of witnesses on his or her behalf under conditions of equality;

(v) If considered to have infringed the penal law, to have this decision and any measures imposed in consequence thereof reviewed by a higher competent, independent and impartial authority or judicial body according to law;

(vi) To have the free assistance of an interpreter if the child cannot understand or speak the language used;

(vii) To have his or her privacy fully respected at all stages of the proceedings.

3. States Parties shall seek to promote the establishment of laws, procedures, authorities and institutions specifically applicable to children alleged as, accused of, or recognized as having infringed the penal law, and in particular:

(a) The establishment of a minimum age below which children shall be presumed not to have the capacity to infringe the penal law;

(b) Whenever appropriate and desirable, measures for dealing with such children without resorting to judicial proceedings, providing that human rights and legal safeguards are fully respected.

4. A variety of dispositions, such as care, guidance and supervision orders; counseling; probation; foster care; education and vocational training programmes and other alternatives to institutional care shall be available to ensure that children are dealt with in a manner appropriate to their well-being and proportionate both to their circumstances and the offence.

* * *

2. United Nations Standard Minimum Rules for the Administration of Juvenile Justice (The Beijing Rules)

PART ONE

GENERAL PRINCIPLES

1. Fundamental perspectives

1.1 Member States shall seek, in conformity with their respective general interests, to further the well-being of the juvenile and her or his family.

1.2 Member States shall endeavour to develop conditions that will ensure for the juvenile a meaningful life in the community, which during that period in life when she or he is most susceptible to deviant behaviour, will foster a process of personal development and education that is as free from crime and delinquency as possible.

1.3 Sufficient attention shall be given to positive measures that involve the full mobilization of all possible resources, including the family, volunteers and other community groups, as well as schools and other community institutions, for the purpose of promoting the well-being of the juvenile, with a view to reducing the need for intervention under the law, and of effectively, fairly and humanely dealing with the juvenile in conflict with the law.

1.4 Juvenile justice shall be conceived as an integral part of the national development process of each country, within a comprehensive framework of social justice for all juveniles, thus, at the same time, contributing to the protection of the young and the maintenance of a peaceful order in society.

1.5 These Rules shall be implemented in the context of economic, social and cultural conditions prevailing in each Member State.

1.6 Juvenile justice services shall be systematically developed and coordinated with a view to improving and sustaining the competence of personnel involved in the services, including their methods, approaches and attitudes.

Commentary

These broad fundamental perspectives refer to comprehensive social policy in general and aim at promoting juvenile welfare to the greatest possible extent, which will minimize the necessity of intervention by the juvenile justice system, and in turn, will reduce the harm that may be caused by any intervention. Such care measures for the young, before the onset of delinquency, are basic policy requisites designed to obviate the need for the application of the Rules.

Rules 1.1 to 1.3 point to the important role that a constructive social policy for juveniles will play, *inter alia*, in the prevention of juvenile crime and delinquency. Rule 1.4 defines juvenile justice as an integral part of social justice for juveniles, while rule 1.6 refers to the necessity of constantly improving juvenile justice, without falling behind the development of progressive social policy for juveniles in general and bearing in mind the need for consistent improvement of staff services.

Rule 1.5 seeks to take account of existing conditions in Member States which would cause the manner of implementation of particular rules necessarily to be different from the manner adopted in other States.

2. Scope of the Rules and definitions used

2.1 The following Standard Minimum Rules shall be applied to juvenile offenders impartially, without distinction of any kind, for example as to race, colour, sex, language, religion, political or other opinions, national or social origin, property, birth or other status.

2.2 For purposes of these Rules, the following definitions shall be applied by Member States in a manner which is compatible with their respective legal systems and concepts:

(a) A *juvenile* is a child or young person who, under the respective legal systems, may be dealt with for an offence in a manner which is different from an adult;

(b) An *offence* is any behaviour (act or omission) that is punishable by law under the respective legal systems;

(c) A *juvenile offender* is a child or young person who is alleged to have committed or who has been found to have committed an offence.

2.3 Efforts shall be made to establish, in each national jurisdiction, a set of laws, rules and provisions specifically applicable to juvenile offenders and institutions and bodies entrusted with the functions of the administration of juvenile justice and designed:

(a) To meet the varying needs of juvenile offenders, while protecting their basic rights;

(b) To meet the needs of society;

(c) To implement the following rules thoroughly and fairly.

Commentary

The Standard Minimum Rules are deliberately formulated so as to be applicable within different legal systems and, at the same time, to set some minimum standards for the handling of juvenile offenders under any definition of a juvenile and under any system of dealing with juvenile offenders. The Rules are always to be applied impartially and without distinction of any kind.

Rule 2.1 therefore stresses the importance of the Rules always being applied impartially and without distinction of any kind. The rule follows the formulation of principle 2 of the Declaration of the Rights of the Child.

Rule 2.2 defines "juvenile" and "offence" as the components of the notion of the "juvenile offender", who is the main subject of these Standard Minimum Rules (see, however, also rules 3 and 4). It should be noted that age limits will depend on, and are explicitly made dependent on, each respective legal system, thus fully respecting the economic, social, political, cultural and legal systems of Member States. This makes for a wide variety of ages coming under the definition of "juvenile", ranging from 7 years to 18 years or above. Such a variety seems inevitable in view of the different national legal systems and does not diminish the impact of these Standard Minimum Rules.

Rule 2.3 is addressed to the necessity of specific national legislation for the optimal implementation of these Standard Minimum Rules, both legally and practically.

3. Extension of the Rules

3.1 The relevant provisions of the Rules shall be applied not only to juvenile offenders but also to juveniles who may be proceeded against for any specific behaviour that would not be punishable if committed by an adult.

3.2 Efforts shall be made to extend the principles embodied in the Rules to all juveniles who are dealt with in welfare and care proceedings.

3.3 Efforts shall also be made to extend the principles embodied in the Rules to young adult offenders.

Commentary

Rule 3 extends the protection afforded by the Standard Minimum Rules for the Administration of Juvenile Justice to cover:

(a) The so-called "status offences" prescribed in various national legal systems where the range of behaviour considered to be an offence is wider for juveniles than it is for adults (for example, truancy, school and family disobedience, public drunkenness, etc.) (rule 3.1);

(b) Juvenile welfare and care proceedings (rule 3.2);

(c) Proceedings dealing with young adult offenders, depending of course on each given age limit (rule 3.3).

The extension of the Rules to cover these three areas seems to be justified. Rule 3.1 provides minimum guarantees in those fields, and rule 3.2 is considered a desirable step in the direction of more fair, equitable and humane justice for all juveniles in conflict with the law.

4. Age of criminal responsibility

4.1 In those legal systems recognizing the concept of the age of criminal responsibility for juveniles, the beginning of that age shall not be fixed at too low an age level, bearing in mind the facts of emotional, mental and intellectual maturity.

Commentary

The minimum age of criminal responsibility differs widely owing to history and culture. The modern approach would be to consider whether a child can live up to the moral and psychological components of criminal responsibility; that is, whether a child, by virtue of her or his individual discernment and understanding, can be held responsible for essentially anti-social behaviour. If the age of criminal responsibility is fixed too low or if there is no lower age limit at all, the notion of responsibility would become meaningless. In general, there is a close relationship between the notion of responsibility for delinquent or criminal behaviour and other social rights and responsibilities (such as marital status, civil majority, etc.).

Efforts should therefore be made to agree on a reasonable lowest age limit that is applicable internationally.

5. Aims of juvenile justice

5.1 The juvenile justice system shall emphasize the well-being of the juvenile and shall ensure that any reaction to juvenile offenders shall always be in proportion to the circumstances of both the offenders and the offence.

Commentary

Rule 5 refers to two of the most important objectives of juvenile justice. The first objective is the promotion of the well-being of the juvenile. This is the main focus of those legal systems in which juvenile offenders are dealt with by family courts or administrative authorities, but the well-being of the juvenile should also be emphasized in legal systems that follow the criminal court model, thus contributing to the avoidance of merely punitive sanctions. (*See also* rule 14).

The second objective is "the principle of proportionality." This principle is well-known as an instrument for curbing punitive sanctions, mostly expressed in terms of just desserts in relation to the gravity of the offence. The response to young offenders should be based on the consideration not only of the gravity of the offence but also of personal circumstances. The individual circumstances of the offender (for example social status, family situation, the harm caused by the offence or other factors affecting personal circumstances) should influence the proportionality of the reactions (for example by having regard to the offender's endeavour to indemnify the victim or to her or his willingness to turn to a wholesome and useful life).

By the same token, reactions aiming to ensure the welfare of the young offender may go beyond necessity and therefore infringe upon the fundamental rights of the young individual, as has been observed in some juvenile justice systems. Here, too, the proportionality of the reaction to the circumstances of both the offender and the offence, including the victim, should be safeguarded.

In essence, rule 5 calls for no less and no more than a fair reaction in any given case of juvenile delinquency and crime. The issues combined in the rule may help to stimulate development in both regards: new and innovative types of reactions are as desirable as precautions against any undue widening of the net of formal social control over juveniles.

6. Scope of discretion

6.1 In view of the varying special needs of juveniles as well as the variety of measures available, appropriate scope for discretion shall be allowed at all stages of proceedings and at the different levels of juvenile justice administration, including investigation, prosecution, adjudication and the follow-up of dispositions.

6.2 Efforts shall be made, however, to ensure sufficient accountability at all stages and levels in the exercise of any such discretion.

6.3 Those who exercise discretion shall be specially qualified or trained to exercise it judiciously and in accordance with their functions and mandates.

Commentary

Rules 6.1, 6.2 and 6.3 combine several important features of effective, fair and humane juvenile justice administration: the need to permit the exercise of discretionary power at all significant levels of processing so that those who make determinations can take the actions deemed to be most appropriate in each individual case; and the need to provide checks and balances in order to curb any abuses of discretionary power and to safeguard the rights of the young offender. Accountability and professionalism are instruments best apt to curb broad discretion. Thus, professional qualifications and expert training are emphasized here as a valuable means of ensuring the judicious exercise of discretion in matters of juvenile offenders. (*See also* rules 1.6 and 2.2.) The formulation of specific guidelines on the exercise of discretion and the provision of systems of review, appeal and the like in order to permit scrutiny of decisions and accountability are emphasized in this context. Such mechanisms are not specified here, as they do not easily lend themselves to incorporation into international standard minimum rules, which cannot possibly cover all differences in justice systems.

7. Rights of juveniles

7.1 Basic procedural safeguards such as the presumption of innocence, the right to be notified of the charges, the right to remain silent, the right to counsel, the right to the presence of a parent or guardian, the right to confront and cross-examine witnesses and the right to appeal to a higher authority shall be guaranteed at all stages of proceedings.

Commentary

Rule 7.1 emphasizes some important points that represent essential elements for a fair and just trial and that are internationally recognized in existing human rights instruments. (*See also* rule 14). The presumption of innocence, for instance, is also to be found in article II of the Universal Declaration of Human Rights and in article 14, paragraph 2, of the International Covenant on Civil and Political Rights.

Rules 14 through 22 of these Standard Minimum Rules specify issues that are important for proceedings in juvenile cases, while rule 7.1 affirms the most basic procedural safeguards in a general way.

8. Protection of privacy

8.1 The juvenile's right to privacy shall be respected at all stages in order to avoid harm being caused to her or him by undue publicity or by the process of labelling.

8.2 In principle, no information that may lead to the identification of a juvenile offender shall be published.

Commentary

Rule 8 stresses the importance of the protection of the juvenile's right to privacy. Young persons are particularly susceptible to stigmatization. Criminological research into labelling processes has provided evidence of the detrimental effects (of different kinds) resulting from the permanent identification of young persons as "delinquent" or "criminal."

Rule 8 stresses the importance of protecting the juvenile from the adverse effects that may result from the publication in the mass media of information about the case (for example the names of young offenders, alleged or convicted). The interest of the individual should be protected and upheld, at least in principle (The general contents of rule 8 are further specified in rule 21.).

9. Saving clause

9.1 Nothing in these Rules shall be interpreted as precluding the application of the Standard Minimum Rules for the Treatment of Prisoners adopted by the United Nations and other human rights instruments and standards recognized by the international community that relate to the care and protection of the young.

Commentary

Rule 9 is meant to avoid any misunderstanding in interpreting and implementing the present Rules in conformity with principles contained in relevant existing or emerging international human rights instruments and standards - such as the Universal Declaration of Human Rights, the International Covenant on Economic, Social and Cultural Rights and the International Covenant on Civil and Political Rights, and the Declaration of the Rights of the Child and the Draft Convention on the Rights of the Child. It should be understood that the application of the present Rules is without prejudice to any such international instruments which may contain provisions of wider application. (*See also* rule 27.).

PART TWO

INVESTIGATION AND PROSECUTION

10. Initial contact

10.1 Upon the apprehension of a juvenile, her or his parents or guardian shall be immediately notified of such apprehension, and, where such immediate notification is not possible, the parents or guardian shall be notified within the shortest possible time thereafter.

10.2 A judge or other competent official or body shall, without delay, consider the issue of release.

10.3 Contacts between the law enforcement agencies and a juvenile offender shall be managed in such a way as to respect the legal status of the juvenile, promote the well-being of the juvenile and avoid harm to her or him, with due regard to the circumstances of the case.

Commentary

Rule 10.1 is in principle contained in rule 92 of the Standard Minimum Rules for the Treatment of Prisoners.

The question of release (rule 10.2) shall be considered without delay by a judge or other competent official. The latter refers to any person or institution in the broadest sense of the term, including community boards or police authorities having power to release an arrested person. (*See also* the International Covenant on Civil and Political Rights, art. 9, para. 3.)

Rule 10.3 deals with some fundamental aspects of the procedures and behaviour on the part of the police and other law enforcement officials in cases of juvenile crime. To "avoid harm" admittedly is flexible wording and covers many features of possible interaction (for example the use of harsh language, physical violence or exposure to the environment). Any involvement in juvenile justice processes can be "harmful" to juveniles; the term "avoid harm" should be broadly interpreted, therefore, as causing the least harm possible to the juvenile in the first instance, as well as any additional or undue harm. This is especially important in the initial contact with law enforcement agencies, which might profoundly influence the juvenile's attitude towards the State and society.

Moreover, the success of any further intervention is largely dependent on such initial contacts. Compassion and kind firmness are important in these situations.

11. Diversion

11.1 Consideration shall be given, wherever appropriate, to dealing with juvenile offenders without resorting to formal trial by the competent authority, referred to in rule 14.1 below.

11.2 The police, the prosecution or other agencies dealing with juvenile cases shall be empowered to dispose of such cases, at their discretion, without recourse to formal hearings, in accordance with the criteria laid down for that purpose in the respective legal system and also in accordance with the principles contained in these Rules.

11.3 Any diversion involving referral to appropriate community or other services shall require the consent of the juvenile, or her or his parents or guardian, provided that such decision to refer a case shall be subject to review by a competent authority, upon application.

11.4 In order to facilitate the discretionary disposition of juvenile cases, efforts shall be made to provide for community programmes, such as temporary supervision and guidance, restitution, and compensation of victims.

Commentary

Diversion, involving removal from criminal justice processing and, frequently, redirection to community support services, is commonly practised on a formal and informal basis in many legal systems. This practise serves to hinder the negative effects of subsequent proceedings in juvenile justice administration (for example the stigma of conviction and sentence). In many cases, non-intervention would be the best response. Thus, diversion at the outset and without referral to alternative (social) services may be the optimal response. This is especially the case where the offence is of a non-serious nature and where the family, the school or other informal social control institutions have already reacted, or are likely to react, in an appropriate and constructive manner.

As stated in rule 11.2, diversion may be used at any point of decision-making by the police, the prosecution or other agencies such as the courts, tribunals, boards or councils. It may be exercised by one authority or several or all authorities, according to the rules and policies of the respective systems and in line with the present Rules. It need not necessarily be limited to petty cases, thus rendering diversion an important instrument.

Rule 11.3 stresses the important requirement of securing the consent of the young offender (or the parent or guardian) to the recommended diversionary measure(s). (Diversion to community service without such consent would contradict the Abolition of Forced Labour Convention.). However, this consent should not be left unchallengeable, since it might sometimes be given out of sheer desperation on the part of the juvenile. The rule underlines that care should be taken to minimize the potential for coercion and intimidation at all levels in the diversion process. Juveniles should not feel pressured (for example in order to avoid court appearance) or be pressured into consenting to diversion programmes. Thus, it is advocated that provision should be made for an objective appraisal of the appropriateness of dispositions involving young offenders by a "competent authority upon application." (The "competent authority" may be different from that referred to in rule 14.)

Rule 11.4 recommends the provision of viable alternatives to juvenile justice processing in the form of community-based diversion. Programmes that involve settlement by victim restitution and those that seek to avoid future conflict with the law through temporary supervision and guidance are especially commended. The merits of individual cases would make diversion appropriate, even when more serious offences have been committed (for example first offence, the act having been committed under peer pressure, etc.).

12. Specialization within the police

12.1 In order to best fulfill their functions, police officers who frequently or exclusively deal with juveniles or who are primarily engaged in the prevention of juvenile crime shall be specially instructed and trained. In large cities, special police units should be established for that purpose.

Commentary

Rule 12 draws attention to the need for specialized training for all law enforcement officials who are involved in the administration of juvenile justice. As police are the first point of contact with the juvenile justice system, it is most important that they act in an informed and appropriate manner.

While the relationship between urbanization and crime is clearly complex, an increase in juvenile crime has been associated with the growth of large cities, particularly with rapid and unplanned growth. Specialized police units would therefore be indispensable, not only in the interest of implementing specific principles contained in the present instrument (such as rule 1.6) but more generally for improving the prevention and control of juvenile crime and the handling of juvenile offenders.

13. Detention pending trial

13.1 Detention pending trial shall be used only as a measure of last resort and for the shortest possible period of time.

13.2 Whenever possible, detention pending trial shall be replaced by alternative measures, such as close supervision, intensive care or placement with a family or in an educational setting or home.

13.3 Juveniles under detention pending trial shall be entitled to all rights and guarantees of the Standard Minimum Rules for the Treatment of Prisoners adopted by the United Nations.

13.4 Juveniles under detention pending trial shall be kept separate from adults and shall be detained in a separate institution or in a separate part of an institution also holding adults.

13.5 While in custody, juveniles shall receive care, protection and all necessary individual assistance - social, educational, vocational, psychological, medical and physical - that they may require in view of their age, sex and personality.

Commentary

The danger to juveniles of "criminal contamination" while in detention pending trial must not be underestimated. It is therefore important to stress the need for alternative measures. By doing so, rule 13.1 encourages the devising of new and innovative measures to avoid such detention in the interest of the well-being of the juvenile.

Juveniles under detention pending trial are entitled to all the rights and guarantees of the Standard Minimum Rules for the Treatment of Prisoners as well as the International Covenant on Civil and Political Rights, especially article 9 and article 10, paragraphs 2 (b) and 3.

Rule 13.4 does not prevent States from taking other measures against the negative influences of adult offenders which are at least as effective as the measures mentioned in the rule.

Different forms of assistance that may become necessary have been enumerated to draw attention to the broad range of particular needs of young detainees to be addressed (for example females or males, drug addicts, alcoholics, mentally ill juveniles, young persons suffering from the trauma, for example, of arrest, etc.).

Varying physical and psychological characteristics of young detainees may warrant classification measures by which some are kept separate while in detention pending trial, thus contributing to the avoidance of victimization and rendering more appropriate assistance.

The Sixth United Nations Congress on the Prevention of Crime and the Treatment of Offenders, in its resolution 4 on juvenile justice standards, specified that the Rules, *inter alia*, should reflect the basic principle that pretrial detention should be used only as a last resort, that no minors should be held in a facility where they are vulnerable to the negative influences of adult detainees and that account should always be taken of the needs particular to their stage of development.

PART THREE

ADJUDICATION AND DISPOSITION

14. Competent authority to adjudicate

14.1 Where the case of a juvenile offender has not been diverted (under rule 11), she or he shall be dealt with by the competent authority (court, tribunal, board, council, etc.) according to the principles of a fair and just trial.

14.2 The proceedings shall be conducive to the best interests of the juvenile and shall be conducted in an atmosphere of understanding, which shall allow the juvenile to participate therein and to express herself or himself freely.

Commentary

It is difficult to formulate a definition of the competent body or person that would universally describe an adjudicating authority. "Competent authority" is meant to include those who preside over courts or tribunals (composed of a single judge or of several members), including professional and lay magistrates as well as administrative boards (for example the Scottish and Scandinavian systems) or other more informal community and conflict resolution agencies of an adjudicatory nature.

The procedure for dealing with juvenile offenders shall in any case follow the minimum standards that are applied almost universally for any criminal defendant under the procedure known as "due process of law." In accordance with due process, a "fair and just trial" includes such basic safeguards as the presumption of innocence, the presentation and examination of witnesses, the common legal defence, the right to remain silent, the right to have the last word in a hearing, the right to appeal, etc. (*See also* rule 7.1).

15. Legal counsel, parents and guardians

15.1 Throughout the proceedings the juvenile shall have the right to be represented by a legal adviser or to apply for free legal aid where there is provision for such aid in the country.

15.2 The parents or the guardian shall be entitled to participate in the proceedings and may be required by the competent authority to attend them in the interest of the juvenile. They may, however, be denied participation by the competent authority if there are reasons to assume that such exclusion is necessary in the interest of the juvenile.

Commentary

Rule 15.1 uses terminology similar to that found in rule 93 of the Standard Minimum Rules for the Treatment of Prisoners. Whereas legal counsel and free legal aid are needed to assure the juvenile legal assistance, the right of the parents or guardian to participate as stated in rule 15.2 should be viewed as general psychological and emotional assistance to the juvenile - a function extending throughout the procedure.

The competent authority's search for an adequate disposition of the case may profit, in particular, from the cooperation of the legal representatives of the juvenile (or, for that matter, some other personal assistant who the juvenile can and does really trust). Such concern can be thwarted if the presence of parents or guardians at the hearings plays a negative role, for instance, if they display a hostile attitude towards the juvenile, hence, the possibility of their exclusion must be provided for.

16. Social inquiry reports

16.1 In all cases except those involving minor offences, before the competent authority renders a final disposition prior to sentencing, the background and circumstances in which the juvenile is living or the conditions under which the offence has been committed shall be properly investigated so as to facilitate judicious adjudication of the case by the competent authority.

Commentary

Social inquiry reports (social reports or presentence reports) are an indispensable aid in most legal proceedings involving juveniles. The competent authority should be informed of relevant facts about the juvenile, such as social and family background, school career, educational experiences, etc. For this purpose, some jurisdictions use special social services or personnel attached to the court or board. Other personnel, including probation officers, may serve the same function. The rule therefore requires that adequate social services should be available to deliver social inquiry reports of a qualified nature.

17. Guiding principles in adjudication and disposition

17.1 The disposition of the competent authority shall be guided by the following principles:

(a) The reaction taken shall always be in proportion not only to the circum-stances and the gravity of the offence but also to the circumstances and the needs of the juvenile as well as to the needs of the society;

(b) Restrictions on the personal liberty of the juvenile shall be imposed only after careful consideration and shall be limited to the possible minimum;

(c) Deprivation of personal liberty shall not be imposed unless the juvenile is adjudicated of a serious act involving violence against another person or of persistence in committing other serious offences, unless there is no other appropriate response;

(d) The well-being of the juvenile shall be the guiding factor in the consideration of her or his case.

17.2 Capital punishment shall not be imposed for any crime committed by juveniles.

17.3 Juveniles shall not be subject to corporal punishment.

17.4 The competent authority shall have the power to discontinue the proceedings at any time.

Commentary

The main difficulty in formulating guidelines for the adjudication of young persons stems from the fact that there are unresolved conflicts of a philosophical nature, such as the following:

(a) Rehabilitation versus just dessert;

(b) Assistance versus repression and punishment;

(c) Reaction according to the singular merits of an individual case versus reaction according to the protection of society in general;

(d) General deterrence versus individual incapacitation.

The conflict between these approaches is more pronounced in juvenile cases than in adult cases. With the variety of causes and reactions characterizing juvenile cases, these alternatives become intricately interwoven.

It is not the function of the Standard Minimum Rules for the Administration of Juvenile Justice to prescribe which approach is to be followed but rather to identify one that is most closely in consonance with internationally accepted principles. Therefore the essential elements as laid down in rule 17.1, in particular in subparagraphs (a) and (c), are mainly to be understood as practical guidelines that should ensure a common starting point; if heeded by the concerned authorities (*See also* rule 5), they could contribute considerably to ensuring that the fundamental rights of juvenile offenders are protected, especially the fundamental rights of personal development and education.

Rule 17.1 (b) implies that strictly punitive approaches are not appropriate. Whereas in adult cases, and possibly also in cases of severe offences by juveniles, just dessert and retributive sanctions might be considered to have some merit, in juvenile cases such considerations should always be outweighed by the interest of safeguarding the well-being and the future of the young person.

In line with resolution 8 of the Sixth United Nations Congress, rule 17.1 (b) encourages the use of alternatives to institutionalization to the maximum extent possible, bearing in mind the need to respond to the specific requirements of the young. Thus, full use should be made of the range of existing alternative sanctions and new alternative sanctions should be developed, bearing the public safety in mind. Probation should be granted to the greatest possible extent via suspended sentences, conditional sentences, board orders and other dispositions.

Rule 17.1 (c) corresponds to one of the guiding principles in resolution 4 of the Sixth Congress which aims at avoiding incarceration in the case of juveniles unless there is no other appropriate response that will protect the public safety.

The provision prohibiting capital punishment in rule 17.2 is in accordance with article 6, paragraph 5, of the International Covenant on Civil and Political Rights.

The provision against corporal punishment is in line with article 7 of the International Covenant on Civil and Political Rights and the Declaration on the

Protection of All Persons from Being Subjected to Torture and Other Cruel, Inhuman or Degrading Treatment or Punishment, as well as the Convention against Torture and Other Cruel, Inhuman or Degrading Treatment or Punishment and the draft convention on the rights of the child.

The power to discontinue the proceedings at any time (rule 17.4) is a characteristic inherent in the handling of juvenile offenders as opposed to adults. At any time, circumstances may become known to the competent authority which would make a complete cessation of the intervention appear to be the best disposition of the case.

18. Various disposition measures

18.1 A large variety of disposition measures shall be made available to the competent authority, allowing for flexibility so as to avoid institutionalization to the greatest extent possible. Such measures, some of which may be combined, include:

(a) Care, guidance and supervision orders;

(b) Probation;

(c) Community service orders;

(d) Financial penalties, compensation and restitution;

(e) Intermediate treatment and other treatment orders;

(f) Orders to participate in group counselling and similar activities;

(g) Orders concerning foster care, living communities or other educational settings;

(h) Other relevant orders.

18.2 No juvenile shall be removed from parental supervision, whether partly or entirely, unless the circumstances of her or his case make this necessary.

Commentary

Rule 18.1 attempts to enumerate some of the important reactions and sanctions that have been practised and proved successful thus far, in different legal systems. On the whole they represent promising opinions that deserve replication and further development. The rule does not enumerate staffing requirements because of possible shortages of adequate staff in some regions; in those regions measures requiring less staff may be tried or developed.

The examples given in rule 18.1 have in common, above all, a reliance on and an appeal to the community for the effective implementation of alternative dispositions. Community-based correction is a traditional measure that has taken on many aspects. On that basis, relevant authorities should be encouraged to offer community-based services.

Rule 18.2 points to the importance of the family which, according to article 10, paragraph 1, of the International Covenant on Economic, Social and Cultural Rights, is "the natural and fundamental group unit of society." Within the family, the parents have not only the right but also the responsibility to care for and supervise their children. Rule 18.2, therefore, requires that the separation of children from their parents is a measure of last resort. It may be resorted to only when the facts of the case clearly warrant this grave step (for example, child abuse).

19. Least possible use of institutionalization

19.1 The placement of a juvenile in an institution shall always be a disposition of last resort and for the minimum necessary period.

Commentary

Progressive criminology advocates the use of non-institutional over institutional treatment. Little or no difference has been found in terms of the success of institutionalization as compared to non-institutionalization. The many adverse influences on an individual that seem unavoidable within any institutional setting evidently cannot be outbalanced by treatment efforts. This is especially the case for juveniles, who are vulnerable to negative influences. Moreover, the negative effects, not only of loss of liberty but also of separation from the usual social environment, are certainly more acute for juveniles than for adults because of their early stage of development.

Rule 19 aims at restricting institutionalization in two regards: in quantity ("last resort") and in time ("minimum necessary period"). Rule 19 reflects one of the basic guiding principles of resolution 4 of the Sixth United Nations Congress: a juvenile offender should not be incarcerated unless there is no other appropriate response. The rule, therefore, makes the appeal that if a juvenile must be institutionalized, the loss of liberty should be restricted to the least possible degree, with special institutional arrangements for confinement and bearing in mind the differences in kinds of offenders, offences and institutions. In fact, priority should be given to "open" over "closed" institutions. Furthermore, any facility should be of a correctional or educational rather than of a prison type.

20. Avoidance of unnecessary delay

20.1 Each case shall from the outset be handled expeditiously, without any unnecessary delay.

Commentary

The speedy conduct of formal procedures in juvenile cases is a paramount concern. Otherwise whatever good may be achieved by the procedure and the disposition is at risk. As time passes, the juvenile will find it increasingly difficult, if not impossible, to relate the procedure and disposition to the offence, both intellectually and psychologically.

21. Records

21.1 Records of juvenile offenders shall be kept strictly confidential and closed to third parties. Access to such records shall be limited to persons directly concerned with the disposition of the case at hand or other duly authorized persons.

21.2 Records of juvenile offenders shall not be used in adult proceedings in subsequent cases involving the same offender.

Commentary

The rule attempts to achieve a balance between conflicting interests connected with records or files: those of the police, prosecution and other authorities in improving control versus the interests of the juvenile offender. (*See also* rule 8). "Other duly authorized persons" would generally include, among others, researchers.

22. Need for professionalism and training

22.1 Professional education, in-service training, refresher courses and other appropriate modes of instruction shall be utilized to establish and maintain the necessary professional competence of all personnel dealing with juvenile cases.

22.2 Juvenile justice personnel shall reflect the diversity of juveniles who come into contact with the juvenile justice system. Efforts shall be made to ensure the fair representation of women and minorities in juvenile justice agencies.

Commentary

The authorities competent for disposition may be persons with very different backgrounds (magistrates in the United Kingdom of Great Britain and Northern Ireland and in regions influenced by the common law system; legally trained judges in countries using Roman law and in regions influenced by them; and elsewhere elected or appointed laymen or jurists, members of community-based boards, etc.). For all these authorities, a minimum training in law, sociology, psychology, criminology and behavioral sciences would be required. This is considered as important as the organizational specialization and independence of the competent authority.

For social workers and probation officers, it might not be feasible to require professional specialization as a prerequisite for taking over any function dealing with juvenile offenders. Thus, professional on-the-job instruction would be minimum qualifications.

Professional qualifications are an essential element in ensuring the impartial and effective administration of juvenile justice. Accordingly, it is necessary to improve the recruitment, advancement and professional training of personnel and to provide them with the necessary means to enable them to properly fulfill their functions.

All political, social, sexual, racial, religious, cultural or any other kind of discrimination in the selection, appointment and advancement of juvenile justice personnel should be avoided in order to achieve impartiality in the administration of juvenile justice. This was recommended by the Sixth Congress. Furthermore, the Sixth Congress called on Member States to ensure the fair and equal treatment of women as criminal justice personnel and recommended that special measures should be taken to recruit, train and facilitate the advancement of female personnel in juvenile justice administration.

PART FOUR

NON-INSTITUTIONAL TREATMENT

23. Effective implementation of disposition

23.1 Appropriate provisions shall be made for the implementation of orders of the competent authority, as referred to in rule 14.1 above, by that authority itself or by some other authority as circumstances may require.

23.2 Such provisions shall include the power to modify the orders as the competent authority may deem necessary from time to time, provided that such modification shall be determined in accordance with the principles contained in these Rules.

Commentary

Disposition in juvenile cases, more so than in adult cases, tends to influence the offender's life for a long period of time. Thus, it is important that the competent authority or an independent body (parole board, probation office, youth welfare institutions or others) with qualifications equal to those of the competent authority that originally disposed of the case should monitor the implementation of the disposition. In some countries, a *juge de l'execution des peines* has been installed for this purpose.

The composition, powers and functions of the authority must be flexible; they are described in general terms in rule 23 in order to ensure wide acceptability.

24. Provision of needed assistance

24.1 Efforts shall be made to provide juveniles, at all stages of the proceedings, with necessary assistance such as lodging, education or vocational training, employment or any other assistance, helpful and practical, in order to facilitate the rehabilitative process.

Commentary

The promotion of the well-being of the juvenile is of paramount consideration. Thus, rule 24 emphasizes the importance of providing requisite facilities, services and other necessary assistance as may further the best interests of the juvenile throughout the rehabilitative process.

25. Mobilization of volunteers and other community services

25.1 Volunteers, voluntary organizations, local institutions and other community resources shall be called upon to contribute effectively to the rehabilitation of the juvenile in a community setting and, as far as possible, within the family unit.

Commentary

This rule reflects the need for a rehabilitative orientation of all work with juvenile offenders. Cooperation with the community is indispensable if the directives of the competent authority are to be carried out effectively. Volunteers and voluntary services, in particular, have proved to be valuable resources but are at present under-utilized. In some instances, the cooperation of ex-offenders (including ex-addicts) can be of considerable assistance.

Rule 25 emanates from the principles laid down in rules 1.1 to 1.6 and follows the relevant provisions of the International Covenant on Civil and Political Rights.

PART FIVE

INSTITUTIONAL TREATMENT

26. Objectives of institutional treatment

26.1 The objective of training and treatment of juveniles placed in institutions is to provide care, protection, education and vocational skills, with a view to assisting them to assume socially constructive and productive roles in society.

26.2 Juveniles in institutions shall receive care, protection and all necessary assistance - social, educational, vocational, psychological, medical and physical - that they may require because of their age, sex, and personality and in the interest of their wholesome development.

26.3 Juveniles in institutions shall be kept separate from adults and shall be detained in a separate institution or in a separate part of an institution also holding adults.

26.4 Young female offenders placed in an institution deserve special attention as to their personal needs and problems. They shall by no means receive less care, protection, assistance, treatment and training than young male offenders. Their fair treatment shall be ensured.

26.5 In the interest and well-being of the institutionalized juvenile, the parents or guardians shall have a right of access.

26.6 Inter-ministerial and inter-departmental cooperation shall be fostered for the purpose of providing adequate academic or, as appropriate, vocational training to institutionalized juveniles, with a view to ensuring that they do not leave the institution at an educational disadvantage.

Commentary

The objectives of institutional treatment as stipulated in rules 26.1 and 26.2 would be acceptable to any system and culture. However, they have not yet been attained everywhere, and much more has to be done in this respect.

Medical and psychological assistance, in particular, are extremely important for institutionalized drug addicts, violent and mentally ill young persons.

The avoidance of negative influences through adult offenders and the safeguarding of the well-being of juveniles in an institutional setting, as stipulated in rule 26.3, are in line with one of the basic guiding principles of the Rules, as set out by the Sixth Congress in its resolution 4. The rule does not prevent States from taking other measures against the negative influences of adult offenders, which are at least as effective as the measures mentioned in the rule (*See also* rule 13.4).

Rule 26.4 addresses the fact that female offenders normally receive less attention than their male counterparts, as pointed out by the Sixth Congress. In particular, resolution 9 of the Sixth Congress calls for the fair treatment of female offenders at every stage of criminal justice processes and for special attention to their particular problems and needs while in custody. Moreover, this rule should also be considered in the light of the Caracas Declaration of the Sixth Congress, which *inter alia*, calls for equal treatment in criminal justice administration, and against the background of the Declaration on the Elimination of Discrimination against Women and the Convention on the Elimination of All Forms of Discrimination against Women.

The right of access (rule 26.5) follows from the provisions of rules 7.1, 10.1, 15.2 and 18.2. Inter-ministerial and inter-departmental cooperation (rule 26.6) are of particular importance in the interest of generally enhancing the quality of institutional treatment and training.

27. Application of the Standard Minimum Rules for the Treatment of Prisoners adopted by the United Nations

27.1 The Standard Minimum Rules for the Treatment of Prisoners and related recommendations shall be applicable as far as relevant to the treatment of juvenile offenders in institutions, including those in detention pending adjudication.

27.2 Efforts shall be made to implement the relevant principles laid down in the Standard Minimum Rules for the Treatment of Prisoners to the largest possible extent so as to meet the varying needs of juveniles specific to their age, sex and personality.

Commentary

The Standard Minimum Rules for the Treatment of Prisoners were among the first instruments of this kind to be promulgated by the United Nations. It is generally agreed that they have had a world-wide impact. Although there are still countries where implementation is more an aspiration than a fact, those Standard Minimum Rules continue to be an important influence in the humane and equitable administration of correctional institutions.

Some essential protections covering juvenile offenders in institutions are contained in the Standard Minimum Rules for the Treatment of Prisoners (accommodation, architecture, bedding, clothing, complaints and requests, contact with the outside world, food, medical care, religious service, separation of ages, staffing, work, etc.) as are provisions concerning punishment and discipline, and restraint for dangerous offenders. It would not be appropriate to modify those Standard Minimum Rules according to the particular characteristics of institutions for juvenile offenders within the scope of the Standard Minimum Rules for the Administration of Juvenile Justice.

Rule 27 focuses on the necessary requirements for juveniles in institutions (rule 27.1) as well as on the varying needs specific to their age, sex and personality (rule 27.2). Thus, the objectives and content of the rule interrelate to the relevant provisions of the Standard Minimum Rules for the Treatment of Prisoners.

28. Frequent and early recourse to conditional release

28.1 Conditional release from an institution shall be used by the appropriate authority to the greatest possible extent, and shall be granted at the earliest possible time.

28.2 Juveniles released conditionally from an institution shall be assisted and supervised by an appropriate authority and shall receive full support by the community.

Commentary

The power to order conditional release may rest with the competent authority, as mentioned in rule 14.1 or with some other authority. In view of this, it is adequate to refer here to the "appropriate" rather than to the "competent" authority.

Circumstances permitting, conditional release shall be preferred to serving a full sentence. Upon evidence of satisfactory progress towards rehabilitation, even offenders who had been deemed dangerous at the time of their institutionalization can be conditionally released whenever feasible. Like probation, such release may be conditional on the satisfactory fulfillment of the requirements specified by the relevant authorities for a period of time established in the decision, for example relating to "good behaviour" of the offender, attendance in community programmes, residence in half-way houses, etc.

In the case of offenders conditionally released from an institution, assistance and supervision by a probation or other officer (particularly where probation has not yet been adopted) should be provided and community support should be encouraged.

29. Semi-institutional arrangements

29.1 Efforts shall be made to provide semi-institutional arrangements, such as half-way houses, educational homes, day-time training centres and other such appropriate arrangements that may assist juveniles in their proper reintegration into society.

Commentary

The importance of care following a period of institutionalization should not be underestimated. This rule emphasizes the necessity of forming a net of semi-institutional arrangements.

This rule also emphasizes the need for a diverse range of facilities and services designed to meet the different needs of young offenders re-entering the community and to provide guidance and structural support as an important step towards successful reintegration into society.

PART SIX

RESEARCH, PLANNING, POLICY FORMULATION AND EVALUATION

30. Research as a basis for planning policy formulation and evaluation

30.1 Efforts shall be made to organize and promote necessary research as a basis for effective planning and policy formulation.

30.2 Efforts shall be made to review and appraise periodically the trends, problems and causes of juvenile delinquency and crime as well as the varying particular needs of juveniles in custody.

30.3 Efforts shall be made to establish a regular evaluative research mechanism built into the system of juvenile justice administration and to collect and analyse relevant data and information for appropriate assessment and future improvement and reform of the administration.

30.4 The delivery of services in juvenile justice administration shall be systematically planned and implemented as an integral part of national development efforts.

Commentary

The utilization of research as a basis for an informed juvenile justice policy is widely acknowledged as an important mechanism for keeping practises abreast of advances in knowledge and the continuing development and improvement of the juvenile justice system. The mutual feedback between research and policy is especially important in juvenile justice. With rapid and often drastic changes in the life styles of the young and in the forms and dimensions of juvenile crime, the societal and justice responses to juvenile crime and delinquency quickly become outmoded and inadequate.

Rule 30 thus establishes standards for integrating research into the process of policy formulation and application in juvenile justice administration. The rule draws particular attention to the need for regular review and evaluation of existing programmes and measures and for planning within the broader context of overall development objectives.

A constant appraisal of the needs of juveniles, as well as the trends and problems of delinquency, is a prerequisite for improving the methods of formulating appropriate policies and establishing adequate interventions, at both formal and informal levels. In this context, research by independent persons and bodies should be facilitated by responsible agencies, and it may be valuable to obtain and to take into account the views of juveniles themselves, not only those who come into contact with the system.

The process of planning must particularly emphasize a more effective and equitable system for the delivery of necessary services. Towards that end, there should be a comprehensive and regular assessment of the wide-ranging, particular needs and problems of juveniles and an identification of clear-cut priorities. In that connection, there should also be a coordination in the use of existing resources, including alternatives and community support that would be suitable in setting up specific procedures designed to implement and monitor established programmes.

* * *

3. United Nations Rules for the Protection of Juveniles Deprived of Their Liberty

ANNEX

United Nations Rules for the Protection of Juveniles Deprived of their Liberty

I. FUNDAMENTAL PERSPECTIVES

1. The juvenile justice system should uphold the rights and safety and promote the physical and mental well-being of juveniles. Imprisonment should be used as a last resort.

2. Juveniles should only be deprived of their liberty in accordance with the principles and procedures set forth in these Rules and in the United Nations Standard Minimum Rules for the Administration of Juvenile Justice (The Beijing Rules). Deprivation of the liberty of a juvenile should be a disposition of last resort and for the minimum necessary period and should be limited to exceptional cases. The length of the sanction should be determined by the judicial authority, without precluding the possibility of his or her early release.

3. The Rules are intended to establish minimum standards accepted by the United Nations for the protection of juveniles deprived of their liberty in all forms, consistent with human rights and fundamental freedoms, and with a view to counteracting the detrimental effects of all types of detention and to fostering integration in society.

4. The Rules should be applied impartially, without discrimination of any kind as to race, colour, sex, age, language, religion, nationality, political or other opinion, cultural beliefs or practises, property, birth or family status, ethnic or social origin, and disability. The religious and cultural beliefs, practises and moral concepts of the juvenile should be respected.

5. The Rules are designed to serve as convenient standards of reference and to provide encouragement and guidance to professionals involved in the management of the juvenile justice system.

6. The Rules should be made readily available to juvenile justice personnel in their national languages. Juveniles who are not fluent in the language spoken by the personnel of the detention facility should have the right to the services of an interpreter free of charge whenever necessary, in particular during medical examinations and disciplinary proceedings.

an interpreter free of charge whenever necessary, in particular during medical examinations and disciplinary proceedings.

7. Where appropriate, States should incorporate the Rules into their legislation or amend it accordingly and provide effective remedies for their breach, including compensation when injuries are inflicted on juveniles. States should also monitor the application of the Rules.

8. The competent authorities should constantly seek to increase the awareness of the public that the care of detained juveniles and preparation for their return to society is a social service of great importance, and to this end active steps should be taken to foster open contacts between the juveniles and the local community.

9. Nothing in the Rules should be interpreted as precluding the application of the relevant United Nations and Human Rights instruments and standards, recognized by the international community, that are more conducive to ensuring the rights, care and protection of juveniles, children and all young persons.

10. In the event that the practical application of particular Rules contained in sections II to V, inclusive, presents any conflict with the Rules contained in the present section, compliance with the latter shall be regarded as the predominant requirement.

II. SCOPE AND APPLICATION OF THE RULES

11. For the purposes of the Rules, the following definitions should apply:

(a) A juvenile is every person under the age of 18. The age limit below which it should not be permitted to deprive a child of his or her liberty should be determined by law;

(b) The deprivation of liberty means any form of detention or imprisonment or the placement of a person in a public or private custodial setting, from which this person is not permitted to leave at will, by order of any judicial, administrative or other public authority.

12. The deprivation of liberty should be effected in conditions and circumstances which ensure respect for the human rights of juveniles. Juveniles detained in facilities should be guaranteed the benefit of meaningful activities and programmes which would serve to promote and sustain their health and self-respect, to foster their sense of responsibility and encourage those attitudes and skills that will assist them in developing their potential as members of society.

13. Juveniles deprived of their liberty shall not for any reason related to their status be denied the civil, economic, political, social or cultural rights to which they are entitled under national or international law, and which are compatible with the deprivation of liberty.

14. The protection of the individual rights of juveniles with special regard to the legality of the execution of the detention measures shall be ensured by the competent authority, while the objectives of social integration should be secured by regular inspections and other means of control carried out, according to international standards, national laws and regulations, by a duly constituted body authorized to visit the juveniles and not belonging to the detention facility.

15. The Rules apply to all types and forms of detention facilities in which juveniles are deprived of their liberty. Sections I, II, IV and V of the Rules apply to all detention facilities and institutional settings in which juveniles are detained, and section III applies specifically to juveniles under arrest or awaiting trial.

16. The Rules shall be implemented in the context of the economic, social and cultural conditions prevailing in each Member State.

III. JUVENILES UNDER ARREST OR AWAITING TRIAL

17. Juveniles who are detained under arrest or awaiting trial ("untried") are presumed innocent and shall be treated as such. Detention before trial shall be avoided to the extent possible and limited to exceptional circumstances. Therefore, all efforts shall be made to apply alternative measures. When preventive detention is nevertheless used, juvenile courts and investigative bodies shall give the highest priority to the most expeditious processing of such cases to ensure the shortest possible duration of detention. Untried detainees should be separated from convicted juveniles.

18. The conditions under which an untried juvenile is detained should be consistent with the rules set out below, with additional specific provisions as are necessary and appropriate, given the requirements of the presumption of innocence, the duration of the detention and the legal status and circumstances of the juvenile. These provisions would include, but not necessarily be restricted to, the following:

(a) Juveniles should have the right of legal counsel and be enabled to apply for free legal aid, where such aid is available, and to communicate regularly with their legal advisers. Privacy and confidentiality shall be ensured for such communications;

(b) Juveniles should be provided, where possible, with opportunities to pursue work, with remuneration, and continue education or training, but should not be required to do so. Work, education or training should not cause the continuation of the detention;

(c) Juveniles should receive and retain materials for their leisure and recreation as are compatible with the interests of the administration of justice.

IV. THE MANAGEMENT OF JUVENILE FACILITIES

A. *Records*

19. All reports, including legal records, medical records and records of disciplinary proceedings, and all other documents relating to the form, content and details of treatment, should be placed in a confidential individual file, which should be kept up to date, accessible only to authorized persons and classified in such a way as to be easily understood. Where possible, every juvenile should have the right to contest any fact or opinion contained in his or her file so as to permit rectification of inaccurate, unfounded or unfair statements. In order to exercise this right, there should be procedures that allow an appropriate third party to have access to and to consult the file on request. Upon release, the records of juveniles shall be sealed, and, at an appropriate time, expunged.

20. No juvenile should be received in any detention facility without a valid commitment order of a judicial, administrative or other public authority. The details of this order should be immediately entered in the register. No juvenile should be detained in any facility where there is no such register.

B. *Admission, registration, movement and transfer*

21. In every place where juveniles are detained, a complete and secure record of the following information should be kept concerning each juvenile received:

(a) Information on the identity of the juvenile;

(b) The fact of and reasons for commitment and the authority therefor;

(c) The day and hour of admission, transfer and release;

(d) Details of the notifications to parents and guardians on every admission, transfer or release of the juvenile in their care at the time of commitment;

(e) Details of known physical and mental health problems, including drug and alcohol abuse.

22. The information on admission, place, transfer and release should be provided without delay to the parents and guardians or closest relative of the juvenile concerned.

23. As soon as possible after reception, full reports and relevant information on the personal situation and circumstances of each juvenile should be drawn up and submitted to the administration.

24. On admission, all juveniles shall be given a copy of the rules governing the detention facility and a written description of their rights and obligations in a language they can understand, together with the address of the authorities competent to receive complaints, as well as the address of public or private agencies and organizations which provide legal assistance. For those juveniles who are illiterate or who cannot understand the language in the written form, the information should be conveyed in a manner enabling full comprehension.

25. All juveniles should be helped to understand the regulations governing the internal organization of the facility, the goals and methodology of the care provided, the disciplinary requirements and procedures, other authorized methods of seeking information and of making complaints, and all such other matters as are necessary to enable them to understand fully their rights and obligations during detention.

26. The transport of juveniles should be carried out at the expense of the administration in conveyances with adequate ventilation and light, in conditions that should in no way subject them to hardship or indignity. Juveniles should not be transferred from one facility to another arbitrarily.

C. *Classification and placement*

27. As soon as possible after the moment of admission, each juvenile should be interviewed, and a psychological and social report identifying any factors relevant to the specific type and level of care and programme required by the juvenile should be prepared. This report, together with the report prepared by a medical officer who has examined the juvenile upon admission, should be forwarded to the director for purposes of determining the most appropriate placement for the juvenile within the facility and the specific type and level of care and programme required and to be pursued. When special rehabilitative treatment is required, and the length of stay in the facility permits, trained personnel of the facility should prepare a written, individualized treatment plan

specifying treatment objectives and time-frame and the means, stages and delays with which the objectives should be approached.

28. The detention of juveniles should only take place under conditions that take full account of their particular needs, status and special requirements according to their age, personality, sex and type of offence, as well as mental and physical health, and which ensure their protection from harmful influences and risk situations. The principal criterion for the separation of different categories of juveniles deprived of their liberty should be the provision of the type of care best suited to the particular needs of the individuals concerned and the protection of their physical, mental and moral integrity and well-being.

29. In all detention facilities juveniles should be separated from adults, unless they are members of the same family. Under controlled conditions, juveniles may be brought together with carefully selected adults as part of a special programme that has been shown to be beneficial for the juveniles concerned.

30. Open detention facilities for juveniles should be established. Open detention facilities are those with no or minimal security measures. The population in such detention facilities should be as small as possible. The number of juveniles detained in closed facilities should be small enough to enable individualized treatment. Detention facilities for juveniles should be decentralized and of such size as to facilitate access and contact between the juveniles and their families. Small-scale detention facilities should be established and integrated into the social, economic and cultural environment of the community.

D. *Physical environment and accommodation*

31. Juveniles deprived of their liberty have the right to facilities and services that meet all the requirements of health and human dignity.

32. The design of detention facilities for juveniles and the physical environment should be in keeping with the rehabilitative aim of residential treatment, with due regard to the need of the juvenile for privacy, sensory stimuli, opportunities for association with peers and participation in sports, physical exercise and leisure-time activities. The design and structure of juvenile detention facilities should be such as to minimize the risk of fire and to ensure safe evacuation from the premises. There should be an effective alarm system in case of fire, as well as formal and drilled procedures to ensure the safety of the juveniles. Detention facilities should not be located in areas where there are known health or other hazards or risks.

33. Sleeping accommodations should normally consist of small group dormitories or individual bedrooms, while bearing in mind local standards. During

sleeping hours there should be regular, unobtrusive supervision of all sleeping areas, including individual rooms and group dormitories, in order to ensure the protection of each juvenile. Every juvenile should, in accordance with local or national standards, be provided with separate and sufficient bedding, which should be clean when issued, kept in good order and changed often enough to ensure cleanliness.

34. Sanitary installations should be so located and of a sufficient standard to enable every juvenile to comply, as required, with their physical needs in privacy and in a clean and decent manner.

35. The possession of personal effects is a basic element of the right to privacy and essential to the psychological well-being of the juvenile. The right of every juvenile to possess personal effects and to have adequate storage facilities for them should be fully recognized and respected. Personal effects that the juvenile does not choose to retain or that are confiscated should be placed in safe custody. An inventory thereof should be signed by the juvenile. Steps should be taken to keep them in good condition. All such articles and money should be returned to the juvenile on release, except in so far as he or she has been authorized to spend money or send such property out of the facility. If a juvenile receives or is found in possession of any medicine, the medical officer should decide what use should be made of it.

36. To the extent possible juveniles should have the right to use their own clothing. Detention facilities should ensure that each juvenile has personal clothing suitable for the climate and adequate to ensure good health, and which should in no manner be degrading or humiliating. Juveniles removed from or leaving a facility for any purpose should be allowed to wear their own clothing.

37. Every detention facility shall ensure that every juvenile receives food that is suitably prepared and presented at normal meal times and of a quality and quantity to satisfy the standards of dietetics, hygiene and health and, as far as possible, religious and cultural requirements. Clean drinking water should be available to every juvenile at any time.

E. *Education, vocational training and work*

38. Every juvenile of compulsory school age has the right to education suited to his or her needs and abilities and designed to prepare him or her for return to society. Such education should be provided outside the detention facility in community schools wherever possible and, in any case, by qualified teachers through programmes integrated with the education system of the country so that, after release, juveniles may continue their education without difficulty. Special attention should be given by the administration of the detention facilities to the

education of juveniles of foreign origin or with particular cultural or ethnic needs. Juveniles who are illiterate or have cognitive or learning difficulties should have the right to special education.

39. Juveniles above compulsory school age who wish to continue their education should be permitted and encouraged to do so, and every effort should be made to provide them with access to appropriate educational programmes.

40. Diplomas or educational certificates awarded to juveniles while in detention should not indicate in any way that the juvenile has been institutionalized.

41. Every detention facility should provide access to a library that is adequately stocked with both instructional and recreational books and periodicals suitable for the juveniles, who should be encouraged and enabled to make full use of it.

42. Every juvenile should have the right to receive vocational training in occupations likely to prepare him or her for future employment.

43. With due regard to proper vocational selection and to the requirements of institutional administration, juveniles should be able to choose the type of work they wish to perform.

44. All protective national and international standards applicable to child labour and young workers should apply to juveniles deprived of their liberty.

45. Wherever possible, juveniles should be provided with the opportunity to perform remunerated labour, if possible within the local community, as a complement to the vocational training provided in order to enhance the possibility of finding suitable employment when they return to their communities. The type of work should be such as to provide appropriate training that will be of benefit to the juveniles following release. The organization and methods of work offered in detention facilities should resemble as closely as possible those of similar work in the community, so as to prepare juveniles for the conditions of normal occupational life.

46. Every juvenile who performs work should have the right to an equitable remuneration. The interests of the juveniles and of their vocational training should not be subordinated to the purpose of making a profit for the detention facility or a third party. Part of the earnings of a juvenile should normally be set aside to constitute a savings fund to be handed over to the juvenile on release. The juvenile should have the right to use the remainder of those earnings to purchase articles for his or her own use or to indemnify the victim

injured by his or her offence or to send it to his or her family or other persons outside the detention facility.

F. *Recreation*

47. Every juvenile should have the right to a suitable amount of time for daily free exercise, in the open air whenever weather permits, during which time appropriate recreational and physical training should normally be provided. Adequate space, installations and equipment should be provided for these activities. Every juvenile should have additional time for daily leisure activities, part of which should be devoted, if the juvenile so wishes, to arts and crafts skill development. The detention facility should ensure that each juvenile is physically able to participate in the available programmes of physical education. Remedial physical education and therapy should be offered, under medical supervision, to juveniles needing it.

G. *Religion*

48. Every juvenile should be allowed to satisfy the needs of his or her religious and spiritual life, in particular by attending the services or meetings provided in the detention facility or by conducting his or her own services and having possession of the necessary books or items of religious observance and instruction of his or her denomination. If a detention facility contains a sufficient number of juveniles of a given religion, one or more qualified representatives of that religion should be appointed or approved and allowed to hold regular services and to pay pastoral visits in private to juveniles at their request. Every juvenile should have the right to receive visits from a qualified representative of any religion of his or her choice, as well as the right not to participate in religious services and freely to decline religious education, counselling or indoctrination.

H. *Medical care*

49. Every juvenile shall receive adequate medical care, both preventive and remedial, including dental, ophthalmological and mental health care, as well as pharmaceutical products and special diets as medically indicated. All such medical care should, where possible, be provided to detained juveniles through the appropriate health facilities and services of the community in which the detention facility is located, in order to prevent stigmatization of the juvenile and promote self-respect and integration into the community.

50. Every juvenile has a right to be examined by a physician immediately upon admission to a detention facility, for the purpose of recording any evidence

of prior ill-treatment and identifying any physical or mental condition requiring medical attention.

51. The medical services provided to juveniles should seek to detect and should treat any physical or mental illness, substance abuse or other condition that may hinder the integration of the juvenile into society. Every detention facility for juveniles should have immediate access to adequate medical facilities and equipment appropriate to the number and requirements of its residents and staff trained in preventive health care and the handling of medical emergencies. Every juvenile who is ill, who complains of illness or who demonstrates symptoms of physical or mental difficulties, should be examined promptly by a medical officer.

52. Any medical officer who has reason to believe that the physical or mental health of a juvenile has been or will be injuriously affected by continued detention, a hunger strike or any condition of detention should report this fact immediately to the director of the detention facility in question and to the independent authority responsible for safeguarding the well-being of the juvenile.

53. A juvenile who is suffering from mental illness should be treated in a specialized institution under independent medical management. Steps should be taken, by arrangement with appropriate agencies, to ensure any necessary continuation of mental health care after release.

54. Juvenile detention facilities should adopt specialized drug abuse prevention and rehabilitation programmes administered by qualified personnel. These programmes should be adapted to the age, sex and other requirements of the juveniles concerned, and detoxification facilities and services staffed by trained personnel should be available to drug- or alcohol dependent juveniles.

55. Medicines should be administered only for necessary treatment on medical grounds and, when possible, after having obtained the informed consent of the juvenile concerned. In particular, they must not be administered with a view to eliciting information or a confession, as a punishment or as a means of restraint. Juveniles shall never be testers in the experimental use of drugs and treatment. The administration of any drug should always be authorized and carried out by qualified medical personnel.

I. *Notification of illness, injury and death*

56. The family or guardian of a juvenile and any other person designated by the juvenile have the right to be informed of the state of health of the juvenile on request and in the event of any important changes in the health of the juvenile. The director of the detention facility should notify immediately the

family or guardian of the juvenile concerned, or other designated person, in case of death, illness requiring transfer of the juvenile to an outside medical facility, or a condition requiring clinical care within the detention facility for more than 48 hours. Notification should also be given to the consular authorities of the State of which a foreign juvenile is a citizen.

57. Upon the death of a juvenile during the period of deprivation of liberty, the nearest relative should have the right to inspect the death certificate, see the body and determine the method of disposal of the body. Upon the death of a juvenile in detention, there should be an independent inquiry into the causes of death, the report of which should be made accessible to the nearest relative. This inquiry should also be made when the death of a juvenile occurs within six months from the date of his or her release from the detention facility and there is reason to believe that the death is related to the period of detention.

58. A juvenile should be informed at the earliest possible time of the death, serious illness or injury of any immediate family member and should be provided with the opportunity to attend the funeral of the deceased or go to the bedside of a critically ill relative.

J. *Contacts with the wider community*

59. Every means should be provided to ensure that juveniles have adequate communication with the outside world, which is an integral part of the right to fair and humane treatment and is essential to the preparation of juveniles for their return to society. Juveniles should be allowed to communicate with their families, friends and other persons or representatives of reputable outside organizations, to leave detention facilities for a visit to their home and family and to receive special permission to leave the detention facility for educational, vocational or other important reasons. Should the juvenile be serving a sentence, the time spent outside a detention facility should be counted as part of the period of sentence.

60. Every juvenile should have the right to receive regular and frequent visits, in principle once a week and not less than once a month, in circumstances that respect the need of the juvenile for privacy, contact and unrestricted communication with the family and the defence counsel.

61. Every juvenile should have the right to communicate in writing or by telephone at least twice a week with the person of his or her choice, unless legally restricted, and should be assisted as necessary in order effectively to enjoy this right. Every juvenile should have the right to receive correspondence.

62. Juveniles should have the opportunity to keep themselves informed regularly of the news by reading newspapers, periodicals and other publications, through access to radio and television programmes and motion pictures, and through the visits of the representatives of any lawful club or organization in which the juvenile is interested.

K. *Limitations of physical restraint and the use of force*

63. Recourse to instruments of restraint and to force for any purpose should be prohibited, except as set forth in rule 64 below.

64. Instruments of restraint and force can only be used in exceptional cases, where all other control methods have been exhausted and failed, and only as explicitly authorized and specified by law and regulation. They should not cause humiliation or degradation, and should be used restrictively and only for the shortest possible period of time. By order of the director of the administration, such instruments might be resorted to in order to prevent the juvenile from inflicting self-injury, injuries to others or serious destruction of property. In such instances, the director should at once consult medical and other relevant personnel and report to the higher administrative authority.

65. The carrying and use of weapons by personnel should be prohibited in any facility where juveniles are detained.

L. *Disciplinary procedures*

66. Any disciplinary measures and procedures should maintain the interest of safety and an ordered community life and should be consistent with the upholding of the inherent dignity of the juvenile and the fundamental objective of institutional care, namely, instilling a sense of justice, self-respect and respect for the basic rights of every person.

67. All disciplinary measures constituting cruel, inhumane or degrading treatment shall be strictly prohibited, including corporal punishment, placement in a dark cell, closed or solitary confinement or any other punishment that may compromise the physical or mental health of the juvenile concerned. The reduction of diet and the restriction or denial of contact with family members should be prohibited for any purpose. Labour should always be viewed as an educational tool and a means of promoting the self-respect of the juvenile in preparing him or her for return to the community and should not be imposed as a disciplinary sanction. No juvenile should be sanctioned more than once for the same disciplinary infraction. Collective sanctions should be prohibited.

68. Legislation or regulations adopted by the competent administrative authority should establish norms concerning the following, taking full account of the fundamental characteristics, needs and rights of juveniles:

(a) Conduct constituting a disciplinary offence;

(b) Type and duration of disciplinary sanctions that may be inflicted;

(c) The authority competent to impose such sanctions;

(d) The authority competent to consider appeals.

69. A report of misconduct should be presented promptly to the competent authority, which should decide on it without undue delay. The competent authority should conduct a thorough examination of the case.

70. No juvenile should be disciplinarily sanctioned except in strict accordance with the terms of the law and regulations in force. No juvenile should be sanctioned unless he or she has been informed of the alleged infraction in a manner appropriate to the full understanding of the juvenile, and given a proper opportunity of presenting his or her defence, including the right of appeal to a competent impartial authority. Complete records should be kept of all disciplinary proceedings.

71. No juveniles should be responsible for disciplinary functions except in the supervision of specified social, educational or sports activities or in self-government programmes.

M. *Inspection and complaints*

72. Qualified inspectors or an equivalent duly constituted authority not belonging to the administration of the facility should be empowered to conduct inspections on a regular basis and to undertake unannounced inspections on their own initiative, and should enjoy full guarantees of independence in the exercise of this function. Inspectors should have unrestricted access to all persons employed by or working in any facility where juveniles are or may be deprived of their liberty, to all juveniles and to all records of such facilities.

73. Qualified medical officers attached to the inspecting authority or the public health service should participate in the inspections, evaluating compliance with the rules concerning the physical environment, hygiene, accommodation, food, exercise and medical services, as well as any other aspect or conditions of institutional life that affect the physical and mental health of juveniles. Every juvenile should have the right to talk in confidence to any inspecting officer.

74. After completing the inspection, the inspector should be required to submit a report on the findings. The report should include an evaluation of the compliance of the detention facilities with the present rules and relevant provisions of national law, and recommendations regarding any steps considered necessary to ensure compliance with them. Any facts discovered by an inspector that appear to indicate that a violation of legal provisions concerning the rights of juveniles or the operation of a juvenile detention facility has occurred should be communicated to the competent authorities for investigation and prosecution.

75. Every juvenile should have the opportunity of making requests or complaints to the director of the detention facility and to his or her authorized representative.

76. Every juvenile should have the right to make a request or complaint, without censorship as to substance, to the central administration, the judicial authority or other proper authorities through approved channels, and to be informed of the response without delay.

77. Efforts should be made to establish an independent office (ombudsman) to receive and investigate complaints made by juveniles deprived of their liberty and to assist in the achievement of equitable settlements.

78. Every juvenile should have the right to request assistance from family members, legal counsellors, humanitarian groups or others where possible, in order to make a complaint. Illiterate juveniles should be provided with assistance should they need to use the services of public or private agencies and organizations which provide legal counsel or which are competent to receive complaints.

N. *Return to the community*

79. All juveniles should benefit from arrangements designed to assist them in returning to society, family life, education or employment after release. Procedures, including early release, and special courses should be devised to this end.

80. Competent authorities should provide or ensure services to assist juveniles in re-establishing themselves in society and to lessen prejudice against such juveniles. These services should ensure, to the extent possible, that the juvenile is provided with suitable residence, employment, clothing, and sufficient means to maintain himself or herself upon release in order to facilitate successful reintegration. The representatives of agencies providing such services should be consulted and should have access to juveniles while detained, with a view to assisting them in their return to the community.

V. PERSONNEL

81. Personnel should be qualified and include a sufficient number of specialists such as educators, vocational instructors, counsellors, social workers, psychiatrists and psychologists. These and other specialist staff should normally be employed on a permanent basis. This should not preclude part-time or volunteer workers when the level of support and training they can provide is appropriate and beneficial. Detention facilities should make use of all remedial, educational, moral, spiritual, and other resources and forms of assistance that are appropriate and available in the community, according to the individual needs and problems of detained juveniles.

82. The administration should provide for the careful selection and recruitment of every grade and type of personnel, since the proper management of detention facilities depends on their integrity, humanity, ability and professional capacity to deal with juveniles, as well as personal suitability for the work.

83. To secure the foregoing ends, personnel should be appointed as professional officers with adequate remuneration to attract and retain suitable women and men. The personnel of juvenile detention facilities should be continually encouraged to fulfil their duties and obligations in a humane, committed, professional, fair and efficient manner, to conduct themselves at all times in such a way as to deserve and gain the respect of the juveniles, and to provide juveniles with a positive role model and perspective.

84. The administration should introduce forms of organization and management that facilitate communications between different categories of staff in each detention facility so as to enhance cooperation between the various services engaged in the care of juveniles, as well as between staff and the administration, with a view to ensuring that staff directly in contact with juveniles are able to function in conditions favourable to the efficient fulfillment of their duties.

85. The personnel should receive such training as will enable them to carry out their responsibilities effectively, in particular training in child psychology, child welfare and international standards and norms of human rights and the rights of the child, including the present Rules. The personnel should maintain and improve their knowledge and professional capacity by attending courses of in-service training, to be organized at suitable intervals throughout their career.

86. The director of a facility should be adequately qualified for his or her task, with administrative ability and suitable training and experience, and should carry out his or her duties on a full-time basis.

87. In the performance of their duties, personnel of detention facilities should respect and protect the human dignity and fundamental human rights of all juveniles, in particular, as follows:

(a) No member of the detention facility or institutional personnel may inflict, instigate or tolerate any act of torture or any form of harsh, cruel, inhuman or degrading treatment, punishment, correction or discipline under any pretext or circumstance whatsoever;

(b) All personnel should rigorously oppose and combat any act of corruption, reporting it without delay to the competent authorities;

(c) All personnel should respect the present Rules. Personnel who have reason to believe that a serious violation of the present Rules has occurred or is about to occur should report the matter to their superior authorities or organs vested with reviewing or remedial power;

(d) All personnel should ensure the full protection of the physical and mental health of juveniles, including protection from physical, sexual and emotional abuse and exploitation, and should take immediate action to secure medical attention whenever required;

(e) All personnel should respect the right of the juvenile to privacy, and, in particular, should safeguard all confidential matters concerning juveniles or their families learned as a result of their professional capacity;

(f) All personnel should seek to minimize any differences between life inside and outside the detention facility which tend to lessen due respect for the dignity of juveniles as human beings.

* * *

4. United Nations Guidelines for the Prevention of Juvenile Delinquency (The Riyadh Guidelines) (excerpts)

I. Fundamental Principles

1. The prevention of juvenile delinquency is an essential part of the crime prevention in society. By engaging in lawful, socially useful activities and adopting a humanistic orientation towards society and outlook on life, young persons can develop non-criminogenic attitudes.

2. The successful prevention of juvenile delinquency requires efforts on the part of the entire society to ensure the harmonious development of adolescents, with respect for and promotion of their personality from early childhood.

3. For the purposes of the interpretation of the present Guidelines, a child-centered orientation should be pursued. Young persons should have an active role and partnership within society and should not be considered as mere objects of socialization or control.

4. In the implementation of the present Guidelines, in accordance with national legal systems, the well-being of young persons from their early childhood should be the focus of any preventive programme.

5. The need for and the importance of progressive delinquency prevention policies and the systematic study and the elaboration of measures should be recognized. These should avoid criminalizing and penalizing a child for behaviour that does not cause serious damage to the development of the child or harm to others. Such policies and measures should involve:

(a) The provision of opportunities, in particular educational opportunities, to meet the varying needs of young persons and to serve as a supportive framework for safeguarding the personal development of all young persons, particularly those who are demonstrably endangered or at social risk and are in need of special care and protections;

(b) Specialized philosophies and approaches for delinquency prevention, on the basis of laws, processes, institutions, facilities and a service delivery network aimed at reducing the motivation, need and opportunity for, or conditions giving rise to, the commission of infractions;

(c) Official intervention to be pursued primarily in the overall interest of the young person and guided by fairness and equity;

(d) Safeguarding the well-being, development, rights and interests of all young persons;

(e) Consideration that youthful behaviour or conduct that does not conform to overall social norms and values is often part of the maturation and growth process and tends to disappear spontaneously in most individuals with the transition to adulthood;

(f) Awareness that, in the predominant opinion of experts, labelling a young person as "deviant", "delinquent" or "pre-delinquent" often contributes to the development of a consistent pattern of undesirable behaviour by young persons.

6. Community-based services and programmes should be developed for the prevention of juvenile delinquency, particularly where no agencies have yet been established. Formal agencies of social control should only be utilized as a means of last resort.

III. General Prevention

9. Comprehensive prevention plans should be instituted at every level of government and include the following:

(a) In-depth analyses of the problem and inventories of programmes, services, facilities and resources available;

(b) Well-defined responsibilities for the qualified agencies, institutions and personnel involved in preventive efforts;

(c) Mechanisms for the appropriate co-ordination of prevention efforts between governmental and non-governmental agencies;

(d) Policies, programmes and strategies based on prognostic studies to be continuously monitored and carefully evaluated in the course of implementation;

(e) Methods for effectively reducing the opportunity to commit delinquent acts;

(f) Community involvement through a wide range of services and programmes;

(g) Close interdisciplinary co-operation between national, state, provincial and local governments, with the involvement of the private sector, representative citizens of the community to be served, and labour, child-care, health education, social, law enforcement and judicial agencies in taking concerted action to prevent juvenile delinquency and youth crime;

(h) Youth participation in delinquency prevention policies and processes, including recourse to community resources, youth self-help, and victim compensation and assistance programmes;

(i) Specialized personnel at all levels.

VI. Legislation and Juvenile Justice Administration

52. Governments should enact and enforce specific laws and procedures to promote and protect the rights and well-being of all young persons.

53. Legislation preventing the victimization, abuse, exploitation and the use for criminal activities of children and young persons should be enacted and enforced.

54. No child or young person should be subjected to harsh or degrading correction or punishment measures at home, in schools or in any other institutions.

55. Legislation and enforcement aimed at restricting and controlling accessibility of weapons of any sort to children and young persons should be pursued.

56. In order to prevent further stigmatization, victimization and criminalization of young persons, legislation should be enacted to ensure that any conduct not considered an offence or not penalized if committed by an adult is not considered an offence and not penalized if committed by a young person.

57. Consideration should be given to the establishment of an office of ombudsman or similar independent organ, which would ensure that the status, rights and interests of young persons are upheld and that proper referral to available services is made. The ombudsman or other organ designated would also supervise the implementation of the Riyadh Guidelines, the Beijing rules and the Rules for the Protection of Juveniles Deprived of their Liberty. The ombudsman or other organ would, at regular intervals, publish a report on the progress made and on the difficulties encountered in the implementation of the instrument. Child advocacy services should also be established.

58. Law enforcement and other relevant personnel, of both sexes, should be trained to respond to the special needs of young persons and should be familiar with and use, to the maximum extent possible, programmes and referral possibilities for the diversion of young persons from the justice system.

59. Legislation should be enacted and strictly enforced to protect children and young persons from drug abuse and drug traffickers.

* * *

H. CRIMINAL JUSTICE POLICY

How to achieve success in criminal justice strategies is a concern that has frequently occupied the General Assembly. In 1980, it adopted an eight-point declaration, known as the Caracas Declaration, which recognizes the relationship between crime and the need to improve social conditions and to encourage the development of social policy that will assist in preventing crime.

As shown in the preceding sections, the Seventh United Nations Congress on the Prevention of Crime and the Treatment of Offenders, held in Milan in 1985, adopted a variety of concrete recommendations and principles. It also recognized the relationship between crime prevention, development, and a new international economic order, calling for a systematic approach to crime prevention and criminal justice and for an integrated understanding of the criminal justice system as part of social policy.

The Guiding Principles for Crime Prevention and Criminal Justice in the Context of Development and a New International Economic Order focus *inter alia* on the responsiveness of the criminal justice system to development and human rights, including the role of the mass media and education.

The Seventh Congress also adopted basic principles on the independence of the judiciary, which highlight important considerations concerning the qualifications, selection and training of persons selected for judicial office; their conditions of service and tenure; the obligation to professional secrecy; the need for personal immunity from civil suits for monetary damages for acts or omissions in the exercise of their judicial functions; and the principle that they shall be subject to suspension or removal only for reasons of incapacity or behaviour that renders them unfit to discharge their duties.

1. Caracas Declaration

I. *Declares* the following:

1. The success of criminal justice systems and strategies for crime prevention, especially in the light of the growth of new and sophisticated forms of crime and the difficulties encountered in the administration of criminal justice, depends above all on the progress achieved throughout the world in improving social conditions and enhancing the quality of life; it is thus essential to review traditional crime prevention strategies based exclusively on legal criteria.

2. Crime prevention and criminal justice should be considered in the context of economic development, political systems, social and cultural values and social change, as well as the context of the new international economic order.

3. It is a matter of great importance and priority that programmes for crime prevention and the treatment of offenders should be based on the social, cultural, political and economic circumstances of each country, in a climate of freedom and respect for human rights, that Member States should develop an effective capacity for the formulating and planning of criminal policy, and that all crime-prevention policies should be co-ordinated with strategies for social, economic, political and cultural development.

5. Member States should ensure that those responsible for the functioning of the criminal justice system at all levels should be properly qualified for their tasks and should perform them in a manner which is independent of personal or group interest.

6. Criminal policy and the administration of justice should be based on principles that will guarantee the equality of everyone before the law without any discrimination, as well as the effective right of defence and the existence of judicial organs that are equal to the task of providing speedy and fair justice and of ensuring greater security and protection of the rights and freedoms of all people.

7. Continuous efforts should be made to seek new approaches and to develop better techniques for crime prevention and the treatment of offenders, and to that end criminal law should be developed in such a way as to play an effective and important role in creating stable social conditions free from oppression and manipulation.

8. The family, school and work have a vital part to play in encouraging the development of social policy and of positive attitudes that will assist in preventing crime, and these factors should be taken into consideration in national planning and in the development of criminal policy and crime prevention programmes.

2. Guiding Principles for Crime Prevention and Criminal Justice in the Context of Development and a New International Economic Order (excerpts)

ANNEX

A. Crime prevention and a new international economic order

International order and national structures

1. In view of the relationship between crime prevention, development and a new international economic order, changes in the economic and social structure should be accompanied by appropriate reforms in criminal justice, so as to ensure the responsiveness of the penal system to the basic values and goals of society, as well as to the aspirations of the international community.

Victim compensation

12. The necessary legislative and other measures should be taken in order to provide the victims of crimes with effective means of legal protection, including compensation for damage suffered by them as a result of the crimes.

B. National development and the prevention of crime

Systematic approach

15. Crime prevention and criminal justice should not be treated as isolated problems to be tackled by simplistic, fragmentary methods, but rather as complex and wide-ranging activities requiring systematic strategies and differentiated approaches in relation to:

(a) The socio-economic, political and cultural context and circumstances of the society in which they are applied;

(b) The developmental stage, with special emphasis on the changes taking place and likely to occur and the related requirements;

(c) The respective traditions and customs, making maximum and effective use of human indigenous options.

Crime prevention as part of social policy

21. The criminal justice system, besides being an instrument to effect control and deterrence, should also contribute to the objective of maintaining peace and

order for equitable social and economic development, redressing inequalities and protecting human rights. In order to relate crime prevention and criminal justice to national development targets, efforts should be made to secure the necessary human and material resources, including the allocation of adequate funding, and to utilize as much as possible all relevant institutions and resources of society, thus ensuring the appropriate involvement of the community.

C. The responsiveness of the criminal justice system to development and human rights

Development and fundamental human rights

23. Socio-economic programmes and national planning should be conducive to the promotion, protection and efficacy of social justice, fundamental freedoms and human rights. Existing socio-economic policies and programmes should be examined in the light of their implications for the achievement of those objectives.

Legal systems, criminal justice and development

24. Legal systems, including criminal justice, should be instrumental in promoting beneficial and equitable development and due regard to human rights and social justice considerations, in ensuring that those performing judicial or quasi-judicial functions exercise them in a manner that is independent of personal or group interest and in maintaining impartiality in the staffing of the courts, in the conduct of criminal court proceedings and in the provision of public access to them.

Periodic reappraisal of criminal justice policies and practises

25. There should be in every country, regardless of its stage of development, a periodic reappraisal of the existing criminal justice policies and practises in relation to both formal and informal means of social control, so as to foster their socio-economic, cultural and other changes.

Written laws and societal structures and values

26. The conflicts existing in many countries between indigenous institutions and traditions for the solution of socio-legal problems and the frequently imported or superimposed foreign legislation and codes should be reviewed with a view to assuring that official norms appropriately reflect current societal values and structures.

Unrestricted access to the legal system

27. Legal systems should endeavour, through appropriate policies aimed at overcoming socio-economic, ethnic, cultural and political inequalities or disparities whenever they exist, to optimize access to justice for all segments of society, especially the most vulnerable ones. Appropriate mechanisms for legal aid and the protection of basic human rights, in accordance with the demands of justice, should be established wherever they do not exist. Legal systems should also provide readily available, less costly and non-cumbersome procedures for the peaceful settlement of disputes and litigation or arbitration, so as to ensure prompt and just parajudicial and judicial action for everybody while offering the means for widespread legal assistance for the effective defence of all those in need.

Community participation

28. Various forms of community participation should be explored and encouraged in order to create suitable alternatives to purely judicial interventions, which would provide more readily accessible methods of administering justice, such as mediation, arbitration and conciliation courts. Community participation in all phases of crime prevention and criminal justice processes should, therefore, be further promoted and strengthened, paying full attention to the protection of human rights.

Mass media and education

29. The role of the mass media and its impact on aspects of crime prevention and criminal justice should be examined and evaluated, since public perceptions of criminal policies and public attitudes are central to the effectiveness and fairness of the legal system. In this connection, the mass media should be encouraged to contribute positively to the education of the public on issues of crime prevention and criminal justice, as an important tool of socialization, together with programmes of civic and legal education.

Human rights, social justice and effective crime prevention

30. While protecting human rights and promoting social justice, improvements in the effectiveness of crime prevention and criminal justice policies should be encouraged through the use of community and other alternatives to incarceration, by avoiding unnecessary delay in the administration of justice, by fostering staff training evaluation and by scientific and technological innovations and action-oriented research, especially when there is need to maximize limited financial and human resources.

Traditional forms of social control

31. When new crime prevention measures are introduced, necessary precautions should be taken not to disrupt the smooth and effective functioning of traditional systems, full attention being paid to the preservation of cultural identities and the protection of human rights.

New forms of crime and criminal sanctions

32. Criminal sanctions, generally applied to counteract conventional criminality, should also be oriented towards new forms and dimensions of crime through the adoption of new legislative instruments and measures adequate to meet the challenges and by means of innovative techniques for detection, investigation, prosecution and sentencing. Appropriate instruments and mechanisms for international co-operation should likewise be devised and applied in order to cope effectively with such new and dangerous manifestations of crime.

Overall-re-examination of criminal justice measures

33. The limited resources of the criminal justice system should be allocated on the basis of careful consideration of the benefits and costs associated with alternative strategies, taking into account not only the direct and indirect costs of crime, but also the social consequences associated with its control. In this connection, constant efforts should be made to consider the use of alternatives to judicial intervention and institutionalization procedures, including community-oriented alternatives, thus decreasing the level of undue criminalization and penalization and reducing its social and human costs.

Modern technology and potential for abuses

34. New developments in science and technology should be used everywhere in the interest of the people and thus also for effective crime prevention. However, since modern technology may produce new forms of crime, appropriate measures should be taken against potential abuses. In particular, as computer systems may result in the accumulation of personal data that could be used to violate human rights, including the right to privacy, or to engage in other abuses, appropriate safeguards should be adopted, confidentiality ensured and a system of individual access to such data and of correction of errors should be established, together with appropriate procedures for expurgating such data in order to alleviate these and other discriminatory aspects deriving from their possible abuse.

Social marginality and inequality

35. In view of the staggering dimensions of social, political, cultural and economic marginality of many segments of the population in certain countries, criminal policies should avoid transforming such deprivation into likely conditions for the application of criminal sanctions. Effective social policies should, on the contrary, be adopted to alleviate the plight of the disadvantaged, and equality, fairness and equity in the processes of law enforcement, prosecution, sentencing and treatment should be ensured so as to avoid discriminatory practises based on socio-economic, cultural, ethnic, national or political backgrounds, on sex or on material means. It is necessary to proceed from the principle that the establishment of genuine social justice in the distribution of material and spiritual goods among all members of society, the elimination of all forms of exploitation and of social and economic inequality and oppressions, and the real assurance of all basic human rights and freedoms represent a principal hope for the successful combating of crime and its eradication from the life of society in general.

* * *

3. Basic Principles on the Independence of the Judiciary (excerpts)

The following basic principles, formulated to assist Member States in their task of securing and promoting the independence of the judiciary should be taken into account and respected by Governments within the framework of their national legislation and practise and be brought to the attention of judges, lawyers, members of the executive and the legislature and the public in general. The principles have been formulated principally with professional judges in mind, but they apply equally, as appropriate, to lay judges, where they exist.

Independence of the judiciary

1. The independence of the judiciary shall be guaranteed by the State and enshrined in the Constitution or the law of the country. It is the duty of all governmental and other institutions to respect and observe the independence of the judiciary.

2. The judiciary shall decide matters before them impartially, on the basis of facts and in accordance with the law, without any restrictions, improper influences, inducements, pressures, threats or interferences, direct or indirect, from any quarter or for any reason.

3. The judiciary shall have jurisdiction over all issues of a judicial nature and shall have exclusive authority to decide whether an issue submitted for its decision is within its competence as defined by law.

4. There shall not be any inappropriate or unwarranted interference with the judicial process, nor shall judicial decisions by the courts be subject to revision. This principle is without prejudice to judicial review or to mitigation or commutation by competent authorities of sentences imposed by the judiciary, in accordance with the law.

5. Everyone shall have the right to be tried by ordinary courts or tribunals using established legal procedures. Tribunals that do not use the duly established procedures of the legal process shall not be created to displace the jurisdiction belonging to the ordinary courts or judicial tribunals.

6. The principle of the independence of the judiciary entitles and requires the judiciary to ensure that judicial proceedings are conducted fairly and that the rights of the parties are respected.

7. It is the duty of each Member State to provide adequate resources to enable the judiciary to properly perform its functions.

Freedom of expression and association

8. In accordance with the Universal Declaration of Human Rights, members of the judiciary are like other citizens entitled to freedom of expression, belief, association and assembly; provided, however, that in exercising such rights, judges shall always conduct themselves in such a manner as to preserve the dignity of their office and the impartiality and independence of the judiciary.

9. Judges shall be free to form and join associations of judges or other organizations to represent their interests, to promote their professional training and to protect their judicial independence.

Qualifications, selection and training

10. Persons selected for judicial office shall be individuals of integrity and ability with appropriate training or qualifications in law. Any method of judicial selection shall safeguard against judicial appointments for improper motives. In the selection of judges, there shall be no discrimination against a person on the grounds of race, colour, sex, religion, political or other opinion, national or social origin, property, birth or status, except that a requirement, that a candidate for judicial office must be a national of the country concerned, shall not be considered discriminatory.

Conditions of service and tenure

11. The term of office of judges, their independence, security, adequate remuneration, conditions of service, pensions and the age of retirement shall be adequately secured by law.

12. Judges, whether appointed or elected, shall have guaranteed tenure until a mandatory retirement age or the expiration of their term of office, where such exists.

13. Promotion of judges, wherever such a system exists, should be based on objective factors, in particular, ability, integrity and experience.

14. The assignment of cases to judges within the court to which they belong is an internal matter of judicial administration.

Professional secrecy and immunity

15. The judiciary shall be bound by professional secrecy with regard to their deliberations and to confidential information acquired in the course of their duties other than in public proceedings, and shall not be compelled to testify on such matters.

16. Without prejudice to any disciplinary procedure or to any right of appeal or to compensation from the State, in accordance with national law, judges should enjoy personal immunity from civil suits for monetary damages for improper acts or omissions in the exercise of their judicial functions.

Discipline, suspension and removal

17. A charge or complaint made against a judge in his/her judicial and professional capacity shall be processed expeditiously and fairly under an appropriate procedure. The judge shall have the right to a fair hearing. The examination of the matter at its initial stage shall be kept confidential, unless otherwise requested by the judge.

18. Judges shall be subject to suspension or removal only for reasons of incapacity or behaviour that renders them unfit to discharge their duties.

19. All disciplinary, suspension or removal proceedings shall be determined in accordance with established standards of judicial conduct.

20. Decisions in disciplinary, suspension or removal proceedings should be subject to an independent review. This principle may not apply to the decisions

of the highest court and those of the legislature in impeachment or similar proceedings.

* * *

I. CODES OF CONDUCT

The term "code" refers to a systematic collection of principles and rules, which often contain not only pre-existing but also new rules. While there are obvious risks to "premature codification" and some would prefer a decentralized case-law development of legal rules, there is much to be said for the current trend to adopt codes of conduct, particularly in the field of the administration of justice.

The 1979 code of conduct for law enforcement officials provides a concise set of rules with commentary, which is well designed for the purpose of facilitating the education of said officials and concretising their terms of reference, thus allowing an evaluation of their actions, particularly in cases of alleged abuse of force.

One would have thought that the 1982 Principles of Medical Ethics would be superfluous to doctors who are already bound by the Hippocratic oath. Unfortunately, experience shows that too many medical doctors have applied their knowledge and skills in order to assist in the interrogation of prisoners and that some have directly participated in torture. These six principles adopted by the General Assembly are intended to mobilize shame against this abominable violation of medical ethics.

The 1990 Basic Principles on the Use of Force and Firearms by Law Enforcement officials comprise 26 provisions aimed at preventing the use of excessive force *inter alia* by appropriate training and equipment of law enforcement officials, and, where necessary, by punishment of officials guilty of arbitrary or abusive use of force and firearms.

The 1990 Guidelines on the Role of Prosecutors comprise 24 articles, which stress *inter alia* the importance of appropriate education and training, particularly on the ideals and ethical duties of their office. The office of prosecutors shall be strictly separated from judicial functions, and prosecutors shall refrain from initiating or continuing prosecutions when an impartial investigation shows the charge to be unfounded.

Similarly, the 1990 Basic Principles on the Role of Lawyers sets forth in 29 points the obligation of lawyers to maintain the honour and dignity of their profession as essential agents of the administration of justice. Codes of professional conduct for lawyers are to be established and violations thereof should be promptly and fairly investigated under appropriate procedures.

1. Code of Conduct for Law Enforcement Officials

The General Assembly,

Considering that the purposes proclaimed in the Charter of the United Nations include the achievement of international cooperation in promoting and encouraging respect for human rights and for fundamental freedoms for all without distinction as to race, sex, language or religion,

Recalling, in particular, the Universal Declaration of Human Rights and the International Covenants on Human Rights,

Recalling also the Declaration on the Protection of All Persons from Being Subjected to Torture and Other Cruel, Inhuman or Degrading Treatment or Punishment, adopted by the General Assembly in its resolution 3452 (XXX) of 9 December 1975,

Mindful that the nature of the functions of law enforcement in the defence of public order and the manner in which those functions are exercised have a direct impact on the quality of life of individuals as well as of society as a whole,

Conscious of the important task which law enforcement officials are performing diligently and with dignity, in compliance with the principles of human rights,

Aware nevertheless, of the potential for abuse which the exercise of such duties entails,

Recognizing that the establishment of a code of conduct for law enforcement officials is only one of several important measures for providing the citizenry served by law enforcement officials with protection of all their rights and interests,

Recognizing that there are additional important principles and prerequisites for the humane performance of law enforcement functions, namely:

(a) That, like all agencies of the criminal justice system, every law enforcement agency should be representative of and responsive and accountable to the community as a whole,

(b) That the effective maintenance of ethical standards among law enforcement officials depends on the existence of a well-conceived, popularly accepted and humane system of laws,

(c) That every law enforcement official is part of the criminal justice system, the aim of which is to prevent and control crime, and that the conduct of every functionary within the system has an impact on the entire system,

(d) That every law enforcement agency, in fulfillment of the first premise of every profession, should be held to the duty of disciplining itself in complete conformity with the principles and standards herein provided and that the actions of law enforcement officials should be responsible to public scrutiny, whether exercised by a review board, a ministry, a procuracy, the judiciary, an ombudsman, a citizens' committee or any combination thereof, or any other reviewing agency,

(e) That standards as such lack practical value unless their content and meaning, through education and training and through monitoring, become part of the creed of every law enforcement official,

Adopts the Code of Conduct for Law Enforcement Officials set forth in the annex to the present resolution and decides to transmit it to Governments with the recommendation that favourable consideration should be given to its use within the framework of national legislation or practise as a body of principles for observance by law enforcement officials.

ANNEX

Code of Conduct for Law Enforcement Officials

Article 1

Law enforcement officials shall at all times fulfil the duty imposed upon them by law, by serving the community and by protecting all persons against illegal acts, consistent with the high degree of responsibility required by their profession.

Commentary

(a) The term "law enforcement officials" includes all officers of the law, whether appointed or elected, who exercise police powers, especially the powers of arrest or detention.

(b) In countries where police powers are exercised by military authorities, whether uniformed or not, or by State security forces, the definition of law enforcement officials shall be regarded as including officers of such services.

(c) Service to the community is intended to include particularly the rendition of services of assistance to those members of the community who by reason of personal, economic, social or other emergencies are in need of immediate aid.

(d) This provision is intended to cover not only all violent, predatory and harmful acts, but extends to the full range of prohibitions under penal statutes. It extends to conduct by persons not capable of incurring criminal liability.

Article 2

In the performance of their duty, law enforcement officials shall respect and protect human dignity and maintain and uphold the human rights of all persons.

Commentary

(a) The human rights in question are identified and protected by national and international law. Among the relevant international instruments are the Universal Declaration of Human Rights, the International Covenant on Civil and Political Rights, the Declaration on the Protection of All Persons from Being Subjected to Torture and Other Cruel, Inhuman or Degrading Treatment or Punishment, the United Nations Declaration on the Elimination of All Forms of Racial Discrimination, the International Convention on the Elimination of All Forms of Racial Discrimination, the International Convention on the Suppression and Punishment of the Crime of *Apartheid*, the Convention on the Prevention and Punishment of the Crime of Genocide, the Standard Minimum Rules for the Treatment of Prisoners and the Vienna Convention on Consular Relations.

(b) National commentaries to this provision should indicate regional or national provisions identifying and protecting these rights.

Article 3

Law enforcement officials may use force only when strictly necessary and to the extent required for the performance of their duty.

Commentary

(a) This provision emphasizes that the use of force by law enforcement officials should be exceptional; while it implies that law enforcement officials may be authorized to use force as is reasonably necessary under the circumstances for the prevention of crime or in effecting or assisting in the lawful arrest of offenders or suspected offenders, no force going beyond that may be used.

(b) National law ordinarily restricts the use of force by law enforcement officials in accordance with a principle of proportionality. It is to be understood that such national principles of proportionality are to be respected in the interpretation of this provision. In no case should this provision be interpreted to authorize the use of force which is disproportionate to the legitimate objective to be achieved.

(c) The use of firearms is considered an extreme measure. Every effort should be made to exclude the use of firearms, especially against children. In general, firearms should not be used except when a suspected offender offers armed resistance or otherwise jeopardizes the lives of others and less extreme measures are not sufficient to restrain or apprehend the suspected offender. In every instance in which a firearm is discharged, a report should be made promptly to the competent authorities.

Article 4

Matters of a confidential nature in the possession of law enforcement officials shall be kept confidential, unless the performance of duty or the needs of justice strictly require otherwise.

Commentary

By the nature of their duties, law enforcement officials obtain information which may relate to private lives or be potentially harmful to the interests, and especially the reputation, of others. Great care should be exercised in safeguarding and using such information, which should be disclosed only in the performance of duty or to serve the needs of justice. Any disclosure of such information for other purposes is wholly improper.

Article 5

No law enforcement official may inflict, instigate or tolerate any act of torture or other cruel, inhuman or degrading treatment or punishment, nor may any law enforcement official invoke superior orders or exceptional circumstances such as a state of war or a threat of war, a threat to national security, internal political instability or any other public emergency as a justification of torture or other cruel, inhuman or degrading treatment or punishment.

Commentary

(a) This prohibition derives from the Declaration on the Protection of All Persons from Being Subjected to Torture and Other Cruel, Inhuman or Degrading Treatment or Punishment, adopted by the General Assembly, according to which:

"[Such an act is] an offence to human dignity and shall be condemned as a denial of the purposes of the Charter of the United Nations and as a violation of the human rights and fundamental freedoms proclaimed in the Universal Declaration of Human Rights [and other international human rights instruments]."

(b) The Declaration defines torture as follows:

"... torture means any act by which severe pain or suffering, whether physical or mental, is intentionally inflicted by or at the instigation of a public official on a person for such purposes as obtaining from him or a third person information or confession, punishing him for an act he has committed or is suspected of having committed, or intimidating him or other persons. It does not include pain or suffering arising only from inherent in or incidental to, lawful sanctions to the extent consistent with the Standard Minimum Rules for the Treatment of Prisoners."

(c) The term "cruel, inhuman or degrading treatment or punishment" has not been defined by the General Assembly but should be interpreted so as to extend the widest possible protection against abuses, whether physical or mental.

Article 6

Law enforcement officials shall ensure the full protection of the health of persons in their custody and, in particular, shall take immediate action to secure medical attention whenever required.

Commentary

(a) "Medical attention", which refers to services rendered by any medical personnel, including certified medical practitioners and paramedics, shall be secured when needed or requested.

(b) While the medical personnel are likely to be attached to the law enforcement operation, law enforcement officials must take into account the judgment of such personnel when they recommend providing the person in custody with appropriate treatment through, or in consultation with, medical personnel from outside the law enforcement operation.

(c) It is understood that law enforcement officials shall also secure medical attention for victims of violations of law or of accidents occurring in the course of violations of law.

Article 7

Law enforcement officials shall not commit any act of corruption. They shall also rigorously oppose and combat all such acts.

Commentary

(a) Any act of corruption, in the same way as any other abuse of authority, is incompatible with the profession of law enforcement officials. The law must be enforced fully with respect to any law enforcement official who commits an act of corruption, as Governments cannot expect to enforce the law among their citizens if they cannot, or will not, enforce the law against their own agents and within their agencies.

(b) While the definition of corruption must be subject to national law, it should be understood to encompass the commission or omission of an act in the performance of or in connection with one's duties, in response to gifts, promises or incentives demanded or accepted, or the wrongful receipt of these once the act has been committed or omitted.

(c) The expression "act of corruption" referred to above should be understood to encompass attempted corruption.

Article 8

Law enforcement officials shall respect the law and the present Code. They shall also, to the best of their capability, prevent and rigorously oppose any violations of them.

Law enforcement officials who have reason to believe that a violation of the present Code has occurred or is about to occur shall report the matter to their superior authorities and, where necessary, to other appropriate authorities or organs vested with reviewing or remedial power.

Commentary

(a) This Code shall be observed whenever it has been incorporated into national legislation or practise. If legislation or practise contains stricter provisions than those of the present Code, those stricter provisions shall be observed.

(b) The article seeks to preserve the balance between the need for internal discipline of the agency on which public safety is largely dependent, on the one hand, and the need for dealing with violations of basic human rights, on the other. Law enforcement officials shall report violations within the chain of command and take other lawful action outside the chain of command only when no other remedies are available or effective. It is understood that law enforcement officials shall not suffer administrative or other penalties because they have reported that a violation of this Code has occurred or is about to occur.

(c) The term "appropriate authorities or organs vested with reviewing or remedial power" refers to any authority or organ existing under national law, whether internal to the law enforcement agency or independent thereof, with statutory, customary or other power to review grievances and complaints arising out of violations within the purview of this Code.

(d) In some countries, the mass media may be regarded as performing complaint review functions similar to those described in subparagraph (c) above. Law enforcement officials may, therefore, be justified if, as a last resort and in accordance with the laws and customs of their own countries and with the provisions of article 4 of the present Code, they bring violations to the attention of public opinion through the mass media.

(e) Law enforcement officials who comply with the provisions of this Code deserve the respect, the full support and the cooperation of the community and of the law enforcement agency in which they serve, as well as the law enforcement profession.

* * *

2. Principles of Medical Ethics relevant to the Role of Health Personnel, Particularly Physicians, in the Protection of Prisoners and Detainees against Torture and Other Cruel, Inhuman or Degrading Treatment or Punishment

ANNEX

Principles of medical ethics relevant to the role of health personnel, particularly physicians, in the protection of prisoners and detainees against torture and other cruel, inhuman or degrading treatment or punishment

Principle 1

Health personnel, particularly physicians, charged with the medical care of prisoners and detainees have a duty to provide them with protection of their physical and mental health and treatment of disease of the same quality and standard as is afforded to those who are not imprisoned or detained.

Principle 2

It is a gross contravention of medical ethics, as well as an offence under applicable international instruments, for health personnel, particularly physicians, to engage, actively or passively, in acts which constitute participation in, complicity in, incitement to or attempts to commit torture or other cruel, inhuman or degrading treatment or punishment.

Principle 3

It is a contravention of medical ethics for health personnel, particularly physicians, to be involved in any professional relationship with prisoners or detainees the purpose of which is not solely to evaluate, protect or prove their physical and mental health.

Principle 4

It is a contravention of medical ethics for health personnel, particularly physicians:

(a) To apply their knowledge and skills in order to assist in the interrogation of prisoners and detainees in a manner that may adversely affect the physical or mental health or condition of such prisoners or detainees and which is not in accordance with the relevant international instruments;

(b) To certify, or to participate in the certification of, the fitness of prisoners or detainees for any form of treatment or punishment that may adversely affect their physical or mental health and which is not in accordance with the relevant international instruments, or to participate in any way in the infliction of any such treatment or punishment which is not in accordance with the relevant international instruments.

Principle 5

It is a contravention of medical ethics for health personnel, particularly physicians, to participate in any procedure for restraining a prisoner or detainee unless such a procedure is determined in accordance with purely medical criteria as being necessary for the protection of the physical or mental health or the safety of the prisoner or detainee himself, of his fellow prisoners or detainees, or of his guardians, and presents no hazard to his physical or mental health.

Principle 6

There may be no derogation from the foregoing principles on any ground whatsoever, including public emergency.

* * *

3. Basic Principles on the Use of Force and Firearms by Law Enforcement Officials

ANNEX

Basic Principles on the Use of Force and Firearms by Law Enforcement Officials

Whereas the work of law enforcement officials is a social service of great importance and there is, therefore, a need to maintain and, whenever necessary, to improve the working conditions and status of these officials,

Whereas a threat to the life and safety of law enforcement officials must be seen as a threat to the stability of society as a whole,

Whereas law enforcement officials[1] have a vital role in the protection of the right to life, liberty and security of the person, as guaranteed in the Universal Declaration of Human Rights and reaffirmed in the International Covenant on Civil and Political Rights,

Whereas the Standard Minimum Rules for the Treatment of Prisoners provide for the circumstances in which prison officials may use force in the course of their duties,

Whereas article 3 of the Code of Conduct for Law Enforcement Officials provides that law enforcement officials may use force only when strictly necessary and to the extent required for the performance of their duty,

---

[1]In accordance with the commentary to article 1 of the Code of Conduct for Enforcement Officials, the term "law enforcement officials" includes all officers of the whether appointed or elected, who exercise police powers, especially the powers of arres detention. In countries where police powers are exercised by military authorities, whe uniformed or not, or by State security forces, the definition of law enforcement officials be regarded as including officers of such services.

Whereas the preparatory meeting for the Seventh United Nations Congress on the Prevention of Crime and the Treatment of Offenders, held at Varenna, Italy, agreed on elements to be considered in the course of further work on restraints on the use of force and firearms by law enforcement officials,

Whereas the Seventh Congress, in its resolution 14, *inter alia,* emphasizes that the use of force and firearms by law enforcement officials should be commensurate with due respect for human rights,

Whereas the Economic and Social Council, in its resolution 1986/10, section IX, of 11 May 1986, invited Member States to pay particular attention in the implementation of the Code to the use of force and firearms by law enforcement officials, and the General Assembly, in its resolution 41/149 of 4 December 1986, *inter alia*, welcomed this recommendation made by the Council,

Whereas it is appropriate that, with due regard to their personal safety, consideration be given to the role of law enforcement officials in relation to the administration of justice, to the protection of the right to life, liberty and security of the person, to their responsibility to maintain public safety and social peace and to the importance of their qualifications, training and conduct,

The basic principles set forth below, which have been formulated to assist Member States in their task of ensuring and promoting the proper role of law enforcement officials, should be taken into account and respected by Governments within the framework of their national legislation and practise, and be brought to the attention of law enforcement officials as well as other persons, such as judges, prosecutors, lawyers, members of the executive branch and the legislature, and the public.

General provisions

1. Governments and law enforcement agencies shall adopt and implement rules and regulations on the use of force and firearms against persons by law enforcement officials. In developing such rules and regulations, governments and law enforcement agencies shall keep the ethical issues associated with the use of force and firearms constantly under review.

2. Governments and law enforcement agencies should develop a range of means as broad as possible and equip law enforcement officials with various types of weapons and ammunition that would allow for a differentiated use of force and firearms. These should include the development of non-lethal incapacitating weapons for use in appropriate situations, with a view to increasingly restraining the application of means capable of causing death or injury to persons. For the same purpose, it should also be possible for law

enforcement officials to be equipped with self-defensive equipment such as shields, helmets, bulletproof vests and bulletproof means of transportation, in order to decrease the need to use weapons of any kind.

3. The development and deployment of non-lethal incapacitating weapons should be carefully evaluated in order to minimize the risk of endangering uninvolved persons, and the use of such weapons should be carefully controlled.

4. Law enforcement officials, in carrying out their duty, shall, as far as possible, apply non-violent means before resorting to the use of force and firearms. They may use force and firearms only if other means remain ineffective or without any promise of achieving the intended result.

5. Whenever the lawful use of force and firearms is unavoidable, law enforcement officials shall:

(a) Exercise restraint in such use and act in proportion to the seriousness of the offence and the legitimate objective to be achieved;

(b) Minimize damage and injury, and respect and preserve human life;

(c) Ensure that assistance and medical aid are rendered to any injured or affected persons at the earliest possible moment;

(d) Ensure that relatives or close friends of the injured or affected person are notified at the earliest possible moment.

6. Where injury or death is caused by the use of force and firearms by law enforcement officials, they shall report the incident promptly to their superiors, in accordance with principle 22.

7. Governments shall ensure that arbitrary or abusive use of force and firearms by law enforcement officials is punished as a criminal offence under their law.

8. Exceptional circumstances such as internal political instability or any other public emergency may not be invoked to justify any departure from these basic principles.

Special provisions

9. Law enforcement officials shall not use firearms against persons except in self-defence or defence of others against the imminent threat of death or serious injury, to prevent the perpetration of a particularly serious crime involving grave threat to life, to arrest a person presenting such a danger and resisting their

authority, or to prevent his or her escape, and only when less extreme means are insufficient to achieve these objectives. In any event, intentional lethal use of firearms may only be made when strictly unavoidable in order to protect life.

10. In the circumstances provided for under principle 9, law enforcement officials shall identify themselves as such and give a clear warning of their intent to use firearms, with sufficient time for the warning to be observed, unless to do so would unduly place the law enforcement officials at risk or would create a risk of death or serious harm to other persons, or would be clearly inappropriate or pointless in the circumstances of the incident.

11. Rules and regulations on the use of firearms by law enforcement officials should include guidelines that:

(a) Specify the circumstances under which law enforcement officials are authorized to carry firearms and prescribe the types of firearms and ammunition permitted;

(b) Ensure that firearms are used only in appropriate circumstances and in a manner likely to decrease the risk of unnecessary harm;

(c) Prohibit the use of those firearms and ammunition that cause unwarranted injury or present an unwarranted risk;

(d) Regulate the control, storage and issuing of firearms, including procedures for ensuring that law enforcement officials are accountable for the firearms and ammunition issued to them;

(e) Provide for warnings to be given, if appropriate, when firearms are to be discharged;

(f) Provide for a system of reporting whenever law enforcement officials use firearms in the performance of their duty.

Policing unlawful assemblies

12. As everyone is allowed to participate in lawful and peaceful assemblies, in accordance with the principles embodied in the Universal Declaration of Human Rights and the International Covenant on Civil and Political Rights, Governments and law enforcement agencies and officials shall recognize that force and firearms may be used only in accordance with principles 13 and 14.

13. In the dispersal of assemblies that are unlawful but nonviolent, law enforcement officials shall avoid the use of force or, where that is not practicable, shall restrict such force to the minimum extent necessary.

14. In the dispersal of violent assemblies, law enforcement officials may use firearms only when less dangerous means are not practicable and only to the minimum extent necessary. Law enforcement officials shall not use firearms in such cases, except under the conditions stipulated in principle 9.

Policing persons in custody or detention

15. Law enforcement officials, in their relations with persons in custody or detention, shall not use force, except when strictly necessary for the maintenance of security and order within the institution, or when personal safety is threatened.

16. Law enforcement officials, in their relations with persons in custody or detention, shall not use firearms, except in self defence or in the defence of others against the immediate threat of death or serious injury, or when strictly necessary to prevent the escape of a person in custody or detention presenting the danger referred to in principle 9.

17. The preceding principles are without prejudice to the rights, duties and responsibilities of prison officials, as set out in the Standard Minimum Rules for the Treatment of prisoners, particularly rules 33, 34 and 54.

Qualifications, training and counselling

18. Governments and law enforcement agencies shall ensure that all law enforcement officials are selected by proper screening procedures, have appropriate moral, psychological and physical qualities for the effective exercise of their functions and receive continuous and thorough professional training. Their continued fitness to perform these functions should be subject to periodic review.

19. Governments and law enforcement agencies shall ensure that all law enforcement officials are provided with training and are tested in accordance with appropriate proficiency standards in the use of force. Those law enforcement officials who are required to carry firearms should be authorized to do so only upon completion of special training in their use.

20. In the training of law enforcement officials, Governments and law enforcement agencies shall give special attention to issues of police ethics and human rights, especially in the investigative process, to alternatives to the use of force and firearms, including the peaceful settlement of conflicts, the understand-

ing of crowd behaviour, and the methods of persuasion, negotiation and mediation, as well as to technical means, with a view to limiting the use of force and firearms. Law enforcement agencies should review their training programmes and operational procedures in the light of particular incidents.

21. Governments and law enforcement agencies shall make stress counselling available to law enforcement officials who are involved in situations where force and firearms are used.

Reporting and review procedures

22. Governments and law enforcement agencies shall establish effective reporting and review procedures for all incidents referred to in principles 6 and 11 (f). For incidents reported pursuant to these principles, Governments and law enforcement agencies shall ensure that an effective review process is available and that independent administrative or prosecutorial authorities are in a position to exercise jurisdiction in appropriate circumstances. In cases of death and serious injury or other grave consequences, a detailed report shall be sent promptly to the competent authorities responsible for administrative review and judicial control.

23. Persons affected by the use of force and firearms or their legal representatives shall have access to an independent process, including a judicial process. In the event of the death of such persons, this provision shall apply to their dependents accordingly.

24. Governments and law enforcement agencies shall ensure that superior officers are held responsible if they know, or should have known, that law enforcement officials under their command are resorting, or have resorted, to the unlawful use of force and firearms, and they did not take all measures in their power to prevent, suppress or report such use.

25. Governments and law enforcement agencies shall ensure that no criminal or disciplinary sanction is imposed on law enforcement officials who, in compliance with the Code of Conduct for Law Enforcement Officials and these basic principles refuse to carry out an order to use force and firearms, or who report such use by other officials.

26. Obedience to superior orders shall be no defence if law enforcement officials knew that an order to use force and firearms resulting in the death or serious injury of a person was manifestly unlawful and had a reasonable opportunity to refuse to follow it. In any case, responsibility also rests on the superiors who gave the unlawful orders.

* * *

4. Guidelines on the Role of Prosecutors

ANNEX

Guidelines on the role of prosecutors

Whereas in the Charter of the United Nations the peoples of the world affirm, *inter alia*, their determination to establish conditions under which justice can be maintained, and proclaim as one of their purposes the achievement of international cooperation in promoting and encouraging respect for human rights and fundamental freedoms without distinction as to race, sex, language or religion,

Whereas the Universal Declaration of Human Rights enshrines the principles of equality before the law, the presumption of innocence and the right to a fair and public hearing by an independent and impartial tribunal,

Whereas frequently there still exists a gap between the vision underlying those principles and the actual situation,

Whereas the organization and administration of justice in every country should be inspired by those principles, and efforts undertaken to translate them fully into reality,

Whereas prosecutors play a crucial role in the administration of justice, and rules concerning the performance of their important responsibilities should promote their respect for and compliance with the above mentioned principles, thus contributing to fair and equitable criminal justice and the effective protection of citizens against crime,

Whereas it is essential to ensure that prosecutors possess the professional qualifications required for the accomplishment of their functions, through improved methods of recruitment and legal and professional training, and through the provision of all necessary means for the proper performance of their role in combating criminality, particularly in its new forms and dimensions,

Whereas the General Assembly, by its resolution 34/169 of 17 December 1979, adopted the Code of Conduct for Law Enforcement Officials, on the recommendation of the Fifth United Nations Congress on the Prevention of Crime and the Treatment of Offenders,

Whereas in resolution 16 of the Sixth United Nations Congress on the Prevention of Crime and the Treatment of Offenders, the Committee on Crime Prevention and Control was called upon to include among its priorities the elaboration of guidelines relating to the independence of judges and the selection, professional training and status of judges and prosecutors,

Whereas the Seventh United Nations Congress on the Prevention of Crime and the Treatment of Offenders adopted the Basic Principles on the Independence of the Judiciary, subsequently endorsed by the General Assembly in its resolutions 40/32 of 29 November 1985 and 40/146 of 13 December 1985,

Whereas the Declaration of Basic Principles of Justice for Victims of Crime and Abuse of Power, recommends measures to be taken at the international and national levels to improve access to justice and fair treatment, restitution, compensation and assistance for victims of crime,

Whereas, in resolution 7 of the Seventh Congress, the Committee was called upon to consider the need for guidelines relating, *inter alia*, to the selection, professional training and status of prosecutors, their expected tasks and conduct, means to enhance their contribution to the smooth functioning of the criminal justice system and their cooperation with the police, the scope of their discretionary powers, and their role in criminal proceedings, and to report thereon to future United Nations congresses,

The Guidelines set forth below, which have been formulated to assist Member States in their tasks of securing and promoting the effectiveness, impartiality and fairness of prosecutors in criminal proceedings should be respected and taken into account by Governments within the framework of their national legislation and practise, and should be brought to the attention of prosecutors, as well as other persons, such as judges, lawyers, members of the executive and the legislature and the public in general. The present Guidelines have been formulated principally with public prosecutors in mind, but they apply equally, as appropriate to prosecutors appointed on an *ad hoc* basis.

Qualifications, selection and training

1. Persons selected as prosecutors shall be individuals of integrity and ability, with appropriate training and qualifications.

2. States shall ensure that:

(a) Selection criteria for prosecutors embody safeguards against appointments based on partiality or prejudice excluding any discrimination against a person on the grounds of race, colour, sex, language, religion, political or other opinion, national, social or ethnic origin, property, birth, economic or other status, except that it shall not be considered discriminatory to require a candidate for prosecutorial office to be a national of the country concerned;

(b) Prosecutors have appropriate education and training and should be made aware of the ideals and ethical duties of their office, of the constitutional and statutory protections for the rights of the suspect and the victim, and of human rights and fundamental freedoms recognized by national and international law.

Status and conditions of service

3. Prosecutors, as essential agents of the administration of justice, shall at all times maintain the honour and dignity of their profession.

4. States shall ensure that prosecutors are able to perform their professional functions without intimidation, hindrance, harassment, improper interference or unjustified exposure to civil, penal or other liability.

5. Prosecutors and their families shall be physically protected by the authorities when their personal safety is threatened as a result of the discharge of prosecutorial functions.

6. Reasonable conditions of service of prosecutors, adequate remuneration and, where applicable, tenure, pension and age of retirement shall be set out by law or published rules or regulations.

7. Promotion of prosecutors, wherever such a system exists, shall be based on objective factors, in particular professional qualifications, ability, integrity and experience, and decided upon in accordance with fair and impartial procedures.

Freedom of expression and association

8. Prosecutors like other citizens are entitled to freedom of expression, belief, association and assembly. In particular, they shall have the right to take part in public discussion of matters concerning the law, the administration of justice and the promotion and protection of human rights and to join or form local, national or international organizations and attend their meetings, without suffering professional disadvantage by reason of their lawful action or their membership in a lawful organization. In exercising these rights, prosecutors shall always conduct themselves in accordance with the law and the recognized standards and ethics of their profession.

9. Prosecutors shall be free to form and join professional associations or other organizations to represent their interests, to promote their professional training and to protect their status.

Role in criminal proceedings

10. The office of prosecutors shall be strictly separated from judicial functions.

11. Prosecutors shall perform an active role in criminal proceedings, including institution of prosecution and, where authorized by law or consistent with local practise, in the investigation of crime, supervision over the legality of these investigations, supervision of the execution of court decisions and the exercise of other functions as representatives of the public interest.

12. Prosecutors shall, in accordance with the law, perform their duties fairly, consistently and expeditiously, and respect and protect human dignity and uphold human rights, thus contributing to ensuring due process and the smooth functioning of the criminal justice system.

13. In the performance of their duties, prosecutors shall:

(a) Carry out their functions impartially and avoid all political, social, religious, racial, cultural, sexual or any other kind of discrimination;

(b) Protect the public interest, act with objectivity, take proper account of the position of the suspect and the victim, and pay attention to all relevant circumstances, irrespective of whether they are to the advantage or disadvantage of the suspect;

(c) Keep matters in their possession confidential, unless the performance of duty or the needs of justice require otherwise;

(d) Consider the views and concerns of victims when their personal interests are affected and ensure that victims are informed of their rights in accordance with the Declaration of Basic Principles of Justice for Victims of Crime and Abuse of Power.

14. Prosecutors shall not initiate or continue prosecutions or shall make every effort to stay proceedings, when an impartial investigation shows the charge to be unfounded.

15. Prosecutors shall give due attention to the prosecution of crimes committed by public officials, particularly corruption, abuse of power, grave violations of human rights and other crimes recognized by international law and, where authorized by law or consistent with local practise, the investigation of such offences.

16. When prosecutors come into possession of evidence against suspects that they know or believe on reasonable grounds was obtained through recourse to unlawful methods, which constitute a grave violation of the suspect's human rights, especially involving torture or cruel, inhuman or degrading treatment or punishments or other abuses of human rights, they shall refuse to use such evidence against anyone other than those who used such methods, or inform the Court accordingly, and shall take all necessary steps to ensure that those responsible for using such methods are brought to justice.

Discretionary functions

17. In countries where prosecutors are vested with discretionary functions, the law or published rules or regulations shall provide guidelines to enhance fairness and consistency of approach in taking decisions in the prosecution process, including institution or waiver of prosecution.

Alternatives to prosecution

18. In accordance with national law, prosecutors shall give due consideration to waiving prosecutions, discontinuing proceedings conditionally or unconditionally, or diverting criminal cases from the formal justice system, with full respect for the rights of suspect(s) and the victim(s). For this purpose; states should fully explore the possibility of adopting diversion schemes not only to alleviate excessive court loads, but also to avoid the stigmatization of pretrial detention, indictment and conviction, as well as the possible adverse effects of imprisonment.

19. In countries where prosecutors are vested with discretionary functions as to the decision whether or not to prosecute a juvenile, special considerations shall be given to the nature and gravity of the offence, protection of society and the personality and background of the juvenile. In making that decision, prosecutors shall particularly consider available alternatives to prosecution under the relevant juvenile justice laws and procedures. Prosecutors shall use their best efforts to take prosecutory action against juveniles only to the extent strictly necessary.

Relations with other government agencies or institutions

20. In order to ensure the fairness and effectiveness of prosecution, prosecutors shall strive to cooperate with the police, the courts, the legal profession, public defenders and other government agencies or institutions.

Disciplinary proceedings

21. Disciplinary offences of prosecutors shall be based on law or lawful regulations. Complaints against prosecutors which allege that they acted in a manner clearly out of the range of professional standards shall be processed expeditiously and fairly under appropriate procedures. Prosecutors shall have the right to a fair hearing. The decision shall be subject to independent review.

22. Disciplinary proceedings against prosecutors shall guarantee an objective evaluation and decision. They shall be determined in accordance with the law, the code of professional conduct and other established standards and ethics and in the light of the present Guidelines.

Observance of the Guidelines

23. Prosecutors shall respect the present Guidelines. They shall also, to the best of their capability, prevent and actively oppose any violations thereof.

24. Prosecutors who have reason to believe that a violation of the present Guidelines has occurred or is about to occur shall report the matter to their superior authorities and, where necessary, to other appropriate authorities or organs vested with reviewing or remedial power.

* * *

5. Basic Principles on the Role of Lawyers

ANNEX

Basic Principles on the Role of Lawyers

Whereas in the Charter of the United Nations the peoples of the world affirm, *inter alia*, their determination to establish conditions under which justice can be maintained, and proclaim as one of their purposes the achievement of international cooperation in promoting and encouraging respect for human rights and fundamental freedoms without distinction as to race, sex, language or religion,

Whereas the Universal Declaration of Human Rights enshrines the principles of equality before the law, the presumption of innocence, the right to a fair and public hearing by an independent and impartial tribunal, and all the guarantees necessary for the defence of everyone charged with a penal offence,

Whereas the International Covenant on Civil and Political Rights proclaims, in addition, the right to be tried without undue delay and the right to a fair and public hearing by a competent, independent and impartial tribunal established by law,

Whereas the International Covenant on Economic, Social and Cultural Rights recalls the obligation of States under the Charter to promote universal respect for, and observance of, human rights and freedoms,

Whereas the Body of Principles for the Protection of All Persons under Any Form of Detention or Imprisonment provides that a detained person shall be entitled to have the assistance of, and to communicate and consult with, legal counsel,

Whereas the Standard Minimum Rules for the Treatment of Prisoners recommend, in particular, that legal assistance and confidential communication with counsel should be ensured to untried prisoners,

Whereas the Safeguards guaranteeing protection of those facing the death penalty reaffirm the right of everyone suspected or charged with a crime for which capital punishment may be imposed to adequate legal assistance at all stages of the proceedings, in accordance with article 14 of the International Covenant on Civil and Political Rights,

Whereas the Declaration of Basic Principles of Justice for Victims of Crime and Abuse of Power recommends measures to be taken at the international and national levels to improve access to justice and fair treatment, restitution, compensation and assistance for victims of crime,

Whereas adequate protection of the human rights and fundamental freedoms to which all persons are entitled, be they economic, social and cultural, or civil and political, requires that all persons have effective access to legal services provided by an independent legal profession,

Whereas professional associations of lawyers have a vital role to play in upholding professional standards and ethics, protecting their members from persecution and improper restrictions and infringements, providing legal services to all in need of them, and cooperating with governmental and other institutions in furthering the ends of justice and public interest,

The Basic Principles on the Role of Lawyers, set forth below, which have been formulated to assist Member States in their task of promoting and ensuring the proper role of lawyers, should be respected and taken into account by Governments within the framework of their national legislation and practise and should be brought to the attention of lawyers as well as other persons, such as judges, prosecutors, members of the executive and the legislature, and the public in general. These principles shall also apply, as appropriate, to persons who exercise the functions of lawyers without having the formal status of lawyers.

Access to lawyers and legal services

1. All persons are entitled to call upon the assistance of a lawyer of their choice to protect and establish their rights and to defend them in all stages of criminal proceedings.

2. Governments shall ensure that efficient procedures and responsive mechanisms for effective and equal access to lawyers are provided for all persons within their territory and subject to their jurisdiction, without distinction of any kind, such as discrimination based on race, colour, ethnic origin, sex, language, religion, political or other opinion, national or social origin, property, birth, economic or other status.

3. Governments shall ensure the provision of sufficient funding and other resources for legal services to the poor and, as necessary, to other disadvantaged persons. Professional associations of lawyers shall cooperate in the organization and provision of services, facilities and other resources.

4. Governments and professional associations of lawyers shall promote programmes to inform the public about their rights and duties under the law and the important role of lawyers in protecting their fundamental freedoms. Special attention should be given to assisting the poor and other disadvantaged persons so as to enable them to assert their rights and where necessary call upon the assistance of lawyers.

Special safeguards in criminal justice matters

5. Governments shall ensure that all persons are immediately informed by the competent authority of their right to be assisted by a lawyer of their own choice upon arrest or detention or when charged with a criminal offence.

6. Any such persons who do not have a lawyer shall, in all cases in which the interests of justice so require, be entitled to have a lawyer of experience and competence commensurate with the nature of the offence assigned to them in order to provide effective legal assistance, without payment by them if they lack sufficient means to pay for such services.

7. Governments shall further ensure that all persons arrested or detained, with or without criminal charge, shall have prompt access to a lawyer, and in any case not later than forty-eight hours from the time of arrest or detention.

8. All arrested, detained or imprisoned persons shall be provided with adequate opportunities, time and facilities to be visited by and to communicate and consult with a lawyer, without delay, interception or censorship and in full confidentiality. Such consultations may be within sight, but not within the hearing, of law enforcement officials.

Qualifications and training

9. Governments, professional associations of lawyers and educational institutions shall ensure that lawyers have appropriate education and training and be made aware of the ideals and ethical duties of the lawyer and of human rights and fundamental freedoms recognized by national and international law.

10. Governments, professional associations of lawyers and educational institutions shall ensure that there is no discrimination against a person with respect to entry into or continued practise within the legal profession on the grounds of race, colour, sex, ethnic origin, religion, political or other opinion, national or social origin, property, birth, economic or other status, except that a requirement that a lawyer must be a national of the country concerned shall not be considered discriminatory.

11. In countries where there exist groups, communities or regions whose needs for legal services are not met, particularly where such groups have distinct cultures, traditions or languages or have been the victims of past discrimination, governments, professional associations of lawyers and educational institutions should take special measures to provide opportunities for candidates from these groups to enter the legal profession and should ensure that they receive training appropriate to the needs of their groups.

Duties and responsibilities

12. Lawyers shall at all times maintain the honour and dignity of their profession as essential agents of the administration of justice.

13. The duties of lawyers towards their clients shall include:

(a) Advising clients as to their legal rights and obligations, and as to the working of the legal system in so far as it is relevant to the legal rights and obligations of the clients;

(b) Assisting clients in every appropriate way, and taking legal action to protect their interests;

(c) Assisting clients before courts, tribunals or administrative authorities, where appropriate.

14. Lawyers, in protecting the rights of their clients and in promoting the cause of justice, shall seek to uphold human rights and fundamental freedoms recognized by national and international law and shall at all times act freely and diligently in accordance with the law and recognized standards and ethics of the legal profession.

15. Lawyers shall always loyally respect the interests of their clients.

Guarantees for the functioning of lawyers

16. Governments shall ensure that lawyers (a) are able to perform all of their professional functions without intimidation, hindrance, harassment or improper interference; (b) are able to travel and to consult with their clients freely both within their own country and abroad; and (c) shall not suffer, or be threatened with, prosecution or administrative, economic or other sanctions for any action taken in accordance with recognized professional duties, standards and ethics.

17. Where the security of lawyers is threatened as a result of discharging their functions, they shall be adequately safeguarded by the authorities.

18. Lawyers shall not be identified with their clients or their clients' causes as a result of discharging their functions.

19. No court or administrative authority before whom the right to counsel is recognized shall refuse to recognize the right of a lawyer to appear before it for his or her client unless that lawyer has been disqualified in accordance with national law and practise and in conformity with these principles.

20. Lawyers shall enjoy civil and penal immunity for relevant statements made in good faith in written or oral pleadings or in their professional appearances before a court, tribunal or other legal or administrative authority.

21. It is the duty of the competent authorities to ensure lawyers access to appropriate information, files and documents in their possession or control in sufficient time to enable lawyers to provide effective legal assistance to their clients. Such access should be provided at the earliest appropriate time.

22. Governments shall recognize and respect that all communications and consultations between lawyers and their clients within their professional relationship are confidential.

Freedom of expression and association

23. Lawyers like other citizens are entitled to freedom of expression, belief, association and assembly. In particular, they shall have the right to take part in public discussion of matters concerning the law, the administration of justice and the promotion and protection of human rights and to join or form local, national or international organizations and attend their meetings, without suffering professional restrictions by reason of their lawful action or their membership in a lawful organization. In exercising these rights, lawyers shall always conduct themselves in accordance with the law and the recognized standards and ethics of the legal profession.

Professional associations of lawyers

24. Lawyers shall be entitled to form and join self-governing professional associations to represent their interests, promote their continuing education and training and protect their professional integrity. The executive body of the professional associations shall be elected by its members and shall exercise its functions without external interference.

25. Professional associations of lawyers shall cooperate with Governments to ensure that everyone has effective and equal access to legal services and that lawyers are able, without improper interference, to counsel and assist their clients in accordance with the law and recognized professional standards and ethics.

Disciplinary proceedings

26. Codes of professional conduct for lawyers shall be established by the legal profession through its appropriate organs, or by legislation, in accordance with national law and custom and recognized international standards and norms.

27. Charges or complaints made against lawyers in their professional capacity shall be processed expeditiously and fairly under appropriate procedures. Lawyers shall have the right to a fair hearing, including the right to be assisted by a lawyer of their choice.

28. Disciplinary proceedings against lawyers shall be brought before an impartial disciplinary committee established by the legal profession, before an independent statutory authority, or before a court, and shall be subject to an independent judicial review.

29. All disciplinary proceedings shall be determined in accordance with the code of professional conduct and other recognized standards and ethics of the legal profession and in the light of these principles.

* * *

J. VICTIMS' RIGHTS AND REMEDIES

Critics of the United Nations sometimes say that there are too many codes, principles and rules to protect the human rights of criminals and alleged criminals, whereas the rights of victims of crime frequently appear to be forgotten, or to occupy only a peripheral position on the agenda of the organization.

In 1985, the General Assembly focused its attention on victims, who should always be treated with compassion and respect for their dignity. Moreover, "[t]hey are entitled to access to the mechanisms of justice and to prompt redress, as provided by national legislation." Offenders should make fair restitution to victims. When compensation is not fully available from the offender, States should endeavor to provide such compensation to victims and their families, in particular, dependents of persons who have died or become incapacitated.

In 1988, a Committee of Experts at the International Institute of Higher Studies in Criminal Science in Siracusa, Italy, proposed concrete measures for the implementation of the above Declaration, accompanied by a detailed commentary.

Subsequently, the Eighth United Nations Congress on the Prevention of Crime and the Treatment of Offenders made further recommendations for the effective protection of the human rights of victims of crime and abuse of power.

Moreover, the Sub-Commission on Prevention of Discrimination and Protection of Minorities has turned its attention to this important subject, appointing the former Director of the United Nations Division (now Centre) on Human Rights, Mr. Theo van Boven, Special Rapporteur entrusted with a study concerning the right to restitution, compensation and rehabilitation for victims of gross violations of human rights and fundamental freedoms.

1. Declaration of Basic Principles of Justice for Victims of Crime and Abuse of Power (excerpts)

A. VICTIMS OF CRIME

1. "Victims" means persons who, individually or collectively, have suffered harm, including physical or mental injury, emotional suffering, economic loss or substantial impairment of their fundamental rights, through acts or omissions that

are in violation of criminal laws operative within Member States, including those laws proscribing criminal abuse of power.

2. A person may be considered a victim, under this Declaration, regardless of whether the perpetrator is identified, apprehended, prosecuted or convicted and regardless of the familial relationship between the perpetrator and the victim. The term "victim" also includes, where appropriate, the immediate family or dependents of the direct victim and persons who have suffered harm in intervening to assist victims in distress or to prevent victimization.

3. The provisions contained herein shall be applicable to all, without distinction of any kind, such as race, colour, sex, age, language, religion, nationality, political or other opinion, cultural beliefs or practises, property, birth or family status, ethnic or social origin, and disability.

Access to justice and fair treatment

4. Victims should be treated with compassion and respect for their dignity. They are entitled to access to the mechanisms of justice and to prompt redress, as provided for by national legislation, for the harm that they have suffered.

5. Judicial and administrative mechanisms should be established and strengthened where necessary to enable victims to obtain redress through formal or informal procedures that are expeditious, fair, inexpensive and accessible. Victims should be informed of their rights in seeking redress through such mechanisms.

6. The responsiveness of judicial and administrative processes to the needs of victims should be facilitated by:

(a) Informing victims of their role and the scope, timing and progress of the proceedings and of the disposition of their cases, especially where serious crimes are involved and when they have requested such information;

(b) Allowing the views and concerns of victims to be presented and considered at appropriate stages of the proceedings where their personal interests are affected, without prejudice to the accused and consistent with the relevant national criminal justice system;

(c) Providing proper assistance to victims throughout the legal process;

(d) Taking measures to minimize inconvenience to victims, protect their privacy, when necessary, and ensure their safety, as well as that of their families and witnesses on their behalf, from intimidation and retaliation;

(e) Avoiding unnecessary delay in the disposition of cases and the execution of orders or decrees granting awards to victims;

7. Informal mechanisms for the resolution of disputes, including mediation, arbitration and customary justice or indigenous practises, should be utilized where appropriate to facilitate conciliation and redress for victims.

Restitution

8. Offenders or third parties responsible for their behaviour should, where appropriate, make fair restitution to victims, their families or dependents. Such restitution should include the return of property or payment for the harm or loss suffered, reimbursement of expenses incurred as a result of the victimization, the provision of services and the restoration of rights.

9. Governments should review their practises, regulations and laws to consider restitution as an available sentencing option in criminal cases, in addition to other criminal sanctions.

10. In cases of substantial harm to the environment, restitution, if ordered, should include, as far as possible, restoration of the environment, reconstruction of the infrastructure, replacement of community facilities and reimbursement of the expenses of relocation, whenever such harm results in the dislocation of a community.

11. Where public officials or other agents acting in an official or quasi-official capacity have violated national criminal laws, the victims should receive restitution from the State whose officials or agents were responsible for the harm inflicted. In cases where the Government under whose authority the victimizing act or omission occurred is no longer in existence, the State or Government successor in title should provide restitution to the victims.

Compensation

12. When compensation is not fully available from the offender or other sources, States should endeavour to provide financial compensation to:

(a) Victims who have sustained significant bodily injury or impairment of physical or mental health as a result of serious crimes;

(b) The family, in particular dependents of persons who have died or become physically or mentally incapacitated as a result of such victimization.

General clause

Nothing in this Body of Principles shall be construed as restricting or derogating from any right defined in the International Covenant on Civil and Political Rights.

13. The establishment, strengthening and expansion of national funds for compensation to victims should be encouraged. Where appropriate, other funds may also be established for this purpose, including in those cases where the State of which the victim is a national is not in a position to compensate the victim for the harm.

Assistance

14. Victims should receive the necessary material, medical, psychological and social assistance through governmental, voluntary, community-based and indigenous means.

15. Victims should be informed of the availability of health and social services and other relevant assistance and be readily afforded access to them.

16. Police, justice, health, social service and other personnel concerned should receive training to sensitize them to the needs of victims, and guidelines to ensure proper and prompt aid.

17. In providing services and assistance to victims, attention should be given to those who have special needs because of the nature of the harm inflicted or because of factors such as those mentioned in paragraph 3 above.

B. VICTIMS OF ABUSE OF POWER

18. "Victims" means persons who, individually or collectively, have suffered harm, including physical or mental injury, emotional suffering, economic loss or substantial impairment of their fundamental rights, through acts or omissions that do not yet constitute violations of national criminal laws but of internationally recognized norms relating to human rights.

19. States should consider incorporating into the national law norms proscribing abuses of power and providing remedies to victims of such abuses. In particular, such remedies should include restitution and/or compensation, and necessary material, medical, psychological and social assistance and support.

20. States should consider negotiating multilateral international treaties relating to victims, as defined in paragraph 18.

21. States should periodically review existing legislation and practises to ensure their responsiveness to changing circumstances, should enact and enforce, if necessary, legislation proscribing acts that constitute serious abuses of political or economic power, as well as promoting policies and mechanisms for the prevention of such acts, and should develop and make readily available appropriate rights and remedies for victims of such acts.

* * *

2. Proposed General Assembly Resolution on Measures for Implementation of the Declaration of Basic Principles of Justice for Victims of Crime and Abuse of Power[1]

Implementation Principles for § R4[2]

States should:

R4 (0).1. provide for the widest possible dissemination in all common languages of the text of the Declaration of Basic Principles of Justice for Victims of Crime and Abuse of Power, including the full text of the General Assembly Resolution adopting it as published by the United Nations Department of Public Information

---

[1]The Measures for Implementation were considered by the Committee on Cri Prevention and Control at its Eleventh Session, 5-16 February, 1990, reported at U. Doc. E/1990/31, E/AC.57/1990/8 on 10 April 1990 and in the Official Records of Economic and Social Council, 1990, Supp. No. 10, E/1990/31. The ECOSOC dr resolution "victims of crime and abuse of power", U.N. Doc. E/AC.57/1990/CRP considers the Guide in preambular paragraph [1]five. Additionally, the Eigl Congress was invited to recommend wide distribution of the Measures for Implemen tion and the Guide at U.N. Doc. E/AC.57/1988/NGO/1, substantive paragraph Committee decision 11/113, "Protection of the human rights of victims of crime a abuse of power" recommended that ECOSOC transmit the draft resolution, referri to the implementation measures in preambular paragraph 10 and substantive paragra 2, to the Eighth Congress.

[2]Inasmuch as the paragraphs of the Resolution and of the Declaration are independen numbered the implementation principles for the Resolution are indicated here by an preced the relevant paragraph number.

1986 (U.N. Doc. DPI/895-August 1986 - IOM), and of their own measures to give effect to the Resolution and Declaration;

R4 (0).2. promote non governmental, professional, and public initiatives of all kinds designed to advance policy-making, programme development, training, research, information-sharing, and advocacy on behalf of victims and the prevention of victimization nationally, regionally, and globally;

R4 (0).3. ratify international and regional conventions aimed at preventing victimization and aiding victims, and incorporate their provisions into nationallegislation and administrative regulations and practises;

R4 (0).4. cooperate in efforts to respond to the needs of victims by international and regional intergovernmental and nongovernmental organizations; and

R4 (0).5. publicize international and regional procedures for preventing victimization and providing recourse and assistance to victims.

Commentary to § R4

States should ratify international and regional instruments designed to prevent victimization and provide redress for victims, such as conventions on compensation to victims of violent crime where these exist; those in other parts of the world should develop and ratify similar instruments intended to foster programmes for compensation to victims of crimes of and, in order to curtail victimization as referred to hereinafter, endeavour:

United Nations Resolution	(a) to implement social, health, including mental health, educational, economic and specific crime prevention policies to reduce victimization and encourage assistance to victims in distress;

Implementation Principles for § R4 (a)

States should:

R4 (a).1. establish mechanisms in the planning of economic and social development to forestall potential victimization.

R4 (a).2. promote programmes to ensure the optimal education and training of all professions working with victims such as media, clergy, police, medicine, nursing, psychiatry, psychology and social work.

R4 (a).3. consider the adoption of measures that encourage bystanders to assist persons who are being victimized or who are in danger of being victimized, for example, by mandating intervention in certain situations and providing awards for acts of heroism and assistance.

United Nations Resolution

(b) To promote community efforts and public participation in crime prevention;

Implementation Principle for §R4 (b)

R4 (b).1. States should promote community efforts designed to prevent, detect, disclose, investigate and redress instances of victimization.

Commentary to §R4 (b)

Victimization and its human and material cost can be reduced through community efforts to prevent crime, improve the treatment of victims, and generate solidarity among all members of society. A system which recognizes victims' rights justifies in some way a more liberal application of the rights of the accused.

United Nations Resolution

(c) To review periodically their existing legislation and practises in order to ensure responsiveness to changing circumstances, and to enact and enforce legislation proscribing acts that violate internationally recognized norms relating to human rights, corporate conduct, and other abuses of power;

Implementation Principles of § R4 (c)

States should:

R4 (c).1. review their laws and practises in the light of the United Nations Declaration of Basic Principles of Justice for Victims of Crime and Abuse of Power and take the necessary steps to implement its provisions, including the incorporation of its principles into national laws, regulations, and practises;

R4 (c).2. establish permanent review boards within their legislative and administrative bodies;

R4 (c).3. cooperate with international and regional intergovernmental and nongovernmental organizations in the adoption of uniform legislation, administrative regulations and practises, and codes of conduct designed to prevent persons from taking advantage of *lacunae* and differences in national laws;

R4 (c).4. simplify laws and practises, where appropriate, in order to ensure their flexibility and their comprehensibility to the general public;

R4 (c).5. establish legal administrative safeguards designed to prevent wrongdoers from passing the cost of their violations on to others, such as the State, consumers, the general public, or international organizations; and

R4 (c).6. criminalize or otherwise proscribe conduct causing victimization in the regulations governing law enforcement and military personnel.

Commentary to § R4 (c)

Some States have established task forces to consider the appropriate responses to the needs of victims, and the types of services presently available, with a view to recommending specific improvements in this respect.

In a number of jurisdictions "Victims' Bills of Rights" have been enacted, incorporating basic victim entitlement and related government responsibilities, including guidelines for the police, prosecutors, judges, community workers, and others on how they should treat victims. Examples are the victims' bills of rights enacted by more than 30 states of the United States of America and the declarations adopted by South Australia and Manitoba, Canada. Model sets of standards are under study in Canada and the United States. The Committee of Ministers of the Council of Europe has adopted a set of guidelines on the Position of the Victim in Criminal Law and Procedure (Recommendation R (85) 11). **R4 (c)** looks forward to the further development of the concept of abuse of power than it already achieved in Part B of the Declaration to include matters which may not necessarily be covered already in human rights instruments.

United Nations Resolution	(d) To establish and strengthen the means of detecting, prosecuting and sentencing those guilty of crimes.

Implementation Principles for §R4 (d)

States should:

R4 (d).1. develop ombudsman-type institutions to oversee the implementation of the measure recommended herein and, in particular to provide a channel of recourse for victims;

R4 (d).2. establish effective restraints on the exercise of public and economic power in order to minimize abuses, including, as appropriate, disclosure requirements and the organization of specialized, multidisciplinary teams to aid in the detection, investigation, and sanctioning of such abuses;

R4 (d).3. ensure that authorities in the fields of criminal justice, social welfare, and economic regulations oversee economic enterprises and investigate instances of possible and alleged victimization;

R4 (d).4. ensure that the competent authorities promptly conduct an impartial investigation whenever there is reasonable ground to believe that victimization has occurred;

R4 (d).5. conduct impartial investigations as soon as possible into all deaths and serious physical and mental injuries apparently caused by law enforcement, military administrative, medical and other professional personnel and into all deaths and serious physical and mental injuries apparently in custody or in public institutions, regardless of whether they are called jails, prisons, reformatories, guardhouses, hospitals, mental institutions, or otherwise;

R4 (d).6. prosecute persons who victimize others by committing serious crimes or extradite such persons to another State having jurisdiction;

R4 (d).7. ensure that persons complaining about alleged victimization and witness to alleged victimization are protected from any ill treatment, intimidation, harassment, or retaliation, whether by public officials, personnel of economic enterprises, or any other persons, as a consequence of the complaint or any evidence given; and

R4 (d).8. ensure that public and military officials and agents receive no immunity from prosecution or disciplinary proceedings for victimization that was caused willfully, and that in such prosecutions or proceedings there is no defence of obedience to superior orders in cases in which those orders are manifestly illegal.

United Nations Resolution

(e) To promote disclosure of relevant information to expose official and corporate misconduct to public scrutiny, and other ways of increasing responsiveness to public concerns;

Implementation Principles for § R4 (e)

States should, with due respect to the legitimate interest of the persons concerned:

R4 (e).1. publicize complaints of victimization and increase awareness of the national and supranational avenues for lodging such complaints, the bodies to whom they should be made, and the protections afforded complainants;

R4 (e).2. publicize discoveries of cases of victimization even in the absence of direct complaints, efforts to suppress victimization, and the measures taken against victimizers, including any disciplinary or judicial measures imposed; and

R4 (e).3. encourage the media to investigate and report violations of law and abuses of power.

United Nations Resolution

(f) To promote the observance of codes of conduct and ethical norms, in particular international standards, by public servants, including law enforcement, correctional, medical, social service and military personnel, as well as the staff of economic enterprises;

Implementation Principles for § R4 (f)

States should:

R4 (f).1. formulate and promote the application in practise of instruments and codes of conduct intended to prevent victimization and aid victims, such as the Code of Conduct for Law Enforcement Officials; the Principles of Medical Ethics relevant to the Role of Health Personnel, particularly Physicians, in the Protection of Prisoners and Detainees against Torture and Other Cruel, Inhuman or Degrading Treatment or Punishment; and the Code of Ethics in the Public Service; so that they cover all categories of personnel and ensure personal as well as institutional accountability and disciplinary measures for violations thereof;

R4 (f).2. formulate and promote codes of conduct for economic enterprises, such as the draft United Nations Code of Conduct on Transnational Corporations and the proposals of the Organization for Economic Cooperation and Development relating thereto, providing, with due consideration to the possible economic and other costs to the public, for administrative and disciplinary measures, such as license revocation, closure, punitive damages, and other suitable penalties for the enterprises concerned and their personnel in the case of violations;

R4 (f).3. instruct all public servants, particularly personnel involved in the administration of justice, medical, psychological, and social services and, as appropriate, the staffs of economic enterprises, in the observance of internationally recognized norms relating to human rights; and

R4 (f).4. establish means to review adherence to such codes of conduct, through, for example, the promotion of awareness, systems of investigation of complaints, and judicial or administrative sanctions designed to promote personal accountability for violations of such codes of conduct.

United Nations Resolution

(g) To prohibit practises and procedures conducive to abuse, such as secret places of detention and incommunicado detention;

Implementation Principles for § R4 (g)

R4 (g).1. States should review their laws and practises with regard to arrest, searches, interrogation, and detention in order to ensure that:

(a) the United Nations Standard Minimum Rules for the Treatment of Prisoners are adhered to, and that all detainees are promptly informed in a comprehensible manner of these Rules, including the right to lodge complaints;

(b) procedures governing arrest, searches, interrogation, and detention conform to internationally recognized human rights norms and are clearly set forth in national legislation or regulations that are regularly reviewed;

(c) legal and disciplinary action is taken against persons who fail to comply with the legislation and regulations governing arrest, searches, interrogation, and detention;

(d) detainees are brought before a judicial authority as soon as possible after being taken into custody;

(e) detainees have access to a lawyer to their choice, and free legal counsel is provided to detainees unable to retain a lawyer;

(f) lawyers, family members, physicians, and mental health professionals have access to detainees as soon as possible after detention begins and on a regular basis thereafter;

(g) detainees have regular access to ombudsman-type persons or institutions;

(h) the families of all persons under any form of detention or imprisonment are at all times informed of the whereabouts of such persons;

(i) places of detention and the names of detainees are entered into a central register accessible at all times to the public;

(j) the fate of missing or "disappeared" persons is investigated and an account of their situation is given to their families;

(k) independent inspections of places of detention are conducted at periodic intervals; and

(l) authorities responsible for detention are, as far as possible, separate from those responsible for interrogation;

United Nations Resolution

(h) To co-operate with other States, through mutual judicial and administrative assistance, in such matters as the detection and pursuit of offenders, their extradition and the seizure of their assets, to be used for restitution to the victims;

Implementation Principles for § R4 (h)

States should:

R4 (h).1. extradite persons charged with victimization if the conduct in question has been criminalized, and is subject to the general principles of extradition;

R4 (h).2. eliminate the "political offender" exception to extradition in cases of severe physical injury to specific or random victims; and

R4 (h).3. enforce judgments against persons found responsible by the courts of the other States for victimization.

United Nations Resolution

5. RECOMMENDS that, at the international and regional levels, all appropriate measures

should be taken: (a) To promote training activities designed to foster adherence to United Nations standards and norms and to curtail possible abuses;

Implementation Principles for § R5 (a)

States should:

R5 (a).1. promote adherence to the Declaration, the Resolution adopting it, and other norms designed to minimize victimization and to aid victims by fostering instruction in all schools, colleges, universities, and other educational and public institutions on these norms and the legislation, programmes, and practises of other States regarding the prevention of victimization and the treatment of victims;

R5 (a).2. increase sensitivity and responsiveness to the needs and rights of victims by providing suitable professional training, (including specialized curricula, manuals, guidelines and procedures) for those coming into contact with victims, such as medical, hospital, and social service staff, media personnel, the clergy and all public officials, including the police, prosecutors, and judicial and correctional personnel;

R5 (a).3. sponsor training of government officials and agents and the staffs of economic enterprises in the prevention of victimization and the provision of adequate responses to the needs of victims; and

R5 (a).4. sponsor training in collaboration with the United Nations, its regional and interregional institutes for crime prevention and criminal justice, its specialized agencies, and other intergovernmental, governmental, and nongovernmental bodies.

United Nations Resolution

(b) To sponsor collaborative action-research on ways in which victimization can be reduced and victims aided, and to promote information exchanges on the most effective means of doing so;

Implementation Principles for § R5 (b)

States should:

R5 (b).1.

(a) study the nature and scope of victimization and the actual needs of victims;

(b) compare the relative merits of approaches pursued in different States to prevent victimization and assist victims, including social, health, mental health, education, and economic policies; mediation and arbitration methods; and civil, administrative, and criminal law measures;

(c) develop new methods of obtaining information about all forms of victimization and needs of victims, including victimization surveys;

(d) assess the effectiveness of existing legislation and administrative regulations and practises for the prevention of victimization and for assistance to victims;

(e) ascertain the impact of victimization attributable to possible exploitative action of local, national or multinational economic enterprises;

(f) develop national data and research banks; and

(g) promote international, regional, and bilateral cooperation in research and the exchange of research data, expertise, and experiences.

States should:

R5 (b).2.

(a) encourage the establishment of various mechanisms, including the formation of private groups, to monitor the effectiveness of legislation and administrative regulations and practises and present proposals for modifications thereof in order to prevent victimization and improve the situation of victims; and

(b) allow such organizations access to the personnel and records of State agencies and economic enterprises to the widest extent possible, with due respect to the principles of privacy and confidentiality.

United Nations Resolution

(c) To render direct aid to requesting Governments designed to help them curtail victimization and alleviate the plight of victims;

Implementation Principles for § R5 (c)

States should:

R5 (c).1. share their experience in providing justice and assistance for victims or in introducing changes to implement the Declaration with other States and support international and regional intergovernmental and nongovernmental organizations in their efforts to prevent victimization and respond to the needs of victims.

R5 (c).2. request technical assistance from other States and international and regional intergovernmental and nongovernmental organizations for the prevention of victimization and the improvement of the response to the needs of victims.

R5 (c).3. facilitate the request for and provision of advisory services from international and regional intergovernmental and nongovernmental organizations.

Commentary to § R5 (c)

The United Nations regional institutes such as the Helsinki Institute for Crime Prevention and Control, affiliated with the United Nations, the United Nations Asia and Far East Institute for the Prevention of Crime and the Treatment of Offenders, the United Nations Latin American Institute for the Prevention of Crime and the Treatment of Offenders and the United Nations African Institute for the Prevention of Crime and the Treatment of Offenders, as well as the Council of Europe have already facilitated such exchanges of information through the arrangement of conferences and working groups and through publications. Several Council of Europe recommendations (such as R (85) 11 on the Position of the Victim in the Framework of Criminal Law and Procedure, adopted on 28 June 1985) deal with victimization. More planning is needed to create working groups and advisory services.

United Nations Resolution

(d) To develop ways and means of providing recourse for victims where national channels may be insufficient;

Implementation Principles for § R5 (d)

States should be encouraged to:

R5 (d).1. contribute to intergovernmental and nongovernmental funds for the compensation of and assistance to victims;

R5 (d).2. collaborate with international and regional intergovernmental and nongovernmental organizations in providing recourse for victims; and

R5 (d).3. cooperate in the effort to improve United Nations human rights procedures by making them more open, fairer, speedier, and geared to providing the optimum means of helping victims.

United Nations Resolution

6. REQUESTS the Secretary-General to invite Member States to report periodically to the General Assembly on the implementation of the Declaration, as well as on measures taken by them to this effect;

Implementation Principles for § R6

R6.1. States should report, when requested, to international and regional intergovernmental and nongovernmental organizations and designated bodies on the incidence of victimization and on the extent to which present legislation and practises are consistent with the Resolution and the Declaration, on measures taken nationally to implement them, and on assistance that might be required from the international community.

R6.2. The Secretary-General is requested to report periodically on the measures taken internationally and by Member States to implement the Resolution and the Declaration in such a manner as to encourage the development of effective implementation procedures.

United Nations Resolution

7. ALSO REQUESTS the Secretary-General to make use of the opportunities, which all relevant bodies and organizations within the United Nations system offer, to assist Member States, whenever necessary, in improving ways and means of protecting victims both at the national level and through international cooperation;

Implementation Principles for § R7

The Secretary-General is requested to:

R7.1. invite interested States and organizations, including the specialized agencies of the United Nations system and other relevant intergovernmental and nongovernmental organizations to establish and promote international and regional mechanisms for exchanging information and encouraging the implementation of the Resolution and the Declaration;

R7.2. designate an international centre as a clearinghouse promoting the international exchange of information on the implementation of the Resolution and the Declaration. Such a clearinghouse should, *inter alia*, provide information on model legislation as well as on research techniques, education and training;

R7.3 request that States provide information related to the implementation of the Resolution and the Declaration either directly to interested States upon request, or to international or regional institutes or bodies that are in a position to act as clearinghouses for such information; and

R7.4. urge that United Nations funding agencies, particularly the United Nations Development Program, and the Department of Technical Cooperation for Development, and individual States provide technical assistance and training in the means of preventing victimization and providing for the needs of victims for law enforcement, media, clergy, justice, health, mental health and social service professionals, and those working in related fields. Such international assistance could also be provided through regional and nongovernmental agencies.

Commentary to § R7

One function of the clearinghouse referred to above should be to serve as a source of relevant reports, brochures, and audiovisual materials. It should also facilitate the exchange of personnel and the organization of conferences and seminars. Nongovernmental organizations have contributed significantly to this effort. For example, the International Institute of Higher Studies in Criminal Sciences has organized a meeting of experts on the Declaration; the World Society of Victimology has organized workshops on the Declaration and has developed an international bibliography on all aspects of victimology; the World Federation for Mental Health held a special Consultation on Meeting the Mental Health Needs of Victims at United Nations Headquarters in New York; the Society for Traumatic Stress has organized similar meetings. Consideration should be given to the issue of costs, particularly in order to facilitate the participation of developing countries. The United Nations regional institutes serving these countries could collaborate in promoting regional initiatives on behalf of victims. International and domestic nongovernmental organizations should be encouraged to contribute to the exchange of ideas and experiences in this regard.

United Nations Resolution

8. FURTHER REQUESTS the Secretary-General to promote the objectives of the Declaration, in particular by ensuring its widest possible dissemination;

Implementation Principles for § R8

The Secretary-General is requested to include the Declaration and the General Assembly Resolution adopting it in all major publications of human rights documents.

United Nations Resolution

9. URGES the specialized agencies and other entities and bodies of the United Nations system, other relevant intergovernmental and non-governmental organizations and the public to cooperate in the implementation of the provisions of the Declaration.

Implementation Principles to § R9

R9.1. States, United Nations entities, and international and interregional intergovernmental and nongovernmental organizations should establish mechanisms for the sharing of knowledge and for the implementation of the Resolution and the Declaration among interested States in the different regions of the world. Such mechanisms should ensure continuity of action throughout the world and be responsive to the range of needs of different States and regions. The United Nations interregional and regional institutes as well as nongovernmental organizations should play a major role in this effort.

R9.2. The United Nations, its specialized agencies and other entities of the United Nations system, subject to the availability of funds, and relevant intergovernmental and nongovernmental organizations should promote cooperation in the implementation of the Resolution and the Declaration through the establishment of an international working group. Such a working group should be created in order to, *inter alia*,

(a) review, encourage, and facilitate the implementation of the Resolution and the Declaration;

(b) review the Resolution and the Declaration and the procedures for implementing it in the light of changing circumstances and make appropriate recommendations to the Secretary-General, interested States, and international and regional intergovernmental and nongovernmental agencies;

(c) draft and encourage the development of model legislation, training and technical assistance programmes, and international conventions consistent with the objective of the Resolution and the Declaration; and

(d) advise the Secretary-General with regard to reports prepared for and by the Secretary-General on the implementation of the Resolution and the Declaration.

R9.3. States should cooperate in the efforts of this and other working groups in this field convened under United Nations auspices and promote the dissemination of their conclusions and recommendations.

R9.4. Interested Governments and organizations should, as soon as possible, initiate practical measures, including the organization of workshops and meetings on specific aspects of implementation of the Resolution and the Declaration. These might include, for example, the development and application of codes of conduct for police and justice personnel and guidelines for the development of suitable training, services and programs. Particular attention should be focused on goal-setting and evaluation in order to improve results in the light of experience.

R9.5. National and international commemorative "years" should be devoted to victims in order to promote measures of prevention and assistance.

Commentary to § R9

The members of the international working group referred to above should be appointed on the recommendation of interested governments. They might also include experts from both governmental and nongovernmental organizations as well as representatives of United Nations entities such as the World Health Organization, the Centre for Human Rights, and the High Commission for Refugees, the International Labor Organization, and the Crime Prevention and Criminal Justice Branch. Consistent with efforts to implement the Resolution and the Declaration, the Secretary-General should make all efforts to support the working group, within existing resources and the availability of extrabudgetary funds.

Measures for Implementation with Regard to Victims of Crime

A. Victims of Crime

United Nations Declaration

1. "Victims" means, persons who, individually or collectively, have suffered harm, including physical or mental injury, emotional suffering, economic loss or substantial impairment of their fundamental rights, though acts or omissions that are in violation of criminal laws operative within Member States, including those laws proscribing criminal abuse of power.

Commentary to § 1

This paragraph defines the scope of the first part of the Declaration. It notes that the provisions in question apply to those who are victims of crimes as determined by laws operative within a state. Such laws may be promulgated at the national, state, or local levels.

United Nations Declaration

2. A person may be considered a victim, under this Declaration, regardless of whether the perpetrator is identified, apprehended, prosecuted or convicted and regardless of the familial relationship between the perpetrator and the victim. The term "victim" also includes, where appropriate, the immediate family or dependents of the direct victim and persons who have suffered harm in intervening to assist victims in distress or to prevent victimization.

Commentary to § 2

This paragraph emphasizes that the Declaration applies to victims even if there has not yet been an authoritative determination of the guilt to the offender. This allows, *inter alia*, for application of the Declaration to civil proceedings and information proceedings. This paragraph also notes that persons other than those who are the immediate and direct victims of the crime may be in need of assistance and access to justice.

United Nations Declaration

3. The provisions contained herein shall be applicable to all, without distinction of any

kind, such as race, colour, sex, age, language, religion, nationality, political or the opinion, cultural beliefs or practises, property, birth or family status, ethnic or social origin, and disability.

Commentary to § 3

This paragraph promotes nondiscrimination. The phrasing is similar to that found in, for example, article 2(1) of the Universal Declaration of Human Rights and article 2(1) of the International Covenant on Civil and Political Rights but includes further specific grounds upon which discrimination is prohibited in the victims context, notably age, nationality, cultural beliefs and practises, and disability. This reflects advances in thinking in the area of discrimination.

United Nations Declaration

Access to justice and fair treatment 4. Victims should be treated with compassion and respect for their dignity. They are entitled to access to the mechanisms of justice and to prompt redress, as provided for by national legislation, for the harm that they have suffered.

Implementation Principles for § 4

States should:

4.1. promote access to the mechanisms of justice and prompt redress by, *inter alia*, providing legal counselling, simplifying procedures where appropriate, and promoting general awareness of the availability of various mechanisms for obtaining justice and redress.

4.2. examine legal procedures in order to ensure the availability of judicial review where appropriate.

Commentary to § 4

The general and specific rights of victims: Victims, as members of the community, have the human rights of all persons, and are entitled to avail themselves of these rights. Furthermore, as victims of crime, they may be granted additional rights and avenues of action by national, state, and local laws.

Victims with special needs: Victims, as do all persons, differ in their ability to deal with adversity. Persons victimized by similar crimes may well vary in their ability to cope with their situation. Special expertise needs to be developed to recognize this heterogeneity of victim's responses so that differing needs may be met.

Groups at special risk: The services designed should also recognize the needs of special groups such as women and children, the disabled, the aged and refugees.

Victim expectations and system resources: Victims, for whom crime is usually a rare occurrence, have an expectation that the criminal justice system, and the police in particular, will react promptly to the crime. Because of the scarcity of resources, however, components of the criminal justice system may establish priorities of their own. The police may, for example, refuse to investigate property crimes involving losses below a certain amount. To the victim, for whom the loss may be a major one, not measurable solely in monetary terms, the disparity between his or her expectations and the reality of the police reaction may be a source of intense disillusionment. This, in turn, may lead to further mental injury and to a diminished willingness to report further incidents of victimization.

Stages of particular importance: The victim's first contact with persons of authority, in particular the police, is important. Those who are first to come into contact with the victim, including the media, should be particularly aware of the dangers of what is known as "secondary victimization", which refers to insensitive treatment of victims by those to whom the victims turn for assistance and support. At later stages in the criminal justice process there may be an even greater possibility that the practitioner in question is not sufficiently aware of the special needs of victims.

Crisis intervention and coping strategies: There is growing understanding in the health, mental health and social service fields of the effects of traumatic stress such as that caused by a crime. Contacts between representatives of these fields and those working in the criminal justice system should be increased, particularly in the planning of training programs, in order to involve persons with knowledge of crisis intervention in contacts between victims and those operating the mechanisms of criminal justice.

For example in the United States and Australia, attention has been given to the first contact of the criminal justice system with the victim, and to a concept called "mental first aid", that is, reassurance should be given to the victim that what occurred to him or her is condemned by society and that the community sympathizes with the victim. The process consists of a responding police officer reassuring the victim that he or she is safe now, that the officer is sorry that this happened to the victim, and, when applicable, that what occurred was not the fault of the victim.

Crisis intervention teams: Some jurisdictions have arranged for a social worker or a specially trained volunteer to accompany the police officer when responding to domestic disturbance calls and when informing family members of a violent crime.

Peer review systems can be used for the sensitization of the police. In Utrecht, the Netherlands, a peer review system has been established in which, after the victim has been questioned by a police detective, a second detective inquires of the victim regarding how he or she was dealt with by the first detective. The responses are used as the basis for further training.

Accessibility of criminal justice system personnel: Criminal justice system personnel, and in particular the police should develop more contacts with the public. The designation of particular police officers, prosecutors, and judges as responsible for victim issues in general, and for matters relating to a particular victim, might be considered. Such experiments have been carried out in, for example, Australia and the Netherlands. In France, the courts have a separate victims' affairs office.

Control over access to justice: Implicit in access to justice is the provision of a means for obtaining a review of a decision taken. Such a review may be carried out by the original decision-maker or by his or her administrative or judicial superior. In the latter case, the superior may amend the decision or direct the original decision-maker to reconsider it. In some situations the victim may also be provided with the opportunity of directly circumventing the original decision.

For example, in the important decision of whether to prosecute, where the prosecutor may decide (when permitted to do so by the respective legal system) that there is no public interest in proceeding against a suspect, or that there is insufficient evidence to do so, states have varying means of redress available to the victim. The victim may request that a superior of the prosecutor review the decision, or that a court do so (in the Federal Republic of Germany, for example, the victim may petition first a superior of the prosecutor and then a court). The victim may also bring a case directly to court. In France, for example, if the court on the motion of the victim decides that the case should be proceeded with, the prosecutor is obliged to take over the prosecution. Finally, in some States, such as Finland and the United Kingdom, the victim may bring a private prosecution for all types of crimes. In some other States, this right is limited to certain petty crimes.

The use of an ombudsman to insure accountability: Several States have an ombudsman to whom complaints may be lodged about the action or omission of civil servants and government authorities. In the Netherlands, a 1985 case dealt with by the ombudsman involved a victim who complained that he had not been informed of the criminal trial of the offender responsible for the victim's loss, and was consequently unable to participate as a *partie civile*. The Ombudsman ruled that the Ministry of Justice should compensate the victim for the losses from the crime. The Ombudsman thus created a new channel of reparation, and established a new mechanism of ensuring accountability.

Definition of redress: Redress includes such matters as financial reparation and the public acknowledgment (through the criminal justice process) of the wrong done to the victim, to the extent that these forms of redress are provided for by the laws of a State. This paragraph does not specify what forms of redress the laws should provide. In some jurisdictions there are strong reservations about permitting the victim the opportunity to have the crime condemned, if this is in conflict with the fundamental goals of criminal policy, such as the need to avoid stigmatization of the offender.

United Nations Declaration

5. Judicial and administrative mechanisms should be established and strengthened where necessary to enable victims to obtain redress through formal or informal procedures that are expeditious, fair, inexpensive and accessible. Victims should be informed of their rights in seeking redress through such mechanisms.

Implementation Principles to § 5

5.1. Where appropriate, the victim should be provided with a choice of proceeding with criminal, administrative, civil, or informal measures. Particular attention should be paid to establishing or expanding the possibility of combining civil claims with criminal proceedings.

5.2. States should provide nonresidents alleging victimization with access to the courts and the necessary assistance.

Commentary to § 5

The choice between criminal, civil, and other types of proceedings: The usual formal mechanism through which criminal victimization is dealt with by society is the criminal justice process. Many States allow for the determination of civil claims in criminal proceedings, for example, through the "*partie civile*", system, "adhesion proceedings", or similar mechanisms. Such a combination of civil and criminal proceedings has several benefits to the victim and the State, ranging from procedural economy to the fact that the presentation of the issues can to a large extent be left to the public prosecutor. Constituting oneself as a party to the criminal proceedings, even if only in connection with the presentation of a civil claim, may provide the victim with such rights as the right to be informed of the different stages of the proceedings and of what action has been taken.

For some crimes, and in particular where the victim and the offender has an existing social relationship, the avoidance of the possible stigmatizing effect of criminal prosecution may involve benefits to both the victim and the offender. In particular, the use of informal procedures has been considered by many to provide a number of benefits over formal procedures. In informal procedures, the two parties immediately concerned with the crime can generally take an active part in deciding on the proper outcome; all underlying circumstances can be considered; and social pressure can often be exerted on the offender to comply with the decision and provide restitution. However, critics of the use of informal procedures (including meditation, arbitration, conciliation, and applied therapeutic techniques) have noted the dangers involved, such as the possible exercise of undue pressure on one or both of the parties.

United Nations Declaration

6. The responsiveness of judicial and administrative processes to the needs of victims should be facilitated by:

(a) Informing victims of their role and the scope, timing and progress of proceedings and of the disposition of their cases, especially where serious crimes are involved and where they have requested such information:

Implementation Principles to §6 (a)

6(a).1. States and voluntary organizations should disseminate information on judicial and administrative processes, through, for example, the publication of brochures outlining the procedures as well as the rights and obligations of victims, and encourage the lodging of complaints of victimization when it occurs, indicating the appropriate recipient of complaints.

6(a).2. States should ensure that judicial and administrative officials provide victims with timely information on procedural and practical issues relevant to their cases, as well as on the scope and relevance of any decisions. Consideration should be given to the designation of a specific agency or official to be responsible for keeping the victim informed, as appropriate, of the progress of the case.

Commentary to § 6 (a)

The initiative for providing information: The responsibility for "informing victims of their role" may be understood as an active obligation of certain officials *sua sponte* or as their passive obligation to respond to inquires made by victims. The Declaration adopts the former interpretation.

It is of particular importance that the information provided be timely, providing the victim with an opportunity to react in an appropriate manner.

Information on procedure and on decisions: The information to be provided to victims may concern procedural matters, such as the general role of the victim in the criminal justice process. Such information may be presented to victims in a booklet or brochure. The information of interest to victims may also include the events and decisions in the particular case.

Designation of responsible agency official: One method of encouraging the provision of information is the designation of a specific agency and, in particular, a specific official responsible for keeping the victim informed. The victim may be informed of the name of the police officer responsible for his or her case. The desk sergeant or another person normally present at the police station may be designated as the contact person for the victim.

The police officer investigating the case may ask the victim if he or she wishes to be kept informed of the progress of the case, and, if so, a notation to this effect is made in the file for the attention of the prosecutor. As long as the case is being dealt with by the police, the police would be responsible for informing the victim of its progress; this responsibility being passed on to the prosecutor along with the file in the case. In some countries, in the case of serious crimes (*e.g.*, rape and homicide), the prosecutor must invite the victim or the family of the victim for a personal discussion, during which the decisions to be made are to be explained.

Providing information on decisions: There may be a statutory obligation requiring the victim to be informed of his or her rights and role and/or of the decisions taken, or the victim may be provided such information on request.

Examples of methods of providing information on procedure: In 1982 the French Ministry of Justice published a book entitled *Guides des droits des victims*. The book was sold at a subsidized price, with part of the proceeds benefitting victim support programmes. The book was written in a simple, easy-to-read style. In several States, brochures have been prepared that outline the criminal justice process as well as the rights and duties of the victim.

United Nations Declaration

(b) Allowing the views and concerns of victims to be presented and considered at appropriate stages of the proceedings where their personal interests are affected, without prejudice to the accused and consistent with the relevant national criminal justice system;

Implementation Principle to § 6 (b)

6(b).1. States should review and, where necessary, improve police and prosecution procedures to ensure that the final judicial or administrative decision-making authority is provided with information on all of the relevant factors surrounding the crime and its impact on the victim.

Commentary to §6 (b)

Understanding of "presentation of views and concerns": The degree to which a victim should be allowed an opportunity to express his or her views and concerns within the criminal justice process has aroused a considerable amount of discussion. This discussion primarily revolves around the issue of whether the victim himself or herself should be allowed an active role, such as the right to be heard at appropriate stages, or whether the views and concerns of the victim are more appropriately presented by other means, such as through the prosecutor. Considerably more research and exchange of experience is needed on the issue. The terms "views and concerns" are in themselves relatively vague. Definitions of their scope could include, for example, views on the losses from or effects of the crime, opinions on what happened and - this is hotly debated in the literature - views of sentence.

The nature of the views and concerns that may be presented: The concern of the victim for restitution from the offenders is widely recognized as legitimate and a matter that should be considered at appropriate stages of the proceedings. Other widely recognized concerns include privacy, safety, and the minimization of inconvenience, matters dealt within subparagraph 6 (d).

There is considerably less agreement on whether the extent of the punishment of the offender, to the extent if it does not consist of restitution as a penal measure, is a legitimate concern of the victim. The involvement of the victim in the determination of punishment may be a factor towards disturbing application of the principles of equality, proportionality, and predictability in the sentencing process. The victim may also become vulnerable to undue pressure from other parties or be subjected to excessive anxiety if he or she is involved in the determination of punishment.

However, there is agreement that the views and concerns of the victim are to be presented only to the extent that (a) this takes place without prejudice to the accused and (b) it is consistent with the relevant national criminal justice system.

The stages of the proceedings: The stage of the proceedings at which the view and concerns of the victim may be presented may be categorized as follows: (a) the investigation and the decision on the prosecution; (b) the trial and the sentencing process; and (c) decisions following conviction, for example, on parole and release from prison.

There appears to be general agreement that the views and concerns of the victim are properly expressed to the police and the prosecutor during stage (a), either personally or though a representative. In respect to the possible release of the suspect on bail as well as the conditions of such release, the victim's concern for his or her safety would appear to be appropriately presented to the prosecutor or to the court.

With regard to stage (b), there appears to be general agreement that the views and concerns of the victim on restitution can properly be presented to the court. Less agreement exists on whether the views and concerns of the victim should be presented to the court when it is deciding on a particular sentence where restitution is not involved and the prosecution has been pursued by the State. It is the practise in some States for the victim to have the right to appear before the court in order to convey the impact of the crime, and even argue for a certain sentence. This is in particular possible in those States in which the victim has some prosecutorial rights, such as the right of subsidiary or private prosecution. Generally, however, the opportunity of the victim to inform the court of the effects of the crime is an indirect one, in that this is done by the prosecutor.

The appropriateness of victim involvement in stage (c) is considerably more contentious, although the terms and conditions of, for example, the release of the offender from prison may be of legitimate interest to the victim, in particular with respect to future contact of the offender with the victim and his or her family.

Research in the United Kingdom has suggested that victims of violent crime expect to be able to present their views on restitution and on various prosecutorial decisions, but that there is little interest in direct involvement in decision-making.

Provisions for special "victim impact statements" and "victim statements of opinion" have been made in the majority of the states of the United States. In South Australia the Attorney General has outlined a Declaration of Victims' Rights. According to item 14 of this document, the victim is entitled to have the full effects of the crime on him or her made known to the sentencing court.

United Nations Declaration

(c) Providing proper assistance to victims throughout the legal process;

Implementation Principles for § 6 (c)

States should:

6(c).1. provide free legal counsel, where appropriate, to victims.

6(c).2. establish special victim-witness assistance programmes. Such programmes might be developed, for example, in connection with the police department, the prosecutor's office, probation offices, or with the support of voluntary agencies and associations.

6(c).3. ensure effective cooperation among the organs of justice, health, mental health, welfare and other services in order to focus attention on the needs of victims in legal proceedings, in particular the victims' need for emotional support throughout them.

Commentary to § 6 (c)

The meaning of "proper assistance": Since social services and assistance to victims are dealt with separately in paragraph 15, subparagraph 6(c) may be understood to be directed primarily towards assistance related to legal proceedings, in other words primarily to legal aid. Such a view, however, would be overly limited. Victims may also need practical and emotional support in connection with their contacts with the legal system.

The providing of legal counsel: Several States have laws on cost-free legal proceedings, on the basis of which parties to the proceedings who are needy may receive legal counsel paid by the State. In India, for example, the terms of reference of the Legal Aid Boards have been widened to include assistance to indigent victims. In many jurisdictions, however, the availability of such counsel is generally tied to the procedural status of the victim: a victim who, for example, serves only as a witness is generally not entitled to such support, nor is the victim generally provided with counsel during the pretrial stage.

Possible sources of support: some countries have experimented with victim/witness programs based on the prosecutors' offices. Other possible sources of support include the probation authorities, such social workers are often present in criminal courts and see all parties requesting help. Voluntary agencies and groups may also be sources of assistance; examples of some of the more widely-based groups are the National Association of Victim Support Schemes (NAVSS) in the United Kingdom, and the "WEISSE Ring" in Australia, the Federal Republic of Germany, and some cantons in Switzerland. There are also groups interested in assisting the victims of particular crimes, such as consumer-related crimes, domestic violence, and sexual violence.

During 1980s Denmark, Norway, and Sweden adopted an institution of "support persons", who are State-paid persons selected by the victim, who can provide, for example, practical, emotional and legal support through the police investigations and court proceedings. This support is primarily intended for the victims of sexual assault.

United Nations Declaration

(d) Taking measures to minimize inconvenience to victims, protect their privacy, when necessary, and ensure their safety, as well as that of their families and witnesses on their behalf, from intimidation and retaliation;

Implementations Principles for §6 (d)

6(d).1. States should develop guidelines for judicial and administrative personnel, in which due consideration is given to the balancing of priorities and needs of the State and the accused against the inconvenience to the interference with the personal interest of the victim, particularly in connection with the investigation of the case, the time and arrangement of the hearings, and the granting of continuances.

6(d).2. States should review their laws and practises with regard to the payment of compensation to victims and witnesses for any expenses necessarily incurred in assisting the authorities in the investigation of the case or its prosecution in court.

6(d).3. States should review their laws and practises, in particular with regard to the rules of evidence, in order to ensure that property belonging to the victim is returned as soon as possible.

6(d).4. States should review their laws and practises with regard to publicity in criminal proceedings in order to reduce its unwarranted negative consequences for the victim. Special attention should be paid to the interest that victims may have in avoiding publication of their names and addresses, intimate details of the crime, or their relation to the offender.

6(d).5. States should review their laws and practises in order to ensure responsiveness to reports of threats, intimidation, or harassment of victims and witnesses. States should consider granting victims and witnesses special protection by the police and under the criminal law.

6(d).6. Special attention should be given to the protection of the victims of, and witnesses to, crimes committed by public officials or other persons acting in an official or quasi-official capacity.

Commentary to 6 (d)

Minimizing inconvenience: Decisions on such matters as the arrangements for police questioning, the date of court hearings, and the granting of continuances are often made in accordance with system priorities and administrative convenience. In such cases less attention may be paid to the practical effect of such decisions on the victim, for example, to his or her difficulties in arranging for time off from work, the care of children, and transportation to and from the police station or court house. All of these considerations need to be taken into account.

The return of property: In many cases the property of the victim (such as stolen property or soiled clothing) is kept by the police for presentation as evidence in court. However, the evidentiary needs could often be attended to by taking photographs or by preparing sworn statements by, for example, the investigating officer. In Turkey, for example, the law states that whenever the investigation is completed, or even earlier in the case of need, any objects unlawfully taken from the victim, placed in safekeeping, or confiscated shall automatically be returned to the victim unless a party to the proceeding raises an objection.

Expenses: Victims, and witnesses in particular, are generally paid only a small amount (if anything at all) for their time and expense in attending proceedings. Any expenses involved in being questioned by the police are rarely reimbursed. All necessary expenses incurred by the victim should be paid by the State, pending the determination of guilt and the responsibility for costs.

Waiting time: Victims and witnesses are often called to court at the beginning of the court session, despite the fact that, on the basis of practise, an educated guess could be made regarding the time at which the trial in question will actually begin, and whether or not the testimony of the victim or witness will be required on that day. Judges and prosecutors should consider the actual need for summoning victims and witnesses, as well as the interests of the victims and witnesses in being present just to follow the proceedings. In the event that the victims or witnesses are to be present for an extended duration, arrangements should be made for sustenance, child care facilities, and other conveniences.

The protection of privacy: This involves the issue of whether or not photographs and the names and addresses of victims may be published by the media, and whether or not the names of the parties should be posted on court notice boards. The need to protect privacy must be weighed against the principles that the criminal justice process should operate in the open and that freedom of the press should be protected.

In camera proceedings: Trials are normally public proceedings. However, the possibility of *in camera* proceedings generally exists, for example, in the interest of the confidentiality of certain types of intimate information or to protect moral values.

The special protection of certain groups of victims: In several States special attention is given to the need for privacy of victims of sexual assault. For example, publication of details that may lead to the identification of a rape victim is not permitted in the United Kingdom, Canada, or the Netherlands. In the Netherlands the victim of rape may be heard by the investigating judge in private and then does not need to testify in the public hearing.

In several States the judges may remove an abusive defendant or a defendant whose presence clearly causes anxiety to the victim or witness for the duration of his or her testimony. In such cases the testimony is then read to the defendant.

Ensuring safety: Victims, as all members of the community, are entitled to the protection of society against violence and threats. Victims, however, may have special fears, arising, for example, from the uncertainty regarding whether or not the suspect has been released on bail.

Consideration should be given to the special criminalization of the intimidation or harassment of victims and witnesses, as has been done in some States.

In South Australia, the addresses of victims and witnesses are not included in depositions made available to the accused before or at committal proceedings. Victims are not required to state their addresses when being sworn as witnesses in court.

One way in which victims and witnesses can be protected from intimidation while waiting in court is through the arrangement of separate waiting room facilities, so that they do not come into undue contact with the suspect, his or her relatives, or acquaintances.

United Nations Declaration

(e) Avoiding unnecessary delay in the disposition of cases and the execution of orders or decrees granting awards to victims.

Implementation Principles for § 6 (e)

States should:

6(e).1. prepare guidelines on the expeditious handling of cases by judicial and administrative personnel, without prejudice to the rights of the defendant.

6(e).2. review their laws and practises in order to facilitate the collection of awards granted to victims, for example, by assisting victims in the execution of orders or decrees granting such awards and by granting such awards priority over fines and other payments to be made by the offender to the State.

United Nations Declaration

7. Informal mechanisms for the resolution of disputes, including mediation, arbitration, and customary justice or indigenous practises, should be utilized where appropriate to facilitate conciliation and redress for victims.

Implementation Principles for § 7

States should:

7.1. encourage community efforts to resolve disputes in a manner that facilitates redress and conciliation for the victim.

7.2. encourage community efforts to prevent, discover, disclose, and remedy victimization.

Commentary to § 7

China has pioneered the use of non-court dispute settlement mechanisms including mediation and arbitration. Several Western European countries, South Australia and some North American jurisdictions have demonstrated considerable interest in mediation and conciliation programmes. Several experimental programmes are being carried out. The programmes usually involve only a limited number of cases and the results have been mixed. Among the difficulties are securing the support of authorities and the interest of the victims. Among the benefits are the potentially greater degree of victim satisfaction with the outcome than is the case in the criminal justice process, and the potential rehabilitative effects on the offender.

In several Socialist States social courts both in residential areas and in places of employment deal with a range of petty crimes and conflicts. In some States lower court judges must refer certain crimes to such social courts for possible resolution. In the Federal Republic of Germany the institution of the "Schiedsmann" (mediator) fulfills a similar function, as does the "Panchayat" system in India.

Restitution

United Nations Declaration	8. Offenders or third parties responsible for their behaviour should, where appropriate, make fair restitution to victims, their families or dependents. Such restitution should include the return of property or payment for the harm or loss suffered, reimbursement of expenses incurred as a result of the victimization, the provision of service and the restoration of rights;

Implementation Principles for § 8

States should:

8.1. review their laws and practises in order to facilitate early restitution from the offender, for example, by providing that the payment of restitution is to be considered a mitigating factor in sentencing. In determining the amount and conditions of restitution, the ability of the offender to pay should be taken into consideration.

8.2. adopt and strengthen measures for seizing the assets of persons found responsible or victimization for purposes of restitution to the victims.

Commentary to § 8

Desirability of restitution: For many victims restitution for the harm caused by the crime is of primary importance. Many people also believe that the ends of justice demand that if reparation is to be made it should be made by the offender. This is, indeed, the cornerstone of many traditional systems of justice. The Declaration underlines the priority of restitution from the offender over, for example, compensation from the State. However, there may be cases in which the victim is reluctant to accept restitution from the offender, in particular if the restitution is to be paid in periodic payments, where each payment reminds the victim of the harm caused. Difficulties in obtaining restitution may also effectively bar recovery or make recovery a very difficult and drawn out process.

The definition of restitution: "Fair restitution" can be understood in relation to three aspects. The first is the harm suffered by victim: restitution should fairly cover the harm and be neither unreasonably small or large. It should also be fair in relation to the means of the offender and of the victim, which involves a danger of inequitable treatment of otherwise similar cases. Where the respective needs of the victim and the offender are in conflict, the question arises of which should have priority.

Intangible damages: The restitution to which the victim is generally deemed to be entitled includes at least out-of-pocket expenses, for example, for repairs and medical treatment. There is greater diversity among different States on whether the victim is also entitled to payment for pain and suffering and for other intangible harm.

The definition of the provision of services: Some States have experimented with "creative restitution" or "community service", in which the offender provides services directly to the victim (*e.g.*, by repairing the damage or working for the victim) or to the community (*e.g.*, by working on charitable projects).

Facilitation of early restitution: In many States further measures against the offender may be waived under various conditions. One condition, used to a varying extent by the police, prosecutors, and the courts, is that the offender provide restitution to the victim for his or her loss. Because of the difficult human rights issues involved (*e.g.*, the danger that an innocent person may be pressured into making restitution), it is the general practise that this condition be imposed only when the evidence of guilt is clear, as when the suspect admits the crime.

For example, in the Netherlands the prosecutor may ask for the partially suspended fine, which is calculated at the amount of the victim's loss plus twenty percent, on the condition that the victim receives restitution. Thus, the offender must choose between making restitution or paying an even heavier fine.

Another means of promoting early restitution is by taking it into consideration in sentence mitigation. The laws of several countries make specific reference to this.

Presentation of civil claims in civil court proceedings: the possibility of suing an offender in civil court for damages appears to be universal. It also appears, however, that such civil proceedings, although they avoid the stigmatizing effects of criminal proceedings and have more relaxed rules of evidence that favour the plaintiff, may have the disadvantage of being lengthy, complex, and expensive. Furthermore, enforcement of a civil judgment is often dependent solely on the initiative of the victim.

Presentation of civil claims in criminal proceedings: The presentation of civil claims in criminal proceedings, which is a very common feature of systems based on the Continental European and Socialist models, offers the victim several benefits. The proof of the guilt of the offender, as well as the arrangement of the practical details (such as summoning the offender and the witnesses) is generally handled by the prosecutor. In several States the victim may also call on the prosecutor to present the civil claim. This possibility exists, for example in several Socialist States and in the Nordic countries. The mechanisms include the *partie civile* process in, for example, France and Italy, and adhesion proceedings in central and northern Europe.

Difficulties with adhesion proceedings: In some states the courts have proved reluctant to use adhesion proceedings. One of the reasons for this may be the fear that the consideration of civil claims would unduly delay and complicate the criminal proceedings, in particular where the claims are complex or where the civil claims refer to injury or losses the extent of which will not become clear for some time.

Collection of information on loss or harm: One of the practical difficulties facing the victim in presenting a civil claim in criminal proceedings is ascertaining the proper procedure. This difficulty could be alleviated if the criminal justice system actively seeks information on the loss or harm and assists the victim in the presentation of the claim.

Mechanisms for the collection of restitution: Legal means generally exist, in particular through civil proceedings, for the victim to obtain an award of damages. Enforcement of the award, however, often proves difficult. In England the law provides that if a court wishes to impose both a fine and restitution (which is known in the United Kingdom as a "compensation order") but the offender apparently lacks the means to pay both, the court shall issue a compensation order only. In Scotland, the law provides that where both a fine and a "compensation order" have been imposed on an offender for the same crime or for different crimes in the same proceedings, the enforcement of the "compensation order" shall take precedence.

In Switzerland, the law allows the judge to turn over to the victim the proceeds of any fine, bail, or sale of a confiscated object if the victim has suffered considerable harm from the crime and is reduced to a state of need, and it appears that the offender will not repair the damage he has caused through the crime.

United Nations Declaration

9. Governments should review their practises, regulations and laws to consider restitution as an available sentencing option in criminal cases, in addition to other criminal sanctions.

Commentary to § 9

The use of restitution as a supplement to or replacement for punishment, or indeed as punishment itself, is receiving increasing attention. Its possible rehabilitative and deterrent effects are still being debated. There is considerably wider agreement on its reparative effect.

The idea of restitution as a sentencing option has generally been regarded with great favour, especially at a time when many States are in the midst of what is known as a "sentencing crisis" in which effective alternatives are being sought. Certain problems have been noted. For example, the use of restitution may be in conflict with the principles of equality and proportionality in sentencing, in particular when it is considered that offenders have different means and that only some crimes lead to harm or damages for which restitution can be paid.

Despite its inherent difficulties, restitution seems a particularly attractive sentencing option in dealing with petty offences in which the extent of the damages can be readily assessed.

"Compensation orders": In some States, such as Cyprus, England, Scotland, and Wales, in which there has traditionally been a sharp distinction between civil and criminal proceedings, the criminal courts are empowered to issue a "compensation order". Moreover, in certain other States in which civil claims can be presented in criminal proceedings (e.g., the German Democratic Republic, Poland, Portugal, and the Union of Soviet Socialist Republics) the criminal court may issue such an order even if the victim does not present a claim.

United Nations Declaration

10. In cases of substantial harm to the environment, restitution, if ordered, should include, as far as possible, restoration of the environment, reconstruction of the infrastructure, replacement of community facilities and reimbursement of the expenses of relocation, whenever such harm results in the dislocation of a community.

Implementation Principles for § 10

10.1. States should review their laws and practises to ensure that restitution covers all of the harm arising from the crime, and that, to the extent possible, all victims obtain restitution for the harm that they have suffered as a result of the crime.

United Nations Declaration

11. Where public officials or other agents acting in an official or quasi-officials capacity have violated national criminal laws, the victim should receive restitution from the State whose officials or agents were responsible for the harm inflicted. In cases where the Government under whose authority the victimizing act or omission occurred is no longer in existence, the State or Government successor in title should provide restitution to the victims.

Implementation Principles for § 11

11.1. When there is reasonable ground to believe that a public official or other person acting in an official or quasi-official capacity has violated national criminal law resulting in harm to a victim, the competent authorities should conduct a prompt and impartial investigation as a basis for a decision on restitution.

11.2. States should review their laws and practises regarding State liability for the acts of public officials and agents.

11.3. In cases where amnesty or like measures have been granted to wrongdoers, this shall not impair the right of victims to access to justice, restitution, compensation and assistance.

Compensation

United Nations Declaration

12. When compensation is not fully available from the offender or other sources, States should endeavour to provide financial compensation to:

(a) Victims who have sustained significant bodily injury or impairment of physical or mental health as a result of serious crimes;

(b) The family, in particular dependents of persons who have died or become physically or mentally incapacitated as a result of such victimization.

Implementation Principles of § 12

States should:

12.1. review their laws and practises regarding their compensation of the victim in cases in which restitution is not fully available from the offender or other sources, such as private insurance. Such compensation may be provided either within the framework of general programmes of national insurance and welfare or through special compensation programmes covering the victims of crime.

12.2. promote public awareness of availability of State compensation, for example, throughout the preparation of guidelines for judicial and administrative personnel on the information to be provided to victims. Particular attention should be given to informing victims of such compensation programmes soon after the victimization.

12.3. adhere to international and regional instruments on State compensation.

Commentary to § 12

Offenders unable to pay restitution: Research in various States indicates that only a small proportion of victims entitled to restitution actually obtain it from the offender, as the offender often remains unidentified or unapprehended or is unable to pay the restitution.

This fact has encouraged various States to create programmes for the compensation of victims by the State. It has also been noted in many States that the victims of similar misfortunes, such as traffic and industrial accidents, are often guaranteed compensation by the State. The State compensation schemes for the victims of crimes, to which the victims or their dependents may apply when no restitution is forthcoming from the offender or third parties, generally provide compensation for medical expenses, lost income, and, in certain situations, for loss of property.

Rationale: The provision of compensation to the victim by the State can be justified in a number of ways. The most widely accepted principle appears to be that of "social solidarity and equity."

Models: There are several models for State compensation programmes. In many states medical care is available to all citizens, either at no cost or at a minimal cost, regardless of the source of the need for the care. Victims of crime may take advantage of such programmes. Such basic schemes, however, may often prove to be insufficient for the victims of crime, who may also bear, for example, loss of earnings and pain and suffering.

The Council of Europe has adopted a Convention on the Compensation of Victims of Violent Crimes in order to introduce and develop such specific programmes (opened for signature on 24 November 1983). This Convention attempts to set minimum standards and ensure international cooperation. After the Convention enters into force States outside the Council of Europe will be invited to accede to it. It may also be used as a model for regional conventions in other parts of the world.

The New Zealand programme, one of the earliest national programmes has been most often cited as an example for other States to follow. It provides victims of crime with the same level of awards as the victims of industrial and automobile accidents. Similar programmes exist in other jurisdictions. Programmes such as that in Quebec, Canada, provide, in addition, emergency payments pending the final determination of the award. In some jurisdictions, such as the Federal Republic of Germany and the United Kingdom, victims of crime are provided with basic levels of compensation that are not available to other victims.

Some programmes also provide for payments for certain property losses. For example, in Finland, France, and Sweden property losses can be reimbursed on a discretionary basis. In Finland and Sweden payments are also made for property losses arising from crimes committed by escaped prisoners. In the United States of America some jurisdictions waive sovereign immunity for crimes committed by persons released, through gross negligence, by prisons or mental hospitals. Some State schemes have been designed to cover the needs of victims of terrorism.

Should a State wish to introduce or develop a compensation programme it might study the commentary to the Council of Europe Convention, which describes the philosophy behind the programmes, their scope and provisions, and ways of ensuring proper access to them.

Special attention should be devoted to the following issues:

(i) how victims are to be informed about the programme. The role of the responding police officer in informing victims of the programme and recommending ways of obtaining assistance is crucial, as this official is often the victim's main contact with community services.

(ii) the definition of the scope of coverage. References in the programmes to "significant injury" may, for example, refer to injuries requiring medical and/or psychological care.

(iii) the extent of territorial coverage. As many persons visit, immigrate to, or work in States of which they are not citizens, it may be necessary for States to provide compensation to all victims of crime occurring within their boundaries, regardless of the State of citizenship of the offender or the victim.

United Nations Declaration

13. The establishment, strengthening and expansion of national funds for compensation to victims should be encouraged. Where appropriate, other funds may also be established for this purpose, including those cases where the State of which the victim is a national is not in a position to compensate the victim for the harm.

Implementation Principle for § 13

13.1. States should be encouraged to contribute to regional and international intergovernmental and nongovernmental funds for the compensation of and assistance to victims.

Commentary to § 13

Although the costs of compensation programmes are generally insignificant in relation to expenditures on the criminal justice system, there are a number of ways of easing the financial burden on the State.

Some States use monies raised in fines, civil surcharges, or seized from offenders to fund compensation schemes.

States could provide fiscal exemption to donors so that these persons would be encouraged to contribute to such funds.

International funds may need to be created to deal with problems of refugees and displaced persons and similar cases where the State of which the victims are nationals is unwilling or unable to provide compensation.

Assistance

United Nations Declaration

14. Victims should receive the necessary material, medical, psychological and social assistance through governmental, voluntary, community-based and indigenous means.

Implementation Principles for § 14

States should:

14.1. encourage the development of means for the identification of the needs and desires of victims, develop services appropriate to those needs and study the effect of various services provided.

14.2. consider the establishment of special crisis intervention services to assist victims.

14.3. encourage the development of programmes designed to identify and help victims in need of services and support (so-called "out-reach" program). These programmes should address both the short-term and long-term effects of victimization.

14.4. review their basic medical, psychological, and social services to ensure that they are responsive to the needs of victims. Guidelines should be developed regarding how these services should deal with victims, for example, in structuring their responses and their referrals to other services. Training should be provided to persons coming into contact with victims such as medical, hospital, psychological, and social service, police, prosecution, judicial, and correctional personnel, the clergy and the media.

14.5. encourage the development of specialized and voluntary services for assistance to victims including self-help groups, either in connection with judicial and administrative agencies or as independent services.

14.6. make special efforts to provide information and services relating to the prevention of crime.

Commentary to § 14

Surveys of the needs of victims reveal that victims require assistance in recovering from loss, injury, and emotional trauma as well as help in participating in the criminal justice system and in obtaining social services. They often need practical and emotional support. Often, they also request information on how to prevent further victimization, both during the court proceedings and, in general, in the community.

General and specific services: In many States victims use basic social, health, mental health, religious and criminal justice system services for many of their victimization-related needs. Often these services are well equipped for their general purposes, but are not organized in ways that are sensitive to the specific needs of victims. Specialized training within the services and interdisciplinary shared work can be particularly beneficial both in improving services and in identifying the appropriate referrals.

In many States primary health care, family and community groups provide support for victims. The World Health Organization has expressed an interest in encouraging this type of support.

In some States specialized services have been established for victims. These are often voluntary and do not have a permanent financial basis. Such service include crisis centers or shelters for women who have been battered or sexually assaulted, victim assistance services in police departments, and a variety of victim support programmes. The programmes in the United Kingdom are being coordinated in order to work out joint policies for programmes concerned with the aged, probation, social services, citizen advice, police, and lawyers.

Such specialized programmes seek to provide counselling and information by meeting with the victims or responding to telephone calls. Some of the programmes provide treatment for victims suffering from severe emotional trauma, provide an accompanying person in court, and, in some cases, mediation on behalf of the victim. The United Kingdom model also seeks to offer recognition and reassurance to the victims of burglaries and personal thefts in order to prevent dissatisfaction and alienation from the community as a whole and from the criminal justice system in particular.

Prevention: Up to the present, prevention services to reduce victimization have been relatively limited. However, many of the programmes for police and social worker intervention in family violence also seek to prevent recurrences. In addition, some of the police-based victim services programmes provide victims with basic information on measures that they can take in order to protect themselves and their property. Agencies for the protection of consumers provide another example of assistance with prevention.

Community agencies: States should encourage private organizations, voluntary agencies, and community-based and self-help groups to improve their services by providing funding, training and support for their efforts. Methods of informing victims about such services or of facilitating "outreach" should be developed by the police and other criminal justice agencies.

Relationships among organizations:

There is a special need to promote the exchange of experiences and ideas among organizations working with victims. National associations such as those in the Federal Republic of Germany, France, and the Netherlands, the United Kingdom, and the United States disseminate publications and guidelines, promote legislation, and arrange conferences that could be useful to States planning to initiate such programmes.

Funding for such services promoting and providing assistance could be raised through private contributions and general revenues. Some jurisdictions in North America are using fines and taxes on offenders for these purposes.

United Nations Declaration

15. Victims should be informed of the availability of health and social services and other relevant assistance, and be readily afforded access to them.

Implementation Principle for § 15

15.1. States should promote the widest possible dissemination of information on available services and assistance. States should also encourage the activity of voluntary and community groups in this area.

Commentary to § 15

Information: Booklets and brochures have been introduced in several States in order to explain the types of services available to victims.

Since the police are generally the first officials to be contacted by victims, and the police have the means to communicate with central agencies, they can easily provide the victim with appropriate information. Guidelines have been developed in some jurisdictions on how the police can manage both their enforcement and investigative duties at the same time that they provide this vital assistance to victims.

Linking victims to services: "Outreach" to victims has been shown to be a necessity in a number of different States, as victims may not see themselves as being in need or find the confidence to turn to the authorities or services. Research has also indicated that the stereotypes concerning which victims need what kind of assistance is misleading. Effective outreach for immediate needs can be provided by the police alerting the services as soon as possible after a crime is reported, thus allowing the services to determine to whom outreach should be made. This requires a close relationship between the services and the police.

Effective means need to be developed to increase community and professional awareness of the long-term effects of victimization.

Self-referral (where the victim himself or herself turns to the service) works well with specialized agencies that focus on specific types of crime or issues with which victims easily identify. Self-referral can co-exist with outreach programmes.

United Nations Declaration

16. Police, justice, health, social service and other personnel concerned should receive training to sensitize them to the needs of victims, and guidelines to ensure proper and prompt aid.

Implementation Principles for § 16

States should:

16.1. review the general training of all judicial and administrative personnel who come into contact with victims in order to ensure that they receive training sensitizing them to the needs and rights of victims, and in order to promote cooperation among the various services concerned.

16.2. in particular review the special training of those who deal with the victims of serious crimes of violence and of those who deal with victims in a crisis situation.

16.3. promote the implementation of guidelines for the treatment of victims by reviewing practises to ensure that all personnel concerned adhere to them.

Commentary to § 16

Multi-service delivery: Many different professionals work with victims. In addition to the professionals specifically named in the Declaration, mention may be made of psychologists, the clergy and members of the media. Each needs to be trained to know how to react to the effects of victimization, how to react to victims and what information to provide to them. Each has much to contribute, and share, and reciprocal training may be beneficial.

Some jurisdictions have developed protocols that specify how various professionals should balance their other responsibilities with those of responding to the victim. For example, judges in the United States of America have drafted recommended judicial practises. The United States National Organization for Victim Assistance has developed a variety of protocols for police, prosecutors, probation officers, and others.

At the present time few curricula provide training on the initial response to victims. Victim assistance and information could be made part of the basic qualifying examinations for police, justice, and social service personnel. In addition, special immediate and long-term needs of victims should also be part of the regular curricula for the training of health professionals such as physicians, psychiatrists, psychologists, social workers, nurses, and of the clergy and members of the media.

Continuing education may also be helpful. As an example, seminars could be organized for judges and senior police personnel for discussion of these issues and to motivate them to become better informed and respond in an improved manner to the needs of victims. Such seminars could also deal with the benefits offered by the many victim-specific services, which are already involved in many areas of professional training in North America and the United Kingdom.

Development of training programmes: Attention should be given in the training of practitioners to the psychology of grief and loss, not only of the immediate victim, but also of members of his or her family. Outside experts should be used, where appropriate, in training professionals in existing services.

In the development of training programmes, attention should be given to general training of all personnel working with victims and post-traumatic stress. Training programmes should take account of demographic factors and should clearly address the widely-held, but erroneous, assumption that most of those effected by trauma and sudden loss can rely on close family members or neighbours for emotional support, and investigate the best strategies to rectify this situation which is often termed a "conspiracy of silence."

United Nations Declaration

17. In providing services and assistance to victims, attention should be given to those who have special needs because of the nature of the harm inflicted or because of

factors such as those mentioned in paragraph 3 above.

Implementation Principles to § 17

17.1. Victims who are more vulnerable to certain effects of crime because they are, for example, very young, old or infirm, should receive special attention. Similarly, attention should be given to the economically disadvantaged and to those who have been the victims of especially traumatic crimes.

17.2. The nature of these special needs should be determined in a systematic manner, for example, through surveys and investigations by interagency working groups.

Commentary to § 17

Special programmes: Several States have established special programmes for more vulnerable groups of victims. For example, the sexual assault crisis centres and shelters for battered women try to respond to the unique needs of these victims. Special programmes have been developed for child victims of sexual assault. Self-help or support groups could also play a useful role, particularly in the case of major crimes that are likely to affect future life and attitudes.

Although the need for special programmes is being increasingly recognized, few States have established programmes for the aged or for those suffering from a very traumatic crime. However, many countries have major national agencies for groups such as the elderly and children. These agencies should be more involved in meetings on victim treatment in order to encourage better collaboration and the exchange of ideas. A major programme for the elderly has been developed in the United Kingdom. This programme assists in the development of victim support programmes, provides funds, produces brochures, and sponsors research on the effects of crime on the elderly, the fear of crime, and crime prevention. Another agency in the United Kingdom deals with young children, taking prosecutions to court and training professionals in such issues as child abuse and incest. A number of local agencies and a hot line in London assist victims of racial harassment; these are particularly intended for Asian victims who suffer repeated harassment in their neighbourhoods.

Measures for Implementation with Regard to Victims of Abuse of Power

B. Victims of Abuse of Power

United Nations Declaration

18. "Victims" means persons who, individually or collectively, have suffered harm, including physical or mental injury, emotional suffering, economic loss or through acts or omissions that do not yet constitute violations of national criminal laws but of internationally recognized norms relating to human rights.

Implementation Principles for § 18

18.1. States should review their law and practises with a view to improving the position of victims of violations of internationally recognized norms relating to human rights, including norms of international law protecting the life, liberty, personal security, and well being of individuals and groups under Article 38 of the Statute of the International Court of Justice. The sources of international law under Article 38 are international conventions, whether general or particular, establishing rules expressly recognized by the contesting States; international custom, as evidence of a general practise accepted as law; the general principles of law recognized by "civilized nations"; and subject to article 59 of the Statute of the International Court of Justice, judicial decisions and the teachings of the most highly qualified publicists of the various nations, as subsidiary means for the determination of rules of law.

18.2. In reviewing their laws and practises, States should particularly provide for victims of violations of, *inter alia*:

(a) the Universal Declaration of Human Rights;

(b) the International Covenant on Civil and Political Rights;

(c) the International Covenant on Economic, Social and Cultural Rights;

(d) the Convention on the Prevention and Punishment of the Crime of Genocide;

(e) the International Convention on the Suppression and Punishment of the Crime of *Apartheid*;

(f) the Slavery and Slave Related Practises Conventions;

(g) the Standard Minimum Rules for the Treatment of Prisoners;

(h) the Convention on the Protection of All Persons from Being Subjected to Torture and Other Cruel, Inhuman or Degrading Treatment or Punishment;

(i) the Code of Conduct for Law Enforcement Officials;

(j) the Principles of Medical Ethics Relevant to the Role of Health Personnel, Particularly Physicians, in the Protection of Prisoners and Detainees against Torture and Other Cruel, Inhuman or Degrading Treatment or Punishment, and the Guiding Principles for Crime Prevention and Criminal Justice in the context of Development and a New International Economic Order;

(k) the Conventions against the Seizure of Diplomats and Taking of Hostages;

(l) Crimes against Humanity;

(m) Crimes against Peace; and

(n) War Crimes.

United Nations Declaration

19. States should consider incorporating into the national law norms proscribing abuses of power and providing remedies to victims of such abuses. In particular, such remedies should include restitution and/or compensation, and necessary material, medical, psychological and social assistance and support.

Implementation Principles for § 19

States should:

19.1. enact legislation criminalizing or otherwise proscribing violations of internationally recognized norms relating to human rights;

19.2. enact legislation guaranteeing to victims of abuse of power the rights conferred upon victims of crime under Part A hereof, namely Access to Justice and Fair Treatment, Restitution, Compensation and Assistance.

19.3. ratify international human rights treaties, standards, and norms and those international criminal law conventions which embody the protection of individual and collective human rights and incorporate them into national laws and State practise; and

19.4. ensure that legal or disciplinary action is taken against persons who fail to comply with legislation or regulations governing arrest, searches, interrogations, and detention.

Commentary to § 19

Since victims of abuse of power have often been deprived of access to justice, special efforts should be made to fully provide such access notwithstanding the possible unavailability of destruction of evidence, including the possibility of class actions and/or other avenues of collective redress. The provision of restitution/compensation is a key means of furnishing symbolic redress as well as material relief for such victims. Among the few precedents which exist in this respect is restitution policy for the victims of National Socialist persecution (*See* U.N. Doc. A/CONF. 121/6/39-41).

Victims of abuse of power often face hardships additional to those faced by victims of crime, e.g. isolation and ostracism during and subsequent to their victimization because of public fear. They are thus in particular need of systems of social support as well as specialized treatment (e.g., for victims of torture).

United Nations Declaration

20. States should consider negotiating multilateral international treaties relating to victims as defined in paragraph 18.

Implementation Principles for § 20

States should:

20.1. ratify regional and international conventions on violations of internationally recognized norms relating to human rights and incorporate these norms into national legislation and administrative regulations and practises.

20.2. submit reports when requested to international and regional intergovernmental and nongovernmental organizations concerning the extent of violations of internationally recognized norms relating to human rights and the effectiveness of various means of preventing them and aiding victims.

United Nations Declaration

21. States should periodically review existing legislation and practises to ensure their

responsiveness to changing circumstances, should enact and enforce, if necessary, legislation proscribing acts that constitute serious abuses of political or economic power, as well as promoting policies and mechanisms for the prevention of such acts, and should develop and make readily available appropriate rights and remedies for victims of such acts.

Implementation Principle to § 21

21.1. States should institute reporting procedures in respect of victims of abuse of power pursuant to treaty obligations or requests of United Nations bodies.

Commentary to § 21

The periodic review should include further exploration of the concept of abuse of power and the possible broadening of that concept beyond the matters covered in human rights treaties, as envisaged by the General Assembly resolution, operative paragraph 4 (b).

* * *

3. Protection of the Human Rights of Victims of Crime and Abuse of Power

Concerned that crime and victimization continue to pose serious problems, affecting both individuals and entire groups and often transcending national frontiers,

Emphasizing the need for preventive action and measures for the fair and humane treatment of victims, whose needs have often been ignored,

Recognizing the importance of the Declaration of Basic Principles of Justice for Victims of Crime and Abuse of Power,[3] which provides standards and guidelines for redress and assistance to such victims and which needs to be widely disseminated and applied in practise,

---

[3]G.A. Res. 40/34, annex.

Welcoming the efforts made to date to develop appropriate means for the implementation of the Declaration, and to further its application at the national, regional and international levels,

Stressing the need for social solidarity, which requires the establishment of close links between members of society to guarantee social peace and respect for the rights of victims, as well as the need to provide adequate mechanisms and measures through which redress and assistance for victims can be provided nationally, regionally and internationally,

Considering the key role of law enforcement agencies, prosecutors, lawyers and the judiciary in the implementation of the Declaration,

Bearing in mind the relevant provisions of the Convention against Torture and Other Cruel, Inhuman or Degrading Treatment or Punishment adopted by the General Assembly in resolution 39/46 of 10 December 1984,

Bearing in mind also the work being carried out by the Committee on Crime Prevention and Control,

Recalling the Cairo Declaration on Law Enforcement and the Human Rights of Victims, adopted by the International Symposium held at Cairo from 22 to 25 January 1989,

Recalling also the report prepared by the ad hoc committee of experts at the International Institute of Higher Studies in Criminal Sciences, held at Syracuse, Italy in May 1986, as revised by a colloquium of leading non-governmental organizations active in crime prevention, criminal justice and the treatment of offenders and victims, held at Milan, Italy, in November-December 1987,

Recalling further the recommendation of the Economic and Social Council in its resolution 1990/22 of 24 May 1990 that Member States and the United Nations regional and interregional institutes should take the necessary steps to provide professional and other persons dealing with victims with suitable training in issues concerning victims, taking into account the model training curricula developed for this purpose,[4]

1. *Takes note with appreciation* of Economic and Social Council resolutions 1989/57 of 24 May 1989 and 1990/22;

---

[4]*See* E/AC.57/1990/NGO/3.

2. *Recommends* that, in the implementation of the said resolution, the Committee on Crime Prevention and Control should take into account the important proposals already made by the community of concerned non-governmental organizations;

3. *Calls upon* States to take into account the provisions of the Declaration of Basic Principles of Justice for Victims of Crime and Abuse of Power in framing their national legislation;

4. *Recommends* that Governments should consider the availability of public and social support services for victims of crime and abuse of power and foster culturally appropriate programmes for victim assistance, information and compensation;

5. *Requests* the Secretary-General to make appropriate provisions to study the feasibility of establishing an international fund, within the framework of the United Nations crime prevention and criminal justice programme, for the compensation of, and assistance to, victims of transnational crimes and for the promotion of international research, data collection and dissemination and the establishment of policy guidelines in this respect;

6. *Recommends* that States should prepare training programmes based on the principles of the Declaration, aimed at defining and disseminating the rights of victims of crime and abuse of power, which should be part of the curricula of faculties of law, criminological institutes, law enforcement training centres and judicial colleges;

7. *Calls upon* States to exchange, both at the international and regional levels, information and experiences related to the means used to implement their legal and social provisions concerned with the protection of victims of crime and abuse of power;

8. *Recommends* that the United Nations and other organizations concerned strengthen their technical co-operation activities in order to help Governments to implement the Declaration and other relevant guidelines and to strengthen international co-operation in this respect;

9. *Requests* the Secretary-General to distribute widely the Guide for Practitioners on the Basic Principles of Justice for Victims of Crime and Abuse of

Power[5] and the Measures for Implementation for the Declaration of Basic Principles of Justice for Victims of Crime and Abuse of Power.[6]

* * *

4. Study Concerning the Right to Restitution, Compensation and Rehabilitation for Victims of Gross Violations of Human Rights and Fundamental Freedoms

Preliminary report submitted by Mr. Theo van Boven, Special Rapporteur

I. RELEVANT EXISTING INTERNATIONAL NORMS

A. International human rights norms (global and regional human rights instruments)

9. A number of both universal and regional human rights instruments contain express provisions relating to the right of every individual to an "*effective remedy*" by competent national tribunals for acts violating human rights which are granted to him by the constitution or by law. Such formulation is contained in article 8 of the Universal Declaration of Human Rights. The notion of an "effective remedy" is also included in article 2 (3) (a) of the International Covenant on Civil and Political Rights and in article 6 of the Declaration on the Elimination of All Forms of Racial Discrimination.

10. Some human rights instruments refer to a more particular "*right to be compensated* in accordance with the law" (art. 10 of the American Convention on Human Rights) or the "*right to an adequate compensation*" (art. 21 (2) of the African Charter on Human and Peoples' Rights).

11. Even more specific are the provisions of article 9 (5) of the International Covenant on Civil and Political Rights and of article 5 (5) of the European Convention for the Protection of Human Rights and Fundamental Freedoms which refer to the "*enforceable right to compensation.*" Similarly, the Convention against Torture and Other Cruel, Inhuman or Degrading Treatment or Punishment contains a provision providing for the victim of torture a redress

---

[5]*See* A/CONF.144/20, annex.

[6]E/AC.57/1988/NGO/1.

and "*enforceable right to fair and adequate compensation, including the means for as full rehabilitation as possible*" (art. 14 (1)).

12. In some instruments, a specific provision is contained indicating that compensation is due *in accordance with law* or with *national law* (art. 14 (6) of the International Covenant on Civil and Political Rights and art. 11 of the Declaration on the Protection of All Persons from Being Subjected to Torture and Other Cruel, Inhuman or Degrading Treatment or Punishment).

13. Provisions relating to reparation or satisfaction of damages are contained in the International Convention on the Elimination of All Forms of Racial Discrimination, article 6 of which provides for the right to seek "*just and adequate reparation or satisfaction for any damage suffered.*" The ILO Convention concerning Indigenous and Tribal Peoples in Independent Countries also refers to "*fair compensation for damages*" (art. 15 (2)), to "*compensation in money*" and "*under appropriate guarantees*" (art. 16 (4)), and to full compensation "*for any loss or injury*" (art. 16 (5)).

14. The American Convention on Human Rights speaks of "*compensatory damages*" (art. 68) and provides that the consequences of the measure or situation that constituted the breach of the right or freedom "*be remedied*" and that "*fair compensation be paid to the injured party*" (art. 63 (1)).

15. The Convention on the Right of the Child contains a provision to the effect that State's Parties shall take all appropriate measures to promote "*physical and psychological recovery and social reintegration of a child victim ...*" (art. 39).

B. Norms in the area of crime prevention and criminal justice

16. Substantial provisions relating to various questions of restitution, compensation and assistance for victims of crime are contained in the Declaration of Basic Principles of Justice for Victims of Crime and Abuse of Power (General Assembly resolution 40/34 of 29 November 1985). The Declaration provides for the following:

(a) Victims are entitled to prompt redress for the harm that they have suffered;

(b) They should be informed of their rights in seeking redress;

(c) Offenders or third parties should make fair restitution to victims, their families or dependents. Such restitution should include the return of property or payment for the harm or loss suffered, reimbursement of expenses incurred as a result of the victimization, the provision of services and the restoration of rights;

(d) When compensation is not fully available from the offender or other sources, States should endeavour to provide financial compensation;

(e) Victims should receive the necessary material, medical, psychological and social assistance and support.

The Declaration also provides that Governments should review their practises, regulations and laws to consider restitution as an available sentencing option in criminal cases, in addition to other criminal sanctions (principle 9).

17. The United Nations Standard Minimum Rules for the Administration of Juvenile Justice ("The Beijing Rules") contains a specific provision to the effect that "in order to facilitate the discretionary disposition of juvenile cases, efforts shall be made to provide for community programmes, such as temporary supervision and guidance, restitution, and compensation of victims."

C. International humanitarian law norms

18. Article 3 of the Hague Convention Regarding the Laws and Customs of Land Warfare provides for the obligation of the contracting party to pay indemnity in case of violation of the regulations. Article 41 of the IV Hague Convention also provides for the right to demand an indemnity for the losses sustained in cases of violations of the clauses of the armistice by individuals.

19. The Four Geneva Conventions of 12 August 1949 contain similar articles providing that "No High Contacting Party shall be allowed to absolve itself or any other High Contracting Party of any liability incurred by itself or another High Contracting Party" in respect of grave breaches involving such acts as "willful killing, torture or inhuman treatment, including biological experiments, willfully causing great suffering or serious injury to body or health, and extensive destruction and appropriation of property, not justified by military necessity and carried out unlawfully and wantonly."[7]

---

[7]See articles 50 and 51 of the Geneva Convention for the Amelioration of the Condition of the Wounded and Sick in Armed Forces in the Field; article 51 and 52 of the Geneva Convention for the Amelioration of the Condition of the Wounded, Sick and Shipwrecked Members of Armed Forces at Sea; articles 130 and 131 of the Geneva Convention Relative to the Treatment of Prisoners of War; and articles 147 and 148 of the Geneva Convention Relative to the Protection of Civilian Persons in Time of War.

20. Article 68 of the Geneva Convention to the Treatment of Prisoners of War contains specific provisions with regard to claims for compensation by a prisoner of war.

21. Article 55 of the Geneva Convention Relative to the Protection of Civilian Persons in Time of War provides that the Occupying Power "shall make arrangements to ensure that fair value is paid for any requisitioned goods."

22. Finally, Protocol I (Protocol additional to the Geneva Conventions of 12 August 1949, and Relating to the Protection of Victims of International Armed Conflicts), states in its article 91 that a Party to the conflicts which violates the provisions of the Conventions or of this Protocol "shall ... be liable to pay compensation."

II. THE RIGHT TO RESTITUTION, COMPENSATION AND REHABILITATION UNDER CUSTOMARY INTERNATIONAL LAW

23. The right to restitution, compensation and rehabilitation is intimately linked with the concept of State responsibility. It is interesting to note that the significance of the well-established international law of State responsibility for the international law of human rights has so far received only scant attention. In the following paragraphs, some important aspects of the international law of State responsibility will be highlighted, with a particular focus on the question of reparation. In this regard it is, of course, relevant to refer to the codification effort of the International Law Commission. This Commission has so far adopted 35 draft articles on State responsibility.

24. State responsibility is the obligation of a State to make reparation arising from a failure to comply with an obligation under international law. State responsibility applies in the case of an act or omission in violation of an international legal obligation, attributable to the delinquent State, resulting in injury to the claimant State (*see also* draft article 3, International Law Commission). In the judgement on the Chorzów Factory (Indemnity) Case, the Permanent Court of International Justice ruled:

> "It is a principle of international law, and even a general conception of law, that any breach of an engagement invokes an obligation to make reparation. [...] reparation is the indispensable complement of a failure to apply a convention, and there is no necessity for this to be stated in the convention itself."[8]

---

[8] 1928 P.C.I.J., Series A, No. 17, p. 29.

State responsibility can result from actions directly attributable to the State through its agents (original responsibility) or from actions that only indirectly involve the State (vicarious responsibility).

Reparation

25. The basic principles governing reparations for breaches of international obligations were established by the Permanent Court of International Justice in the Chorzów Factory (Indemnity) Case as follows:

> "The essential principles contained in the actual notion of an illegal act - a principle which seems to be established by international practise and in particular by the decisions of arbitral tribunals - is that reparation must, as far as possible, wipe out all consequences of the illegal act and re-establish the situation which would, in all probability, have existed if that act had not been committed. Restitution in kind, or, if this is not possible, payment of a sum corresponding to the value which a restitution in kind would bear; the award, if need be, of damages for loss sustained which would not be covered by restitution in kind or payment in place of it - such are the principles which should serve to determine the amount of compensation due for an act contrary to international law."[9]

The four main forms of reparation are restitution, indemnity, satisfaction and declaratory judgement.

A. *Restitution*

26. Restitution in kind is designed to re-establish the situation which would have existed if the wrongful act or omission had not taken place, by performance of the obligation which the State failed to discharge: revocation of the unlawful act, return of property wrongfully removed or abstention from further wrongful conduct. The Permanent Court of International Justice implied in its decision in the Chorzów Factory (Indemnity) Case, that restitution is the normal form of reparation and indemnity could only take place if restitution in kind is not possible.

B. *Indemnity*

27. This is in practise the most usual form of reparation. The indemnity should compensate for all damage which results from the unlawful act, including a profit

---

[9]*Id.* at 47.

which would have been possible in the ordinary course of events, but not prospective gains which are highly problematical, too remote or speculative. The basic test is the certainty of the damage. It is not essential that the damage should have already taken place for compensation to be recoverable. The possibility of punitive or exemplary damages is a matter of some debate in international law. It is generally believed, however, that the imposition of such damages would go beyond the jurisdiction conferred on the International Court of Justice and beyond the jurisdiction normally attributed to arbitral tribunals.

C. *Satisfaction*

28. Satisfaction may be defined as any measure which the author of a breach of duty is bound to take under customary law or under an agreement by the parties to a dispute, apart from restitution or compensation. There are three objects of satisfaction which are often cumulative: (a) apologies or other acknowledgement of wrongdoing, e.g., by means of payment of an indemnity; (b) the prosecution and punishment of the individuals concerned; and (c) the taking of measures to prevent a recurrence of the harm. There is no evidence under international law of a rule that provides that satisfaction is alternative to and, on being given, exclusive of a right to compensation for the breach of duty.

D. *Declaratory judgement*

29. A declaratory judgement of a court as to the illegality of the act of the defendant State constitutes in some cases a measure of satisfaction (or reparation in the broad sense). In various instances, the International Court of Justice has been willing to give declaratory judgements, using such formulas as that a State "...is under a duty immediately to cease and refrain from all such acts as may constitute breaches of the foregoing legal obligations."[10]

---

[10]Case Concerning Military and Paramilitary Activities Against Nicaragua, Merits, ICJ Reports of Judgements, Advisory Opinions and Orders (1986), p. 149, para. 12.

K. COMPLAINTS AND REPORTING PROCEDURES

Standard-setting alone will not guarantee the observance of human rights. Specialized bodies, such as the Human Rights Committee, the Committee Against Torture and the Committee on the Elimination of Racial Discrimination, have been established to monitor State compliance with their obligations under the various conventions.

Besides the periodic reporting obligations of State parties, there are procedures for complaints that a State may formulate against the alleged non-compliance of another State. These procedures have not yet been utilized.

Individual complaints procedures are envisaged under the Optional Protocol to the International Covenant on Civil and Political Rights, under article 14 to the International Convention on the Elimination of All Forms of Racial Discrimination and under article 22 of the Convention Against Torture.

The Centre for Human Rights has also issued a useful "Fact Sheet" entitled "Communications Procedures," which is intended to facilitate public understanding of these procedures, so that persons who claim that their rights have been violated can avail themselves of this avenue of international redress, provided, of course, that they have exhausted domestic remedies.

Decisions by the Human Rights Committee, however, are not self-executing. Therefore, the Committee has established a "follow-up" procedure to determine the extent of State compliance with its recommendations.

1. International Covenant on Civil and Political Rights

Article 41

1. A State Party to the present Covenant may at any time declare under this article that it recognizes the competence of the Committee to receive and consider communications to the effect that a State Party claims that another State Party is not fulfilling its obligations under the present Covenant. Communications under this article may be received and considered only if submitted by a State Party which has made a declaration recognizing in regard to itself the competence of the Committee. No communication shall be received by the Committee if it concerns a State Party which has not made such a declaration. Communications received under this article shall be dealt with in accordance with the following procedure:

a. If a State Party to the present Covenant considers that another State Party is not giving effect to the provisions of the present Covenant, it may, by written communication, bring the matter to the attention of that State Party. Within three months after the receipt of the communication, the receiving State shall afford the State which sent the communication an explanation or any other statement in writing clarifying the matter which should include, to the extent possible and pertinent, reference to domestic procedures and remedies taken, pending, or available in the matter;

b. If the matter is not adjusted to the satisfaction of both States Parties concerned within six months after the receipt by the receiving State of the initial communication, either State shall have the right to refer the matter to the Committee, by notice given to the Committee and to the other State;

c. The Committee shall deal with a matter referred to it only after it has ascertained that all available domestic remedies have been invoked and exhausted in the matter, in conformity with the generally recognized principles of international law. This shall not be the rule where the application of the remedies is unreasonably prolonged;

d. The Committee shall hold closed meetings when examining communications under this article;

e. Subject to the provisions of subparagraph (c), the Committee shall make available its good offices to the States Parties concerned with a view to a friendly solution of the matter on the basis of respect for human rights and fundamental freedoms as recognized in the present Covenant;

f. In any matter referred to it, the Committee may call upon the States Parties concerned, referred to in subparagraph (b), to supply any relevant information;

g. The States Parties concerned, referred to in subparagraph (b), shall have the right to be represented when the matter is being considered in the Committee and to make submissions orally and/or in writing;

h. The Committee shall, within twelve months after the date of receipt of notice under subparagraph (b), submit a report:

> (i) If a solution within the terms of subparagraph (e) is reached, the Committee shall confine its report to a brief statement of the facts and of the solution reached;

(ii) If a solution within the terms of subparagraph (e) is not reached, the Committee shall confine its report to a brief statement of the facts; the written submissions and record of the oral submissions made by the States Parties concerned shall be attached to the report.

In every matter, the report shall be communicated to the States Parties concerned.

2. The provisions of this article shall come into force when ten States Parties to the present Covenant have made declarations under paragraph 1 of this article. Such declarations shall be deposited by the States Parties with the Secretary-General of the United Nations, who shall transmit copies thereof to the other States Parties. A declaration may be withdrawn at any time by notification to the Secretary-General. Such a withdrawal shall not prejudice the consideration of any matter which is the subject of a communication already transmitted under this article; no further communication by any State Party shall be received after the notification of withdrawal of the declaration has been received by the Secretary-General, unless the State Party concerned has made a new declaration.

* * *

2. Optional Protocol to the International Covenant on Civil and Political Rights

Article 1

A State Party to the Covenant that becomes a Party to the present Protocol recognizes the competence of the Committee to receive and consider communications from the individuals subject to its jurisdiction who claim to be victims of a violation by the State Party of any of the rights set forth in the Covenant. No communication shall be received by the Committee if it concerns a State Party to the Covenant which is not a Party to the present Protocol.

Article 2

Subject to the provisions of article 1, individuals who claim that any of their rights enumerated in the Covenant have been violated and who have exhausted all available domestic remedies may submit a written communication to the Committee for consideration.

Article 3

The Committee shall consider inadmissible any communication under the present Protocol which is anonymous, or which it considers to be an abuse of the right of submission of such communications or to be incompatible with the provisions of the Covenant.

Article 4

1. Subject to the provisions of article 3, the Committee shall bring any communications submitted to it under the present Protocol to the attention of the State Party to the present Protocol alleged to be violating any provision of the Covenant.

2. Within six months, the receiving State shall submit to the Committee written explanations or statements clarifying the matter and the remedy, if any, that may have been taken by that State.

Article 5

1. The Committee shall consider communications received under the present Protocol in the light of all written information made available to it by the individual and by the State Party concerned.

2. The Committee shall not consider any communication from an individual unless it has ascertained that:

(a) The same matter is not being examined under another procedure of international investigation or settlement;

(b) The individual has exhausted all available domestic remedies.

This shall not be the rule where the application of the remedies is unreasonably prolonged.

3. The Committee shall hold closed meetings when examining communications under the present Protocol.

4. The Committee shall forward its views to the State Party concerned and to the individual.

Article 6

The Committee shall include in its annual report under article 45 of the Covenant a summary of its activities under the present Protocol.

* * *

3. International Convention on the Elimination of All Forms of Racial Discrimination (excerpts)

Article 14

1. A State Party may at any time declare that it recognizes the competence of the Committee to receive and consider communications from individuals or groups of individuals within its jurisdiction claiming to be victims of a violation by that State Party of any of the rights set forth in this Convention. No communications shall be received by the Committee if it concerns a State Party which has not made such a declaration.

2. Any State Party which makes a declaration as provided for in paragraph 1 of this article may establish or indicate a body within its national legal order which shall be competent to receive and consider petitions from individuals and groups of individuals within its jurisdiction who claim to be victims of a violation of any of the rights set forth in this Convention and who have exhausted other available local remedies.

3. A declaration made in accordance with paragraph 1 of this article and the name of any body established or indicated in accordance with paragraph 2 of this article shall be deposited by the State Party concerned with the Secretary-General of the United Nations, who shall transmit copies thereof to the other States Parties. A declaration may be withdrawn at any time by notification to the Secretary-General, but such a withdrawal shall not affect communications pending before the Committee.

4. A register of petitions shall be kept by the body established or indicated in accordance with paragraph 2 of this article, and certified copies of the register shall be filed annually through appropriate channels with the Secretary-General on the understanding that the contents shall not be publicly disclosed.

5. In the event of failure to obtain satisfaction from the body established or indicated in accordance with paragraph 2 of this article, the petitioner shall have the right to communicate the matter to the Committee within six months.

6. *a.* The Committee shall confidentially bring any communication referred to it to the attention of the State Party alleged to be violating any provision of this Convention, but the identity of the individual or groups of individuals concerned shall not be revealed without his or their express consent. The Committee shall not receive anonymous communications.

   b. Within three months, the receiving State shall submit to the Committee written explanations or statements clarifying the matter and the remedy, if any, that may have been taken by that State.

7. *a.* The Committee shall consider communications in the light of all information made available to it by the State Party concerned and by the petitioner. The Committee shall not consider any communication from a petitioner unless it has ascertained that the petitioner has exhausted all available domestic remedies. However, this shall not be the rule where the application of the remedies is unreasonably prolonged.

   b. The Committee shall forward its suggestions and recommendations, if any, to the State Party concerned and to the petitioner.

8. The Committee shall include in its annual report a summary of such communications and, where appropriate, a summary of the explanations and statements of the States Parties concerned and of its own suggestions and recommendations.

9. The Committee shall be competent to exercise the functions provided for in this article only when at least ten State Parties to this Convention are bound by declarations in accordance with paragraph 1 of this article.

* * *

4. Convention Against Torture and Other Cruel, Inhuman or Degrading Treatment or Punishment

Article 21

1. A State Party to this Convention may at any time declare under this article that it recognizes the competence of the Committee to receive and consider communications to the effect that a State Party claims that another State Party is not fulfilling its obligations under this Convention. Such communications may be received and considered according to the procedures laid down in this article only if submitted by a State Party which has made a declaration recognizing in

regard to itself the competence of the Committee. No communication shall be dealt with by the Committee under this article if it concerns a State Party which has not made such a declaration. Communications received under this article shall be dealt with in accordance with the following procedure:

(a) If a State Party considers that another State Party is not giving effect to the provisions of this Convention, it may, by written communication, bring the matter to the attention of that State Party. Within three months after the receipt of the communication the receiving State shall afford the State which sent the communication an explanation or any other statement in writing clarifying the matter, which should include, to the extent possible and pertinent, reference to domestic procedures and remedies taken, pending or available in the matter;

(b) If the matter is not adjusted to the satisfaction of both States Parties concerned within six months after the receipt by the receiving State of the initial communication, either State shall have the right to refer the matter to the Committee, by notice given to the Committee and to the other State;

(c) The Committee shall deal with a matter referred to it under this article only after it has ascertained that all domestic remedies have been invoked and exhausted in the matter, in conformity with the generally recognized principles of international law. This shall not be the rule where the application of the remedies is unreasonably prolonged or is unlikely to bring effective relief to the person who is the victim of the violation of this Convention;

(d) The Committee shall hold closed meetings when examining communications under this article;

(e) Subject to the provisions of subparagraph (c), the Committee shall make available its good offices to the States Parties concerned with a view to a friendly solution of the matter on the basis of respect for the obligations provided for in this Convention. For this purpose, the Committee may, when appropriate, set up an *ad hoc* conciliation commission;

(f) In any matter referred to it under this article, the Committee may call upon the States Parties concerned, referred to in subparagraph (b), to supply any relevant information;

(g) The States Parties concerned, referred to in subparagraph (b), shall have the right to be represented when the matter is being considered by the Committee and to make submissions orally and/or in writing;

(h) The Committee shall, within twelve months after the date of receipt of notice under subparagraph (b), submit a report:

(i) If a solution within the terms of subparagraph (e) is reached, the Committee shall confine its report to a brief statement of the facts and of the solution reached;

(ii) If a solution within the terms of subparagraph (e) is not reached, the Committee shall confine its report to a brief statement of the facts; the written submissions and record of the oral submissions made be the written submissions and record of the oral submissions made by the States Parties concerned shall be attached to the report. In every matter, the report shall be communicated to the States Parties concerned.

2. The provisions of this article shall come into force when five States Parties to this Convention have made declarations under paragraph 1 of this article. Such declarations shall be deposited by the States Parties with the Secretary-General of the United Nations, who shall transmit copies thereof to the other States Parties. A declaration may be withdrawn at any time by notification to the Secretary-General. Such a withdrawal shall not prejudice the consideration of any matter which is the subject of a communication already transmitted under this article; no further communication by any State Party shall be received under this article after the notification of withdrawal of the declaration has been received by the Secretary-General, unless the State Party concerned has made a new declaration.

Article 22

1. A State Party to this Convention may at any time declare under this article that it recognizes the competence of the Committee to receive and consider communications from or on behalf of individuals subject to its jurisdiction who claim to be victims of a violation by a State Party of the provisions of the Convention. No communication shall be received by the Committee if it concerns a State Party which has not made such a declaration.

2. The Committee shall consider inadmissible any communication under this article which is anonymous or which it considers to be abuse of the right of submission of such communications or to be incompatible with the provisions of this Convention.

3. Subject to the provisions of paragraph 2, the Committee shall bring any communications submitted to it under this article to the attention of the State Party to this Convention which has made a declaration under paragraph 1 and is

alleged to be violating any provisions of the Convention. Within six months, the receiving State shall submit to the Committee written explanations or statements clarifying the matter and the remedy, if any, that may have been taken by that State.

4. The Committee shall consider communications received under this article in the light of all information made available to it by or on behalf of the individual and by the State Party concerned.

5. The Committee shall consider communications received under this article in the light of all information made available to it by or on behalf of the individual and by the State Party concerned if

(a) the same matter has not been, and is not being examined under another procedure of international investigation or settlement;
(b) the individual has exhausted all available domestic remedies; this shall not be the rule where the application of the remedies is unreasonably prolonged or is unlikely to bring effective relief to the person who is the victim of the violation of this Convention.

6. The Committee shall hold closed meetings when examining communications under this article.

7. The Committee shall forward its views to the State Party concerned and to the individual.

8. The provisions of this article shall come into force when five States Parties to this Convention have made declarations under paragraph 1 of this article. Such declarations shall be deposited by the States Parties with the Secretary-General of the United Nations, who shall transmit copies thereof to the other States Parties. A declaration may be withdrawn at any time by notification to the Secretary-General. Such a withdrawal shall not prejudice the consideration of any matter which is the subject of a communication already transmitted under this article; no further communication by or on behalf of an individual shall be received under this article after the notification of withdrawal of the declaration

has been received by the Secretary-General, unless the State Party has made a new declaration.

* * *

5. Enforced or Involuntary Disappearances

Establishment of a working group

The subsequent establishment, in 1980, of the Working Group on Enforced or Involuntary Disappearances by the United Nations Commission on Human Rights was thus inspired by the United Nations General Assembly. It was the first mechanism set up within the framework of the United Nations Human Rights Programme to deal with human rights violations in an issue-oriented manner, irrespective of where they were reported to have occurred. Subsequent years have seen the establishment of other thematic procedures in related fields, such as the appointment of Special Rapporteurs on Summary or Arbitrary Executions and on the Question of Torture.

A new mechanism

In implementing its broad mandate, the Working Group has developed a totally novel, unorthodox mechanism for dealing with complaints about human rights violations. It receives and examines reports on disappearances submitted by relatives of missing persons or human rights organizations acting on their behalf. After determining whether those reports comply with a number of criteria, the Working Group transmits individual cases to the Governments concerned, requesting them to carry out investigations and to inform the Working Group of their results. The Working Group deals with the numerous individual cases of human rights violations on a purely humanitarian basis, irrespective of the ratification by Governments of existing legal instruments providing for an individual complaints procedure. The Working Group acts essentially as a channel of communication between the families of the missing persons and Governments and so far has successfully developed a dialogue, aimed at solving cases, with the majority of Governments concerned. It has also initiated an urgent action procedure under which the Working Group's Chairman is authorized to process cases of recent disappearances in between Group sessions, thus helping to avoid any delays in its endeavours to save human lives. Dealing with individual cases constitutes the bulk of the Working Group's activity. It has, however, also examined the phenomenon on a more abstract level by studying, *inter alia*, the extent to which a variety of civil and political, as well as social, economic and cultural rights are being violated by the practise of enforced disappearance of persons. In addition, it has studied preventive and remedial legal or institutional mechanisms at the national level, in particular during visits to countries which, following a request by the United Nations Commission on Human Rights, have extended invitations to the Working Groups.

The Working Group meets three times a year for six to eight working days. It has traditionally held one meeting outside of Geneva, Switzerland, in order to hear the cases of relatives and witnesses who, otherwise, would not have been able to appear before it. Missions have also been made to the following countries: Mexico and Cyprus (1982), Bolivia (1984), Peru (1985 and 1986), Guatemala (1987) and Colombia (1988).

III. Methods of work

The Working Group's methods of work are based on its mandate as stipulated in the United Nations Commission on Human Rights resolution 20 (XXXVI) and are specifically geared to its main objective. That objective is to assist families in determining the fate and whereabouts of their missing relatives who, having disappeared, are situated outside the protective precinct of the law. To this end, the Working Group endeavours to establish a channel of communication between the families and the Governments concerned, in order to ensure that sufficiently documented and clearly identified individual cases which the families, directly or indirectly, have brought to the Working Group's attention are investigated and the whereabouts of the missing person clarified. The Working Group's role ends when the fate and whereabouts of the missing person have been clearly established as a result of investigations by the Government or the family, irrespective of whether that person is alive or dead. The Working Group does not concern itself with the question of determining responsibility for specific cases of disappearance or for other human rights violations which may have occurred in the course of disappearances. The nature of its activity is strictly humanitarian.

An example of enforced or involuntary disappearance may be shown in the following: a clearly identified person is detained against his will by officials of a branch or level of government or by an organized group of organized private individuals allegedly acting on behalf of, or with the support, permission or acquiescence of the Government. These forces then conceal the whereabouts of that person or refuse to disclose his fate or to acknowledge that the person was detained.

The Working Group does not deal with situations of international armed conflict, in view of the competence of the International Committee of the Red Cross (ICRC) in such situations, as determined by the Geneva Conventions of 12 August 1949 and the additional Protocols thereto.

In transmitting cases of disappearances, the Working Group deals exclusively with Governments, basing itself on the principle that Governments must assume responsibility for any violation of human rights on their territory. If, however, disappearances are attributed to terrorist or insurgent movements fighting the Government on its own territory, the Working Group has refrained from processing them. The Working Group considers that, as a matter of principle, such groups may not be approached with a view to investigating or clarifying disappearances for which they are held responsible.

Admissibility

Reports on disappearances are considered admissible by the Working Group when they originate from the family or friends of the missing person. Such reports may, however, be channelled to the Working Group through representatives of the family, Governments, intergovernmental organizations, humanitarian organizations and other reliable sources. They must be submitted in writing with a clear indication of the identity of the sender.

In order to enable Governments to carry out meaningful investigations, the Working Group provides them with information containing at least a minimum of basic data. In addition, the Working Group constantly urges the sources of reports to furnish as many details as possible on the identity of the missing person (if available, identity card numbers) and the circumstances of the disappearance. The Working Group requires the following minimum elements:

Full name of the missing person;

Date of disappearance, i.e., day, month and year of arrest or abduction, or day, month and year when the missing person was last seen. When the missing person was last seen in a detention centre, an approximate indication is sufficient.

Place of arrest or abduction or where the missing person was last seen (at least an indication of town or village);

Parties presumed to have carried out the arrest or abduction or to hold the missing person in unacknowledged detention; and,

Steps taken to determine the fate or whereabouts of the missing person or at least an indication that efforts to resort to domestic remedies were aggravated or have otherwise been inconclusive.

Reported cases

Reported cases of disappearances are placed before the Working Group for detailed examination during its sessions. Those which fulfil the requirements as outlined above are transmitted, upon the Working Groups' specific authorization, to the Governments concerned, with a request to carry out investigations and to inform the Working Group of their results. The reported cases are communicated by letter from the Working Group's Chairman to the Government concerned through the Permanent Representative to the United Nations.

In the case of the disappearance of a pregnant woman, the child presumed to have been born during the mother's captivity is mentioned in the description of the mother's case. The child is treated as a separate case when witnesses have reported that the mother actually gave birth to a child during detention.

Cases that occurred within the three months preceding receipt of the report by the Working Group are cabled directly to the concerned ministers of foreign affairs. Their transmission can be authorized by the Chairman on the basis of a specific delegation of power given to him by the Working Group. Cases which occurred prior to the three-month limit but not more than one year before the date of their receipt by the Secretariat, provided that they had some connection with a case which occurred within the three-month period, can be transmitted between sessions by letter upon authorization by the Chairman.

Reports on a disappearance indicating that officials from more than one country were directly responsible for or involved in a disappearance are communicated to both the Government of the country where the disappearance occurred and the Government of the country whose officials or agents were alleged to have participated in the arrest or the abduction of the missing person. However, such cases are counted only in the statistics of the country in which the person was reportedly held in detention or last seen.

At least once a year, the Working Group reminds every Government concerned on the cases which have not yet been clarified. Furthermore, at any time during the year, any Government may request the summaries of the outstanding and/or clarified cases which the Working Group has transmitted to it.

Replies from Governments

All replies received from Governments on reports of disappearances are examined by the Working Group and forwarded to the sources of those reports who are invited to make observations and/or provide additional details on the cases.

If the reply clearly indicates where the missing person is (whether alive or dead) and if that information is sufficiently definite for the family to be reasonably expected to accept it, the Working Group considered the case clarified at the session following the receipt of that information.

If the reply provides definite information on the missing person's fate after the reported date of disappearance, but does not unambiguously specify the person's present whereabouts (indicating, for instance, that the person was released from prison some time ago or that he is free, without stating where), the Committee must await a reply from the source. If the source does not respond within six months of the date on which the Government's reply was communicated to it, the case is considered clarified. If the source contests the Government's information on reasonable grounds, the Government is so informed and invited to comment.

If the source provides well-documented information that a case has erroneously been considered clarified, because the Government's reply referred to a different person, does not correspond to the reported situation or has not reached the source within the six-month period described above, the Working Group re-submits the case to the Government requesting it to comment. In such instances the case is again listed among the outstanding cases and a specific explanation is given in the Working Group's report to the United Nations Commission on Human Rights, indicating the errors or discrepancies.

Any substantive additional information which the source submits on an outstanding case is placed before the Working Group and, following its approval, transmitted to the Government concerned. If the additional information received amounts to a clarification of the case, the Government is so informed.

The Working Group retains cases on its files as long as the exact whereabouts of the missing persons have not been determined. This principle is not affected by changes of government in a given country. However, the Working Group accepts the closure of a case on its files when the competent authority specified in the relevant national law pronounces, with the concurrence of the relatives and other interested parties, the presumption of death of a person reported missing.

IV. How to report cases of disappearances

Information on the enforced or involuntary disappearance of a person may be submitted in any written form—in urgent cases preferably by cable, telex or telefax—to the Working Group on Enforced or Involuntary Disappearances of the Commission on Human Rights, c/o the United Nations Centre for Human Rights, 1211 Geneva 10, Switzerland (cable address: UNATIONS Geneva; telex 289696; fax 339879). Even when a particular case is submitted by a non-governmental organization, all requests for action by the Working Group must originate from the family or friends of the missing person. The report must give a clear indication of the identity of the person or organization making the reports, and must include a contact address. If the author of the report is not a relative of the missing person, but acts directly or indirectly upon the family's request, he should remain in contact with the family, in order to be able to inform them about the results of the Working Group's endeavours. Any replies obtained on the missing person's fate or whereabouts are for the exclusive information of the relatives.

As is explained more fully in chapter III, a report should contain the following minimum information:

Full name;

Day, month and year of disappearance;

Place of disappearance;

Those considered responsible;

Information about search.

Experience has shown that information on the enforced or involuntary disappearance of a person varies greatly in detail by reason of the nature of each case and the surrounding circumstances. Forms designed to assist relatives in formulating reports on disappearances can be obtained from the United Nations Centre for Human Rights. While it is important to receive as much information as possible, missing details should not prevent the submission of reports. However, the Working Group can only process clearly identified individual cases containing the minimum elements of information outlined in chapter III.

* * *

6. Communications Procedures

The system at work

Every month members of the Sub-Commission on Prevention of Discrimination and Protection of Minorities—human rights experts who serve in their personal capacity—receive from the United Nations Secretary-General a list of communications, with short descriptions in each case, and any replies sent in by Governments. The list is also supplied to members of the Commission on Human Rights.

A five-member Working Group of the Sub-Commission meets for two weeks each year, just before the Sub-Commission's annual session. The Group considers all the communications and Governments' replies, and selects for the attention of the Sub-Commission cases where there seems to be reliable evidence of a consistent pattern of gross violations of human rights and fundamental freedoms, i.e. situations affecting a large number of people over a protracted period of time.

A majority of the Working Group's members is needed to refer a communication to the Sub-Commission. No further action is taken on communications which the Working Group does not pass on to the Sub-Commission.

The Sub-Commission then considers the communications brought before it by the Working Group and has to decide whether to refer situations where there appears to be a consistent pattern of human rights violations to the Commission on Human Rights.

Subsequently, it is the turn of the Commission to determine whether a thorough study of a particular situation is needed, with a report and recommendations to the Economic and Social Council. The Commission may also decide to appoint an *ad hoc* committee to make an investigation, but this requires the consent of the State where the violations are alleged to have happened.

ABC of a human rights communication

To decide what communications may be accepted for examination, the Sub-Commission on Prevention of Discrimination and Protection of Minorities has drawn up rules of procedures.[1]

The first of these rules is that the aim of the communication must not be inconsistent with the principles of the United Nations Charter, the Universal Declaration of Human Rights, or other applicable human rights treaties, conventions, etc.

A communication will be admitted only if consideration shows there are reasonable grounds to believe—also taking into account any replies sent by the Governments concerned—that there is a consistent pattern of gross and reliably attested violations of human rights and fundamental freedoms.

Communications may be admitted when they come from people—individuals or groups—who claim to be victims of human rights violations. They may also be admitted when they come from any person or groups of people which has direct, reliable knowledge of violations. When non-governmental organizations

---

[1]Sub-Commission, E.S.C. Res. 1 (XXIV) of 13 August 1971.

(NGOs) present communications on violations, the conditions are that the NGO is acting in good faith in accordance with recognized principles of human rights, and that it has direct, reliable evidence of the situation it is describing.

Anonymous communications are inadmissible as are those based only on reports in the mass media.

Each communication must describe the facts, the purpose of the petition, and the rights that have been violated. As a rule, a communication will not be considered if the language is abusive or if it contains insulting remarks about the State against which the complaint is directed. If the other requirements are fulfilled once the abusive language has been deleted, such communications may nevertheless, be considered.

No communication will be admitted if it runs counter to the principles of the United Nations Charter, or if it shows political motivations.

The domestic remedies must have been exhausted before a communication is considered—unless it can be shown convincingly that solutions at the national level would be ineffective or that they would extend over an unreasonable length of time.

The rules of procedure, finally, seek to avoid overlapping with other existing procedures, and the repeated submission of communications already dealt with by the United Nations.

Communications intended for handling under the "1503" procedure may be addressed to:

Centre for Human Rights
United Nations Office at Geneva
1211 Geneva 10, Switzerland

Dialogue with Governments

With the passage of time, United Nations human rights procedures have become more readily accepted and recognized by Governments, and their co-operation in the work of the Commission on Human Rights has grown steadily. The Commission works through direct contacts to establish a dialogue with the Governments of countries where human rights violations are alleged to have occurred. These contacts are made either by the United Nations Secretary-General or by special representatives or independent experts who are appointed by the Commission and who report to it.

A number of steps have been taken aimed at enhancing Governments' co-operation under the "1503" procedure. In 1972 the Sub-Commission underlined the importance of receiving replies from Governments to allegations of human rights violations contained in the communications received. In 1974 the Commission itself decided to refer the documents on complaints to the Governments concerned, and to invite them to make written comments. At the same time the Sub-Commission was instructed to inform such Governments of its intention to refer a situation to the commission and to invite observations in writing. A five-member Working Group of the Commission has been appointed annually since 1974 to examine the material transmitted by the Sub-Commissions, and the observations of Governments, and to recommend a course of action to take on each case. This body is known as the Working Group on Situations. Its recommendations also go to the Governments concerned, which have the right to be represented during the Commission's debate, and while its decision is adopted.

Confidentiality

All actions taken under the "1503" procedure remain confidential unless the Commission reports thereon to the Economic and Social Council. Until that stage is reached, the meetings of all human rights bodies involved are held in private and the confidentiality of their records and the documents they handle is preserved.

Since 1978, however, the Chairman of the Commission on Human Rights has announced in public session the names of countries which have been under examination. The Chairman makes a distinction between countries where the Commission continues to keep a human rights situation under review, and those where it has been decided to take no further action.

The Economic and Social Council sometimes decides—on its own initiative, after the study of a particular situation has ended, or on the recommendation of the Commission on Human Rights—that secrecy may be lifted. This was the case with Equatorial Guinea in 1979, Argentina and Uruguay in 1985, and the Philippines in 1986. In 1987, the Council decided that the confidential report by the Special Representative of the Commission on the human rights situation in Haiti should be made public.

"Optional Protocol" procedure

The International Covenant on Civil and Political Rights and its Optional Protocol entered into force on 23 March 1976. A State which is a party to the Covenant and to the Protocol recognizes that the United Nations Human Rights Committee—a body of 18 experts, appointed in their personal capacity, which meets three times a year—can receive and consider communications from individuals who claim that their human rights have been violated by that State.

Of the 122 States which had acceded to or ratified the Covenant by August, 1993, 73 had accepted the competence of the Committee to deal with individual complaints. These States are: Algeria, Angola, Argentina, Armenia, Australia, Austria, Barbados, Belarus, Benin, Bolivia, Bulgaria, Cameroon, Canada, Central African Republic, Chile, Colombia, Congo, Costa Rica, Cyprus, Czech Republic, Denmark, Dominican Republic, Ecuador, Equatorial Guinea, Estonia, Finland, France, Gambia, Guinea, Guyana, Hungary, Iceland, Ireland, Italy, Jamaica, Libyan Arab Jamahiriya, Lithuania, Luxembourg, Madagascar, Malta, Mauritius, Mongolia, Nepal, Netherlands, New Zealand, Nicaragua, Niger, Norway, Panama, Peru, Philippines, Poland, Portugal, Republic of Korea, Romania, Russian Federation, Saint Vincent and the Grenadines, San Marino, Senegal, Seychelles, Slovakia, Slovenia, Somalia, Spain, Suriname, Sweden, Togo, Trinidad and Tobago, Ukraine, Uruguay, Venezuela, Zaire and Zambia.

Communications from individuals are considered by the Committee in closed meetings. Their letters, and other documents of the Committee, remain confidential.

Between 1977 and 1993, the Committee had received 552 communications involving 43 States. In 121 of the 161 cases where the Committee has concluded its work and made known its views, violations of the Covenant have been established. It takes between six months and one year to decide whether a communication is admissible, and the Committee's views on the merits may follow a year or two later. The entire process of dealing with a complaint is normally completed within two to three years.

Is it admissible?

A communication, to be considered, must not be anonymous and it must come from a person, or persons who live under the jurisdiction of a State which is a party to the Optional Protocol. Normally, a communication should be sent in by the individual who claims that his or her rights, as set out in the Covenant on Civil and Political Rights, have been violated by that State. When it seems that the alleged victim cannot submit the communication, the Committee may consider a communication from another person, who justifies his authority to act on behalf of the alleged victim. An unrelated third party having no apparent links with the alleged victim cannot submit the communication.

The complaint, naturally, has to be compatible with the provisions of the Covenant, and it cannot be considered if the same problem is being examined under another international procedure of investigation or settlement. All domestic remedies must have been exhausted before the complaint is placed before the Committee.

Even before deciding whether a communication is admissible or not, the Committee—or its Working Group on Communications—may ask the alleged victim or the State concerned to provide additional written information or observations and set a time-limit. If the State replies at this stage, the person complaining receives a copy for comment. If the case is referred back to the author only for more information, and is then found to be inadmissible, nothing will have been transmitted to the State. The Committee may decide to drop a complaint without a written decision; for example, when the author withdraws it, or shows in some other way that he does not wish to go on with the matter.

At the end of this fact sheet there is a model which shows how a communication to the Human Rights Committee should be set out. Communications intended for handling under the Optional Protocol should be addressed to:

Human Rights Committee
c/o Centre for Human Rights
United Nations Office at Geneva
1211 Geneva 10, Switzerland.

Assessing a complaint

Once a communication has been declared admissible, the Committee asks the State concerned to explain or clarify the problem and state whether anything has been done to settle it. A limit of six months is set for the State party's reply. Then the author of the complaint is given an opportunity to comment on the State's reply. After that, the Committee expresses its views and sends them to the State concerned and to the author of the complaint.

The Committee puts individuals who complain and the States which are alleged to have violated their rights on an equal footing throughout its proceedings. Each has an opportunity to comment on the other's arguments.

Calling a halt . . .

People who allege that they are victims of human rights violations may need protection before the Committee has had time to make its final views known. Without prejudging the merits of complaints, the Committee has sometimes had to give an interim opinion to particular States. Pending study of one case, the Committee informed a State that the alleged victim "having sought refuge in country X, should not be handed over or expelled to country Y." On another occasion, the Committee expressed concern over the state of health of an alleged victim, and asked the Government to have him examined urgently by a competent medical body. The Committee also asked for a copy of the body's report. There have also been decisions asking a State not to carry out a death sentence while a communication is under examination.

Decisions are announced

While a communication is being considered by the Human Rights Committee, the proceedings are totally confidential. The Committee's findings—views on communications which have been declared admissible and examined on the merits, and decisions declaring others inadmissible—are always made public.

A selection of the Committee's decisions under the Optional Protocol is being published. Volume I of this series, covering the 2nd to the 16th sessions of the Committee, was published in 1985. Volume II, covering the 17th to the 32 sessions, is due for publication in 1989.

How do the procedures differ?

The major difference between the procedure under resolution 1503 (XLVIII) and under the Optional Protocol to the International Covenant on Civil and Political Rights is that the former covers the examination of *situations*, and the latter is concerned with the examination of *individual complaints*: isolated instances of alleged violations of human rights. But there are other ways of telling the two procedures apart.

- The "1503" procedure is based on a resolution of a United Nations body: the Economic and Social Council. To make it work, the voluntary co-operation of States is indispensable. The "Optional Protocol" procedure takes its authority from an international treaty under which the States parties have bound themselves to accept a specific procedure for examining claims brought against them.

- The "1503" procedure applies to all States. Under the Optional Protocol, the procedure applies only to States which have acceded to or ratified the Covenant and Protocol.

- Violations of all human rights and fundamental freedoms are covered by the former, while the latter is concerned only with those civil and political rights which are protected by the International Covenant on Civil and Political Rights.

- Any person, group of persons or non-governmental organization may invoke the "1503" procedure if they have direct or second-hand knowledge of the alleged violations. A communication under the Optional Protocol must either be signed by the alleged victim or by someone with authority to act on his or her behalf.

- The authors of communications under the "1503" procedure are not involved at any stage in its implementation, nor are they informed of any action taken by the United Nations—unless it is made public. The authors are merely informed by the United Nations Secretariat that their communications have been received, that copies have been sent to the States concerned, and that summaries will be handed to members of the Sub-Commission on the Prevention of Discrimination and Protection of Minorities and to the members of the Commission on Human Rights. The author of a communication put before the Human Rights Committee under the Optional Protocol, on the other hand, has full standing. He is informed of all actions taken by the Committee or its Working Group on Communications. The State concerned is also kept informed. The author has the opportunity to comment on any written submission by the State.

Other avenues

Two other procedures are available to people who believe that their human rights are being violated. They have been established under the International Convention on the Elimination of All Forms of Racial Discrimination, and the Convention against Torture and Other Cruel, Inhuman or Degrading Treatment or Punishment.

Elimination of racial discrimination

Individuals or groups of people who claim that their rights, as set out in the International Convention on the Elimination of All Forms of Racial Discrimination, are being violated, may—as laid down in article 14 of the Convention—write to the United Nations Committee on the Elimination of Racial Discrimination (CERD), asking that their complaint be considered. They must first have exhausted all domestic remedies.

Eighteen of the 137 States that had ratified or acceded to the Convention by the end of 1993 recognize the competence of the Committee to receive and consider communications under article 14. They are: Algeria, Australia, Bulgaria, Costa Rica, Denmark, Ecuador, France, Hungary, Iceland, Italy, Netherlands, Norway, Peru, Russian Federation, Senegal, Sweden, Ukraine and Uruguay.

Communications intended for handling by the Committee should be addressed to:

> Committee on the Elimination of Racial Discrimination
> c/o Centre for Human Rights
> United Nations Office at Geneva
> 1211 Geneva 10, Switzerland.

The Committee cannot receive a communication if it concerns a State which, although a party to the Convention, does not recognize the competence of the Committee to do so.

Convention against Torture

Under article 22 of the Convention against Torture and Other Cruel, Inhuman or Degrading Treatment or Punishment, individuals who claim to be victims of a violation of the rights protected by the Convention and who have exhausted all the domestic possibilities of recourse may write to the Committee against Torture, asking for consideration of their case. As of 31 July 1993, 34 of the 77 States which have ratified or acceded to the Convention had recognized the competence of the Committee to receive and consider communications of this kind. These States are: Algeria, Argentina, Australia, Austria, Bulgaria, Canada, Croatia, Cyprus, Denmark, Ecuador, Finland, France, Greece, Hungary, Italy, Liechtenstein, Luxembourg, Malta, Monaco, Netherlands, New Zealand, Norway, Poland, Portugal, Russian Federation, Slovenia, Spain, Sweden, Switzerland, Togo, Tunisia, Turkey, Uruguay and Yugoslavia.

Communications intended for handling by the Committee should be addressed to:

> Committee against Torture
> c/o Centre for Human Rights
> United Nations Office at Geneva
> 1211 Geneva 10, Switzerland.

The Committee cannot receive communications which concern States not recognizing its competence under article 22 of the Convention. (For more information, please refer to *Fact Sheet No. 4, Methods of Combating Torture* and *Fact Sheet No. 15* on the *Committee Against Torture.*)

Status of women

Two lists dealing with violations of human rights are prepared annually for the United Nations Commission on the Status of Women by the Centre for Social

Development and Humanitarian Affairs, based in Vienna. One is a non-confidential list containing summaries of communications which concern the promotion of the status of women in the political, economic, social, civil and educational fields. The other is a confidential list which contains summaries of communications on alleged violations which affect the status of women.

Communications intended for handling by the Commission on the Status of Women should be addressed to:

United Nations Commission on the Status of Women
Centre for Social Development and Humanitarian Affairs
United Nations Office at Vienna
Vienna International Centre
P.O. Box 500, 1400 Vienna, Austria

Model communication

Date: ____________________

Communication to:

The Human Rights Committee
c/o Centre for Human Rights
United Nations Office
8-14 avenue de la Paix
1211 Geneva 10, Switzerland,

submitted for consideration under the Optional Protocol to the International Covenant on Civil and Political Rights

I. Information concerning the author of the communication

Name ______________________________
First name(s) ______________________
Nationality ________________________
Profession _________________________
Date and place of birth ____________________________________
Present address ____

____

Address for exchange of confidential correspondence (if other than present adress) ____

____

Submitting the communication as:

(*a*) Victim of the violation or violations set forth below ☐

(*b*) Appointed representative/legal counsel of the alleged victim(s) ☐

(*c*) Other ☐

If box (*c*) is marked, the author should explain:

(i) In what capacity he is acting on behalf of the victim(s) (e.g. family relationship or other personal links with the alleged victim(s)):

____

(ii) Why the victim(s) is (are) unable to submit the communication himself (themselves):

____

An unrelated third party having no link to the victim(s) cannot submit a communication on his (their) behalf.

II. Information concerning the alleged victim(s) (if other than the author)

Name ______________________________
First name(s) ______________________________
Nationality ______________________________
Profession ______________________________
Date and place of birth ______________________________
Present address or whereabouts ______________________________

____

III. State concerned/articles violated/domestic remedies

Name of the State party (country) to the International Covenant and the Optional Protocol against which the communication is directed:

____

Articles of the International Covenant on Civil and Political Rights allegedly violated:

____

Steps taken by or on behalf of the alleged victim(s) to exhaust domestic remedies—recourse to the courts or other public authorities, when and with what results (if possible, enclose copies of all relevant judicial or administrative decisions):

If domestic remedies have not been exhausted, explain why:

IV. Other International procedures

Has the same matter been submitted for examination under another procedure of international investigation or settlement (e.g. the Inter-American Commission on Human Rights, the European Commission on Human Rights)? If so, when and with what results?

V. Facts of the claim

Detailed description of the facts of the alleged violation or violations (including relevant dates)*

Author's signature: ______________________________

*Add as many pages as needed for this description.

* * *

7. Application of the International Covenant on Civil and Political Rights under the Optional Protocol by the Human Rights Committee (excerpts)

by Alfred de Zayas/Jakob Th. Möller/Torkel Opsahl

1. Procedure on Admissibility and Merits

Consideration of communications under the Optional Protocol takes place in closed meetings (Art. 5 [3] of the Optional Protocol). All documents pertaining to the work of the Committee under the Optional Protocol (submissions from the parties and other working documents of the Committee) are confidential.

a) Admissibility

Once a communication has been registered, the Committee must decide whether it is admissible under the Optional Protocol. The requirements for admissibility, which are contained in Articles 1,2,3 and 5 (2) of the Optional Protocol, are listed in Rule 90 of the Committee's provisional rules of procedure, pursuant to which the Committee shall ascertain:

(a) That the communication is not anonymous and that it emanates from an individual, or individuals, subject to the jurisdiction of a State party to the Protocol;

(b) That the individual claims to be a victim of a violation by that State party of any of the rights set forth in the Covenant. Normally, the communication should be submitted by the individual himself or by his representative; the Committee may, however, accept for consideration a communication submitted on behalf of an alleged victim when it appears that he is unable to submit the communication himself;

(c) That the communication does not constitute an abuse of the right of submission under the Protocol;

(d) That the communication is not incompatible with the provisions of the Covenant;

(e) That the same matter is not being examined under another procedure of international investigation or settlement;

(f) That the individual has exhausted all available domestic remedies.

Unlike in the procedure before the European Commission (Article 26 of the European Convention), there is *no* requirement under the Optional Protocol that the author submit his communication to the HRC within six months from the exhaustion of domestic remedies in the State concerned.

Under Rule 91(1) the Committee or its Working Group on Communications may request the State party concerned or the author of the communication to submit, within a time-limit which is indicated in each such decision (normally six weeks or two months), additional written information or observations relevant to the question of admissibility of the communication. Such a request does not imply that any decision has been taken on the question of admissibility (Rule 91 [3]). If the case is referred to the State party at this stage, any reply received from it is transmitted to the author to give him an opportunity to comment thereon. If the case is only referred back to the author for clarifications under Rule 91 and is subsequently declared inadmissible, no transmittal to the State party may have taken place. The Committee may also decide to discontinue or suspend consideration of a communication, for example, if its author indicates that he wants to withdraw the case or if the Committee has lost touch with the author. A decision to declare a communication inadmissible (or otherwise to discontinue or suspend consideration of it) may, in a clear case, be taken without referring the case to the State party for its observations. The decision to declare a communication admissible or inadmissible rests with the Committee only, not with its Working Group.

b) Merits

If a communication is declared admissible, the Committee proceeds to consider the substance of the complaint. In accordance with Article 4 of the Optional Protocol, it requests the State party concerned to submit to the Committee "explanations or statements clarifying the matter and the remedy, if any, which may have been taken" by it. Under Article 4 (2), the State Party has a time-limit of six months in which to submit its observations. When these observations are received by the Secretariat, the author is given an opportunity to comment thereon. The Committee then normally formulates its views and forwards them to the State party and to the author of the communication, in accordance with Article 5 (4) of the Optional Protocol. The State party may be requested to transmit a copy of the views to an imprisoned victim. Before the adoption of final views, further information may be sought from the State party or the author by means of an interim decision. Throughout the proceedings, the principle of equality of arms prevails. Unless a communication is declared inadmissible without referral to the State party (or otherwise discontinued before referral to the State party), both parties are given an opportunity to comment on each other's submissions.

c) Interim Measures

Rule 86 of the Committee's provisional rules of procedure provides that the Committee may, prior to the forwarding of its final views on a communication, inform the State party whether interim measures of protection may be desirable to avoid irreparable damage to the victim of the alleged violation. Such request for interim measures does not imply a determination of the merits of the communication. The Committee has had occasion to request interim measures in a number of cases, *e.g.*, No. 22/1977 (*O.E. v. S.*) where it informed the State party of the view of the Committee "that pending further consideration of the case, the alleged victim, having sought refuge in S., should not be handed over or expelled to Country X". In an interim decision relating to another case, the Committee expressed concern over the state of health of the alleged victim and requested the State party "as a matter of urgency to arrange for him to be examined by a competent medical board and . . . to furnish the Committee with a copy of the board's report" (No. 10/1977, *Altesor v. Uruguay*). Most recently, at its 28th session in July 1986, the Committee adopted an interim decision requesting a State party to refrain from carrying out a death sentence pending further examination of the question of admissibility of a communication placed before it at that session.

2. Evidence and Burden of Proof

Thus far the Committee has not developed any independent fact-finding functions under the Optional Protocol, but it is required pursuant to Article 5 (1) of the Optional Protocol to consider "all written information made available to it" by the parties.

With respect to the burden of proof, the Committee has established in a number of cases dealing with alleged violations of Articles 6 (right to life), 7 (torture and ill-treatment) and 9 (arbitrary arrest, disappeared persons), that

> this cannot rest alone on the author of the communication, especially considering that the author and the State party do not always have equal access to the evidence and that frequently the State party alone has access to relevant information. It is implicit in Article 4 (2) of the Optional Protocol that the State party has the duty to investigate in good faith all allegations of violation of the Covenant by evidence submitted by the author of the communication, and to furnish to the Committee the information available to it. In cases where the author has submitted to the Committee allegations supported by substantial witness testimony, as in this case, and where further clarification of the case depends on the information exclusively in the hands of the State party, the Committee may consider such allegations as substantiated in the absence of satisfactory evidence and

explanations to the contrary from the State party (No. 30/1978, *Bleier v. Uruguay*).

Furthermore, the Committee has held that "a refutation of [the author's] allegation in general terms is not sufficient" (No. 11/1977, *Grille Motta v. Uruguay*).

(From: II. Issues Considered by the Committee)

1. Criteria for Admissibility under the Optional Protocol

It is convenient to distinguish the issues which mainly concern the various conditions for considering communications, (admissibility criteria under the Optional Protocol) from the substantive issues concerning the rights and freedoms under the Covenant (2. below). The criteria for proceeding with a communication always depends, directly or indirectly, on the terms of the Optional Protocol.

a) The Standing of the Author (Optional Protocol Arts. 1 and 2)

Normally, a communication should be submitted by the individual himself or by his representative; the Committee may, however, accept for consideration a communication submitted on behalf of an alleged victim when it appears that he is unable to submit the communication himself (Rule 90 [1] [b]). In practise, the Committee has accepted communication not only from a duly authorized legal representative, but also from close family members acting on behalf of alleged victims. In other cases the Committee has found that the author of a communication lacked standing. In case No. 128/1982 (*L.A. v. Uruguay*), the author was a member of a non-governmental organization and had taken interest in the alleged victim's situation. He claimed to have authority to act because he believed "that every prisoner treated unjustly would appreciate further investigation of his case by the Human Rights Committee". The Committee decided that the author lacked standing and declared the communication inadmissible. The Human Rights Committee has thus established through a number of decisions on admissibility that a communication submitted by a third party on behalf of an alleged victim can only be considered if the author justifies his authority to submit the communication.

The Committee has also held that an organization as such cannot submit a communication. In case No. 163/1984 (*C. et al. v. Italy*) it stated: "According to Article 1 of the Optional Protocol, only individuals have the right to submit a communication. To the extent, therefore, that the communication originates from the [organization], it has to be declared inadmissible because of lack of personal standing". Similarly, in case No. 104/1981 (*J.T. v. Canada*), the Committee declared a communication inadmissible, partly because "the W. G. Party is an association and not an individual, and as such cannot submit a communication to the Committee under the Optional Protocol."

b) The Victim

The Committee has clarified in case No. 35/1978 (*Aumeeruddy-Cziffra et al. v. Mauritius*) that

> a person can only claim to be a victim in the sense of Article 1 of the Optional Protocol if he or she is actually affected. It is a matter of degree how concretely this requirement should be taken. However, no individual can in the abstract, by a way of an *actio popularis*, challenge a law or practise claimed to be contrary to the Covenant. If the law or practise has not already been concretely applied to the detriment of that individual, it must in any event be applicable in such a way that the alleged victim's risk of being affected is more than a theoretical possibility.

That is, a person is not a victim unless he has personally suffered a violation of his rights. In case No. 61/1979 (*Leo Hertzberg et al. v. Finland*) the Committee stressed

> that it has only been entrusted with the mandate of examining whether an individual has suffered an actual violation of his rights. It cannot review in the abstract whether national legislation contravenes the Covenant, although such legislation may, in particular circumstances, produce adverse effects which directly affect the individual, making him thus a victim in the sense contemplated by Article 1 and 2 of the Optional Protocol.

At its twenty-second session of July 1984 the Committee was again confronted with this problem. In declaring Communication No. 163/1984 (*C. et al. v. Italy*) inadmissible the Committee explained that

> the author of a communication must himself claim, in a substantiated manner, to be the victim of a violation by the State party concerned. It is not the task of the Human Rights Committee, acting under the Optional Protocol, to review *in abstracto* national legislation as to its compliance with obligations imposed by the Covenant. It is true that, in some circumstances, a domestic law may by its mere existence directly violate the rights of individuals under the Covenant. In the present case, however, the authors of the communication have not demonstrated that they are themselves actually and personally affected by Article 9 of Law No. 638 of 11 November 1983. Consequently, the Committee is unable, in accordance with the terms of the Optional Protocol, to consider their complaints.

At its 24th session in April 1985 the Committee declared Communication No. 187/1985 (*J.H. v. Canada*) inadmissible because

> [t]he author of the present communication has not put forward any facts to indicate that he is or has been a victim of discrimination in violation of the provisions of the Covenant. An allegation to the effect that past or present promotion policies are generally to the detriment of English-speaking members of the Canadian Armed Forces is not sufficient in this respect. The Committee, accordingly, concludes that the author has not shown that he has a claim under Article 2 of the Optional Protocol.

d) Individuals Subject to a State Party's Jurisdiction

In several cases the Committee has had to address the question whether an alleged victim is "subject to the jurisdiction" of the State party for the purposes of Article 1 of the Optional Protocol. In case No. 110/1981 (*A. Viana Acosta v. Uruguay*), the State party contended that the communication was inadmissible because the alleged victim had been released from imprisonment and "he left the country to live abroad and he was therefore not subject to jurisdiction" of the State party. The Committee noted in its views that

> by virtue of Article 2, Paragraph 1 of the Covenant, each State party undertakes to respect and to ensure to "all individuals within its territory and subject to its jurisdiction" the rights recognized in the Covenant. Article 1 of the Optional Protocol was clearly intended to apply to individuals subject to the jurisdiction of the State party concerned at the time of the alleged violation of the Covenant. This was manifestly the object and purpose of Article 1.

The same question was dealt with in case No. 25/1978 (*C. Améndola and G. Baritussio v. Uruguay*).

A related issue arises when the alleged violation of the human rights of a national of a State party occurs when that person is not residing in his country at the time of the alleged violation. This was the situation in case No. 57/1979 (*S. Vidal Martins v. Uruguay*) where the author, while living abroad, requested the renewal of her passport. It was the Committee's view that

> the issue of a passport to a Uruguayan citizen is clearly a matter within the jurisdiction of the Uruguayan authorities and he is "subject to the jurisdiction" of Uruguay for that purpose. Moreover a passport is a means of enabling him "to leave any country, including his own", as required by Article 12 (2) of the Covenant. It therefore follows from the very nature of

> the right that, in case of a citizen resident abroad it imposes obligations both on the State of residence and on the State of nationality.

The Committee expressed a similar view when it declared case No. 125/1982 admissible. It stated: "The question of the issue of a passport by [the State party] to a nation [of the State party] wherever he may be, is clearly a matter within the jurisdiction of the [State party's] authorities and he is `subject to the jurisdiction' of [the State party] for that purpose".

e) Preclusion under Article 5 (2) (a) of the Optional Protocol if the Same Matter is Being Examined under another Procedure of International Investigation or Settlement

The Optional Protocol precludes the competence of the Committee to consider cases which are simultaneously being examined under other procedures of international investigation or settlement, such as the procedures of the Inter-American Commission on Human Rights (IACHR) and the European Commission of Human Rights (ECHR). When this situation arises, the practise of the Committee has been to instruct the Secretariat to explain to the author that consideration by the Committee is precluded under Article 5 (2) (a) of the Optional Protocol. In the majority of such cases (which have concerned examination of the same matter of the Inter-American Commission on Human Rights) the authors have then withdrawn their communications from the IACHR in order to enable the Committee to proceed with its examination. In one case the author preferred to withdraw the case from the Human Rights Committee in order to have it considered by the European Commission of Human Rights. Simultaneous consideration by the Human Rights Committee and the IACHR is, however, possible under certain conditions. Thus in the case No. 10/1977 (*Alberto Altesor v. Uruguay*) the Committee concluded "that it is not prevented from considering the communication submitted to it by the authors on 10 March 1977 by reason of the subsequent complaint made by an unrelated third party under the procedure of IACHR. The rationale for this decision was explained in case No. 74/1979 (*M.A. Estrella v. Uruguay*) where the Committee observed that the provision of Article 5 (2) (a) "cannot be so interpreted as to imply that an unrelated third party, acting without the knowledge and consent of the alleged victim, can preclude the latter from having access to the Human Rights Committee".

As to what constitutes the "same matter", the Committee decided in case No. 6/1977 (*M. Millan Sequeira v. Uruguay*) that a two-line reference to the person concerned in a case before the Inter-American Commission on Human Rights, which listed in a similar manner the names of hundreds of other person allegedly detained in the country, "did not constitute the same matter as that described in detail by the author in his communication to the Human Rights Committee".

The Committee has also held that the submission of a similar case concerning a third party to another international procedure does not constitute the "same matter". Thus in case No. 75/1980 (*D. Fanili v. Italy*) the Committee explained: ". . . the concept of the 'same matter' within the meaning of Article 5 (2) (a) of the Optional Protocol must be understood as including the same claim concerning the same individual submitted by him or someone else who has the standing to act on his behalf before the other international body".

In the first case placed before it under the Optional Protocol, the Committee had occasion to determine that the examination of a particular human rights situation in a given country under Economic and Social Council resolution 1503 (XLVIII) — which governs a procedure for the examination of situations which appear to reveal "a consistent pattern of gross and reliably attested violations of human rights and fundamental freedoms" — does not, within the meaning of Article 5 (2) (a) of the Optional Protocol, constitute an examination of the "same matter", as a claim by an individual submitted to the Human Rights Committee under the Optional Protocol. The procedure governed by Economic and Social Council resolution 1503 (XLVIII) therefore does not bar the Human Rights Committee from considering an individual case. Also in one of the early cases considered, the Human Rights Committee determined that a procedure established by a non-governmental organization (such as the Inter-Parliamentary Council of the Inter-Parliamentary Union) does not constitute a procedure of international investigation or settlement within the meaning of Article 5 (2) (a) of the Optional Protocol.

With respect to Communications Nos. 146/1983 and 148 to 154/1983 (*Baboeram-Adhin et al. v. Suriname*) the Committee observed

> that a study by an intergovernmental organization either of the human rights situation in a given country (such as that by the IACHR) or a study of the trade union rights situation in a given country (such as the issues examined by the Committee on Freedom of Association of the International Labour Organization [ILO], or of a human rights problem of a more global character (such as that of the Special Rapporteur of the Commission on Human Rights on summary or arbitrary executions), although such studies might refer to or draw on information concerning individuals, cannot be seen as being the same matter as the examination of individual cases within the meaning of Article 5 (2) (a) of the Optional Protocol. Secondly, a procedure established by non-governmental organizations (such as Amnesty International, the International Commission of Jurists or the International Committee of the Red Cross, irrespective of the latter's standing in international law) does not constitute a procedure of international investigation or settlement within the meaning of Article 5 (2) (a) of the Optional Protocol.

f) Reservations by States Parties

Several States parties have further limited the competence of the Human Rights Committee to deal with communications under the Optional Protocol. With reference to Article 5 (2) (a) the Governments of Denmark, France, Iceland, Italy, Luxembourg, Norway, Spain and Sweden made reservations upon ratification of the Optional Protocol, precluding the competence of the Committee to consider a communication from an individual if the matter has already been examined under another procedure of international investigation or settlement. This reservation goes beyond the provision in the Optional Protocol which only precludes consideration with respect to cases simultaneously being examined elsewhere, but not with respect to cases which have been dealt with under another procedure. In case No. 121/1982 (*A. M. v. Denmark*), the author had first submitted his communication to the European Commission of Human Rights, which had declared it inadmissible as manifestly ill-founded. The Committee at its sixteenth session concluded that it was not competent to consider the communication in the light of the State party's reservation. In a subsequent case concerning another State party (*O. F. v. Norway*) the author first approached the European Commission of Human Rights but was informed by its Secretariat that it was already too late to submit an application. The State party itself informed the Committee that it would not object to the admissibility of the communication on the basis of its reservation, because the case had not been examined by the European Commission of Human Rights.

In a more recent case No. 168/1984 (*V. O. v. Norway*) the State party pleaded its reservation and the Committee found the objection to be dispositive of the matter. At its twenty-fifth session, the Committee, in declaring the communication inadmissible, shed further light on the meaning of the term "the same matter", as applied to communications submitted both to the Committee and to another international body:

> The Committee notes that the Norwegian reservation to Article 5 (2) of the Optional Protocol stipulates that the Committee shall lack competence to consider a communication if "the same matter" has already been examined under other international procedures. This phrase in the view of the Committee refers, with regard to identical parties, to the complaints advanced and facts adduced in support of them. Thus the Committee finds that the matter that is before the Committee now is in fact the same matter that was examined by the European Commission. While fully understanding the circumstances which have led the author to make a communication under the Covenant, the Committee finds that the State party's reservation operates to preclude it from examining the communication.

g) Exhaustion of Domestic Remedies

Pursuant to Article 5 (2) (b) of the Optional Protocol the Committee shall not consider any communication unless it has ascertained that the author has exhausted all available domestic remedies. The rule of exhaustion is a general rule of international body of investigation or settlement unless and until he has exhausted the means available to him in the State concerned for redressing his injuries, whether by appeal to the domestic courts or to the administrative authorities. This is a reasonable rule which is predicated both on practicality and on due respect for the sovereignty of States. A number of communications before the Committee have been declared inadmissible on this ground (*e.g.*, Nos. 26/1978, 39/1978 and 41/1979). In its decisions on admissibility, the Committee has clarified the meaning of Article 5 (2) (b) of the Optional Protocol, explaining *inter alia* that "exhaustion of domestic remedies can be required only to the extent that these remedies are effective and available" and in case No. 89/1981 (*Muhonen v. Finland*) the Committee further clarified that an "extraordinary remedy of seeking the annulment of the decisions of the Ministry of Justice" does not constitute an effective remedy within the meaning of Article 5 (2) (b) of the Optional Protocol.

In a number of early cases Uruguay contended that the authors had failed to exhaust domestic remedies. It submitted to the Committee a general description of remedies provided under the law of Uruguay, without, however, linking these remedies to the specific circumstances of each case. The Committee considered that this was insufficient and informed the State party that it would be necessary to give "details of the remedies which it submitted had been available to the author in the circumstances of his case, together with evidence that there would be a reasonable prospect that such remedies would be effective" (No. 4/1977, *William Torres Ramírez v. Uruguay*).

The provisional rules of procedure also provide that a decision on admissibility may be reviewed in the light of any explanations or statements submitted by the State party under Article 4 (2) of the Optional Protocol (Rule 93 [43]). Such a review requires the State party to give "specific details of domestic remedies which it claims to have been available to the alleged victim, together with evidence that there would be a reasonable prospect that such remedies would be effective".

In case No. 113/1981 (*F. L. v. Canada*) the Committee first declared the communication admissible at its nineteenth session, but it invited the State party to submit additional information on available domestic remedies. At its twenty-fourth session in April 1985, the Committee revised its prior decision as follows:

> Pursuant to Rule 93 (4) of its provisional rules of procedure, the Human Rights Committee has reviewed its decision on admissibility of 25 July 1983. On the basis of the additional information provided by the Canadian Government, the Committee concludes that the authors could have obtained redress for the violation complained of by seeking a declaratory judgement. The committee has stressed in other cases that remedies the availability of which is not reasonably evident cannot be invoked by the Government to the detriment of the author in proceedings under the Optional Protocol. According to the detailed explanations contained in the submission of 17 February 1984, however, the legal position appears to be sufficiently clear in that the specific remedy of a declaratory judgement was available and, if granted, would have been an effective remedy against the authorities concerned . . .
> In the light of the above considerations, the Committee finds that it is precluded under Article 5 (2) (b) of the Optional Protocol from considering the merits of the case and decides:
>
> 1. The decision of 25 July 1983 is set aside.
>
> 2. The communication is inadmissible.

h) Incompatibility

The Committee can consider communications only insofar as they relate to alleged violations of rights contained in the International Covenant on Civil and Political Rights. Communications relating to alleged violations of other rights must therefore be declared inadmissible *ratione materiae* as incompatible with the provisions of the Covenant. For instance, the Committee at its seventh session had to declare Communication No. 53/1979 (*K. B. v. Norway*) inadmissible because "the right to dispose of property, as such, is not protected by any provision of the International Covenant on Civil and Political Rights". Similarly, at its eighteenth session, the Committee declared Communication No. 129/1982 (*I. M. v. Norway*) inadmissible because "the assessment of taxable income and allocation of houses are not themselves matters to which the Covenant applies".

In case No. 117/1981 (*F. A. v. Italy*) the authors had claimed that the extradition proceedings, initiated by Italy against the alleged victim, at that time living in France, constituted a violation of the Covenant. At its twenty-first session the Committee declared that the claim was without foundation. "There is no provision of the Covenant making it unlawful for a State party to seek extradition of a person from another country. This claim is therefore inadmissible under Article 3 of the Optional Protocol; as incompatible with the provisions of the Covenant, *ratione materiae*".

i) Substantiation of Allegations

Although at the stage of admissibility an author of a communication need not prove the alleged violation, he must submit sufficient evidence in substantiation of his allegation as will constitute a *prima facie* case. The Committee has declared a number of communications inadmissible on the ground of non-substantiation of allegations.

The Optional Protocol has no provision to declare communications inadmissible on the ground of being "manifestly ill-founded" (as in the European system, Article 27 (2) of the European Convention). The Committee has recently disposed of such cases by declaring that the author "has no claim under Article 2 of the Optional Protocol" (*e.g.*, Nos. 170/1984, *E. H. v. Finland*; 173/1984, *M. F. v. Netherlands*; 174/1984, *J. K. v. Canada*; and 187/1985, *J. H. v. Canada*).

j) Abuse of the Right of Submission

Under Article 3 of the Optional Protocol, the Committee shall declare inadmissible a communication which it considers to be an abuse of the right of submission. In case No. 72/1980 (*K. L. v. Denmark*), where the author had alleged violations of rights not protected in the Covenant, had failed to substantiate in fact or law other allegations which pertained to rights protected by the Covenant and had himself indicated that he still intended to pursue further domestic remedies, the Committee concluded that "in these circumstances, the submission of the communication must be regarded as an abuse of the right of submission under Article 3 of the Optional Protocol".

The Committee, however, has been reluctant to declare communications inadmissible on the ground of abuse and prefers to declare them "incompatible" with the Covenant under Article 3 of the Optional Protocol. For instance, in case No. 104/1981 (*J. T. v. Canada*) the author claimed a violation by Canada of his right to freedom of expression under Article 19 of the Covenant, because he had been prevented from disseminating anti-Semitic messages through the telephone and postal systems. The Committee found that Canada had an obligation under Article 20 (2) of the Covenant to prohibit such advocacy of racial or religious hatred. "In the Committee's opinion therefore, the communication is, in respect of this claim, incompatible with the provisions of the Covenant, within the meaning of Article 3 of the Optional Protocol".

k) Competence of the Committee *vis-à-vis* National Law and Decisions

Several of the conditions for admissibility already examined are at the same time, broadly speaking, limitations on the competence of the Committee. Communications must directly or indirectly emanate from the alleged victim and must relate to facts relevant in time and subject-matter; if not, they are declared inadmissible as incompatible *ratione personae, temporis* or *materiae*, respectively.

In practise, it is often necessary to elaborate on the limited competence of the Committee as regards the subject-matter complained of, especially when the victim questions national law and decisions. Here it should be recalled that the competence of the Committee derives, of course, from the Covenant and the Optional Protocol and only from these instruments; hence it has no power or function on any other basis and in particular not within national legal systems. It is not a "fourth instance" following the exhaustion of domestic remedies and cannot be used as a forum for pursuing a complaint on the basis of domestic law. As a point of departure, therefore, it must be irrelevant for the Committee whether, for instance, a national law is constitutional or unconstitutional, or whether national courts are right or wrong under national law. What matters is only whether the laws, actions and judgements raise issues concerning or interfere with rights protected under the Covenant. Since the parties often repeat their arguments about national law and decisions, the Committee in number of cases has had to explained the scope of its competence in more detail.

In case No. 58/1979 (*Anna Maroufidou v. Sweden*), the Committee, in its views under Article 5 (4) of the Optional Protocol, delimited its own jurisdiction:

> The Committee takes the view that the interpretation of domestic law is essentially a matter for the courts and authorities of the State party concerned. It is not within the powers or functions of the Committee to evaluate whether the competent authorities of the State party in question have interpreted and applied the domestic law correctly in the case before it under the Optional Protocol, unless it is established that they have not interpreted and applied it in good faith or that it is evident that there has been an abuse of power.

The Committee did not indicate any explicit basis for its caveat regarding bad faith or abuse of power. Of course, neither the covenant nor the Optional Protocol afford any basis for any general competence of the Committee to test the good faith of national authorities or check their possible abuse of power as such. What the Committee appears to have had in mind is that such circumstances are likely to bring the provisions of the Covenant into play.

Hence, the saving clause of the *Maroufidou* case is best understood as indicating that the Committee would have competence when, for instance, it has to test the observance of such Covenant rights as equality before the law (Article 26) and those connected with a fair hearing before courts and tribunals (Article 14). Usually the distance is narrow between subjective bad faith or abuse and objective unfairness, and evidence of the former is therefore relevant to the latter. If applied more generally, i.e. to all "competent authorities of the State party" apart from courts, the *Maroufidou* formula would find only ambiguous and partial support in the Covenant, for example in those provisions which refer to "lawful" acts (of deprivation of liberty, Article 9), or restrictions imposed "in conformity and the law" (Article 21), and perhaps to a certain extent in such general provisions as Article 5 of the Covenant. This is not the place, however, to enter into general discussion of the possibility of *renvoi* from the Covenant to domestic law.

In its subsequent decision in case No. 27/1978 (*L. Pinkney v. Canada*), in which the author claimed that the Canadian courts had failed to evaluate missing evidence in his case and that such evidence would have assisted his defence, the Committee observed that:

> As regards the allegedly missing evidence, it has been established that the question whether it existed, and, if so, whether it would be relevant, was considered both by the trial judge and by the Court of Appeal. It is true that in the absence of the allegedly missing material itself, the Court's findings depended on an assessment of the information before them. However, it is not the function of the Committee to examine whether this assessment by the Courts was based on errors of fact, or to review their application of Canadian law, but only to determine whether it was made in circumstances indicating that the provisions of the Covenant were not observed.
>
> The Committee recalls that *Mr. Pinkney* was unable to convince the courts that such evidence would in any way have assisted his defence. Such a point is normally one on which the assessment of the domestic courts must be decisive.

More recently, at its twenty-third session, the Committee declared Communication No. 174/1984 (*J. K. v. Canada*) inadmissible and observed that it was beyond its competence "to review findings of fact made by national tribunals or to determine whether national tribunals properly evaluate new evidence submitted on appeal".

Notwithstanding this evident restrictions on the Committee's competence, the consideration of the communications under the Optional Protocol, as indicated above, requires the Committee to evaluate specific facts and to test in concrete cases the compatibility of national law, as applied, with the provisions of the Covenant. Somewhat related to this function is the Committee's authority to interpret the Covenant. In case No. 50/1979 (*G. van Duzen v. Canada*) the Committee observed that

> its interpretation and application of the International Covenant on Civil and Political Rights has to be based on the principle that the terms and concepts of the Covenant are independent of any particular national system of law and of all dictionary definitions. Although the terms of the Covenant are derived from long traditions within many nations, the Committee must now regard them as having an autonomous meaning. The parties have made extensive submissions, in particular as regards the meaning of the word "penalty" and as regards relevant Canadian law and practise. The Committee appreciates their relevance for the light they shed on the nature of the issue in dispute. On the other hand, the meaning of the word "penalty" in Canadian law is not, as such, decisive. Whether the word "penalty" in Article 15 (1) should be interpreted narrowly or widely, and whether it applies to different kinds of penalties, "criminal" and "administrative", under the Covenant, must depend on other factors. Apart from the text of Article 15 (1), regard must be had, *inter alia*, to its object and purpose.

The Committee has also had the opportunity of pronouncing itself on its general mandate in connection with the issue whether the Committee has a right to have direct access to individuals who claim to be victims of violations of their rights under the Covenant and who are detained by a State party. The Committee has maintained that its mandate necessarily covers this right of direct access. One State party, however, had challenged this position. In the Committee's views under Article 5 (4) of the Optional Protocol in case No. 63/1979 (*V. Setelich v. Uruguay*) the Committee rejected the contention that it had

> exceeded its mandate when in its decision of 24 October 1980, it requested the State party to afford to *Raúl Sendic Antonaccio* the opportunity to communicate directly with the Committee. The Committee rejects the State party's argument that a victim's right to contact the committee directly is invalid in the case of persons imprisoned in Uruguay. If governments had the right to erect obstacles to contacts between victims and the Committee, the procedure established by the Optional Protocol would, in many instances, be rendered meaningless. It is a prerequisite for the effective application of the Optional Protocol that detainees should be able to communicate directly with the Committee. The contention that International Covenant and the Protocol apply only to States, as subjects of international law, and that, in consequence, these instruments are not directly applicable to individuals is devoid of legal foundation in cases where a State has recognized the competence of the Committee to receive and consider communications from individuals under the Optional Protocol. That being so, denying individuals who are victims of an alleged violation their right to bring the matter before the Committee is tantamount to denying the mandatory nature of the Optional Protocol.

In subsequent cases the Committee has established the practise of requesting State parties to forward copies of the Committee's view to detained victims. For instance, in case No. 84/1981 (*Dermit Barbato v. Uruguay*), the Committee stated "that the State party is under an obligation . . to transmit a copy of these views to *Guillermo Dermit*." (See also the view in cases Nos. 88/1981, 106/1981, and 43/1979.)

a) Article 6: The Right to Life

The right to life is dealt with generally in Paragraph 1 of Article 6 of the Covenant, while Paragraphs 2 to 6 mostly concern the application of the death penalty.

There have been relatively few communications before the Committee involving Article 6 of the Covenant. In case No. 45/1979 (*P. Camargo v. Colombia*), the Committee, commenting generally on Article 6, stated *inter alia*;

> The requirements that the right [to life] shall be protected by law and that no one shall be arbitrarily deprived of his life mean that the law must strictly control and limit the circumstances in which a person may be deprived of his life by the authorities of a State. In the present case it is evident from the fact that seven persons lost their lives as a result of the deliberate action of the police that the deprivation of life was intentional. Moreover, the police action was apparently taken without warning to the victims and without giving them any opportunity to surrender to the police patrol or to offer any explanation of their presence or intentions. . .

The Committee concluded:

> that the action of the police resulting in the death of Mrs. *Maria Fanny Suárez de Guerrero* was disproportionate to the requirements of law enforcement in the circumstances of the case and that she was arbitrarily deprived of her life contrary to Article 6 (1) of the International Covenant on Civil and Political Rights. Inasmuch as the police action was made justifiable as a matter of Colombian law by Legislative Decree No. 0070 of 20 January 1978, the right to life was not adequately protected by the law of Colombia as required by Article 6 (1). . .
>
> The Committee is accordingly of the view that the State party should take the necessary measures to compensate the husband of *Mrs. Maria Fanny Suárez de Guerrero* for the death of his wife and to ensure that the right to life is duly protected by amending the law.

Perhaps the leading cases dealing with Article 6 are Nos. 146/1983 and 148 to 154/1983 (*Kanta Baboeram-Adhin et al. v. Suriname*) decided by the Committee at its 24th session. In its view under Article 5 (4) of the Optional Protocol the Committee declared:

> Article 6 (1) of the Covenant provides:
>
> "Every human being has the inherent right to life. This right shall be protected by law. No one shall be arbitrarily deprived of his life."
>
> The right enshrined in this article is the supreme right of the human being. It follows that the deprivation of life by the authorities of the State is a matter of the utmost gravity. This follows from the article as a whole and in particular is the reason why paragraph 2 of the article lays down that the death penalty may be imposed only for the most serious crimes. The requirements that the right shall be protected by law and that no one shall be arbitrarily deprived of his life mean that the law must strictly control and limit the circumstances in which a person may be deprived of his life by the authorities of a State. In the present case it is evident from the fact that 15 prominent persons lost their lives as a result of the deliberate action of the military police that the deprivation of life was intentional. The State party has failed to submit any evidence proving that these persons were shot while trying to escape.
>
> The Human Rights Committee, acting under Article 5 (4) of the Optional Protocol to the International Covenant on Civil and Political Rights, is of the view that the victims were arbitrarily deprived of their lives contrary to Article 6 (1) of the International Covenant does not find it necessary to consider assertions that other provisions of the Covenant were violated.
>
> The Committee therefore urges the State party to take effective steps (i) to investigate the killings of December 1982; (ii) to bring to justice any persons found to be responsible for the death of the victims, (iii) to pay compensation to the surviving families; and (iv) to ensure that the right to life is duly protected in Suriname.

In case No. 84/1981 (*Dermit Barbato v. Uruguay*), the Committee observed that whilst it could not arrive at a definite conclusion as to whether the victim had committed suicide, was driven to suicide or was killed by others while in custody, "the inescapable conclusion is that in all the circumstances the Uruguayan authorities either by act or by omission were responsible for not taking adequate measures to protect his life, as required by Article 6 (1) of the Covenant".

The fate of so-called "disappeared persons" has also been dealt with in connection with Article 6. Thus in case No. 30/1978 (*Bleier v. Uruguay*), the Committee found that the fact of the disappearance of *Eduardo Bleier* in October 1975 did not alone establish that he was arrested by the Uruguayan authorities.

> But, the allegation that he was so arrested and detained is confirmed (i) by the information, unexplained and substantially unrefuted by the State party, that *Eduardo Bleiers's* name was on a list of prisoners read out once a week at an army unit in Montevideo where his family delivered clothing for him and received his dirty clothing until the summer of 1976, and (ii) by the testimony of other prisoners that they saw him in Uruguayan detention centres . . . It is therefore the Committee's view that . . . there are serious reasons to believe that the ultimate violation of Article 6 has been perpetrated . . . [T]he Committee urges the Uruguayan Government to reconsider its position in this case and to take effective steps . . . to establish what has happened to *Eduardo Bleier* since October 1975, to bring to justice any persons found to be responsible for his death, disappearance or ill-treatment, and to pay compensation to him or his family for any injury which he has suffered.

b) Article 7: The Right not to be Subjected to Torture or to Cruel, Inhuman or Degrading Treatment

Article 7, which prohibits torture and other cruel, inhuman or degrading treatment or punishment, has been invoked in a number of cases, mostly concerning Uruguay (in particular Nos. 4/1977, 5/1977, 8/1977, 9/1977, 11/1977, 25/1978, 28/1978, 33/1978, 37/1978, 52/1979, 63/1979, 73/1980, and 110/1981).

In these cases the authors have made detailed descriptions of various forms of torture and other cruel treatment allegedly inflicted upon the victims (such as beatings, electric shocks, immersion in water to a point near suffocation, burning with cigarettes and prolonged forced standing). Some of the authors identified by name the persons who had allegedly engaged in the torture. In all the cases listed above the Committee found violations of Article 7.

The Committee has found it at times difficult to circumscribe the content of Article 7. It has therefore in a number of cases made findings of violations of Article 7 together with Article 10 (1), as in case No. 49/1979 (*D. Marais v. Madagascar*), where the victim had been held *incommunicado* for several years in a "cell measuring 1 meter (m.) by 2 m. in the basement of the political police prison at Ambohibao." Similarly, in case No. 115/1982 (*John Wight v. Madagascar*), because the victim "was kept in a solitary room at the [political police prison] chained to a bed spring on the floor, with minimal clothing and a severe rationing of food, and because during hospitalization he was "chained to the floor. . . and held totally *incommunicado.*"

In case No. 107/1981 (*Quinteros v. Uruguay*) the Committee found that mental anguish suffered by a mother because of the disappearance of her daughter also constitutes a violation of Article 7:

> The Committee understands the anguish and stress caused to the mother by the disappearance of her daughter and by the continuing uncertainty concerning her fate and whereabouts. The author has the right to know what has happened to her daughter. In these respects, she too is a victim of the violations of the Covenant suffered by her daughter, in particular of Article 7.

c) Article 9: The Right to Liberty and Security of Person

aa) Arbitrary Arrest and Detention (Article 9 [1])

Although many communications submitted to the Committee claim that the victim has been subjected to arbitrary arrest and detention, this allegation has proved to be difficult to establish, since States parties have been able to show in most cases that the deprivation of liberty was carried out according to the law of the State concerned. In the absence of an independent fact-finding machinery, the Committee has experienced considerable difficulty in determining whether in the circumstances of each case the deprivation of liberty could be deemed arbitrary. In cases, however, where the facts indicated that no arrest warrant had been issued or that the victim was not released from imprisonment after serving his term or after issuance of a release order, the Committee has found violations of Article 9 (1). Thus, we have the example of case No. 25/1978 (*C. Améndola and G. Baritussio v. Uruguay*), where one of the victims was kept in detention for over one month after fully serving her term of detention, and the other victim was "subjected to arbitrary detention under the 'prompt security measures' until 12 August 1978 after having signed on 15 August 1974 the document for her provisional release". Similarly in case No. 37/1979 (*Soriano de Bouton v. Uruguay*) the victim "was not released until one month after an order for her release was issued by the military court"; and in case No. 33/1978 (*Leopoldo Buffo Caraballal v. Uruguay*) the victim "was not released until approximately six or seven months after an order for his release was issued by the military court."

In case No. 56/1979 (*Lilian Celiberti v. Uruguay*), the victim had been abducted by agents of the State party in another country, brought across the border and charged with "subversive association". The Committee found a violation of Article 9 (1), "because the act of abduction into Uruguayan territory constituted an arbitrary arrest and detention."

In case No. 16/1977 (*D. Monguya Mbenge v. Zaire*), the Committee found that *Abraham Oyabi* had been "arrested on 1 September 1977 in order to force him to disclose the whereabouts of *Simon Biyanga* and that he was not released from detention until late in 1978 or early in 1979. The State party has not claimed that there was any criminal charge against him. In the view of the Committee, therefore, he was subjected to arbitrary arrest and detention contrary to Article 9 of the Covenant."

The "disappearance" of a person has also been found to entail a violation of Article 9 when evidence indicates the responsibility of the State party (No. 30/1978, *Bleier v. Uruguay*). Similarly, in case No. 107/1981 (*Quinteros v. Uruguay*), the Committee found that the evidence showed that "on 28 June 1976, *Elena Quinteros* was arrested on the grounds of the Embassy of Venezuela at Montevideo by at least one member of the Uruguayan police force and that in August 1976 she was held in a military detention centre in Uruguay. . ." Although the State party claimed to have no knowledge of these events, the Committee concluded that the author had submitted sufficient evidence to sustain a finding of a violation of Article 9.

bb) The Right to be Brought Promptly Before a Judge and Tried within a Reasonable Time (Article 9[3])

One of the most fundamental rights of persons who have been arrested or detained on a criminal charge is the right to be brought "promptly" before a judicial officer, and to "trial within a reasonable time". The Committee has received many communications concerning alleged violations of this right, but it has not yet established the precise meaning of the terms used in Article 9 (3) of the Covenant. However, the relevant general comment, adopted by the Committee at its sixteenth session, sheds some light on these issues. In particular, "promptly" is held to mean that "delays must not exceed a few days", while the total length of "detention pending trial" is "another matter", and should be "as short as possible".

In its views under the Optional Protocol the Committee has been less explicit in distinguishing these different elements of Article 9 (3). It has held, however, that the article had been breached with respect to a victim who had been arrested on 24 March 1977 and detained until 9 January 1978 (*i.e.* over nine months) without having been brought before a judge (No. 90/1981, *Lueye Magana ex-Philibert v. Zaire*). In another case of an established breach the victim was arrested on 2 December 1980, was kept *incommunicado* and not brought before a judicial authority until 23 March 1981, i.e. over three months later (No. 84/1981, *Dermit Barbato v. Uruguay*). (*See also* Nos. 5/1977, 6/1977, 8/1977, 10/1977, 11/1977, 28/1978, 32/1978, 33/1978, 37/1978, 44/1979, 52/1979, 63/1979, 66/1979, and 73/1980). On the other hand, the Committee found no violation of Article 9 (3) where the person was arrested on 28 September 1978 and charged before a military examining judge on 7 November 1978, i.e. six weeks later (No. 43/1979, *Drescher v. Uruguay*). Perhaps this finding fails to bear out the difference between judicial review of the arrest and detention, which shall take place "promptly", and the trial, which shall follow "within a reasonable time". For the latter purpose six weeks is not particularly long, while for the former it would certainly be, as suggested by the different terms for the two matters. To prepare the trial is a different and much more time-consuming task than to establish the basis for pre-trial detention.

cc) The Right to Challenge the Lawfulness of one's Arrest and Detention (Article 9 [4]).

The Committee has considered many communications in which the authors have alleged that the right to take proceedings before a court in order to challenge their arrest has been violated, in particular because they were denied the remedy of *habeas corpus*. The Committee found a violation of Article 9 (4) in cases where it established that the victims had no way of challenging their arrest, because the remedy of *habeas corpus* was not applicable to persons arrested under the so-called "prompt security measures" in the State party concern (Nos. 4/1977, 5/1977, 6/1977, 8/1977, 9/1977, 10/1977, 11/1977, 25/1978, 28/1978, 32/1978, 33/1978, 37/1978, 43/1979, and 44/1979.)

In case No. 46/1979 (*O. Fals Borda et al. v. Colombia*), the Committee noted: "As to the allegations of breaches of the provisions of Article 9 of the Covenant, it has been established that the alleged victims did not have recourse to *habeas corpus*". The Committee concluded that the provision had been violated because the victims "could not themselves take proceedings in order that a court might decide without delay on the lawfulness of their detention".

For one of the two victims in this case a breach was also found of Article 9 (3). It would seem to follow that a person detained on a specific criminal charge may invoke both Paragraph 3 and Paragraph 4 of Article 9. But many of the cases of breaches of Article 9 (4) confirm that this right is independent of such a charge and arises, in particular, when someone is detained on security grounds, which is often the justification given for political detention. Whether or not such detention is considered as compatible with Article 9 as a whole (not arbitrary *etc.*), there must be a possibility of court review as required under Article 9 (4). This right also has potential application in many other cases.

dd) The Right to Compensation for Unlawful Arrest or Detention (Article 9[5])

In a number of cases the Committee has expressed the view that the State party is under an obligation "to provide effective remedies to the victim, including compensation in accordance with Article 9 (5) of the Covenant" (No. 9/1977; *see also* 8/1977, 25/1978, 90/1981, 107/1981, 132/1982). Compensation under Article 9 (1), but also breaches of Article 9 (3) and (4). Furthermore, the Committee has frequently recommended that the State party pay compensation to victims of violations of other articles of the Covenant such as Articles 6, 7, 10 and 14. (See *e.g.*, Nos. 30/1978, 45/1979, 52/1979, 70/1980 and 146/148—154/1983). The duty to do so may be said to follow from Article 2 (3) of the Covenant.

d) Article 10: The Right to be Treated Humanely during Imprisonment

A violation of the first Paragraph of this Article, which provides that all persons deprived of their liberty shall be treated with respect for the inherent dignity of the human person, has been found in a number of cases, including case No. 49/1979 (*D. Marais v. Madagascar*), where the victim had been held "in a cell measuring 1 m. by 2 m. in the basement of the political police prison at Ambohibao and has been held *incommunicado* ever since:, in case No. 109/1981 (*Gómez de Voituret v. Uruguay*), "because *Teresa Gómez de Voituret* was kept in solitary confinement for several months in conditions which failed to respect the inherent dignity of the human person", in case No. 85/1981 (*Romero v. Uruguay*), "because *Hector Alfredo Romero* has not been treated with humanity and with respect for the inherent dignity of the human person, in particular because he was kept *incommunicado* at an unknown place of detention for several months (from November 1976 to the middle of 1977) during which time his fate and his whereabouts were unknown". (*See also* Nos. 4/1977, 5/1977, 8/1977, 10/1977, 25/1977, 27/1978, 30/1978, 33/1978, 44/1979, 56/1979, 63/1979, 70/1980 and 115/1982).

Paragraph 2 of Article 10 provides for the right of accused persons to be segregated from convicted persons and prescribes special treatment for juveniles. In case No. 27/1978 (*L. Pinkney v. Canada*) the Committee noted:

> that the requirement of Article 10 (2) of the Covenant that "accused persons shall, save in exceptional circumstances, be segregated from convicted persons" means that they shall be kept in separate quarters (but not necessarily in separate buildings). The Committee would not regard the arrangements described by the State party whereby convicted persons work as food servers and cleaners in the remand area of the prison as being incompatible with Article 10 (2) (a), provided that contacts between the two

classes of prisoners are kept strictly to a minimum necessary for the performance of those tasks.

g) Article 14: The Right to a Fair Hearing

Article 14 of the Covenant, as the Committee has observed,

> is of a complex nature and . . . different aspects of its provisions will need specific comments. All of these provisions are aimed at ensuring the proper administration of justice, and to this end uphold a series of individual rights such as equality before the courts and tribunals and the right to a fair and public hearing by a competent, independent and impartial tribunal established by law. This is how the Committee began its recent general comment on Article 14.

Indeed, the right to a fair hearing in court is one of the cornerstones of the Covenant as a guarantee of the rule of law. This general comment with its 19 paragraphs is most comprehensive of all so far adopted, but by no means exhausts the numerous issues of principle and practise arising in the interpretation and application of Article 14. One may expect, for example, that the Committee will soon have to consider the scope of Article 14 (1), which lays down the most important principles for a fair hearing. The Committee has yet to clarify the extent to which Article 14 applies not only to procedures for the determination of criminal charges against individuals but also to procedures to determine "rights and obligations in a suit at law". Besides private law disputes, which clearly must be covered, matters such as the rights and obligations of individuals towards the State are likely to be brought up for consideration. But how broadly does Article 14 guarantee a right to a court hearing in such "public law disputes"? In other words, the question of a right to judicial review of administrative action arises.

So far, no communication raising this problem has reached the stage of the merits. However, in a complex decision in case No. 112/1981 (*Y.L. v. Canada*) concerning a complaint about decisions by a pension review board, the Committee found that the guarantees of Article 14 (1) did not apply because a "suit at Law" was not involved. The Communication was declared inadmissible. Experiences of similar bodies suggest that it may become a prominent area of controversy in the years to come.

Apart from this uncertainty about the full scope of Article 14 (1), other issues of principle are looming in the background. It may be noted that the rest of the Article — Paragraphs (2) to (7) — concerns only criminal procedures, which the Covenant regulates in much more detail than other court procedures.

The general comment referred to elaborates on many principles in a more general way than the Committee has done in its view under the Optional Protocol, stating, for instance, that the "presumption of innocence" in criminal cases implies "a duty for all public authorities to refrain from prejudging the outcome of the trial". In other words, the presumption must be respected not only by the judge, particularly in connection with the burden of proof and the extension to all accused persons of the benefit of the doubt (*in dubio pro reo*), but also by other public authorities dealing with such persons. Until they are proven guilty according to law, the presumption prevails, particularly in connection with the treatment of accused persons and with the issuance of statements about them, e.g. to the press.

The case-law under the Optional Protocol so far has applied the requirements of Article 14 mainly to victims of defective criminal proceedings in Uruguay, as the following summary will show. In particular, the right to a fair and public hearing (Art. 14 [1]) and some of the minimum guarantees of the defendant (Art. 14 [3]) have been highlighted in a number of cases.

aa) Fair and Public Hearing by a Competent, Independent and Impartial Tribunal (Article 14 [1])

In case No. 70/1980 (*Elsa Cubas v. Uruguay*) the Committee made findings of fact that the victim "was tried *in camera*, the trial was conducted without her presence and the judgement was not rendered in public" and held that these facts revealed a violation of Article 14 (1) "because she did not have a fair and public hearing". Similarly, in case No. 10/1977 (*Alberto Altesor v. Uruguay*), the Committee found that Article 14 (1) had been violated "because he did not have a fair and public hearing". In case No. 44/1979 (*A. Pietroroia v. Uruguay*), the Committee made a finding of fact that the victim was sentenced "in a closed trial, conducted in writing and without his presence . . . and the judgement of the Court was not made public", and based thereon a finding of a violation of Article 14 (1). (*See also* cases No. 28/1978, and 32/1978.)

bb) Minimum Guarantees in the Determination of any Criminal Charge (Article 14 [3])

— The Right to Communicate with Counsel (Article 14 [3] [b])

Violations of Article 14 (3) have been found in numerous cases, *e.g.* No. 83/1981 (*V. Martínez Machado v. Uruguay*) "because the conditions of his detention from November 1980 to May 1981 effectively barred him from access to legal assistance", and No. 49/1970 (*D. Marais v. Madagascar*) "because he has been denied adequate opportunity to communicate with his counsel, . . . and because his right to the assistance of his counsel to represent him and prepare his defence has been interfered with by the Malagasy authorities", and No. 115/1982 (*J. Wight v. Madagascar*) "because during a ten-month period . . . while criminal charges against him were being investigated and determined, he was kept *incommunicado* without access to legal counsel."

— The Right to Legal Assistance of One's Own Choosing (Article 14 [3] [b])

In a number of cases the Committee has found that the victims were denied the right to defend themselves through counsel of their own choosing and were compelled to accept *ex officio* counsel in violation of Article 14 (3) (b) and (d), (No. 52/1979, 56/1979, and 73/1980).

> Thus in case No. 52/1979 (*López Burgos v. Uruguay*), the Committee noted: The State party has stated that *López Burgos* was not prevented from choosing his own legal counsel. It has not, however, refuted witness testimony indicating that López Burgos and others arrested with him, including *Monica Soliño* and *Inés Quadros*, whose parents are attorneys, were forced to agree to *ex officio* legal counsel.

— The Right to Have Adequate Time and Facilities for the Preparation of one's Defence (Article 14 [3] [b])

In case No. 158/1983 (*O. F. v. Norway*) the author had been found guilty of driving his automobile at a speed exceeding that allowed by the traffic law and of failing to furnish information to an official register about a business firm which he operated. He claimed that he was not able to adequately prepare his defence because the Court did not provide him with copies of all relevant documents about the traffic violation. In declaring the case inadmissible, the Committee noted

> that from 26 August to the date of the hearing on 21 October 1982 the author could have examined, personally or through his lawyer, documents relevant to his case at the police station. He chose not to do so, but requested that copies of all documents be sent to him. The Committee notes that the Covenant does not explicitly provide for a right of a charged person to be furnished with copies of all relevant documents in a criminal investigation, but does provide that he shall "have adequate time and facilities for the preparation of his defence and to communicate with counsel of his own choosing." Even if all the allegations of the author were to be accepted as proven, there would be no ground for asserting that a violation of Article 14 (3) (b) occurred.

— The Right to be Tried without Undue Delay (Article 14 [3] [c])

A violation of this provision of the Covenant is frequently accompanied by a violation of the right to be brought promptly before a judge and tried within a reasonable time (Article 9 [3]). Thus far the Committee has not defined the relevant terms or suggested a rule of thumb, because it must consider the particular circumstances of each communication. In case No. 43/1979 (*A. Drescher Caldas v. Uruguay*) a victim who had been arrested on 28 September 1978 and tried before a military court in July 1979 (10 months later) was deemed to have suffered a violation of his right to be tried without undue delay. The Committee has also found a violation of Article 14 (3) (c) in case No.80/1980 (*S. Vasilskis v. Uruguay*), where the victim was arrested some years before the entry into force of the Covenant and the Optional Protocol and was not tried until some time after entry into force of these instruments for the State concerned. In that case the victim had been arrested on 4 June 1972, the Covenant and Optional Protocol had entered into force on 23 March 1976 for the State party concerned and judgement was not pronounced by the court of first instance until 14 December 1977. (*See also* Nos. 4/1977, 5/1977, 6/1977, 8/1977, 10/1977, 27/1978, 28/1978, 32/1978, 33/1978, 44/1979, 46/1979, 52/1979, 56/1979, 63/1979, 70/1980, and 73/1980.)

— The Right to Free Legal Assistance (Article 14 [3] [d])

In case No. 158/1983 (*O. F. v. Norway*) the author, who had been found guilty of two minor offences and sentenced to pay a fine of NKr. 1,000.—claimed, *inter alia*, that Article 14 (3) (d) had been violated in his case. The Committee observed in this connection:

> The Covenant foresees free legal assistance to a charged person "in any case where the interests of justice so require and without payment by him in any such case if he does not have sufficient means to pay for it". The author has failed to show that in his particular case the "interests of justice" would have required the assignment of a lawyer at the expense of the State party.

The author's communication was declared inadmissible.

—The Right to Examine Witnesses (Article [3] [e])

In case No. 63/1979 (*V. Setelich v. Uruguay*) the Committee found a violation of Article 14 (3) (e) because the victim "was denied the opportunity to obtain the attendance and examination of witnesses on his behalf."

— The Right not to Incriminate Oneself (Article [3] [g])

The use of forced confessions in order to convict accused persons has been found by the Committee to be in violation of Article 14 (3) (g) in cases No. 52/1979 and 73/1980.

Thus in case No. 52/1979 (*López Burgos v. Uruguay*), the author had submitted written witness testimony by four ex-detainees who asserted "that *López Burgos* and several others were forced under threats to sign false statements which were subsequently used in the legal proceedings against them". In its views the Committee noted: "The State party has not refuted the author's allegations that Mr. *López Burgos* was forced to sign false testimony against himself and that this testimony was used in the trial against him."

cc) The Right to Review of Conviction and Sentence (Article 14 [5])

In case No. 64/1979 (*Salgar de Montejo v. Colombia*), the Committee noted that the expression "according to law" in Article 14 (5) of the Covenant is not intended to leave the very existence of the right to review to the discretion of the States parties, since the rights are those recognized by domestic law. Rather, what is to be determined "according to law" is the modalities by which the review by a higher tribunal is to be carried out. The Committee found that the facts of the case disclosed a violation of Article 14 (5), because the victim "was denied the right to review of her conviction by a higher tribunal."

In case No. 27/1978 (*L. Pinkney v. Canada*) the author had appealed his conviction to the British Columbia Court of Appeal. The production of the transcripts of the lower court proceedings, however, was delayed for two and a half years. The author alleged that this delay was excessive and prejudicial to his exercise of the right to appeal. The Committee observed "that the right under Article 14 (3) (c) to be tried without undue delay should be applied in conjunction with the right under Article 14 (5) to review by a higher tribunal, and that consequently there was in this case a violation of both of these provisions taken together."

h) Article 15: *Nulla poena sine lege*

In case No. 28/1978 (*L. Weinberger Weisz v. Uruguay*), the Committee found that Article 15 had been violated "because the penal law was applied retroactively against" the victim: the charge of conspiracy (*Asociación para delinquir*) was found to be tantamount to prosecution for membership in a political party, which had been lawful at the time when the victim was affiliated with it and which had been banned only afterwards. (*See also* Nos. 44/1979, 46/1979, and 91/1981.)

The purpose of the main principle of Article 15 is to protect individuals against *ex post facto* criminal laws operating to their detriment. The last sentence of Paragraph 1 of Article 15 departs from this safeguard when this purpose is absent; on the contrary, it not only allows, but prescribes the retroactive operation of a new law imposing a "lighter penalty". The Committee has been seised of two cases where it was claimed that a new law changing the conditions of parole should have been applied retroactively to two convicted persons. In the specific circumstances of the cases the Committee decided that no violation of the Covenant had taken place (Nos. 50/1979, *Van Duzen v. Canada*; 55/1979, *MacIsaac v. Canada*).

The Committee found that it had not been shown in either of the two cases that the alleged victim had in fact been adversely affected by the non-retroactive application of the new rules. It therefore left open several difficult questions of interpretation such as whether the duty of States parties to extend the benefit of a "lighter penalty" retroactively, despite its broad wording, must not have inherent limitations. Certain reservations and interpretative declarations have limited it to "cases in progress", i.e. before sentence is passed. In another case (No. 46/1979, *Fals Borda et al. v. Colombia*), the Committee in an *obiter dictum* seems to have assumed that this clause is inapplicable after the rejection of appeals. If not, States parties when introducing lighter penalties would seem to have to provide for review of earlier sentences without any explicit time limit.

p) Article 26: Discrimination on the Ground of Sex

The committee found a violation of Article 26 in case No. 35/1978 (*Aumeeruddy-Cziffra et al. v. Mauritius* [also referred to above in relation to Articles 17, 23 and 25]), where the State party's immigration law and deportation law subjected foreign husbands of native women to certain restrictions, whereas foreign wives of native men were not so subjected.

q) Article 27: Protection of Minorities

Article 27 has been invoked before the Committee primarily in connection with the rights of Canadian Indians to their cultural heritage. In case No. 24/1977 (*Sandra Lovelace v. Canada*), a native Indian had been denied by operation of the Indian Act, the legal right to reside on an Indian reserve because she had married a non-Indian. She later divorced. The Committee found a breach of Article 27. It considered that for purposes of Article 27 she must still be considered among "persons belonging" to the minority concerned; and although the right to reside in the reserve was not as such guaranteed by Article 27, access to her native culture and language had in fact been denied to her in a way which the Committee held to be unjustified. It also made reference to other provisions of the Covenant invoked by Mrs. Lovelace. Canada subsequently informed the

Committee that the Indian Act had been duly amended, so as to remove therefrom any discriminatory provisions.

* * *

8. Manual on Human Rights Reporting Under Six Major International Human Rights Instruments (excerpts)

The International Covenant on Economic, Social and Cultural Rights

by Philip Alston

The International Covenant on Economic, Social and Cultural Rights (hereinafter, the "Covenant", or "ICESCR") was adopted by the General Assembly of the United Nations pursuant to resolution 2200A (XXI) of 16 December 1966. It entered into force on 3 September 1976, in accordance with article 27. As of September 1990 the Covenant had been ratified or acceded to by 95 States.

A. The Reporting Process

(a) The Covenant and its reporting requirements

The Covenant is the twin sibling of the International Covenant on Civil and Political Rights. Each of the Covenants elaborates on some of the rights contained in the Universal Declaration of Human Rights and there is some overlap in content between the two. Most importantly, however, the preamble to the Covenant recognizes that the human rights ideal can only be achieved "if conditions are created whereby everyone may enjoy his economic, social and cultural rights, as well as his civil and political rights". (The preamble to the Covenant on Civil and Political Rights expresses the identical sentiment but reverses the order in which the two sets of rights are listed.) Thus, this Covenant cannot be viewed in isolation from the other and both the means and the objectives laid down in the Covenant on Civil and Political Rights should be borne in mind in reporting on the Covenant on Economic, Social and Cultural Rights.

Under article 2(1) of the Covenant, each State party "undertakes to take steps . . . with a view to achieving progressively the full realization of the rights recognized . . .". The obligation is made subject to the availability of resources, but the scope of that qualification is limited (as discussed below, in connection with article 2). Moreover, article 2(2) of the Covenant, which requires States to guarantee that the relevant rights will be exercised without discrimination, is not subject to resource constraints. In other words, if the resources are available to enable any degree of enjoyment of a given right, then it must be under circumstances that do not discriminate. Similarly, article 3 which provides for affirmative measures to ensure the equal rights of men and women, is not made subject to the availability of resources.

Before considering the nature of the reporting obligation it is appropriate to note that the body which monitors compliance with States' parties obligations under the Covenant is the Committee on Economic, Social and Cultural Rights (hereinafter referred to as "the Committee"). It does so under the aegis of the United Nations Economic and Social Council which is the body formally entrusted with that responsibility under the Covenant. Before the Committee began its work in 1987, the Council was assisted in its task by the Sessional Working Group of Governmental Experts (hereinafter referred to as "the Sessional Working Group").

The principal obligation of States parties to the Covenant is to implement its provisions at the national level. The obligation to report to an international body, which is the focus of the present Manual, is essentially a means of promoting the implementation of that obligation. Article 16(1) states, in the following terms, the obligation to report.

—Text of article 16(1)

> **The States Parties to the present Covenant undertake to submit in conformity with this part of the Covenant reports on the measures which they have adopted and the progress made in achieving the observance of the rights recognized herein.**

The nature of the report to be submitted is further elaborated upon in article 17(2) which provides that "[r]eports may indicate factors and difficulties affecting the degree of fulfillment of obligations under the present Covenant". Taken together, these provisions make it clear that States parties reports are required to deal not only with the progress made but also with cases where appropriate progress has not been made. The Committee has made this clear on a number of occasions, and particularly when States reports have sought to portray only the positive developments in the country concerned. Such reports are not considered to satisfy the requirements of the Covenant.

In 1976, shortly after the Covenant came into force, the Economic and Social Council instituted a three phase reporting cycle according to which States parties were required to report, initially at three-yearly intervals, on different clusters of rights (articles 6-9, 10-12 and 13-15). This system meant that a complete initial reporting cycle took nine years. The cycle for subsequent, or periodic, reports took only six years to complete but meant that a State party was required to submit a report under the Covenant every two years. This programme of reporting was considered by the Committee to be unduly burdensome upon States and to reflect an excessively compartmentalized approach to the rights recognized in the Covenant.

A new reporting cycle was thus introduced (Economic and Social Council resolution 1988/4) as a result of which States parties are now requested to submit an initial report, dealing with the entire Covenant, within two years of the Covenant's entry into force for the State concerned. Every five years thereafter a single, comprehensive, periodic report is required. At its fourth session, the Committee drew up a revised schedule for the submission of reports with a view to ensuring a smooth transition from the old to the new periodicity.

These arrangements are without prejudice to the Committee's ability to request a State party to submit additional information to supplement that already provided in a report by the State concerned.

(b) Guidelines for reporting under the Covenant

General guidelines dealing both with the form and content of reports were established shortly after the Covenant's entry into force in 1976. However, in response to the recent introduction of an entirely new reporting cycle, and in the light of various perceived inadequacies in the approach reflected in the original guidelines, the Committee began the process of revising the guidelines at its second session and completed the process with the adoption of new guidelines at its fifth session.

The guidelines are intended to provide guidance to states parties in the preparation of their reports. By following them as closely as possible, reporting officers will minimize the risk that their reports are deemed to be inadequate in scope and insufficient in detail. The guidelines also provide a uniformly applicable framework within which the Committee can work and enable it to demonstrate a consistency of approach from one report to another. Finally, the guidelines are designed to reduce the amount of duplication of information requested by the various treaty bodies.

The Committee's guidelines do not distinguish between initial and periodic reports. The same information is requested in relation to each, although it is unnecessary to repeat in a periodic report information already provided in a previous report.

The guidelines are divided into two parts. The first, or general, part requests a country profile dealing with matters such as information about the land and its people, the general political structure, the economic, social and cultural characteristics of the country and the general legal framework within which human rights are protected. This part of the guidelines is now common to the reporting guidelines prepared for all the United Nations human rights treaty bodies and it is assumed that the reporting State can simply reproduce a standard profile, updated if necessary, whenever reporting to any of the relevant treaty bodies. Part one of the guidelines is as follows:

—Text of part one of the reporting guidelines regarding the form and contents of reports to be submitted by States parties under articles 16 and 17 of the International Covenant on Economic, Social and Cultural Rights

A. *General part of the report*

1. *Country profile*

(a) *Land and people*

This section should contain information on the main geographic, ethnic linguistic, demographic and religious characteristics of the country and its population.

(b) *General political structure*

This section should contain information on the main geographic, ethnic linguistic, demographic and religious characteristics of the country and its population.

(b) *General political structure*

This section should briefly describe the political history and framework, the type of government and the organization of the executive, legislative and judicial organs.

(c) *Economic, social and cultural characteristics*

This section should include information on such indicators as gross national product (GNP), per capita income, functional distribution of income (i.e., relation of labour/capital income proportion in the public and private sectors of economy), rate of inflation, balances of trade and payment, external debt, rate of unemployment and literacy rate.

(ii) What remedies are available to an individual who claims that any of his/her rights have been violated; and what systems of compensation exist for victims;

(iii) Whether any of the rights referred to in the various conventions are protected either in the Constitution or by separate legislation and, if so, whether provisions exist in the Constitution or such specific legislation for derogations and under what circumstances;

(iv) Whether the provisions of the various international human rights instruments can be invoked before, and directly enforced by, the courts, other tribunals or administrative authorities or whether they have to be transformed into internal laws or administrative regulations in order to be enforced by the authorities concerned.

2. *Information and publicity concerning the Covenant on Economic, Social and Cultural Rights and the country's reports to the Committee*

(a) In what manner and to what extent has the text of the Covenant been disseminated? Has it been translated into local languages and how have copies of such translations been distributed? Is assistance from the United Nations required in this regard (if so, please specify)?

(b) What government agencies prepared the report? Were inputs sought or received from any sources other than from the Government?

(c) How widely available is the report? Has its content been the subject of public debate?

3. *Legal status and specific implementation of the Covenant on Economic, Social and Cultural Rights*

(In so far as not fully dealt with under section 1 (d) above).

(a) In what manner has the right to self-determination been implemented?

(b) What is the status of the Covenant in domestic law? Are any of the rights contained in the Covenant directly applicable by courts and other authorities? Give details of such application.

(c) Which of the rights stipulated in the Covenant are recognized in the Constitution or other legislation? Attach the texts of such provisions and give details of their application by courts and other authorities.

(d) Which of the rights are specifically subject to non-discrimination provisions in national law? Attach the text of such provisions.

(e) Has the ratification of the Covenant given rise to any modification of the relevant domestic law?

(f) To what extent and in what manner are non-nationals not guaranteed the rights recognized in the Covenant? What justification is there for any difference?

4. *The role of international co-operation in the implementation of the Covenant on Economic, Social and Cultural Rights*

If your State participates in development co-operation, is any effort made to ensure that it is used, on a priority basis, to promote the realization of economic, social and cultural rights?

Part two of the guidelines then deals, on an article-by-article basis, with each of the substantive rights recognized in articles 6 to 15 of the Covenant. (For the text of the guidelines, see under the relevant articles below.) There are three matters to which the Committee has attached particular importance in relation to reporting on these articles. The first is that matters which have been adequately dealt with under arrangements for reporting to other United Nations agencies or other human rights treaty bodies need not necessarily be treated again *in extenso* reports required under the Covenant. Detailed cross-referencing to the relevant reports and if appropriate, comments on the outcome of consideration of that report may be sufficient. This is designed to reduce the burden of having to report on virtually identical issues to a number of different bodies and accords with the provision of article 17(3) of the Covenant.

—Text of article 17(3)

> **Where relevant information has previously been furnished to the United Nations or to any specialized agency by any State Party to the present Covenant, it will not be necessary to reproduce that information, but a precise reference to the information so furnished will suffice.**

By the same token, this arrangement does not in any way preclude a matter on which a report has been submitted to another appropriate body from being taken up and examined in detail by the Committee. Various elements — such as the passage of time, the availability of new information, a perceived difference in approach between the relevant provision of the Covenant and that of another instrument, or a particular interest in an issue by the Committee — might lead the Committee to undertake such an examination.

The second matter to which the Committee has attached particular importance is the need to report not only on relevant factors but also on any difficulties encountered in securing realization of the rights recognized in the Covenant. The guidelines emphasize that this requires a detailed description not only of the legal and administrative situation but also of the *de facto* situation. Negative developments, frustrated aspirations and other difficulties should be reported upon, in addition to information on positive developments. Indeed, the Committee has tended to look much more favourably upon reports which are frank and recognize shortcomings in performance or achievement than on reports which identify only items of `good news'.

The third matter is the provision of appropriate Statistics, wherever available. If they are not available the Committee should also be informed of that fact. The Committee has noted that such information should be presented in context so as to provide an indication of both the progress already achieved as well as of the goals which have yet to be achieved.

In order to promote a better understanding of the various provisions of the Covenant, the Committee has instituted two approaches, of which reporting officers, in particular, should be aware. The first is the adoption, from time to time, of **general comments**. The purposes of these comments, which are in most respects comparable to the purposes served by those adopted by the Human Rights Committee, are discussed further below. The second is the **general discussion** that the Committee seeks to hold at each of its sessions, in which it focuses on a particular right, such as the right to food or the right to housing. These discussions are reported upon in the Committee's reports and intended to shed light on some of the issues that arise in considering the requirements associated with specific provisions of the Covenant.

* * *

The International Covenant on Civil and Political Rights

By Fausto Pocar

The International Covenant on Civil and Political Rights (hereinafter, the "Covenant", or "ICCPR") was adopted by the General Assembly of the United Nations with resolution 2200 A (XXI) of 16 December 1966. It entered into force on 23 March 1976, in accordance with article 459. As of October 1990, the Covenant has been ratified or acceded to by 92 States.

A. The Reporting Process

(a) The Covenant and its reporting requirements

Under article 2(1) of the Covenant, each State party undertakes to respect and to ensure to all individuals within its territory and subject to its jurisdiction the rights recognized, and specifically listed and dealt with, in Part III of the Covenant, without distinction of any kind, such as race, colour, sex, language, religion, political or other opinion, national or social origin, property, birth, or other status. The Covenant itself addresses the implementation of this fundamental international treaty obligation of States parties in the subsequent paragraphs of article 2. It points out that each State party has to take the necessary steps, in accordance with its constitutional processes and the provisions of the Covenant, to adopt legislative and other measures required to give effect to the rights recognized in the Covenant. Such measures shall in any case include effective remedies for victims of violations of their rights and freedoms, possibly in a judicial form and enforceable by competent authorities when granted.

In connection with this provision, and parallel to it, the Covenant requires States parties to submit reports on the measures adopted by them on the progress made in the enjoyment of the rights defined in the Covenant, and on any factors and difficulties that may affect the implementation of the Covenant. This obligation is set forth in article 40, which also describes the main characteristics of the monitoring system based on reporting.

—Text of article 40

> **1. The States Parties to the present Covenant undertake to submit reports on the measures they have adopted which give effect to the rights recognized herein and on the progress made in the enjoyment of those rights;**
>
> **(a) Within one year of the entry into force of the present Covenant for the States Parties concerned;**
>
> **(b) Thereafter whenever the Committee so requests.**
>
> **2. All reports shall be submitted to the Secretary-General of the United Nations, who shall transmit them to the Committee for consideration. Reports shall indicate the factors and difficulties, if any, affecting the implementation of the present Covenant.**

3. The Secretary-General of the United Nations may, after consultation with the Committee, transmit to the specialized agencies concerned copies of such parts of the reports as may fall within their field of competence.

4. The Committee shall study the reports submitted by the States Parties to the present Covenant. It shall transmit its reports, and such general comments as it may consider appropriate, to the States Parties. The Committee may also transmit to the Economic and Social Council these comments along with the copies of the reports it has received from States Parties to the present Covenant.

5. States Parties to the present Covenant may submit to the Committee observations on any comments that may be made in accordance with paragraph 4 of this article.

According to article 40(1) to (3), each State party is required to submit within one year of its entry into force an initial report covering the rights enshrined in the Covenant. Subsequent reports are due upon request by the Human Rights Committee (hereinafter, "the Committee"). Therefore, the submission of any report constitutes a treaty obligation. Regarding the initial report, this obligation is explicitly stated in the Covenant; in regard to subsequent reports, it derives from the powers conferred upon the Committee by the Covenant.

In exercising its powers, the Committee has decided in principle to establish a specific periodicity for the submission of States reports. Based on a decision adopted by the Committee in 1981 and amended in 1982 (U.N.Doc. CCPR/C/19/Rev. 1), States parties which have submitted their initial reports before July 1981 are requested to submit subsequent reports every five years after the consideration of their initial reports. Other States parties are required to submit subsequent reports to the Committee every five years from the date when the initial report was due. This decision is without prejudice to the power of the Committee to request a subsequent report whenever it deems appropriate. The date for the submission of a State party's next periodic report may be deferred in cases where a State party, following the examination of its report and at the request of the Committee, submits additional information, and provided that such additional information is considered at a meeting with representatives of the reporting State.

As to the substance of the reporting obligation undertaken by States parties, article 40 gives only general indications. It refers to measures adopted to give effect to the protected rights, to progress made in their enjoyment, and to any factors or difficulties affecting the implementation of the Covenant.

(b) Guidelines for reporting under the Covenant

The Committee has prepared general guidelines regarding the form and contents of reports. These guidelines are intended to provide guidance to States parties in their reporting activities and to avoid general and incomplete presentations. They are further designed to ensure that reports are presented in a uniform manner and that they offer a complete picture of the situation in each State regarding the implementation of rights contained in the Covenant. This formal structure provides a uniform character to the reports and enables the Committee to perform its supervisory duties in its consideration of reports, and at the same time offers an opportunity to other States parties fully to appreciate how the obligations under the Covenant are carried out by each State party.

The Committee has issued separate general guidelines for initial and for subsequent reports. They follow the same structural pattern, but differ to a certain extent in the emphasis they place on reporting under the individual provisions of the Covenant.

According to a decision taken by the Committee in 1977 (U.N. Doc. CCPR/C/5), the initial report should observe the following guidelines.

—Text of the general guidelines for initial reports

Part one: general. This part should describe briefly the general legal framework within which civil and political rights are protected in the reporting State. In particular it should indicate:

(i) Whether any of the rights referred to in the Covenant are protected either in the Constitution or by a separate "Bill of Rights", and if so, what provisions are made in the Constitution or in the Bill of Rights for derogations and in what circumstances;

(ii) Whether the provisions of the Covenant can be invoked before and directly enforced by the courts, other tribunals or administrative authorities or whether they have to be transformed into internal laws or administrative regulations to be enforced by the authorities concerned;

(iii) What judicial, administrative or other competent authorities have jurisdiction affecting human rights;

(iv) What remedies are available to an individual who claims that any of his rights have been violated;

(v) What other measures have been taken to ensure the implementation of the provisions of the Covenant.

Part two: information in relation to each of the articles in parts I, II and III of the Covenant. This part should describe in relation to the provisions of each article:

(i) The legislative, administrative or other measures in force in regard to each right;

(ii) Any restrictions or limitations even of a temporary nature imposed by law or practise or any other manner on the enjoyment of the right;

(iii) Any other factors or difficulties affecting the enjoyment of the right by persons within the jurisdiction of the State;

(iv) Any other information on the progress made in the enjoyment of the right.

The report should be accompanied by copies of the principal legislative and other texts referred to in the report. These will be made available to members of the Committee. It should be noted, however, that, for reasons of expense, they will not normally be reproduced for general distribution with the report except to the extent that the reporting State specifically so requests. It is desirable therefore that, when a text is not actually quoted in or annexed to the report itself, the report should contain sufficient information to be understood without reference to it.

States reports should always follow the format recommended by the Committee.

The first part should be of a general nature and provide background information on the context within which civil and political rights are ensured in the reporting State. To this end, the status of the Covenant in the domestic legal order needs to be clarified. The Committee seeks information on how the Covenant becomes part of then national legislation, namely either by means of corresponding provisions in the Constitution or a separate Bill of Rights and in internal laws, or through its direct applicability, granting rights to individuals that can be invoked directly before and enforced by State courts and other authorities. Moreover, specific information should be provided on the remedies available in domestic law to individuals claiming a violation of their rights as contained in the Covenant. Finally, this part of the report should describe any other step taken by the State's authorities to implement the Covenant and the role of national institutions in supervising and implementing the protected rights. (Part one of the guidelines is now common to the reporting guidelines prepared for all United Nations human rights treaty bodies. For the text of the consolidated guidelines for the initial part of the reports of States parties see the annex at the end of part one of the Manual.)

The second part of the report should then be devoted, on an article-by-article basis, to the description of measures taken to realize each specific right set forth in the Covenant. In this respect, a detailed description should be made of any restrictions affecting the enjoyment of each protected right, as well as any other difficulty encountered by the State in implementing them. In order to get a complete and comprehensive picture of the actual level of implementation reached by the State party, the information provided to the Committee should refer not only to measures adopted in the legislative field, but also to the judicial and administrative practise, and even, as the case may be, to activities of bodies other than State organs, as far as they are relevant to the enjoyment of any specific right. Since the State party is under an obligation both to respect and to ensure the rights under the Covenant, negative as well as positive measures taken by the authorities are relevant, and, as far as applicable, should be dealt with under each article. For the Committee, it is important to obtain a clear understanding of the legal and the *de facto* situation in the reporting State.

The Committee recently also decided to adopt certain measures to follow up on its views on communications under the Optional Protocol to the Covenant. At its thirty-ninth session in 1990, the Committee amended its guidelines for the submission of initial and periodic reports by adding a new paragraph, which reads as follows:

> "*When a State party to the Covenant is also a party to the Optional Protocol, and if in the period under review in the Report the Committee has issued Views finding that the State party has violated provisions of the Covenant, the Report should include a section explaining what action has been taken relating to the communication concerned. In particular, the State party should indicate what remedy it has afforded the author of the communication whose rights the Committee found to have been violated.*"

Accordingly, States parties to whom the provision of this new paragraph of the guidelines applies, are expected to include the appropriate information in their reports to the Committee.

For details on periodic reporting, see section C below.

The Committee has adopted a number of **general comments** in accordance with article 40(4) of the Covenant. These general comments reflect the experience gained by the Committee in the consideration of reports. At the same time, they are intended to assist States parties in fulfilling their reporting obligations. Therefore, States parties should pay attention to these general comments when preparing reports. (For more details on general comments, see below.)

* * *

The International Convention on the Elimination of all Forms of Racial Discrimination

By Luis Valencia Rodriguez

The International Convention on the Elimination of All Forms of Racial Discrimination (hereinafter, "the Convention") was adopted by the General Assembly of the United Nations with resolution 2106 A (XX) of 21 December 1965. It entered into force on 4 January 1969 in accordance with article 19. As of August 1990, the Convention had been ratified or acceded to by 129 States.

A. The Reporting Process

(a) The Convention and its reporting requirements

The preamble to the Convention sets out some of the considerations of the States parties for preparing this instrument. The States parties express their conviction that "any doctrine of superiority based on racial differentiation is scientifically false, morally condemnable, socially unjust and dangerous", and they reaffirm that "discrimination between human beings on the grounds of race, colour or ethnic origin is an obstacle to friendly and peaceful relations among nations and is capable of disturbing peace and security among peoples".

States, in becoming parties to the Convention, declare their abhorrence of racial discrimination or segregation. They are resolved to adopt all necessary measures to eliminate racial discrimination in all its forms and manifestations, and to prevent and combat racist doctrines and practises in order to promote understanding between races. These ideals are reflected in the substantive provisions of the Convention.

The Convention has been defined as the international community's *only* tool for combating racial discrimination which is at one and the same time universal in reach, comprehensive in scope, legally binding in character, and equipped with built-in measures of implementation, including international machinery — a pioneer in the field — responsible for monitoring the actual implementation of their obligations by the contracting sovereign States. This assessment remains valid to this day.

The system of international accountability and international review built into the Convention is the reporting procedure, in which the Committee on the Elimination of Racial Discrimination (hereinafter, "the Committee") plays the central role. States parties are required to submit periodic reports on the measures taken by them to implement the Convention. This obligation, which is set forth in article 9 of the Convention, is a treaty obligation binding all States parties to the Convention.

—Text of article 9

> **1. States parties undertake to submit to the Secretary-General of the United Nations, for consideration by the Committee, a report on the legislative, judicial, administrative or other measures which they have adopted and which give effect to the provisions of this Convention: (a) within one year after the entry into force of the Convention for the State concerned; and (b) thereafter every two years and whenever the Committee so requests. The Committee may request further information from the States Parties.**
>
> **2. The Committee shall report annually, through the Secretary-General, to the General Assembly of the United Nations on its activities and may make suggestions and general recommendations based on the examination of the reports and information received from the State Parties. Such suggestions and general recommendations shall be reported to the General Assembly together with comments, if any, from States Parties.**

According to article 9, consequently, two kinds of reports have to be submitted. The initial report must be submitted by the State party within one year of the entry into force of the Convention. Periodic reports must be submitted at two-year intervals, and upon request of the Committee. (For a recent change in this periodicity, see section C below). The presentation of both initial and subsequent reports therefore constitutes a treaty obligation specifically contained in the Convention, and as a consequence, is binding for all States parties.

As to the substance of the reporting obligation undertaken by States parties, article 9 gives only general indications. It refers to measures adopted by the States parties to give effect to the provisions of the Convention. The Committee prepared guidelines to assist States parties in fulfilling their obligations under the Convention.

(b) Guidelines for reporting under the Convention

Initial and periodic reports should be prepared in accordance with the general guidelines established by the Committee for the preparation of reports. A communication to States parties was first adopted by the Committee in 1970. At its twenty-first session in 1980, the Committee adopted general guidelines on the form and contents of reports by States parties, which replaced the communication. At its twenty-fifth session in 1982, the Committee adopted additional guidelines for the implementation of article 7 of the Convention.

According to these general guidelines, reports from States parties should always be presented in two parts. A first part (entitled "Part one — general") should provide general background information and a second part (entitled "Part two — information in relation to articles 2 to 7 of the Convention") should deal individually with each of the substantive provisions of the Convention.

The format of the guidelines follows exactly this pattern. Therefore, the guidelines for the second part will be discussed jointly with each specific article to which they refer later under subsection (c) Reporting on the substantive provisions.

—Text of the general guidelines concerning the form and contents of reports by States parties

Part one — general. This part should

(a) Describe briefly the policy of eliminating racial discrimination in all its forms and the general legal framework within which racial discrimination as defined in article 1, paragraph 1, of the Convention is prohibited and eliminated in the reporting State, and the recognition, enjoyment or exercise, on an equal footing, of human rights and fundamental freedoms in the political, economic, social, cultural or any other field of public life are promoted and protected;

(b) Indicate whether the provisions of the Convention can be invoked before, and directly enforced by, the courts, other tribunals or administrative authorities or whether they have to be implemented by way of internal laws or administrative regulations in order to be enforced by the authorities concerned:

(c) Provide information in connection with General Recommendation IV, adopted by the Committee on 16 August 1973, in which the Committee invited States parties "to endeavour to include in their reports under article 9 (of the Convention) relevant information on the demographic composition of the population . . ."

Pursuant to this guideline, the Committee expects to receive information from the States parties on their compliance with the obligation assumed under article 1 of the Convention.

—Text of article 1

> **1. In this Convention, the term "racial discrimination" shall mean any distinction, exclusion, restriction or preference based on race, colour, descent, or national or ethnic origin which has the purpose or effect of nullifying or impairing the recognition, enjoyment or exercise, on an equal footing, of human rights and fundamental freedoms in the political, economic, social, cultural or any other field of public life.**
>
> **2. This Convention shall not apply to distinctions, exclusions, restrictions or preferences made by a State Party to this Convention between citizens and non-citizens.**
>
> **3. Nothing in this Convention may be interpreted as affecting in any way the legal provisions of States Parties concerning nationality, citizenship or naturalization, provided that such provisions do not discriminate against any particular nationality.**
>
> **4. Special measures taken for the sole purpose of securing adequate advancement of certain racial or ethnic groups or individuals requiring such protection as may be necessary in order to ensure such groups or individuals equal enjoyment or exercise of human rights or fundamental freedoms shall not be deemed racial discrimination, provided, however, that such measures do not, as a consequence, lead to the maintenance of separate rights for different racial groups and that they shall not be continued**

after the objectives for which they were taken have been achieved.

Article 1 defines the concept of racial discrimination. It is important to emphasize that according to this definition, racial discrimination exists not only when there are distinctions, exclusions, restrictions or preferences based only on race or the colour of the skin, but also when they are a consequence of descent, or national or ethnic origin. It is also necessary to remember that racial discrimination exists when such differences cause the nullification or impairment of the equal recognition, enjoyment or exercise of human rights and fundamental freedoms in all fields of public life.

The essence of this definition is its adherence to the principle of equality, which is later reflected in several of the substantive provisions of the Convention, and in particular in article 5, which contains the right to equality before the law. Although the definition of racial discrimination is different from the statement of article 5, the latter must be taken into account in interpreting the definition. To be sure, equality and non-discrimination can be seen as affirmative and negative statements of the same principle.

One of the main objectives of the Convention is indeed to promote racial equality. As such, the Convention not only aims to achieve *de jure* racial equality, but particularly also *de facto* equality, which allows the various ethnic, racial and national groups to enjoy the same social development. The goal of *de facto* equality is central to the Convention.

In this regard, article 1(4) provides that special measures taken to achieve equality shall not be considered racial discrimination, provided that they are discontinued after the objectives for which they were taken have been achieved.

As the Committee has stated, "In accordance with the Convention, the primary obligation of every State party is to adopt, and to put into effect without delay, a comprehensive national policy for the elimination of racial discrimination in all its forms, utilizing for that purpose all appropriate means. The Convention also provides clear guidelines, with which States parties undertake to comply in the development and application of their respective national policies. Those policies must have as their aim the elimination of racial discrimination in all its forms — whether practised by public authorities, institutions or officials or by private individuals, groups or organizations. Moreover, they must aim not only at combating racial discrimination but also at promoting interracial understanding, tolerance and friendship. Toward these ends, States must be prepared to use both coercion and persuasion — utilizing the power of the law, to prohibit and punish, as well as the power of education and information, to enlighten and persuade".

In accordance with the general guideline for part one of reports, and in light of article 1 of the Convention, States parties should provide three kinds of information. First, they should discuss the policy of the reporting State with regard to racial discrimination and the legal framework of such a policy. Secondly, they should provide information on how the Convention and the rights put forward on it become part of the domestic legal order. And thirdly, the initial report should provide general background information on the reporting State, and make special reference to the demographic composition of the population, and to any problems confronting different ethnic groups. It should provide detailed statistical information on demographic matters that are of interest to the Committee in pursuing the tasks entrusted to it by the Conventions.

This part of the report should enable the Committee to obtain a clear understanding of the overall situation in the reporting State relevant to questions of racial discrimination, such as the racial and ethnic composition of the population, and the existence and number of minority groups, (such as migrant workers, refugees, etc.). In the past, the Committee has sought information on categories such as life expectancy, infant mortality rate, the standing of such groups in the social hierarchy and their political importance in the reporting State, etc. (Part one of the guidelines is now common to the reporting guidelines prepared for all United Nations human rights treaty bodies. For the text of the consolidated guidelines for the initial part of the reports of States parties see the annex at the end of part one of the Manual.)

Information gathered for reporting under other international instruments on rights of vulnerable groups should be consulted for its potential relevance under the present Convention. With regard to article 1(4) of ICERD, those are in particular articles 27 of ICCPR, 2(3) of ICESCR, and 4 (temporary special measures) and 14 of CEDAW.

* * *

The International Convention of the Suppression and Punishment of the Crime of *Apartheid*

By Samba Cor Konate

The International Convention on the Suppression and Punishment of the Crime of *Apartheid* (hereinafter, "the Convention") was adopted by the General Assembly of the United Nations with resolution 3058 (XXVIII) of 30 November 1973. It entered into force on 18 July 1976, in accordance with article XV. As of August 1990, the Convention had been ratified or acceded to by 89 States.

A. The Reporting Process

(a) The Convention and its reporting requirements

Under article 1 of the Convention, States parties declare that *apartheid* is a "crime against humanity", violating the principles of international law, and in particular the Charter of the United Nations. States parties therefore undertake in article IV to adopt the necessary legislative and other measures to suppress and to prevent this crime. They also take steps to prosecute and to punish, within their respective jurisdictions, persons responsible for, or accused of, acts defined as *apartheid* by the Convention.

The responsibility of taking appropriate steps on the national level is complemented by the provision requiring States parties to submit periodic reports on the measures adopted to give effect to the Convention. The basis for the reporting process is contained in article VII.

—Text of article VII

> **1. The States Parties to the present Convention undertake to submit periodic reports to the group established under article IX on the legislative, judicial, administrative or other measures that they have adopted and that give effect to the provisions of the Convention.**
>
> **2. Copies of the reports shall be transmitted through the Secretary-General of the United Nations to the Special Committee on *Apartheid*.**

According to article VII, States parties to the Convention are required to submit reports describing any legislative, judicial, administrative or other measures they have taken to implement the provisions of the Convention. This article clearly indicates that it is not sufficient for States to ratify the Convention; in order to discharge themselves of their responsibilities under this instrument, they must submit reports in accordance with the Convention. The presentation of reports therefore constitutes the same treaty obligation as any other obligation arising under the Convention.

The reports submitted by States parties are considered by a group of three members (the "Group of Three", see later) of the Commission on Human Rights, established in accordance with the article IX.

The Convention itself gives only general indications regarding the periodicity of such reports. The Commission on Human Rights, in its resolution 7 (XXXIV) of 1978, called upon States parties to submit their first report not later than two years after the entry into force of the Convention. The Commission established that subsequent reports should be submitted at two-year intervals. (For a recent change in this recommendation, see section C below.)

The practise followed by the Group of Three, the Commission on Human Rights and the States parties since 1978 has confirmed this periodicity.

(b) Guidelines for reporting under the Convention

The Group of Three decided at its 1978 session to prepare guidelines regarding the form and content of periodic reports by States parties. The purposes of these guidelines is to assist the Groups of Three and the Commission on Human Rights in fulfilling the tasks entrusted to them under the Convention. The guidelines shall also help States parties to report in a comprehensive and structured way on the measures taken to implement the Convention and to improve the consideration of reports. Although an observation of the guidelines is not a treaty obligation, States parties are urged to follow them in the preparation of periodic reports. It should be pointed out that first, as well as subsequent periodic reports should be elaborated on the basis of these same guidelines.

—Text of the general guidelines regarding the form and contents of reports to be submitted by States parties under article VII of the International Convention on the Suppression and Punishment of the Crime of *Apartheid*

(a) Information on the legislative, judicial, administrative or other measures that have been adopted and that give effect to the following provisions of the Convention:

(i) That apartheid is a crime against humanity and that inhuman acts resulting from the policies and practises of apartheid and similar policies and practises of racial segregation and discrimination, as defined in article II of the Convention, are crimes violating the principles of international law, in particular the purposes and principles of the Charter of the United Nations, and constitution a serious threat to international peace and security;

(ii) That organizations, institutions and individuals committing the crime of apartheid are considered criminal.

(b) Information on the legislative, judicial, administrative or other measures that have been adopted and that give effect to the following provisions of the Convention:

(i) The undertaking, as required under article IV (b) of the Convention, to adopt legislative, judicial and administrative measures to prosecute, bring to trial and punish in accordance with their jurisdiction persons responsible for, or accused of, the acts defined in article II of the Convention, whether or not such persons reside in the territory of the States in which the acts are committed or are nationals of that State or some other State or are stateless persons;

(ii) Article III of the Convention, that international criminal responsibility shall be applied, irrespective of the motive involved, to individuals, members of organizations and institutions and representatives of the State, whether residing in the territory of the State in which acts are perpetrated or in some other State, whenever they (1) commit, participate in, directly incite or conspire in the commission of the acts mentioned in article II of the Convention; (2) directly abet, encourage or co-operate in the commission of the crime of apartheid;

(iii) The undertaking, as provided for in article XI of the Convention, to grant extradition in accordance with their legislation and with the treaties in force, in cases enumerated in article II of the Convention;

(c) Information on the legislative, judicial, administrative or other measures that have been adopted and that give effect:

(i) To the undertaking, as required under article IV (a) of the Convention, to adopt any legislative or other measures necessary to suppress as well as to prevent any encouragement of the crime of apartheid and similar segregationist and discriminatory policies or their manifestations and to punish persons guilty of those crimes;

(ii) To acquaint the public as widely as possible with the evils of apartheid and the text of the Convention using all the information and other media at their disposal;

(d) Information on the legislative, judicial, administrative or other measures that have been adopted and that give effect to the undertaking, as required under article VI of the Convention, to accept and carry out in accordance with the Charter of the United Nations the decisions taken by the Security Council aimed at the prevention, suppression and punishment of the crime of *apartheid*, and to co-operate in the implementation of decisions adopted by other competent organs of the United Nations with a view to achieving the purposes of the Convention;

(e) States Parties should endeavour where possible to identify in their periodic reports individuals, organizations, institutions and representatives of States which are alleged to be responsible for the crimes enumerated in article II of the Convention, as well as those against whom legal proceedings have been undertaken by the State party to the Convention;

(f) The reports should contain, as appropriate, decisions of the courts or the competent tribunal of the State party relating to cases falling within the scope of article II of the Convention, as provided for under article V of the Convention, as well as information relating to cases of extradition in accordance with article XI of the Convention;

(g) The report should be accompanied by copies of the principal legislative and other texts referred to in the report. These will be kept in the files of the Secretariat and be made available in the original language to members of the Groups or the Commission on Human Rights for consultation. It would be desirable therefore that, when a text is not actually quoted in or annexed to the report itself, the report should contain sufficient information to be understood without reference to the accompanying texts.

The Group of Three and the Commission on Human Rights have repeatedly stressed the requirement that States parties submit reports — in accordance with the guidelines — and have called the attention of States parties to this treaty obligation.

It is essential for States parties reports to contain information on the procedure that makes this instrument a part of the *corpus juridicium* of the national criminal law code. Since the issue at stake is the implementation of an international legal instrument, States parties are required to provide information on the legislative, judicial, administrative and other measures taken to give effect to the provisions contained in the Convention. Reports should also provide information on any difficulties the reporting State has encountered in its implementation. Reports shall indicate the sanctions that apply in case of proven violation of these norms. Therefore, States parties should not limit themselves to describing their political positions or attitudes towards the politics of *apartheid*.

States parties have to indicate what preventive measures they have adopted to ensure that such crimes are not committed on their territory or by their citizens. States parties shall describe actions undertaken at the national level, in the light of their own experience, to combat the crime of *apartheid*, and provide statistical information on legal actions taken in this regard.

* * *

The Convention on the Elimination of all Forms of Discrimination Against Women

By Zagorka Ilic

The Convention on the Elimination of All Forms of Discrimination against Women (hereinafter, "the Convention") was adopted by the General Assembly of the United Nations with resolution 34/180 of 18 December 1979. It entered into force on 3 September 1981, in accordance with article 27(1). As of June 1990, the Convention had been ratified or acceded to by 103 States.

A. The Reporting Process

(a) The Convention and its reporting requirements

The adoption of the Convention was the culmination of 30 years of work by the United Nations, and in particular by its Commission on the Status of Women, for the advancement of women. In its comprehensiveness the Convention encompasses earlier, more narrowly focused instruments on the subject. Its scope and reach make the Convention an international bill of rights for women.

The preamble acknowledges that despite various United Nations efforts to promote the equality of rights of men and women, "extensive discrimination against women continues to exist" and that such discrimination "violates the principles of equality of rights and respect for human dignity". The preamble goes on to state that discriminatory practises are an obstacle to the equal participation of women in all aspects of the life of their countries, hampering the increased prosperity of society and family. The preamble recognizes women's great contribution to the welfare of the family and to the development of society, and states that changes in the traditional roles for men and women in society and family are needed. By adopting the Convention, the international community expresses its determination to adopt the measures required for the elimination of discrimination against women in all its forms and manifestations.

Under article 2 of the Convention, States parties, in condemning discrimination against women in all its forms, "agree to pursue by all appropriate means and without delay a policy of eliminating discrimination against women". Its subsequent paragraphs and article 3 contain detailed requirements for States parties to take in implementing this instrument at the national level.

In addition to the treaty obligation to implement the Convention at the national level, States parties also undertake the commitment to submit reports on the measures taken to achieve this goal, and on any factors and difficulties encountered in this effort. This obligation is set forth in article 18 of the Convention. The reports are to be considered by a Committee on the Elimination of Discrimination against Women (hereinafter, "the Committee").

—Text of article 18

> **1. States Parties undertake to submit to the Secretary-General of the United Nations, for consideration by the Committee, a report on the legislative, judicial, administrative or other measures which they have adopted to give effect to the provisions of the present Convention and on the progress made in this respect:**
>
> **(a) Within one year after the entry into force for the States concerned;**
>
> **(b) Thereafter at least every four years and further whenever the Committee so requests.**
>
> **2. Reports may indicate factors and difficulties affecting the degree of fulfillment of obligations under the present Convention.**

This article clearly shows that the submission of both initial and subsequent reports is a treaty obligation binding States parties to the Convention. The article also establishes the periodicity for the submission of reports. Initial reports are therefore due within a year after the entry into force of the Convention in a given State, and thereafter at least every four years. The Convention also enables the Committee to request reports at its discretion.

Article 18 indicates what kind of information reports are expected to provide. This includes information on the measures adopted and on the progress made in the implementation of the Convention. Reports should also indicate any factors and difficulties encountered by States parties in this regard.

(b) Guidelines for reporting under the Convention

In order to assist States parties in fulfilling their treaty obligations, the Committee has adopted guidelines for the preparation of reports. These guidelines shall ensure that all the substantive articles of the Convention are covered in a report, and that the reports are presented in a uniform manner so that a complete picture can emerge regarding the implementation of the Convention and the progress achieved in the realization of the rights contained therein.

The Committee has adopted separate guidelines for the preparation of initial reports and for second and subsequent periodic reports. (The latter will be dealt with under section C below.)

—Text of the general guidelines regarding the form and contents of reports received from States parties under article 18

Part one should describe:

(a) As concisely as possible the actual, general, social, economic, political and legal framework within which a State party approaches the elimination of discrimination against women in all its forms, as defined in the Convention;

(b) Any legal and other measures adopted to implement the Convention or their absence as well as any effects which ratification of the Convention has had on the State party's actual, general, social, economic, political and legal framework since entry into force of the Convention for the reporting State;

(c) Whether there are any institutions or authorities which have as their task to ensure that the principle of equality between men and women is complied with in practise, and what remedies are available to women who have suffered discrimination;

(d) The means used to promote and ensure the full development and advancement of women for the purpose of guaranteeing them the exercise and enjoyment of human rights and fundamental freedoms in all fields on a basis of equality with men;

(e) Whether the provisions of the Convention can be invoked before, and directly enforced by, the courts, other tribunals or administrative authorities or whether the provisions of the Convention have to be implemented by way of internal laws or administrative regulations in order to be enforced by the authorities concerned.

Part two should provide specific information in relation to each provision of the Convention:

(a) The constitutional, legislative and administrative provisions or other measures in force;

(b) The developments that have taken place and the programmes and institutions that have been established since the entry into force of the Convention;

(c) Any restrictions or limitations, even of a temporary nature, imposed by law or practise or in any other manner on the enjoyment of each right;

(d) Any other factors or difficulties affecting the exercise and enjoyment of each right;

(e) Any other information on progress made in the fulfillment of each right.

It is recommended that the reports should not be confined to mere lists of legal instruments adopted in the country concerned in recent years but should also include information indicating how these legal instruments are reflected in the actual, economic, political and social realities and general conditions existing in their countries. Data concerning these realities and conditions should also be supplied with a breakdown of the statistics on the category of sex.

States parties are invited to submit copies of the principal legislative, judicial, administrative and other texts referred to in the report so that these can be made available to the Committee. It is desirable therefore that, when a text is not actually quoted in or annexed to the report itself, the report should contain sufficient information to be understood without the actual reference.

The reports should reveal obstacles to the participation of women on an equal basis with men in the political, social, economic and cultural life of their countries, and give information on types and frequencies of cases of non-compliance with the principle of equal rights.

The reports should also pay due attention to the role of women and their full participation in the solution of problems and issues which are referred to in the preamble and which are not covered by the article of the Convention.

The reports and the supplementary documentation should be submitted in one of the working languages of the Committee (Arabic, Chinese, English, French, Russian or Spanish) in as concise a form as possible.

The guidelines recommend that the reports be divided into two parts.

The first part should provide general background information relevant to the situation of women and the implementation of the Convention in the reporting State. Part one, paragraphs (a)-(e), of the guidelines give a detailed catalogue of issues that need to be addressed in this part of the report to enable the Committee to obtain a comprehensive picture of the facts that determine the situation of women in the reporting State. (Part one of the guidelines is now common to the reporting guidelines prepared for all the United Nations Human rights treaty bodies. For the text of the consolidated guidelines for the initial part of the reports of States parties see the annex at the end of part one of the Manual.)

The second part of the report should provide the information requested in part two, paragraphs (a)-(e) of the guidelines on an article-by-article basis. These paragraphs indicate precisely what kind of details the Committee seeks with regard to the implementation of each article of the Convention.

In addition to the guidelines, the Committee has to date adopted a number of **general recommendations**, observations and suggestions in accordance with article 21 and concerning certain articles or specific subjects of the Convention. In general, they deal with matters that give rise to particular concern in the Committee as a result of the consideration of reports. As a consequence, they recommend to States parties to take certain actions in the implementation of an article or to submit certain kinds of information when reporting to the Committee. (These general recommendations and suggestions will mostly be dealt with below under (c) Reporting on the Substantive provisions.) It might also be pointed out that due to the limited amount of time allocated for its meetings, the Committee has not yet had the possibility for a thorough discussion regarding the meaning of particular articles of the Convention (see the work of the Human Rights Committee in this regard, leading to the adoption of the general comments), but it intends to start having such discussions at its tenth session in 1991.

It should be noted that the Committee has always emphasized the importance of including information on any factors or difficulties States parties encounter in fulfilling their obligations under the Convention. The request for this specific kind of information is based on article 18(2) of the Convention, and repeated in the general guidelines.

The Committee also always asks for statistical data broken down by gender so that it can properly appreciate the position of women and any improvements to it in the framework of the substantive provisions of the Convention.

In fact, the Committee addressed this matter in its general recommendation no. 9 (eighth session 1989), entitled "Statistical data concerning the situation of women". It states that statistical information is "absolutely necessary" for the understanding of the real situation of women in reporting States, but that many of the reports received do not provide statistics. The Committee therefore

> "recommends that states parties should make every effort to ensure that their national statistical services responsible for planning national censuses and other social and economic surveys formulate their questionnaires in such a way that data can be desegregated according to gender, with regard to both absolute numbers and percentages, so that interested users can easily obtain information on the citation of women in the particular sector in which they are interested".

The Committee further considered the existence of national machinery and publicity an important element in the implementation of the Convention at national levels. It dealt with the matter in its general recommendation no. 6 (seventh session 1988), entitled "Effective national machinery and publicity". It recommends that States parties:

> "1. Establish and/or strengthen effective national machinery, institutions and procedures, at a high level of Government, and with adequate resources, commitment and authority to:
>
> (a) Advise on the impact on women of all government policies;
>
> (b) Monitor the situation of women comprehensively;
>
> (c) Help formulate new policies and effectively carry out strategies and measures to eliminate discrimination;
>
> 2. Take appropriate steps to ensure the dissemination of the Convention, the reports of the States parties under article 18 and the reports of the Committee in the language of the State concerned;
>
> 3. Seek the assistance of the Secretary-General and the Department of Public Information in providing translations of the Convention and the reports of the Committee;

4. Include in their initial and periodic reports the action taken in respect to this recommendation".

The Convention has proven to be subject to more reservations than any other major international human rights treaty. The Convention itself permits reservations at the time of accession or ratification. It specifies, however, that reservations incompatible with the purpose of the Convention shall not be permitted. Subsequently, it does not indicate which reservations should be considered incompatible or who should decide such questions.

The large number of reservations and of interpretative declarations made by many States parties to the Convention on most of the substantive articles of the Convention has given rise to great concern among other States parties, and some of them have objected to them without, however, ever declaring that the Convention not be in force between the State party entering a reservation and the State party expressing its concern.

The Committee itself as well as the States parties in their annual meetings and the General Assembly have taken up the issue repeatedly. It is the opinion of many that such reservations could affect the full implementation of the Convention. The Committee has consistently encouraged reporting States to review any reservations made regarding the Convention and to withdraw them as soon as possible. This matter is routinely discussed by members of the Committee during the general observations and comments made regarding States parties reports.

* * *

The Convention Against Torture and Other Cruel, Inhuman or Degrading Treatment or Punishment

By Joseph Voyame

The Convention against Torture and Other Cruel, Inhuman or Degrading Treatment or Punishment (hereinafter, "the Convention") was adopted by the General Assembly of the United Nations with resolution 39/46 of 10 December 1984. It entered into force on 27 June 1987, in accordance with article 27(1). As of June 1990, the Convention had been ratified or acceded to by 52 States.

A. The Reporting Process

(a) The Convention and its reporting requirements

According to article 2(1) of the Convention, each State party must take effective legislative, administrative, judicial and other measures to prevent any acts of torture, as defined in article 1 of the Convention, from being committed in any territory under its jurisdiction. Paragraphs 2 and 3 of article 2 specify that such acts are not justifiable by exceptional circumstances, nor by order from a superior officer or a public authority. These provisions apply also to other cruel, inhuman or degrading treatment or punishment (throughout this chapter, only the term "torture" will be used).

In addition to this provision, States parties assume a series of obligations contained in articles 3 to 16 of the Convention. In particular, States parties must proceed immediately to an impartial investigation when there is reasonable ground to believe that an act of torture has been committed (article 12). Furthermore, any individual who alleges to have been tortured must have the right to complain (article 13); and the victim -- or in the event of the victim's death, his family -- must be ensured fair and adequate compensation (article 14).

In order to ensure the implementation of these obligations, the Convention requires States parties to report periodically on the measures taken to give effect to the rights enshrined in the Convention. This obligation is contained in article 19, which also outlines the procedure for the examination of reports.

—Text of article 19

> **1. The States Parties shall submit to the Committee, through the Secretary-General of the United Nations, reports on the measures they have taken to give effect to their undertakings under this Convention, within one year after the entry into force of the Convention for the State Party concerned. Thereafter the States Parties shall submit supplementary reports every four years on any new measures taken and such other reports as the Committee may request.**
>
> **2. The Secretary-General of the United Nations shall transmit the reports to all States Parties.**
>
> **3. Each report shall be considered by the Committee which may make such general comments on the report as it may consider appropriate and shall forward these to the State Party concerned. That State Party may respond with any observations it chooses to the Committee.**
>
> **4. The Committee may, at its discretion, decide to include any comments made by it in accordance with paragraph 3 of**

this article, together with the report made in accordance with article 24. If so requested by the State Party concerned, the Committee may also include a copy of the report submitted under paragraph 1 of this article.

Given this provision of the Convention, each State party must submit, within a year of its entry into force for the given State, an initial report on the measures taken to implement the obligations resulting from the Convention. Subsequently, each State party must submit a supplementary report every four years, as well as any other report requested by the Committee.

As far as the content of these reports is concerned, the Convention gives only very general indications. However, in November 1989, the Committee prepared and adopted general guidelines on the form and content of initial reports to be submitted in accordance with article 19(1) of the Convention (document CAT/C/4/Rev.1). As of June 1990, the Committee had adopted guidelines just for initial reports. Since the Convention entered into force only at 27 June 1987, the first supplemental report according to the provision of article 19(1) will be due only after 27 June 1992.

(b) Guidelines for reporting under the Convention

The guidelines prepared by the Committee are intended to assist States parties in the elaboration and the presentation of their initial reports; they should facilitate the preparation of sufficiently comprehensive and detailed reports. The guidelines further aim at a uniform presentation of reports; they therefore assist the Committee in the performance of its duties, and offer an opportunity to all states parties to appreciate clearly how the obligations under the Convention are carried out by each State party.

—Text of the general guidelines regarding the form and contents of initial reports

Part I: information of general nature

This part should:

(a) Describe briefly the general legal framework within which torture as defined in Article 1, paragraph 1, of the Convention as well as the other cruel, inhuman or degrading treatment or punishment are prohibited and eliminated in the reporting State;

(b) Indicate whether the reporting State is a party to an international instrument or has national legislation which does or may contain provisions of wider application that those provided for under the Convention;

(c) Indicate whether the provisions of the Convention can be invoked before and directly enforced by the courts, other tribunals or administrative authorities or whether they have to be transformed into internal laws or administrative regulations to be enforced by the authorities concerned;

(d) Indicate what judicial, administrative or other competent authorities have jurisdiction over matters dealt with in the Convention and provide information on cases actually dealt with by those authorities during the reporting period;

(e) Indicate what remedies are available to an individual who claims to have been a victim of torture or other cruel, inhuman or degrading treatment or punishment and what rehabilitation programmes are available to victims of torture;

(f) Describe briefly the actual situation as regards the practical implementation of the Convention in the reporting State and indicate any factors and difficulties affecting the degree of fulfillment of the obligations of the reporting State under the Convention.

Part II: information in relation to each of the articles in part I of the Convention

This part should provide specific information relating to the implementation by the reporting State of articles 2 to 16 of the Convention, in accordance with the sequence of those articles and their respective provisions. It should include in relation to the provisions of each article:

(a) The legislative, judicial, administrative or other measures in force which give effect to those provisions;

(b) Any factors or difficulties affecting the practical implementation of those provisions;

(c) Any information on concrete cases and situations where measures giving effect to those provisions have been enforced including any relevant statistical data.

The report should be accompanied by sufficient copies in one of the working languages (English, French, Russian or Spanish) of the principal legislative and the texts referred to in the report. These will be made available to members of the Committee. It should be noted, however, that they will not be reproduced for general distribution with the report. It is desirable therefore that, when a text is not actually quoted in or annexed to the report itself, the report should contain sufficient information to be understood without reference to it. The text of national legislative provisions relevant to the implementation of the Convention should be quoted in the report.

The reports submitted by States parties should always be divided into two parts.

The first part of the report should be of a general nature. It should provide basic information and describe the context within which the prohibition of torture is guaranteed in the reporting State. The following principal aspects ought to be addressed: the report should precisely indicate the status of the Convention in the domestic legal order, and in particular it should clarify whether for the convention to become part of the domestic legal order, it is necessary to be explicitly and completely reiterated in the Constitution or in another legislative act of the State party. Should that be a requirement, the report should provide information on the legislative act incorporating the Convention in the domestic legal order and its impact. Otherwise, the report should specify whether ratification of or accession to the Convention in itself leads to the incorporation of the Convention and to the obligation for the State's agents to apply directly the provisions of the Convention, as well as to the possibility for individuals to invoke directly the rights conferred on them by the Convention. Furthermore, the first part should describe the organizational structure of the State party, namely the legislative, executive and judicial powers and their responsibilities. This part should report which judicial, administrative or other authorities are in charge of implementing the various provisions of the Convention. Finally, this part should assess the *de facto* situation with regard to torture in the reporting State, and should torture still exist, it should give the reasons why it could not yet be abolished completely. (Part one of the guidelines is now common to the reporting guidelines prepared for all the United Nations human rights treaty bodies. For the text of the consolidated guidelines for the initial part of the reports of States parties see the annex at the end of part one of the Manual.)

The second part of the report should provide detailed information on an article-by-article basis on how the reporting State is implementing articles 2 to 16 of the Convention. With regard to each individual article, the report should provide information on the legislative, administrative and judicial measures taken to give effect to the provisions of the article under consideration, as well as information on any concrete cases of the application of those measures. In all instances, available statistical information should be included.

Reports, however, must also mention any cases of violation of the Convention, and should describe the reasons for such violations and the measures taken to remedy the situation. In fact, for the Committee it is important to obtain a clear picture not only of the legal situation, but also of the *de facto* situation in the reporting State.

The report itself must contain the most important domestic legal provisions pertaining to the Convention so that they are easily accessible. It is also necessary to attach other relevant laws and regulations to the report, as well as the texts of any administrative or judicial decisions rendered or measures adopted in direct or indirect application of the Convention. To the extent possible, these texts must be submitted in one of the working languages of the Committee, i.e. English, French, Russian or Spanish.

* * *

9. Model Questionnaire

Model questionnaire to be completed by persons alleging arbitrary arrest or detention[2]

I. Identity of the person arrested or detained

1. Family name ______________________________

2. First name ______________________________

3. Sex:

   Male ☐ Female ☐

4. Birth date or age (at the time of detention) ________________

5. Nationality(ies) ______________________________

6. *(a)* Identity document (if any) ____________________

   (b) Issued by ______________________________

   (c) On (date) ______________________________

[2]A separate questionnaire must be completed for each case of alleged arbitrary arrest or detention. As far as possible, all details requested should be given. Nevertheless, failure to do so will not necessarily result in the inadmissibility of the communication.

(*d*) No. ______________________________

7. Profession and/or activity (if believed to be relevant to the arrest/detention)

____

____

8. Address of usual residence ______________________________

____

II. Arrest[3]

1. Date of arrest ______________________________

2. Place of arrest (as detailed as possible):

____

____

____

____

3. Forces who carried out the arrest or are believed to have carried it out:

____

4. Did they show a warrant or other decision by a public authority?

Yes ☐ No ☐

5. Authority who issued the warrant or decision ______________________________

____

6. Relevant legislation applied (if known) ______________________________

____

____

____

____

[3]For the purpose of this questionnaire, "arrest" refers to the initial act of apprehending a person. "Detention" means and includes detention before, during and after trial. In some cases, only section II, or section III may be applicable. Nonetheless, whenever possible, both sections should be filled in.

III. Detention[4]

1. Date of detention ______________________

2. Duration of detention (if not known, probable duration) __________

3. Forces holding the detainee under custody ______________
____

4. Places of detention (indicate any transfer and present place of detention):
____

5. Authorities that ordered the detention ______________
____

6. Reasons for the detention imputed by the authorities __________
____

7. Relevant legislation applied (if known) ______________
____

IV. Describe the circumstances of the arrest and/or the detention and indicate precise reasons why you consider the arrest or detention to be arbitrary[5]

____

____

V. Indicate internal steps, including domestic remedies, taken especially with the legal and administrative authorities, particularly for the purpose of establishing the detention and, as appropriate, their results or the reasons why such steps or remedies were ineffective or why they were not taken

---

[4]Copies of documents that prove the arbitrary nature of the arrest or detention, or help to better understand the specific circumstances of the case, as well as any other relevant information, may also be attached to this questionnaire.

[5]Copies of documents that prove the arbitrary nature of the arrest or detention, or help to better understand the specific circumstances of the case, as well as any other relevant information, may also be attached to this questionnaire.

____

____

____

____

VI. Full name and address of the person(s) submitting the information (telephone and fax number, if possible)[6]

____

____

____

____

Date ____________________ Signature ____________________________

* * *

[6]If a case is submitted to the Working Group by anyone other than the victim or his family, such person or organization should indicate authorization by the victim or his family to act on their behalf. If, however, the authorization is not readily available, the Working Group reserves the right to proceed without the authorization. All details concerning the person(s) submitting the information to the Working Group, and any authorization provided by the victim or his family, will be kept confidential.

This questionnaire should be addressed to the Working Group on arbitrary detention, Centre for Human Rights, United Nations Office at Geneva, 8-14 avenue de la Paix, 1211 Geneva 10, Switzerland, fax No. (022) 9170123.

10. International Commission of Jurists

THE FOLLOW-UP PROCEDURE OF THE UN HUMAN RIGHTS COMMITTEE

Alfred M. de Zayas[7]

The Human Rights Committee (HRC) was established as the monitoring organ of the International Covenant on Civil and Political Rights (ICCPR), which entered into force on 23 March 1976. It consists of 18 experts elected by States parties to the Covenant, at present 100. Unlike the UN Commission on Human rights, which is composed of delegations from 53 member States of the United Nations, the HRC members serve in their personal capacities and do not represent their countries. As a treaty body, it is not *strictu sensu* a United Nations organ, although it is assisted by the Secretariat, i.e. the Centre for Human Rights in Geneva, and reports annually to the UN General Assembly.

Under the Optional Protocol to the ICCPR, individuals who claim that any of their rights enumerated in the Covenant have been violated and who have exhausted all available domestic remedies may submit written communications to the HRC for examination. Currently 60 States parties to the Covenant have accepted the competence of the HRC to deal with individual complaints by ratifying or acceding to the Optional Protocol. No communication can be received by the HRC if it concerns a State party to the Covenant which is not also a party to the Optional Protocol. Consideration of communications under the Optional Protocol takes place in closed meetings. Final decisions, however, are published in the HRC's annual report to the General Assembly and in a running series entitled "Selected Decisions of the Human Rights Committee" (volumes I and II have been already issued).

The HRC started its work under the Optional Protocol at its second session in 1977. Since then, 472 communications concerning 36 States parties have been registered for consideration. Examination of 125 communications was concluded by the adoption of final decisions on the merits. Violations of provisions of the Covenant were found in 98 cases.

---

[7]This article was written in the author's personal capacity and does not necessarily reflect the opinions of the United Nations Secretariat or of the members of the Human Rights Committee.

"Views" and Remedies

The HRC's decisions on the merits are referred to as "Views" in article 5, paragraph 4, of the Optional Protocol. Although Views read like court judgments, the drafters of the Covenant did not call them so, nor did they confer upon them legally binding force. The Optional Protocol does not provide for an enforcement mechanism. Thus, the Committee's Views are more in the nature of recommendations, which States parties are free to implement or not to the extent they deem appropriate. Considerable moral weight is attached to the HRC's findings, and it may be presumed that when a State voluntarily adheres to the procedure under the Optional Protocol, it does so in good faith and that it undertakes to honour the HRC's recommendations.

Beyond that, a State may provide in its domestic legislation that it will carry out the decisions of the HRC. For instance, pursuant to article 39 of Peruvian Law No. 23,506, a Peruvian citizen who considers that his or her human rights have been violated may appeal to the United Nations Human Rights Committee. Article 40 of the same law provides that the Peruvian Supreme Court will receive the resolutions of the HRC and order their implementation. This law was invoked by Rubén Muñoz Hermoza in a case involving arbitrary dismissal from public service. His communication (No. 203/1986, *Muñoz v. Peru*) was examined by the HRC, which found a violation of his rights under article 14, paragraph 1, of the Covenant.[8]

When the HRC has made a finding of a violation of a provision of the Covenant in its Views, it proceeds to ask the State party to take appropriate steps to remedy the violation. For instance, in a case concerning the disappearance and possible death of the victims, the HRC found that "the right to life enshrined in article 6 of the Covenant and the rights to liberty have not been effectively protected" by the State party. In its Views the Committee stated that "it would welcome information on any relevant measures taken by the State party in respect of the Committee's Views and, in particular, invites the State party to inform the Committee of further developments in the investigation of the disappearance of the Sanjuán brothers" (No. 181/1984, *Sanjuán v. Colombia*).[9] In another case concerning an alien who was held pending extradition, the HRC found that there had been a violation of article 9, paragraph 4, of the Covenant, because the author had been unable to challenge his detention before a court during the initial seven days following the issuance of the detention order. In its

---

[8]Human rights Committee 1989 Report, Official Records of the General Assembly, 44th session, Supplement No. 40/44/40, annex X, section D, paras. 1 and 13.2.

[9]Human rights committee 1990 Report, annex IX, section B, paras. 11 and 12.

Views the HRC observed that "the State party is under an obligation to remedy the violations suffered by the author and to ensure that similar violations do not occur in the future". It indicated that "it would welcome information on any relevant measures taken by the State party in respect of the Committee's views" (No. 291/1988, *Torres v. Finland*).[10] In a case where the author was sentenced to death after a trial, which the HRC held had violated basic guarantees of fair hearing under article 14 of the Covenant, the HRC asked the State party to release the author (No. 250/1987, *Reid v. Jamaica*).[11]

Monitoring Compliance

It is encouraging to note that many States parties have honoured their commitments under the Optional Protocol by releasing prisoners, paying compensation to victims or amending legislation found to be incompatible with the Covenant. In its annual reports to the General Assembly, the HRC has been reporting on these successes. There is, however, no general overview on the degree of State compliance with the Committee's Views.

At its 38th session in March/April 1989, the HRC discussed the question of its powers in relation to the problems of the implementation of its Views. At its 39th session in July 1990, the HRC decided systematically to seek such information. In the past, the HRC had requested information verbally. Furthermore, HRC members have used the opportunity of examining States' reports under article 40 to raise the issue (and, indeed, to present lists of cases to the States' representatives). However, only in a few cases did States forward information to the HRC. Thus, the HRC often had no information on what had happened to a particular victim of a violation of the Covenant after it had issued its Views. Further, the HRC has received letters of complaint from a number of victims stating that their situation remained unchanged or that no appropriate remedy had been provided.

Legal Basis for Follow-Up Procedure

The world community associated great hopes with the establishment of the Human Rights Committee. As the monitoring organ of the most important human rights treaty to date, the HRC was entrusted with a weighty responsibility. Of course, there already existed regional human rights commissions which operated pursuant to regional conventions, but here at last was a multilateral treaty aimed

---

[10] *Id.*, annex IX, section K, para. 9.

[11] *Id.*, annex IX, section J, para. 12.2.

at universal participation and a Committee of distinguished experts from all continents and legal traditions with a truly global perspective.

With the growing recognition of the individual as a subject of international law, bearing both rights and responsibilities, the idea of an international court of human rights with competence to examine complaints of individuals against States and the power to hand down binding judgments has been gaining ground. Admittedly the Human Rights Committee is not such a court, but it does exercise analogous responsibilities and it is the only international body to fulfil this need.

In the earlier years of the Human Rights Committee, members frequently discussed ways and means of increasing co-operation with States parties, especially in respect of the Committee's Views under the Optional Protocol. But doubts were expressed as to the legal basis for any action to be taken by the HRC subsequent to the adoption of Views in a particular case. At the HRC's 17th session in October 1982, some members expressed the opinion that nothing in the Covenant and the Optional Protocol, which circumscribe the HRC's mandate, empowered it to reconsider its Views on communications or to ensure their implementation. Some members expressed their understanding that the HRC was a *sui generis* body with no judicial powers and that the implementation of its Views was left to the good will of the State party concerned. They felt that the question of monitoring the implementation of those Views in the absence of a clear legal mandate to effect might even be contrary to article 2, paragraph 7, of the United Nations Charter relating to non-interference by the United Nations in the internal affairs of sovereign States. Moreover, if States parties wanted to make the Committee's Views binding, they could use the amendment procedure under article 11 of the Protocol, an easier matter in 1982, when there were only 28 States parties to the Protocol.[12]

Other members, however, felt that the HRC could not let its work under the Optional Protocol degenerate into an exercise in futility. They felt that due consideration had to be paid to both the letter and spirit of the Covenant, and that where the Committee believed that certain appropriate action was reasonably open to it, or was not expressly prohibited, the HRC should take it and that the Optional Protocol allowed considerable latitude for interpretation, since many issues were not specifically covered by its provisions.

Gradually a consensus emerged in the HRC that "follow-up" procedures were within its mandate. This is implicit in the preamble to the Optional Protocol, which declares that the HRC receives and considers communications "in order

---

[12]Human Rights Committee 1983 Report, Official Records of the General Assembly, 38th session, supplement No. 40 (A/38/40), p. 93, para. 3.9.

further to achieve the purposes of the Covenant and the implementation of its provisions." To this end it is legitimate for the HRC to engage in exchange with States parties regarding their response to the Committee's Views. The International Court of Justice has affirmed that even in the Absence of specific enabling powers, an international body may act in ways not specifically forbidden for the achievement of its purposes and objectives (Case of Certain Expenses, ICJ Reports 1962). Moreover, the competence to "consider" communications, laid down in article 1 of the Optional Protocol, may be interpreted broadly as encompassing not only the examination of cases up to the rendering of Views but also beyond that to "consider" the measures adopted by a State party to remedy violations of the Covenant found in the course of examination of a communication.

Indeed, certain follow-up competence must be inherent to the effective performance of the HRC's functions. Even if the Committee's Views are not legally binding judgments and the HRC has no power to ensure their enforcement, it must at least have authority to monitor the effect of its Views. This authority can be understood on the basis of the doctrine of implied powers (Reparation for Injuries Suffered in Service of the United Nations, Advisory Opinion, ICJ Report 1949, pp. 174-188), according to which every international organ must be deemed to have certain implied powers. Every procedure of international investigation or settlement (article 5, paragraph 2(b) of Optional Protocol) necessarily must have the means of determining whether a settlement has been reached and whether the settlement is being observed. States parties that voluntarily submit to the Optional Protocol procedure do so in good faith, intending to respect the Committee's Views. Accordingly, the HRC would not be going beyond its mandate by monitoring implementation.

Thus, even if the Optional Protocol is silent on the question of the HRC's powers subsequent to the adoption and transmittal of Views, it does not exclude the development of a reasonable follow-up machinery.

Further, it should not be forgotten that all parties to the Covenant have given the HRC a general competence to request "reports on the measures they have adopted which give effect to the rights recognized herein and on the progress made in the enjoyment of those rights" (article 40, paragraph 1, of the Covenant). Such reports should be submitted "whenever the Committee so requests" (article 40, paragraph 1(b)), e.g. after the adoption of Views under the Optional Protocol. Accordingly, the HRC could request from any State party found to be in violation of the Covenant a brief, separate report on its compliance with the Committee's Views. Such a request might be addressed to States parties one year after the adoption of the Committee's Views. Thus, while formally linked to article 40 of the Covenant, this procedure would function separately from the examination of the regular periodic State reports.

Special Rapporteur

At its 39th session, the HRC decided to adopt these measures to "follow up" on its cases:

- When, in its Views under the Optional Protocol, the Committee makes a finding of a violation, the State party concerned will be asked in the Views itself to inform the Committee of what action it deems appropriate. A time limit will be indicated for the receipt of such information. This time limit shall be determined on the basis of the circumstances of each case; it shall not exceed 180 days.

- States parties have undertaken, under article 2, paragraph 3, of the Covenant, to ensure effective remedies for violations of the Covenant. If no reply is received within the indicated time periods, or if the reply shows that no remedy has been provided, this will henceforth be noted in the Committee's Annual Report. Equally, positive responses and co-operation from States parties will also be included in the Annual Report.

- The Committee's Guidelines for the preparation of Reports, requesting States parties who are also parties to the Optional Protocol, and in respect of whom any finding of a violation had been made in the period under review, shall be amended to include a brief section indicating "measures which they have adopted which give effect to the rights recognized therein" (article 40 of the Covenant) in respect of the authors concerned. Because of the periodicity of Reports under article 40, this information is additional to, and does not replace, the information that is to be given to the Committee under the time limits specified above.

- Should this information not be made available in the relevant periodic Report, questions relating to it will be included by the Committee in its List of questions that it customarily prepares for a State party a few days prior to the examination of the Report, and the matter will be pursued in the dialogue with the state party.

- The Committee will appoint a Special Rapporteur for the Follow-Up of Views.

The Special Rapporteur's duties are as follows:

- To recommend to the Committee action upon all letters of complaint henceforth received from the individuals held, in the Views of the HRC under the Optional Protocol, to have been the victims of a violation, and who claim that no appropriate remedy has been provided.

- To communicate with States parties and, if it deems appropriate, with the victims in respect of such letters already received by the HRC.

- To seek to provide information on any action taken in relation to Views adopted by the HRC to date, when such information has not otherwise been made available. To this end, the Special Rapporteur will communicate with all States parties and victims in respect of whom findings of violations have been made, and to ascertain what action, if any, has been taken. This information, when collected, will also be made available in a future Annual Report.

- To assist the Rapporteur of the Committee in the Preparation of the relevant section of the Annual Report that will henceforth contain detailed information on the follow-up of cases.

- To advise the Committee on the appropriate deadline for the receipt of information on the remedial measures adopted by a State party found to have violated provisions of the Covenant.

- To submit to the Committee, at suitable intervals, recommendations on possible ways of rendering the follow-up procedure more effective."[13]

At this same session, the HRC appointed János Fodor as Special Rapporteur for the Follow-Up of Views for a one-year term. At its 41st, 42nd and 43rd sessions, Mr. Fodor presented progress reports, which are at this stage confidential. The HRC has yet to decide whether such progress reports should be published or whether only certain information contained in them should be incorporated into the Committee's Annual Reports.

Information from States Parties

Prior to the appointment of the Special Rapporteur on the Follow-Up of Views, the HRC had received information from States parties on action taken by them in pursuance of the Committee's Views. For instance, during its 31st session the HRC adopted its Views on case No. 188/1984 (*R. Martinez Portorreal v. the Dominican Republic*). The HRC had found that the author, a human rights lawyer, had been a victim of violations of articles 7, 9 and 10 of the Covenant. During its 39th Session, the government of the Dominican Republic informed the HRC of the measures taken to remedy the violations, in particular, offering Mr. Martinez Portorreal and the members of the Dominican Committee for Human Rights all assurances and guarantees to facilitate their

---

[13]Human Rights Committee 1990 Report, Vol. II, annex XI.

functions and issuing an official passport to Mr. Martinez Portorreal.[14] At its 36th session, the HRC adopted its Views on case No. 238/1987 (*Bolaños v. Ecuador*), finding a violation of article 9, paragraphs 1 and 3, and of article 14, paragraphs 1 and 3(c) of the Covenant, because Mr. Bolaños had been kept in pre-trial detention for six years. The HRC urged the State party to release Mr. Bolaños from detention and to grant him compensation. At its 38th session, the State party informed the HRC that Mr. Bolaños had been released from detention a few weeks after receipt of the Committee's Views, and that the government of Ecuador had endeavoured to remedy the violations against him by assisting him in finding employment.[15]

Subsequent to the appointment of Special Rapporteur in 1990, information is being received in a systematic manner, enabling the HRC to better evaluate the effect of its Views. Two examples are cited here:

- At its 38th session, the HRC adopted its Views on case No. 291/1988 (*M. Torres v. Finland*.[16] The HRC found that there had been a violation of article 9, paragraph 4, of the Covenant because the author, an alien subject to extradition, had been unable to challenge the legality of his detention before a court during certain periods following his arrest. The HRC observed that the State party should "remedy the violations suffered by the author and . . . ensure that similar violations do not occur in the future."

  By verbal note of 15 May 1991, in response to the Special Rapporteur's request, the State party informed the HRC that the Aliens Act had been revised by a Parliamentary Act that took effect on 10 May 1990, in order to make the provisions governing the detention of aliens compatible with the Covenant. Moreover, the Covenant has been incorporated into Finnish domestic law, making it directly applicable before Finnish courts and authorities. According to a decision dated 8 January 1991, the Finnish Ministry of the Interior agreed to pay 7,000 Finnish marks to Mr. Torres as compensation.[17]

---

[14] *Id.*, annex XII, section A.

[15] *Id.*, annex XII, section B.

[16] *Id.*, annex IX, section K.

[17] Human Rights Committee 1991 Report, para. 705.

- During its 39th session, the HRC adopted its Views on case No. 305/1988 (*H. van Alphen v. the Netherlands*).[18] The HRC found a violation of article 9, paragraph 1, of the Covenant because the author, a Dutch lawyer, had been kept in detention for nine weeks in connection with his refusal to co-operate in an investigation against his clients.

  By a verbal note of 15 May 1991, the Netherlands informed the HRC that although it was unable to share the HRC's; conclusions that there had been a violation of article 9, paragraph 1, of the Covenant, it would, "out of respect for the HRC . . .make to Mr. van Alphen an ex-gratia payment in the amount of [Dutch guilders] 5,000."[19]

Thus, it is evident that the HRC is having a direct impact on States parties to the Optional Protocol and also creating international case law. Even if only 60 States are parties to the Optional Protocol, the HRC's jurisprudence is being quoted in national courts and commented on in scholarly journals. As the only quasi-judicial body examining complaints from individuals, the HRC has a distinguished beginning and its pronouncements will not doubt gain in universal recognition. The Committee's Follow-Up Procedure responds to a generally perceived need to know how States parties are implementing its decisions. Publicity about follow-up will in turn enhance the authority of the HRC's decisions. Surely, as more and more States parties voluntarily carry out the HRC's recommendations, other States that would not yet feel bound to comply will find it more difficult to justify non-compliance *vis-à-vis* other States and even *vis-à-vis* their own citizens. Still, it is an unfortunate fact that some States parties have failed to comply or fully to comply with the Committee's Views. Lacking an enforcement mechanism or the power to impose sanctions, the HRC relies on the legal persuasiveness and moral weight of its decisions and on the growing influence of world public opinion.

All in all, there is good reason for optimism, because the trend is clearly toward greater compliance, thereby setting an example for all States. It can be said without fear of contradiction that the Optional Protocol procedure of the Human Rights Committee is emerging as an important tool in the common effort to establish a universal human rights culture. Part of this culture is the increasing public awareness that the United Nations work in the field of standard setting includes the establishment of a monitoring machinery and that decisions of treaty bodies like the Human Rights Committee are being implemented. Indeed, there is nothing as successful as success, and surely the HRC's success in follow-up

---

[18]Human Rights Committee 1990 Report, Annex IX, section M.

[19]Human Rights Committee 1991, Report, para. 707.

will contribute to its effectiveness and reinforce the public's perception that HRC decisions are meaningful expressions of human rights law, and ultimately that real progress is being achieved in the realization of human rights for all.[20]

* * *

[20]For a review of the case law of the HRC, see a recent publication of the Centre for Human Rights entitled "Application of the International Covenant on Civil and Political Rights under the Optional Protocol by the Human Rights Committee", which can be ordered free of charge from the Centre a Reprint No. 1. See also the Centre's Fact Sheet No. 7 on "Communications Procedures", which is available in all UN working languages.

L. DEROGATION

During situations of internal unrest, civil war or public emergency, States frequently restrict the enjoyment of fundamental rights and freedoms.

The International Covenant on Civil and Political Rights envisages the possibility of derogation. A public emergency which threatens the life of the nation must, however, be officially proclaimed. Measures of derogation must be limited to the extent strictly required by the situation and must not involve discrimination.

No derogation from articles 6 (right to life), 7 (prohibition of torture), 8 (paragraphs 1 and 2, prohibition of slavery), 11 (prohibition of imprisonment solely for inability to fulfil a contractual obligation), 15 (prohibition of *ex post facto* legislation), 16 (right to recognition as a person before the law) and 18 (freedom of religion) is allowed.

The Sub-Commission on Prevention of Discrimination and Protection of Minorities has also focused on situations of public emergency that fall short of the threshold of armed conflict, in which the Geneva Red Cross Convention and Protocols would apply. In order to safeguard the minimum rights of persons in these situations between outright war and a peace regime, a number of experts met at the University of Abu/Turku in 1990 in order to adopt a declaration of minimum humanitarian standards. This declaration was subsequently submitted to the Sub-Commission by two of its members. This declaration is currently under review.

1. International Covenant on Civil and Political Rights

Article 4

1. In time of public emergency which threatens the life of the nation and the existence of which is officially proclaimed, the States Parties to the present Covenant may take measures derogating from their obligations under the present Covenant to the extent strictly required by the exigencies of the situation, provided that such measures are not inconsistent with their other obligations under international law and do not involve discrimination solely on the ground of race, colour, sex, language, religion or social origin.

2. No derogation from articles 6, 7, 8 (paragraphs 1 and 2), 11, 15, 16 and 18 may be made under this provision.

3. Any State party to the present Covenant availing itself of the right of derogation shall immediately inform the other States parties to the present Covenant through the intermediary of the Secretary-General of the United Nations, of the provision from which it has derogated and of the reasons by which it was actuated. A further communication shall be made, through the same intermediary, on the date on which it terminates such derogation.

* * *

2. General Comment of the Human Rights Committee on the International Convenant on Civil and Political Rights Adopted on 27 July 1982

1. Article 4 of the Covenant has posed a number of problems for the Committee when considering reports from some States parties. When a public emergency which threatens the life of a nation arises and it is officially proclaimed, a State party may derogate from a number of rights to the extent strictly required by the situation. The State party, however, may not derogate from certain specific rights and may not take discriminatory measures on a number of grounds. The State party is also under an obligation to inform the other States parties immediately, through the Secretary-General, of the derogations it has made including the reasons therefor and the date on which the derogations are terminated.

2. States parties have generally indicated the mechanism provided in their legal systems for the declaration of a state of emergency and the applicable provisions of the law governing derogations. However, in the case of a few States which had apparently derogated from Covenant rights, it was unclear not only whether a state of emergency had been officially declared but also whether rights from which the Covenant allows no derogation had in fact not been derogated from and further whether the other States parties had been informed of the derogations and of the reasons for the derogations.

3. The Committee holds the view that measures taken under article 4 are of an exceptional and temporary nature and may only last as long as the life of the nation concerned is threatened and that, in times of emergency, the protection of human rights becomes all the more important, particularly those rights from which no derogations can be made. The Committee also considers that it is equally important for States parties, in times of public emergency, to inform the other States parties of the nature and extent of the derogations they have made and of the reasons therefor and, further, to fulfil their reporting obligations under article 40 of the Covenant by indicating the nature and extent of each right derogated from together with the relevant documentation.

* * *

3. Declaration of Minimum Humanitarian Standards

Article 1

This Declaration affirms minimum humanitarian standards which are applicable in all situations, including internal violence, disturbances, tensions, and public emergency, and which cannot be derogated from under any circumstances. These standards must be respected whether or not a state of emergency has been proclaimed.

Article 2

These standards shall be respected by, and applied to all persons groups and authorities, irrespective of their legal status and without any adverse discrimination.

Article 3

1. Everyone shall have the right to recognition everywhere as a person before the law. All persons even if their liberty has been restricted, are entitled to respect for their personal honour and convictions, freedom of thought, conscience and religious practises. They shall in all circumstances be treated humanely, without any adverse distinction.

2. The following acts are and shall remain prohibited:

   a) violence to the life, health and physical or mental well-being of persons, in particular, murder, torture, mutilation, rape, as well as cruel, inhuman or degrading treatment or punishment and other outrages upon personal dignity;

   b) collective punishments against persons and their property;

   c) the taking of hostages;

   d) practising, permitting or tolerating the involuntary disappearance of individuals, including their abduction or unacknowledged detention;

   e) pillage;

f) deliberate deprivation of access to necessary food, drinking water and medicine;

g) threats or incitement to commit any of the foregoing acts.

Article 4

1. All persons deprived of their liberty shall be held in recognized places of detention. Accurate information on their detention and whereabouts, including transfers, shall be made promptly available to their family members and counsel or other persons having a legitimate interest in the information.

2. All persons deprived of their liberty shall be allowed to communicate with the outside world including counsel in accordance with reasonable regulations promulgated by the competent authority.

3. The right to an effective remedy, including *habeas corpus*, shall be guaranteed as a means to determine the whereabouts or the state of health of persons deprived of their liberty and for identifying the authority ordering or carrying out the deprivation of liberty. Everyone who is deprived of his or her liberty by arrest or detention shall be entitled to take proceedings by which the lawfulness of the detention shall be decided speedily by a court and his or her release ordered if the detention is not lawful.

4. All persons deprived of their liberty shall be treated humanely, provided with adequate food and drinking water, decent accommodation and clothing, and be afforded safeguards as regards health, hygiene, and working and social conditions.

Article 5

1. Attacks against persons not taking part in acts of violence shall be prohibited in all circumstances.

2. Whenever the use of force is unavoidable, it shall be in proportion to the seriousness of the offence or the objective to be achieved.

3. Weapons or other material or methods prohibited in international armed conflicts must not be employed in any circumstances.

Article 6

Acts or threats of violence the primary purpose or foreseeable effect of which is to spread terror among the population are prohibited.

Article 7

1. The displacement of the population or parts thereof shall not be ordered unless their safety or imperative security reasons so demand. Should such displacements have to be carried out, all possible measures shall be taken in order that the population may be transferred and received under satisfactory conditions of shelter, hygiene, health, safety, and nutrition. Persons or groups thus displaced shall be allowed to return to their homes as soon as the conditions which made their displacement imperative have ceased. Every effort shall be made to enable those so displaced who wish to remain together to do so. Families whose members wish to remain together must be allowed to do so. The persons thus displaced shall be free to move around in the territory, subject only to the safety of the persons involved or reasons of imperative security.

2. No persons shall be compelled to leave their own territory.

Article 8

1. Every human being has the inherent right to life. This right shall be protected by law. No one shall be arbitrarily deprived of his or her life.

2. In addition to the guarantees of the inherent right to life, and the prohibition of genocide, in existing human rights and humanitarian instruments, the following provisions shall be respected as a minimum.

3. In countries which have not yet abolished the death penalty, sentences of death shall be carried out only for the most serious crimes. Sentences of death shall not be carried out on pregnant women, mothers of young children or on children under eighteen years of age at the time of the commission of the offence.

4. No death sentence shall be carried out before the expiration of at least six months from the notification of the final judgment confirming such death sentence.

Article 9

No sentence shall be passed and no penalty shall be executed on a person found guilty of an offence without previous judgment pronounced by a regularly constituted court affording all the judicial guarantees which are recognized as indispensable by the community of nations. In particular:

a) the procedure shall provide for an accused to be informed without delay of the particulars of the offence alleged against him or her, shall provide for a trial within a reasonable time, and shall afford the accused before and during his or her trial all necessary rights and means of defence;

b) no one shall be convicted of an offence except on the basis of individual penal responsibility;

c) anyone charged with an offence is presumed innocent until proved guilty according to law;

d) anyone charged with an offence shall have the right to be tried in his or her presence;

e) no one shall be compelled to testify against himself or herself or to confess guilt;

f) no one shall be liable to be tried or punished again for an offence for which he or she has already been finally convicted or acquitted in accordance with the law and penal procedure;

g) no one shall be held guilty of any criminal offence on account of any act or omission which did not constitute a criminal offence, under applicable law, at the time when it was committed.

Article 10

Every child has the right to the measures of protection required by his or her condition as a minor and shall be provided with the care and aid the child requires. Children who have not yet attained the age of fifteen years shall not be recruited in or allowed to join armed forces or armed groups or allowed to take part in acts of violence. All efforts shall be made not to allow persons below the age of eighteen to take part in acts of violence.

Article 11

If it is considered necessary for imperative reasons of security to subject any person to assigned residence, internment or administrative detention, such decisions shall be subject to a regular procedure prescribed by law affording all the judicial guarantees which are recognized as indispensable by the international community, including the right of appeal or to a periodical review.

Article 12

In every circumstance, the wounded and sick, whether or not they have taken part in acts of violence, shall be protected and treated humanely and shall receive, to the fullest extent practicable and with the least possible delay, the medical care and attention required by their condition. There shall be no distinction among them on any grounds other than their medical condition.

Article 13

Every possible measure shall be taken, without delay, to search for and collect wounded, sick and missing persons and to protect them against pillage and ill- treatment, to ensure their adequate care, and to search for the dead; prevent their being despoiled or mutilated, and to dispose of them with respect.

Article 14

1. Medical and religious personnel shall be respected and protected and shall be granted all available help for the performance of their duties. They shall not be compelled to carry out tasks which are not compatible with their humanitarian missions.

2. Under no circumstances shall any person be punished for having carried out medical activities compatible with the principles of medical ethics, regardless of the person benefitting therefrom.

Article 15

In situations of internal violence, disturbances, tensions or public emergency, humanitarian organizations shall be granted all the facilities necessary to enable them to carry out their humanitarian activities.

Article 16

In observing these standards, all efforts shall be made to protect the rights of groups, minorities and peoples, including their dignity and identity.

Article 17

The observance of these standards shall not affect the legal status of any authorities, groups, or persons involved in situations of internal violence, disturbances, tensions or public emergency.

Article 18

1. Nothing in the present standards shall be interpreted as restricting or impairing the provisions of any international humanitarian or human rights instrument.

2. No restriction upon or derogation from any of the fundamental rights of human beings recognized or existing in any country by virtue of law, treaties, regulations, custom, or principles of humanity shall be admitted on the pretext that the present standards do not recognize such rights or that they recognize them to a lesser extent.

* * *

M. INTERNATIONAL COOPERATION IN PENAL MATTERS, INCLUDING MODEL TREATIES

In light of the increased inter-dependence of the world community, it is only natural that States have sought ways of cooperating more closely in the exchange of information, attainment of evidence, and apprehension and extradition of fugitives.

The growth of organized crime, terrorism, and drug-trafficking has necessitated special guidelines and led to the adoption of a great many bi-treaties as well as multilateral treaties.

In order to facilitate this task, the United Nations General Assembly has adopted model treaties on a variety of subjects, including extradition; mutual assistance in criminal matters; the transfer of proceedings; the prevention of crimes that infringe on the cultural heritage of peoples in the form of movable property; and the transfer of supervision of offenders conditionally sentenced or conditionally released.

1. Prevention and Control of Organized Crime

The Eighth United Nations Congress on the Prevention of Crime and the Treatment of Offenders,

Recognizing that the growing threat of organized crime, with its highly destabilizing and corrupting influence on fundamental social, economic and political institutions, represents a challenge demanding accrued and more effective international co-operation,

Recalling that the Milan Plan of Action,[1] adopted by the Seventh United Nations Congress on the Prevention of Crime and the Treatment of Offenders, recommended that it was imperative to launch a major effort to control and eventually eradicate the destructive phenomena of illicit drug traffic and abuse and of organized crime,

---

[1]*Seventh United Nations Congress on Crime and the Treatment of Offenders*, Milan, Italy, 26 August-6 September 1985, U.N. Do. A/Conf./121/22/Rev.1, Chap. I, sect. A.

Recalling also that the Seventh Congress, in its resolution 1,[2] recommended that the Committee on Crime Prevention and Control should be requested to develop a comprehensive framework of guidelines and standards that would assist Governments in the development of measures to deal with organized crime at the national, regional and international levels,

Recalling further that the General Assembly, in its resolution 40/32 of 29 November 1985, approved the Milan Plan of Action as a useful and effective means of strengthening international co-operation in the field of crime prevention and criminal justice, and endorsed the other resolutions adopted unanimously by the Seventh Congress,

Noting that the General Assembly, in its resolutions 41/107, 42/59 and 43/99, of 4 December 1986, 30 November 1987 and 8 December 1988, respectively, as well as the Economic and Social Council, in its resolutions 1986/10 and 1987/53 of 21 May 1986 and 28 May 1987, respectively, urged Member States to accord priority, *inter alia*, to the implementation of the recommendations contained in the Milan Plan of Action.

Recalling the provisions set forth in the United Nations Convention against Illicit Traffic in Narcotic Drugs and Psychotropic Substances,[3] in 1988,

Recognizing that illicit trafficking in narcotic drugs and psychotropic substances is a criminal activity and that its suppression requires a high priority and concrete action at the national, regional and international levels by all States, including rapid ratification of, and accession to, the United Nations Convention against Illicit Traffic in Narcotic Drugs and Psychotropic Substances,

Noting also that the Economic and Social Council, in its resolution 1989/70 of 24 May 1989, called upon Governments, international organizations and interested non-governmental organizations to co-operate with the Committee on Crime Prevention and Control in giving special attention to promoting international co-operation in combating organized crime,

Noting further that the General Assembly, in its resolution 44/72 of 8 December 1989, reaffirmed the continued validity of the Milan Plan of Action and requested the Eighth Congress, *inter alia*, to propose viable control measures aimed at eradicating the activities of organized crime,

---

[2]*Id.*, sect. E.

[3]E/CONF.82/15 and Corr. 2.

1. *Adopts* the Guidelines contained in the annex to the present resolution as valuable recommendations for national and international action against organized crime;

2. *Urges* Member States to give favourable consideration to their implementation at both national and international levels, as appropriate;

3. *Invites* Member States, on request, to make available to the Secretary-General the provisions of their legislation relating to money laundering, to tracing, monitoring and forfeiture of the proceeds of crime, the monitoring of large-scale cash transactions and other measures enabling these to be made available to such Member States desiring to enact or further develop legislation in these fields.

* * *

ANNEX

Guidelines for the Prevention and Control of Organized Crime

A. National Measures

Preventive Strategies

1. Raising public awareness and mobilizing public support are important elements of any preventive action. Education and promotional programmes and the process of public exposure have been successful in changing community attitudes and in enlisting public support. Measures of this kind can help to counter public revenue fraud and can be further developed and utilized on a systematic basis by targeting areas of special social and economic harm to the community and by enlisting the co-operation of the mass media in playing a positive role.

2. Research into the structure of organized crime and the evaluation of the effectiveness of existing countermeasures should be encouraged, since it can contribute to the establishment of a more informed basis for prevention programmes. For example, research in relation to corruption, its causes, nature and effect, its links to organized crime and anti-corruption measures is a prerequisite to the development of preventive programmes.

3. Possible devices to prevent or minimize the impact of organized crime should be continuously explored. While the whole question of crime prevention is an underdeveloped area in many countries, specific measures in a number of

spheres have been effective. Detailed programmes that are designed to place obstacles in the way of a potential offender, reduce opportunities for crime and make its commission more conspicuous should be encouraged. Fraud control programmes represent a significant and positive step in this direction. Other measures include risk analysis to assess vulnerability to fraud[] control strategies in relation to such areas as system and procedures, management and the supervision of staff, physical security, information and intelligence, computers, investigative strategies and training programmes. The creation of anti-corruption agencies or similar mechanisms should also be pursued. Crime impact studies and the identification of criminogenic factors of new development programmes would provide opportunities for the adoption of remedial and preventive measures at the planning stage.

4. Improvements in the efficiency of law enforcement and criminal justice are important preventive strategies based on more efficient and fair processes that act as a deterrent to crime and strengthen guarantees of human rights. Planning processes designed to integrate and co-ordinate relevant criminal justice agencies that often operate independently of each other, as stressed in the Guiding Principles for Crime Prevention and Criminal Justice in the Context of Development and a New International Order,[4] will also serve as a deterrent to crime.

5. Better training to upgrade skills and professional qualifications of law enforcement and judicial personnel should be undertaken to improve effectiveness, consistency and fairness in national criminal justice systems. Regional and joint training programmes should be developed in order to exchange information on successful techniques and new technology.

6. The efforts of drug-producing countries aimed at the eradication of the illicit production and processing of drugs should be recognized and supported. In particular, developed countries should grant adequate technical and financial assistance for the implementation of crop substitution programmes. The latter should also increase their efforts to achieve a radical reduction in illicit drugs demand and consumption within their national borders.

Criminal legislation

7. Legislation should be encouraged that defines new offences with respect to money laundering and organized fraud and the offence of opening and operating accounts under a false name. Computer crime is another area that requires consideration. In addition, there is a need for reform in civil, fiscal and

---

[4]*Seventh United Nations Congress...*, Chap. I, sect. B.

regulatory legislation that relates to the control of organized crime. Information on significant innovations that have occurred in recent years should be widely shared through the United Nations, with a view to facilitating the development of a solid basis for the harmonization of criminal law dealing with organized crime.

8. Forfeiture of the proceeds of crime represent one of the most significant recent developments. Measures which states could consider in this context might include the following: provision for the freezing or withholding, and the confiscation or forfeiture, of property used in, or derived from the commission of an offence; and orders for pecuniary penalties representing a court assessment of the monetary value of the benefits derived by the offender from the commission of the offence. Viable remedies that have been developed in several countries on those matters should be brought, in a systematic way, to the attention of other interested countries, with a view to their more widespread utilization. The final disposition of property forfeited by one country, at the request of another, may be made subject to bilateral arrangements.

Criminal investigation

9. Attention should be focused on new methods of criminal investigation and the techniques developed in various countries of "following the money trail." Important in this context are the following: orders requiring financial institutions to provide all the information necessary to follow the money trail, including details of accounts belonging to a particular person, and orders requesting them to report suspect or unusual cash transactions to the appropriate authorities. Banks and other financial institutions should not resort to the principle of secrecy once there exists a judicial order issued by the competent judicial authority.

10. The interception of telecommunications and the use of electronic surveillance are also a relevant and effective procedure, subject to human rights considerations.

11. Schemes for the protection of witnesses against violence and intimidation are becoming increasingly important in the criminal investigation and trail process and in enforcement efforts against organized crime. These procedures include the provision of ways of shielding the identity of witnesses from the accused and his lawyer, protected accommodation and physical protection, relocation and monetary support.

Law Enforcement and Criminal Justice Administration

12. Law enforcement plays a crucial role in programmes against organized crime. It is important to ensure that law enforcement agencies have adequate

powers, subject to proper human rights safeguards. Consideration should be given to the necessity of establishing a specialized interdisciplinary agency to deal specifically with organized crime.

13. Major emphasis should also be placed on the application of technical and organizational measures designed to increase the effectiveness of the investigative and sentencing authorities, including prosecutors and the judiciary. Furthermore, courses on professional ethics should be incorporated into the curricula of law enforcement and judicial training institutions. Some of the instruments developed by the United Nations could be used for this purpose, such as the Basic Principles on the Independence of the Judiciary[5] and the Code of Conduct for Law Enforcement Officials.[6]

B. International co-operation

14. The transnational dimensions of organized crime require the urgent development of new and effective co-operative arrangement on a more comprehensive basis. The exchange of information between relevant agencies of Member States is also an important activity that needs to be strengthened and developed further.

15. Governments should vigorously support all useful initiatives by countries and international institutions to combat illicit drug-trafficking, and should warn others of the imminent danger represented by it. All countries must be involved in combating organized crime on the basis of shared concern. In this respect, consistent and continuous global efforts, combining the exchange of the necessary data and operational resources, should be encouraged and undertaken.

16. Model legislation for the forfeiture of the proceeds of crime should be developed and implemented.

17. Specific strategies and methods should be developed for erecting stronger barriers between legitimate financial markets and the market in illegally acquired capital.

18. Technical co-operation in its various forms, with expanded advisory services, should be strengthened in order to share common experiences and innovations and to assist countries in need. International, regional and subregional conferenc-

---

[5] *Id.*, sect. D.

[6] G.A. Res. 34/169, annex.

es bringing together members of the law enforcement, prosecution and judicial authorities should be encouraged.

19. Modern technological advances should be used in the area of passport and travel controls, and efforts should be encouraged to monitor and identify cars, boats and aircraft used in transnational theft or transfer, or for illicit trans-shipments.

20. Data bases containing law enforcement, financial and offender's records should be established or expanded with due regard for the protection of privacy.

21. Mutual assistance, the transfer of criminal proceedings and the enforcement of criminal judgments, including confiscation and forfeiture of illegal assets, as well as extradition procedures, should receive priority attention.

22. Comparative research and data collection related to the issue of transnational organized crime, its causes, its links to domestic instability and other forms of criminality, as well as its prevention and control, should be supported.

23. The United Nations regional and interregional institutes for crime prevention and control and the intergovernmental and non-governmental organizations concerned should give increased attention to the issue of organized crime.

24. The United Nations Development Programme and other funding agencies of the United Nations system, as well as Member States, should be urged to strengthen their support for national, regional and international programmes addressed to the prevention and control of organized crime.

2. Terrorist Criminal Activities

The Eighth United Nations Congress on the Prevention of Crime and the Treatment of Offenders,

Aware of the grave menace that national and international terrorist criminal activities pose to social and political stability and to the lives of countless human beings,

Concerned by the rapid internationalization of these criminal operations,

Convinced that the trends towards the internationalization of terrorist activities makes imperative an appropriate internationally coordinated response of global dimensions,

Recalling that in the Milan Plan of Action[7] the Seventh United Nations Congress on the Prevention of Crime and the Treatment of Offenders affirmed that priority must be given to combating terrorism in all its forms, including, when appropriate, coordinated and concerted action by the international community.

Recalling also that the Seventh Congress, in its resolution 23,[8] requested that the Committee on Crime Prevention and Control should consider the development of recommendations for international action to strengthen law enforcement measures, including extradition procedures and other arrangement for legal assistance and co-operation, with respect to offences of a terrorist nature,

Noting that the General Assembly, in its resolution 40/32 of 29 November 1985, approved the Milan Plan of Action as a useful and effective means of strengthening international co-operation in the field of crime prevention and criminal justice, and endorsed the other resolution adopted unanimously by the Seventh Congress,

Noting further that the General Assembly, in its resolution 41/107, 42/59 and 43/99 of 4 December 1986, 30 November 1987 and 8 December 1988, respectively, as well as the Economic and Social Council, in its resolutions 1986/10 and 1987/53 of 21 May 1986 and 28 May 1987, respectively, urged Member States to accord priority, *inter alia*, to the implementation of the recommendations contained in the Milan Plan of Action,

Aware that the General Assembly, in its resolution 44/72 of 8 December 1989, reaffirmed the continued validity of the Milan Plan of Action and requested the Eighth United Nations Congress on the Prevention of Crime and the Treatment of Offenders, *inter alia*, to propose viable control measures for combating terrorist criminal activities,

Recalling the concern about, and condemnation of, terrorism expressed by the General Assembly in its resolutions 3034 (XXVII), 31/102, 32/147, 34/145, 36/109, 38/130, 40/61, 42/59 and 44/29 of 18 September 1972, 15 December 1983, 9 December 1985, 30 November 1987 and 4 December 1989, respectively,

Recalling also General Assembly resolution 42/159 of 7 December 1987, in which the Assembly, *inter alia,* recognized that the effectiveness of the struggle against terrorism could be enhanced by the establishment of a generally agreed definition of international terrorism,

---

[7]*Seventh United Nations Congress...*, Chap. I, sect. A.

[8]*Id.*, sect. E.

1. *Agrees* that the text of the following annex represents valuable guidance for appropriate, coordinated and concerted action against international terrorism at both the national and international level;

2. *Urges* Member States to given favourable consideration to following this guidance at both the national and the international level.

* * *

ANNEX

Measures against international terrorism[8]

A. Definition

1. Since the first study[9] of international terrorism was conducted by the United Nations in 1972, the international community has been unable to arrive at a universally agreed meaning of what is included in the term "international terrorism." Nor has it reached sufficient general agreement on the measures needed to prevent and control the harmful manifestations of acts of terrorist violence.

2. Without prejudice to the discussion of the subject in the General Assembly of the United Nations and until such time as a universally acceptable definition of international terrorism is agreed, it would be useful to work with a view to identifying behaviour that the international community regards as unacceptable and that requires the application of effective preventive and repressive measures that are consistent with the recognized principles of international law.

3. Furthermore, the international community should understand better the underlying causes that bring about such conduct in order to develop measures for its prevention and control.

---

[9]Measures to prevent international terrorism which endangers or takes innocent human lives or jeopardizes fundamental freedoms, and study of the underlying causes of those forms of terrorism and acts of violence which lie in misery, frustration, grievance and despair and which cause some people to sacrifice human lives, including their own, in an attempt to effect radical changes: Study prepared by the Secretariat in accordance with the decision taken by the Sixth Committee at its 1314th meeting, on 27 September 1972 (A/C.6/418).

B. Identification of the problems

4. Existing international norms may not in certain areas be sufficient to control all forms and manifestations of terrorist violence. Among the issues of concern are: State policies and practises that may be considered by other States as constituting a violation of international treaty obligations; the absence of specific norms on State responsibility regarding the failure to carry out existing international obligations; the abuse of the privilege of diplomatic immunity and the diplomatic pouch; the absence of norms concerning the responsibility of States for acts not prohibited by international law; the absence of international regulation and control of the traffic and trade in arms; the inadequacy of international mechanisms for the peaceful resolution of conflicts and for the enforcement of internationally protected human rights; the lack of universal acceptance of the principles of *aut dedere aut judicare*; and the shortcomings of international co-operation in the effective and uniform prevention and control of all forms and manifestations of terrorist violence.

C. International co-operation for the effective and uniform prevention of terrorism

5. Effective measures for international co-operation in the prevention of terrorist violence should be developed at the international, regional and bilateral levels. These include: co-operation between law enforcement agencies, prosecution authorities and the judiciary; increasing integration and co-operation within the various agencies responsible for law enforcement and criminal justice, with due regard to fundamental human rights; inclusion of modalities of inter-State co-operation in penal matters at all levels of enforcement and criminal justice increasing education and training of law enforcement personnel with regard to crime prevention and modalities of international co-operation in penal matters, including the development of specialized courses on international criminal law and comparative penal law and procedures, as a part of legal education as well as professional and judicial training; and the development of both general educational and public awareness programmes through the mass media in order to enlighten the public on the dangers of terrorist violence.

D. Jurisdiction

6. Greater uniformity in the laws and practises of States concerning criminal jurisdiction should be encouraged, while over-extension of national jurisdiction should be avoided in order to prevent unnecessary legal conflicts between States.

7. Jurisdictional priorities should be established giving territoriality the first priority.

E. Extradition

8. States should endeavor to develop and implement effectively international extradition treaties, be they part of multilateral conventions, regional conventions or bilateral agreements.

9. The political offence exception should not be a bar to extradition for crimes of terrorist violence under existing international convention, except in cases when the requested State undertakes to submit the case to its competent authorities for the purpose of prosecution or transfers the proceedings to another State to conduct the prosecution.

10. States are encouraged to rely on existing extradition provisions in multilateral treaties whenever there is an absence of bilateral treaties.

11. Member States are encouraged to extend their bilateral extradition relationships using as a basis for negotiations the Model Treaty on Extradition elaborated by the United Nations and adopted by the Eighth Congress on the Prevention of Crime and the Treatment of Offenders. In addition, Member States could also consider elaborating multilateral conventions on extradition to remove gaps and loopholes in existing treaties and current extradition procedures.

12. Voluntary return subject to appropriate judicial guarantees, should be encouraged.

F. Mutual assistance and co-operation

13. The prevention and control of terrorist violence depends on effective mutual co-operation and assistance between States in securing evidence with respect to the prosecution or extradition of the offenders.

14. States are encouraged to lend each other the widest possible mutual assistance and co-operation in penal matters, subject to respect for internationally recognized human rights, and to rely on the provision of multilateral treaties and specific regional and bilateral agreements. To achieve this end, the model treaty on mutual assistance in criminal matters constitutes a basis for strengthened international co-operation.

G. Non-applicability of defence

15. Defence based on obedience to superior orders, or acts of State, or immunities granted for the commission of the crime should not apply with respect to persons who have violated international conventions prohibiting acts of terrorist violence.

H. Conduct of States

16. Resort to practises of terrorist violence supported, carried out or acquiesced in by States should be more effectively curbed by the international community, and the United Nations should develop mechanisms for the control of such conduct, particularly through the strengthening of United Nations machinery for the preservation of peace and security and the protection of human rights.

17. Measures by the international community to curb terrorism that is supported, carried out or acquiesced in by States should be encouraged.

I. Targets of high vulnerability

18. A study concerning the feasibility of the development of an international convention that would enhance the protection of targets that are particularly vulnerable, the destruction of which would cause great harm to populations or cause severe damage to society, such as hydroelectricity or nuclear facilities, should be undertaken.

19. The United Nations should assist any country that suffers from terrorism or from the presence of terrorist organizations on its territory to put an end to that phenomenon.

J. Control of weapons, ammunition and explosives

20. States should develop appropriate national legislation for the effective control of weapons, ammunition and explosives and other dangerous materials that find their way into the hands of persons who could use them for the purposes of terrorism.

21. International regulations on the transfer, import, export and storage of such objects should be developed so that customs and border controls can be harmonized to prevent their transnational movement, except for established lawful purposes.

K. Protection of the judiciary and of criminal justice personnel

22. States should adopt measures and policies aimed at the effective protection of the judiciary and of criminal justice personnel, including jurors and lawyers involved in trials of terrorism cases, and should also co-operate between themselves in the implementation of such measures.

L. Protection of victims

23. States should establish appropriate mechanisms for the protection, and introduce relevant legislation as well as allocate sufficient resources for the assistance and relief, of victims of terrorism, in accordance with the Declaration of Basic Principles of Justice for Victims of Crime and Abuse of Power.[10]

24. International exchange of experiences concerning the subject referred to in the previous paragraph should be encouraged.

M. Protection of witnesses

25. States should adopt measures and policies aimed at the effective protection of witnesses of terrorist acts.

26. States with experiences in the field of witness protection programmes should consider lending assistance to other States contemplating similar programmes.

N. Treatment of offenders

27. States should endeavour to diminish existing disparities of sentencing in the field of terrorist offences.

28. Persons charged with, or convicted of, terrorist offences, must be treated without discrimination and in accordance with internationally recognized human rights standards and norms, such as enunciated in the Universal Declaration of Human Rights,[11] the International Covenant on Civil and Political Rights,[12] the Slavery Convention,[13] the Supplementary Convention on the Abolition of Slavery, the Slave Trade, and Institutions and Practises Similar to Slavery, the Abolition of Forced Labour Convention,[14] the Convention against Torture and

---

[10] *Seventh United Nations Congress...*, Chap. I, sect. C.

[11] G.A. Res. 217 A (III).

[12] G.A. Res. 2200 A (XXI), annex.

[13] G.A. Res. 794 (VIII).

[14] *See Human Rights: A Compilation of International Instruments* (United Nations publication, Sales No. E.88.XIV.1), sect. F.

Other Cruel, Inhuman or Degrading Treatment or Punishment[15] and the Standard Minimum Rules for the Treatment of Prisoners.[16]

O. Role of the mass media

29. States should consider the development of guidelines for the mass media or encourage the establishment of voluntary guidelines to control the following: sensationalizing and justifying terrorist violence; disseminating strategic information on potential targets; and disseminating tactical information while terrorist acts are taking place, thereby possibly endangering the lives of innocent civilians and law enforcement personnel or impeding effective law enforcement measures to prevent or control such acts and to apprehend the offenders. These guidelines are in no way intended to restrict the internationally recognized basic human right of freedom of speech and information or to encourage interference in the domestic affairs of other States.

P. Codification of international criminal law and creation of an international criminal court

30. The work of the International Law Commission on codification of aspects of international criminal law should be encouraged. The Committee on Crime Prevention and Control should have an opportunity to present its views.

31. The International Law Commission should be encouraged to continue to explore the possibility of establishing an international criminal court or some other international mechanism to have jurisdiction over persons who have committed offences (including offences connected with terrorism or with illicit trafficking in narcotic drugs or psychotropic substances), in accordance with G.A. Res. 44/39 of 4 December 1989. Similarly, and in the light of the report that the International Law Commission will submit on this particular subject to the General Assembly at its forty-fifth session, the possibility might be considered of establishing an international criminal court or appropriate mechanism with each and all of the procedural and substantive arrangements that might guarantee both its effective operation and absolute respect for the sovereignty and the territorial and political integrity of States and the self-determination of peoples. States could also explore the possibility of establishing separate international criminal courts of regional or sub-regional jurisdiction in which grave international crimes, and particularly terrorism, could be brought to trial and the incorporation of such courts within the United Nations system.

---

[15]G.A. Res. 39/46, annex.

[16]*Human Rights: A Compilation* ..., sect. G.

Q. Enhancing the effectiveness of international cooperation

32. The United Nations, in co-operation with specialized agencies such as the International Civil Aviation Organization, the International Maritime Organization, and the International Atomic Energy Agency, should prepare periodic reports on compliance with existing international conventions, including detailed reporting on incidents and cases (arrest, prosecution, adjudication and sentencing), to be made available for international circulation.

33. States that are signatories to international conventions prohibiting terrorist violence are urged to ratify those conventions at the earliest opportunity and to take effective measures to enforce their provisions.

34. States that are not signatories to international conventions prohibiting terrorist violence are urged to accede to such conventions at the earliest opportunity and to take effective measures to enforce their provisions.

35. States are urged to sign and ratify the Convention for the Suppression of Unlawful Acts against the Safety of Maritime Navigation and the Protocol for the Suppression of Unlawful Acts against the Safety of Fixed Platforms Located on the Continental Shelf, adopted by the conference of the International Maritime Organization, held at Rome in 1988, and the Protocol for the Suppression of Unlawful Acts of Violence at Airports Serving International Civil Aviation, adopted by the International Conference on Air Law, which was convened by the International Civil Aviation Organization at Montreal, from 9 to 24 February 1988.

36. The United Nations should consider developing ways and means of encouraging prevention policies, strategies and action by States to ensure the effective implementation of international conventions, including enhanced co-operation at the law enforcement, prosecution and judicial levels.

37. The central role of the United Nations, and in particular of the Crime Prevention and Criminal Justice Branch, Centre for Social Development and Humanitarian Affairs of the United Nations Office at Vienna, as well as the relevant specialized agencies, should be strengthened in order to fulfil the above-mentioned objectives and other purposes of the Organization, including the preservation of peace, the strengthening of world order and the fight against crime under the rule of law.

* * *

3. Model Treaty on Extradition

ANNEX

Model Treaty on Extradition

Article 1

Obligation to extradite

Each Party agrees to extradite to the other, upon request and subject to the provisions of the present Treaty, any person who is wanted in the requesting State for prosecution for an extraditable offence or for the imposition or enforcement of a sentence in respect of such an offence.[17]

Article 2

Extraditable offences

1. For the purposes of the present Treaty, extraditable offences are offences that are punishable under the laws of both Parties by imprisonment or other deprivation of liberty for a maximum period of at least [one/two] year(s), or by a more severe penalty. Where the request for extradition relates to a person who is wanted for the enforcement of a sentence of imprisonment or other deprivation of liberty imposed for such an offence, extradition shall be granted only if a period of at least [four/six] months of such sentence remains to be served.

2. In determining whether an offence is an offence punishable under the laws of both Parties, it shall not matter whether:

   a. The laws of the Parties place the acts or omissions constituting the main offence within the same category of offence or denominate the offence by the same terminology;

   b. Under the laws of the Parties the constituent elements of the offence differ, it being understood that the totality of the acts or omissions as presented by the requesting State shall be taken into account.

---

[17]Reference to the imposition of a sentence may not be necessary for all countries.

3. Where extradition of a person is sought or an offence against a law relating to taxation, customs duties, exchange, control or other revenue matters, extradition may not be refused on the ground that the law of the requested State does not impose the same kind of tax or duty or does not contain a tax, customs duty or exchange regulation of the same kind as the law of the requesting State.[18]

4. If the request for extradition includes several separate offences each of which is punishable under the laws of both Parties, but some of which do not fulfil the other conditions set out in paragraph 1 of the present article, the requested Party may grant extradition for the latter offences provided that the person is to be extradited for at least one extraditable offence.

Article 3

Mandatory grounds for refusal

Extradition shall not be granted in any of the following circumstances:

a. If the offence for which extradition is requested is regarded by the requested State as an offence of a political nature;[19]

b. If the requested State has substantial grounds for believing that the request for extradition has been made for the purpose of prosecuting or punishing a person on account of that person's race, religion, nationality, ethnic origin, political opinions, sex or status, or that that person's position may be prejudiced for any of those reasons;

c. If the offence for which extradition is requested is an offence under military law, which is not also an offence under ordinary criminal law;

d. If there has been a final judgement rendered against the person in the requested State in respect of the offence for which the person's extradition is requested;

---

[18]Some countries may wish to omit this paragraph or provide an optional ground for refusal under article 4.

[19]Some countries may wish to add the following text: "Reference to an offence of a political nature shall not include any offence in respect of which the Parties have assumed an obligation, pursuant to any multilateral convention, to take prosecutorial action where they do not extradite, or any other offence that the Parties have agreed is not an offence of a political character for the purposes of extradition."

e. If the person whose extradition is requested has, under the law of either Party, become immune from prosecution or punishment for any reason, including lapse of time or amnesty;[20]

f. If the person whose extradition is requested has been or would be subjected in the requesting State to torture or cruel, inhuman or degrading treatment or punishment or if that person has not received or would not receive the minimum guarantees in criminal proceedings, as contained in the International Covenant on Civil and Political Rights, article 14;[21]

g. If the judgement of the requesting State has been rendered *in absentia,* the convicted person has not had sufficient notice of the trial or the opportunity to arrange for his or her defence and he has not had or will not have the opportunity to have the case retried in his or her presence.[22]

Article 4

Optional grounds for refusal

Extradition may be refused in any of the following circumstances:

a. If the person whose extradition is requested is a national of the requested State. Where extradition is refused on this ground, the requested State shall, if the other State so requests, submit the case to its competent authorities with a view to taking appropriate action against the person in respect of the offence for which extradition had been requested;

b. If the competent authorities of the requested State have decided either not to institute or to terminate proceedings against the person for the offence in respect of which extradition is requested;

---

[20]Some countries may wish to make this an optional ground for refusal under article 4.

[21]*See* G.A. Res. 2200 A (XXI), annex.

[22]Some countries may wish to add to article 3 the following ground for refusal: "If there is insufficient proof, according to the evidentiary standards of the requested State, that the person whose extradition is requested is a party to the offence". (See also footnote 47.)

c. If a prosecution in respect of the offence for which extradition is requested is pending in the requested State against the person whose extradition is requested;

d. If the offence for which extradition is requested carries the death penalty under the law of the requesting State, unless that State gives such assurance as the requested State considers sufficient that the death penalty will not be imposed or, if imposed, will not be carried out;[23]

e. If the offence for which extradition is requested has been committed outside the territory of either Party and the law of the requested State does not provide for jurisdiction over such an offence committed outside its territory in comparable circumstances;

f. If the offence for which extradition is requested is regarded under the law of the requested State as having been committed in whole or in part within that State.[24] Where extradition is refused on this ground, the requested State shall, if the other State so requests, submit the case to its competent authorities with a view to taking appropriate action against the person for the offence for which extradition had been requested;

g. If the person whose extradition is requested has been sentenced or would be liable to be tried or sentenced in the requesting State by an extraordinary or *ad hoc* court or tribunal;

h. If the requested State, while also taking into account the nature of the offence and the interests of the requesting State, considers that, in the circumstances of the case, the extradition of that person would be incompatible with humanitarian considerations in view of age, health or other personal circumstances of that person.

Article 5

Channels of communication and required documents

1. A request for extradition shall be made in writing. The request, supporting documents and subsequent communications shall be transmitted

---

[23]Some countries may wish to apply the same restriction to the imposition of a life, or indeterminate, sentence.

[24]Some countries may wish to make specific reference to a vessel under its flag or an aircraft registered under its laws at the time of the commission of the offence.

through the diplomatic channel, directly between the ministries of justice or any other authorities designated by the Parties.

2. A request for extradition shall be accompanied by the following:

a. In all cases,

(i) As accurate a description as possible of the person sought, together with any other information that may help to establish that person's identity, nationality and location;

(ii) The text of the relevant provision of the law creating the offence or, where necessary, a statement of the law relevant to the offence and a statement of the penalty that can be imposed for the offence;

b. If the person is accused of an offence, by a warrant issued by a court or other competent judicial authority for the arrest of the person or a certified copy of that warrant, a statement of the offence for which extradition is requested and a description of the acts or omissions constituting the alleged offence, including an indication of the time and place of its commission;[25]

c. If the person has been convicted of an offence, by a statement of the offence for which extradition is requested and a description of the acts or omissions constituting the offence and by the original or certified copy of the judgement or any other document setting out the conviction and the sentence imposed, the fact that the sentence is enforceable, and the extent to which the sentence remains to be served;

d. If the person has been convicted of an offence in his or her absence, in addition to the documents set out in paragraph 2 (c) of the present article, by a statement as to the legal means

---

[25]Countries that require a judicial assessment of the sufficiency of evidence may wish to add the following clause: "and sufficient proof in a form acceptable under the law of the requested State, establishing, according to the evidentiary standards of that State, that the person is a party to the offence". (*See also* Sect. F., doc. 1, footnote 28.)

available to the person to prepare his or her defence or to have the case retried in his or her presence;

e. If the person has been convicted of an offence but no sentence has been imposed, by a statement of the offence for which extradition is requested and a description of the acts or omissions constituting the offence and by a document setting out the conviction and a statement affirming that there is an intention to impose a sentence.

3. The documents submitted in support of a request for extradition shall be accompanied by a translation into the language of the requested State or in another language acceptable to that State.

Article 6

Simplified extradition procedure

The requested State, if not precluded by its law, may grant extradition after receipt of a request for provisional arrest, provided that the person sought explicitly consents before a competent authority.

Article 7

Certification and authentication

Except as provided by the present Treaty, a request for extradition and the documents in support thereof, as well as documents or other material supplied in response to such a request, shall not require certification or authentication.[26]

Article 8

Additional information

If the requested State considers that the information provided in support of a request for extradition is not sufficient, it may request that additional information be furnished within such reasonable time as it specifies.

---

[26]The laws of some countries require authentication before documents transmitted from other countries can be admitted in their courts and, therefore, would require a clause setting out the authentication required.

Article 9

Provisional arrest

1. In case of urgency the requesting State may apply for the provisional arrest of the person sought pending the presentation of the request for extradition. The application shall be transmitted by means of the facilities of the International Criminal Police Organization, by post or telegraph or by any other means affording a record in writing.

2. The application shall contain a description of the person sought, a statement that extradition is to be requested, a statement of the existence of one of the documents mentioned in paragraph 2 of article 5 of the present Treaty, authorizing the apprehension of the person, a statement of the punishment that can be or has been imposed for the offence, including the time left to be served and a concise statement of the facts of the case, and a statement of the location, where known, of the person.

3. The requested State shall decide on the application in accordance with its law and communicate its decision to the requesting State without delay.

4. The person arrested upon such an application shall be set at liberty upon the expiration of [40] days from the date of arrest if a request for extradition, supported by the relevant documents specified in paragraph 2 of article 5 of the present Treaty, has not been received. The present paragraph does not preclude the possibility of conditional release of the person prior to the expiration of the [40] days.

5. The release of the person pursuant to paragraph 4 of the present article shall not prevent rearrest and institution of proceedings with a view to extraditing the person sought if the request and supporting documents are subsequently received.

Article 10

Decision on the request

1. The requested State shall deal with the request for extradition pursuant to procedures provided by its own law, and shall promptly communicate its decision to the requesting State.

2. Reasons shall be given for any complete or partial refusal of the request.

Article 11

Surrender of the person

1. Upon being informed that extradition has been granted, the Parties shall, without undue delay, arrange for the surrender of the person sought and the requested State shall inform the requesting State of the length of time for which the person sought was detained with a view to surrender.

2. The person shall be removed from the territory of the requested State within such reasonable period as the requested State specifies and, if the person is not removed within that period, the requested State may release the person and may refuse to extradite that person for the same offence.

3. If circumstances beyond its control prevent a Party from surrendering or removing the person to be extradited, it shall notify the other Party. The two Parties shall mutually decide upon a new date of surrender, and the provisions of paragraph 2 of the present article shall apply.

Article 12

Postponed or conditional surrender

1. The requested State may, after making its decision on the request for extradition postpone the surrender of a person sought, in order to proceed against that person, or, if that person has already been convicted, in order to enforce a sentence imposed for an offence other than that for which extradition is sought. In such a case the requested State shall advise the requesting State accordingly.

2. The requested State may, instead of postponing surrender, temporarily surrender the person sought to the requesting State in accordance with conditions to be determined between the Parties.

Article 13

Surrender of property

1. To the extent permitted under the law of the requested State and subject to the rights of third parties, which shall be duly respected, all property found in the requested State that has been acquired as a result of the offence or that may be required as evidence shall, if the requesting State so requests, be surrendered if extradition is granted.

2. The said property may, if the requesting State so requests, be surrendered to the requesting State even if the extradition agreed to cannot be carried out.

3. When the said property is liable to seizure or confiscation in the requested State, it may retain it or temporarily hand it over.

4. Where the law of the requested State or the protection of the rights of third parties so require, any property so surrendered shall be returned to the requested State free of charge after the completion of the proceedings, if that State so requests.

Article 14

Rule of specialty

1. A person extradited under the present Treaty shall not be proceeded against, sentenced, detained, re-extradited to a third State, or subjected to any other restriction of personal liberty in the territory of the requesting State for any offence committed before surrender other than:

a. An offence for which extradition was granted;

b. Any other offence in respect of which the requested State consents.[27] Consent shall be given if the offence for which it is requested is itself subject to extradition in accordance with the present Treaty.[28]

2. A request for the consent of the requested State under the present article shall be accompanied by the documents mentioned in paragraph 2 of article 5 of the present Treaty and a legal record of any statement made by the extradited person with respect to the offence.

3. Paragraph 1 of the present article shall not apply if the person has had an opportunity to leave the requesting State and has not done so within [30/45] days of final discharge in respect of the offence for which that person was

[27]Some countries may wish to add, as a third case, explicit consent of the person.

[28]Some countries may not wish to assume that obligation and may wish to include other grounds in determining whether or not to grant consent.

extradited or if the person has voluntarily returned to the territory of the requesting State after leaving it.

Article 15

Transit

1. Where a person is to be extradited to a Party from a third State through the territory of the other Party, the Party to which the person is to be extradited shall request the other Party to permit the transit of that person through its territory. This does not apply where air transport is used and no landing in the territory of the other Party is scheduled.

2. Upon receipt of such a request, which shall contain relevant information, the requested State shall deal with this request pursuant to procedures provided by its own law. The requested State shall grant the request expeditiously unless its essential interests would be prejudiced thereby.[29]

3. The State of transit shall ensure that legal provisions exist that would enable detaining the person in custody during transit.

4. In the event of an unscheduled landing, the Party to be requested to permit transit may, at the request of the escorting officer, hold the person in custody for [48] hours, pending receipt of the transit request to be made in accordance with paragraph 1 of the present article.

Article 16

Concurrent requests

If a Party receives requests for extradition for the same person from both the other Party and a third State it shall, at its discretion, determine to which of those States the person is to be extradited.

---

[29]Some countries may wish to agree on other grounds for refusal, which may also warrant refusal for extradition, such as those related to the nature of the offence (e.g. political, fiscal, military) or to the status of the person (e.g. their own nationals).

Article 17

Costs

1. The requested State shall meet the cost of any proceedings in its jurisdiction arising out of a request for extradition.

2. The requested State shall also bear the costs incurred in its territory in connection with the seizure and handing over of property, or the arrest and detention of the person whose extradition is sought.[30]

3. The requesting State shall bear the costs incurred in conveying the person from the territory of the requested State, including transit costs.

Article 18

Final provisions

1. The present Treaty is subject to [ratification, acceptance or approval]. The instruments of [ratification, acceptance or approval] shall be exchanged as soon as possible.

2. The present Treaty shall enter into force on the thirtieth day after the day on which the instruments of [ratification, acceptance or approval] are exchanged.

3. The present Treaty shall apply to requests made after its entry into force, even if the relevant acts or omissions occurred prior to that date.

4. Either Contracting Party may denounce the present Treaty by giving notice in writing to the other Party. Such denunciation shall take effect six months following the date on which such notice is received by the other Party.

* * *

---

[30]Some countries may wish to consider reimbursement of costs incurred as a result of withdrawal of a request for extradition or provisional arrest.

4. Model Treaty on Mutual Assistance in Criminal Matters

ANNEX

Article 1

Scope of application[31]

1. The Parties shall, in accordance with the present Treaty, afford to each other the widest possible measure of mutual assistance in investigations or court proceedings in respect of offences the punishment of which at the time of the request for assistance, falls within the jurisdiction of the judicial authorities of the requesting State.

2. Mutual assistance to be afforded in accordance with the present Treaty may include:

a. Taking evidence or statements from persons;

b. Assisting in the availability of detained persons or others to give evidence or assist in investigations;

c. Effecting service of judicial documents;

d. Executing searches and seizures;

e. Examining objects and sites;

f. Providing information and evidentiary items;

g. Providing originals or certified copies of relevant documents and records, including bank, financial, corporate or business records.

3. The present Treaty does not apply to:

---

[31]Additions to the scope of assistance to be provided, such as provisions covering information on sentences passed on nationals of the Parties, can be considered bilaterally. Obviously, such assistance must be compatible with the law of the requested State.

a. The arrest or detention of any person with a view to the extradition of that person;

b. The enforcement in the requested State of criminal judgements imposed in the requesting State except to the extent permitted by the law of the requested State and the Optional Protocol to the present Treaty;

c. The transfer of persons in custody to serve sentences;

d. The transfer of proceedings in criminal matters.

Article 2[32]

Other arrangements

Unless the Parties decide otherwise, the present Treaty shall not affect obligations subsisting between them whether pursuant to other treaties or arrangements or otherwise.

Article 3

Designation of competent authorities

Each Party shall designate and indicate to the other Party an authority or authorities by or through which requests for the purpose of the present Treaty should be made or received.

Article 4[33]

Refusal of assistance

1. Assistance may be refused if:[34]

---

[32]Article 2 recognizes the continuing role of informal assistance between law enforcement agencies and associated agencies in different countries.

[33]Article 4 provides an illustrative list of the grounds for refusal.

[34]Some countries may wish to delete or modify some of the provisions or include other grounds for refusal, such as those related to the nature of the offence (e.g. fiscal), the nature of the applicable penalty (e.g. capital punishment), requirements of shared

a. The requested State is of the opinion that the request, if granted, would prejudice its sovereignty, security, public order *(ordre public)* or other essential public interests;

b. The offence is regarded by the requested State as being of a political nature;

c. There are substantial grounds for believing that the request for assistance has been made for the purpose of prosecuting a person on account of that person's race, sex, religion, nationality, ethnic origin or political opinions or in that that person's position may be prejudiced for any of those reasons;

d. The request relates to an offence that is subject to investigation or prosecution in the requested State or the prosecution of which in the requesting State would be incompatible with the requested State's law on double jeopardy *(ne bis in idem);*

e. The assistance requested requires the requested State to carry out compulsory measures that would be inconsistent with its law and practise had the offence been the subject of investigation or prosecution under its own jurisdiction;

f. The act is an offence under military law, which is not also an offence under ordinary criminal law.

2. Assistance shall not be refused solely on the ground of secrecy of banks and similar financial institutions.

3. The requested State may postpone the execution of the request if its immediate execution would interfere with an ongoing investigation or prosecution in the requested State.

4. Before refusing a request or postponing its execution, the requested State shall consider whether assistance may be granted subject to certain

---

concepts (e.g. double jurisdiction, no lapse of time) or specific kinds of assistance (e.g. interception of telecommunications, performing deoxyribonucleic-acid (DNA) tests). In particular, some countries may law wish to include as grounds for refusal the fact that the act on which the request is based would not be an offence if committed in the territory of the requested State (dual criminality).

conditions. If the requesting State accepts assistance subject to these conditions, it shall comply with them.

5. Reasons shall be given for any refusal or postponement of mutual assistance.

Article 5

Contents of requests

1. Requests for assistance shall include:[35]

a. The name of the requesting office and the competent authority conducting the investigation or court proceedings to which the request relates;

b. The purpose of the request and a brief description of the assistance sought;

c. A description of the facts alleged to constitute the offence and a statement or text of the relevant laws, except in cases of a request for service of documents;

d. The name and address of the person to be served, where necessary;

e. The reasons for and details of any particular procedure or requirement that the requesting State wishes to be followed, including a statement as to whether sworn or affirmed evidence or statements are required;

f. Specification of any time-limit within which compliance with the request is desired;

g. Such other information as is necessary for the proper execution of the request.

2. Requests supporting documents and other communications made pursuant to the present Treaty shall be accompanied by a translation into the language of the requested State or another language acceptable to that State.

---

[35]This list can be reduced or expanded in bilateral negotiations.

3. If the requested State considers that the information contained in the request is not sufficient to enable the request to be dealt with, it may request additional information.

Article 6

Execution of requests[36]

Subject to article 19 of the present Treaty, requests for assistance shall be carried out promptly, in the manner provided for by the law and practise of the requested State. To the extent consistent with its law and practise, the requested State shall carry out the request in the manner specified by the requesting State.

Article 7

Return of material to the requested State

Any property, as well as original records or documents, handed over to the requesting State under the present Treaty shall be returned to the requested State as soon as possible unless the latter waives its right of return thereof.

Article 8[37]

Limitation on use

The requesting State shall not, without the consent of the requested State, use or transfer information or evidence provided by the requested State for investigations or proceedings other than those stated in the request. However, in cases where the charge is altered, the material provided may be used in so far as the offence, as charged, is an offence in respect of which mutual assistance could be provided under the present Treaty.

---

[36]More detailed provisions may be included concerning the provision of information on the time and place of execution of the request and requiring the requested State to inform promptly the requesting State in cases where significant delay is likely to occur or where a decision is made not to comply with the request and the reasons for refusal.

[37]Some countries may wish to omit article 8 or modify it, e.g. restrict it to fiscal offences.

Article 9

Protection of confidentiality[38]

Upon request:

a. The requested State shall use its best endeavours to keep confidential the request for assistance, its contents and its supporting documents as well as the fact of granting of such assistance. If the request cannot be executed without breaching confidentiality, the requested State shall so inform the requesting State, which shall then determine whether the request should nevertheless be executed;

b. The requesting State shall keep confidential evidence and information provided by the requested State, except to the extent that the evidence and information is needed for the investigation and proceedings described in the request.

Article 10

Service of documents[39]

1. The requested State shall effect service of documents that are transmitted to it for this purpose by the requesting State.

2. A request to effect service of summonses shall be made to a requested State not less than [...][40] days before the date on which the appearance of a

---

[38]Provisions relating to confidentiality will be important for many countries but may present problems to others. The nature of the provisions in individual treaties can be determined in bilateral negotiations.

[39]More detailed provisions relating to the service of documents, such as writs and judicial verdicts, can be determined bilaterally. Provisions may be desired for the service of documents by mail or other manner and for the forwarding of proof of service of the documents. For example, proof of service could be given by means of a receipt dated and signed by the person served or by means of a declaration made by the requested State that service has been effected, with an indication of the form and date of such service. One or another of these documents could be sent promptly to the requesting State. The requested State could, if the requesting State so requests, state whether service has been effected in accordance with the law of the requested State. If service could not be effected, the reasons could be communicated promptly by the requested State to the requesting State.

[40]Depending on travel distance and related arrangements.

person is required. In urgent cases, the requested State may waive the time requirement.

Article 11[41]

Obtaining of evidence

1. The requested State shall, in conformity with its law and upon request, take the sworn or affirmed testimony, or otherwise obtain statements of persons or require them to produce items of evidence for transmission to the requesting State.

2. Upon the request of the requesting State, the parties to the relevant proceedings in the requesting State, their legal representatives and representatives of the requesting State may, subject to the laws and procedures of the requested State, be present at the proceedings.

Article 12

Right or obligation to decline to give evidence

1. A person who is required to give evidence in the requested or requesting State may decline to give evidence where either:

   a. The law of the requested State permits or requires that person to decline to give evidence in similar circumstances in proceedings originating in the requested State; or

   b. The law of the requesting State permits or requires that person to decline to give evidence in similar circumstances in proceedings originating in the requesting State.

2. If a person claims that there is a right or obligation to decline to give evidence under the law of the other State, the State where that person is present shall, with respect thereto, rely on a certificate of the competent authority of the other State as evidence of the existence or non-existence of that right or obligation.

---

[41]Article 11 is concerned with the obtaining of evidence in judicial proceedings, the taking of a person's statement by a less formal process and the production of items of evidence.

Article 13

Availability of persons in custody to give evidence or to assist in investigations[42]

1. Upon the request of the requesting State, and if the requested State agrees and its law so permits, a person in custody in the latter State may, subject to his or her consent, be temporarily transferred to the requesting State to give evidence or to assist in the investigations.

2. While the person transferred is required to be held in custody under the law of the requested State, the requesting State shall hold that person in custody and shall return that person in custody to the requested State at the conclusion of the matter in relation to which transfer was sought or at such earlier time as the person's presence is no longer required.

3. Where the requested State advises the requesting State that the transferred person is no longer required to be held in custody, that person shall be set at liberty and be treated as a person referred to in article 14 of the present Treaty.

Article 14

Availability of other persons to give evidence or assist in investigations[43]

1. The requesting State may request the assistance of the requested State in inviting a person:

   a. To appear in proceedings in relation to a criminal matter in the requesting State unless that person is the person charged; or

---

[42]In bilateral negotiations, provisions may also be introduced to deal with such matters as the modalities and time of restitution of evidence and the setting of a time-limit for the presence of the person in custody in the requesting State.

[43]Provisions relating to the payment of the expenses of the person providing assistance are contained in paragraph 3 of article 14. Additional details, such as provision for the payment of costs in advance, can be the subject of bilateral negotiations.

b. To assist in the investigations in relation to a criminal matter in the requesting State.

2. The requested State shall invite the person to appear as a witness or expert in proceedings or to assist in the investigations. Where appropriate, the requested State shall satisfy itself that satisfactory arrangements have been made for the person's safety.

3. The request or the summons shall indicate the approximate allowances and the travel and subsistence expenses payable by the requesting State.

4. Upon request, the requested State may grant the person an advance, which shall be refunded by the requesting State.

Article 15[44]

Safe conduct

1. Subject to paragraph 2 of the present article, where a person is in the requesting State pursuant to a request made under article 13 or 14 of the present Treaty:

a. That person shall not be detained, prosecuted, punished or subjected to any other restrictions of personal liberty in the requesting State in respect of any acts or omissions or convictions that preceded the person's departure from the requested State;

b. That person shall not, without that person's consent, be required to give evidence in any proceeding or to assist in any investigation other than the proceeding or investigation to which the request relates.

2. Paragraph 1 of the present article shall cease to apply if that person, being free to leave, has not left the requesting State within a period of [15] consecutive days, or any longer period otherwise agreed on by the Parties, after

---

[44]The provisions in article 15 may be required as the only way of securing important evidence in proceedings involving serious national and transnational crime. However, as they may raise difficulties for some countries, the precise content of the article, including any additions or modifications, can be determined in bilateral negotiations.

that person has been officially told or notified that his or her presence is no longer required or, having left, has voluntarily returned.

3. A person who does not consent to a request pursuant to article 13 or accept an invitation pursuant to article 14 shall not, by reason thereof, be liable to any penalty or be subjected to any coercive measure, notwithstanding any contrary statement in the request or summons.

Article 16

Provision of publicly available documents and other records[45]

1. The requested State shall provide copies of documents and records in so far as they are open to public access as part of a public register or otherwise, or in so far as they are available for purchase or inspection by the public.

2. The requested State may provide copies of any other document or record under the same conditions as such document or record may be provided to its own law enforcement and judicial authorities.

Article 17

Search and seizure[46]

The requested State shall, in so far as its law permits, carry out requests for search and seizure and delivery of any material to the requesting State for evidentiary purposes, provided that the rights of *bona fide* third parties are protected.

---

[45]The question may arise as to whether this should be discretionary. This provision can be the subject of bilateral negotiations.

[46]Bilateral arrangements may cover the provision of information on the results of search and seizure and the observance of conditions imposed in relation to the delivery of seized property.

Article 18

Certification and authentication[47]

A request for assistance and the documents in support thereof, as well as documents or other material supplied in response to such a request, shall not require certification or authentication.

Article 19

Costs[48]

The ordinary costs of executing a request shall be borne by the requested State, unless otherwise determined by the Parties. If expenses of a substantial or extraordinary nature are or will be required to execute the request, the Parties shall consult in advance to determine the terms and conditions under which the request shall be executed as well as the manner in which the costs shall be borne.

Article 20

Consultation

The Parties shall consult promptly, at the request of either, concerning the interpretation, the application or the carrying out of the present Treaty either generally or in relation to a particular case.

Article 21

---

[47]The laws of some countries require authentication before documents transmitted from other countries can be admitted in their courts, and, therefore, would require a clause setting out the authentication required.

[48]More detailed provisions may be included, for example, the requested State would meet the ordinary cost of fulfilling the request for assistance except that the requesting State would bear (a) the exceptional or extraordinary expenses required to fulfill the request, where required by the requested State and subject to previous consultations; (b) the expenses associated with conveying any person to or from the territory of the requested State, and any fees, allowances or expenses payable to that person while in the requesting State pursuant to a request under article 11, 13 or 14; (c) the expenses associated with conveying custodial or escorting officers; and (d) the expenses involved in obtaining reports of experts.

Final Provisions

1. The present Treaty is subject to (ratification, acceptance or approval). The instruments of (ratification, acceptance or approval) shall be exchanged as soon as possible.

2. The present Treaty shall enter into force on the thirtieth day after the day on which the instruments of (ratification, acceptance or approval) are exchanged.

3. The present Treaty shall apply to requests made after its entry into force, even if the relevant acts or omissions occurred prior to that date.

4. Either Contracting Party may denounce the present Treaty by giving notice in writing to the other Party. Such denunciation shall take effect six months following the date on which it is received by the other Party.

* * *

Optional Protocol to the Model Treaty on Mutual Assistance in Criminal Matters Concerning the Proceeds of Crime[49]

1. In the present Protocol "proceeds of crime" means any property suspected, or found by a court, to be property directly or indirectly derived or realized as a result of the commission of an offence or to represent the value of property and other benefits derived from the commission of an offence.

---

[49]The present Optional Protocol is included on the ground that questions of forfeiture are conceptually different from, although closely related to, matters generally accepted as falling within the description of mutual assistance. However, States may wish to include these provisions in the text because of their importance in dealing with organized crime. Moreover, assistance in forfeiting the proceeds of crime has now emerged as a new instrument in international cooperation. Provisions similar to those outlined in the present Protocol appear in many bilateral assistance treaties. Further details can be provided in bilateral arrangements. One matter that could be considered is the need for other provisions dealing with issues related to bank secrecy. An addition could, for example, be made to paragraph 4 of the present Protocol providing that the requested State shall, upon request, take such measures as are permitted by its law to require compliance with monitoring orders by financial institutions. Provision could be made for the sharing of the proceeds of crime between the Contracting States or for consideration of the disposal of the proceeds on a case-by-case basis.

2. The requested State shall, upon request, endeavour to ascertain whether any proceeds of the alleged crime are located within its jurisdiction and shall notify the requesting State of the results of its inquiries. In making the request, the requesting State shall notify the requested State of the basis of its belief that such proceeds may be located within its jurisdiction.

3. In pursuance of a request made under paragraph 2 of the present Protocol, the requested State shall endeavour to trace assets, investigate financial dealings, and obtain other information or evidence that may help to secure the recovery of proceeds of crime.

4. Where, pursuant to paragraph 2 of the present Protocol, suspected proceeds of crime are found, the requested State shall upon request take such measures as are permitted by its law to prevent any dealing in, transfer or disposal of, those suspected proceeds of crime, pending a final determination in respect of those proceeds by a court of the requesting State.

5. The requested State shall, to the extent permitted by its law, give effect to or permit enforcement of a final order forfeiting or confiscating the proceeds of crime made by a court of the requesting State or take other appropriate action to secure the proceeds following a request by the requesting State.[50]

6. The Parties shall ensure that the rights of *bona fide* third parties shall be respected in the application of the present Protocol.

* * *

5. Model Treaty on the Transfer of Proceedings in Criminal Matters

ANNEX

Desirous of further strengthening international cooperation and mutual assistance in criminal justice, on the basis of the principles of respect for national sovereignty and jurisdiction and of non-interference in the internal affairs of States,

---

[50]The Parties might consider widening the scope of the present Protocol by the inclusion of references to victims' restitution and the recovery of fines imposed as a sentence in a criminal prosecution.

Believing that such cooperation should further the ends of justice, the social resettlement of offenders and the interests of the victims of crime,

Bearing in mind that the transfer of proceedings in criminal matters contributes to effective administration of justice and to reducing conflicts of competence,

Aware that the transfer of proceedings in criminal matters can help to avoid pre-trial detention and thus reduce the prison population,

Convinced, therefore, that the transfer of proceedings in criminal matters should be promoted,

Have agreed as follows:

Article 1

Scope of application

1. When a person is suspected of having committed an offence under the law of a State which is a Contracting Party, that State may, if the interests of the proper administration of justice so require, request another State which is a Contracting Party to take proceedings in respect of this offence.

2. For the purpose of applying the present Treaty, the Contracting Parties shall take the necessary legislative measures to ensure that a request of the requesting State to take proceedings shall allow the requested State to exercise the necessary jurisdiction.

Article 2

Channels of communications

A request to take proceedings shall be made in writing. The request, supporting documents and subsequent communication shall be transmitted through diplomatic channels, directly between the Ministries of Justice or any other authorities designated by the Parties.

Article 3

Required documents

1. The request to take proceedings shall contain or be accompanied by the following information:

a. The authority presenting the request;

b. A description of the act for which transfer of proceedings is being requested, including the specific time and place of the offence;

c. A statement on the results of investigations which substantiate the suspicion of an offence;

d. The legal provisions of the requesting State on the basis of which the act is considered to be an offence;

e. A reasonably exact statement on the identity, nationality and residence of the suspected person.

2. The documents submitted in support of a request to take proceedings shall be accompanied by a translation into the language of the requested State or into another language acceptable to that State.

Article 4

Certification and authentication

Subject to national law and unless the Parties decide otherwise, a request to take proceedings and the documents in support thereof, as well as the documents and other material supplied in response to such a request shall not require certification or authentication.[51]

Article 5

Decision on the request

The competent authorities of the requested State shall examine what action to take on the request to take proceedings in order to comply, as fully as possible, with the request under their own law, and shall promptly communicate their decision to the requesting State.

---

[51]The laws of some countries require authentication before documents transmitted from other countries can be admitted in their courts and, therefore, would require a clause setting out the authentication required.

Article 6

Dual criminality

A request to take proceedings can be complied with only if the act on which the request is based would be an offence if committed in the territory of the requested State.

Article 7

Grounds for refusal

If the requested State refuses acceptance of a request for transfer of proceedings, it shall communicate the reasons for refusal to the requesting State. Acceptance may be refused if:[52]

a. The suspected person is not a national of or ordinary resident in the requested State;

b. The act is an offence under military law, which is not also an offence under ordinary criminal law;

c. The offence is in connection with taxes, duties, customs or exchange;

d. The offence is regarded by the requested State as being of a political nature.

Article 8

The position of the suspected person

1. The suspected person may express to either State his or her interest in the transfer of the proceedings. Similarly, such interest may be expressed by the legal representative or close relatives of the suspected person.

---

[52]When negotiating on the basis of the present Model Treaty, States may wish to add other grounds for refusal or conditions to this list, relating, for example, to the nature or gravity of the offence, to the protection of fundamental human rights, or to considerations of public order.

2. Before a request for transfer of proceedings is made, the requesting State shall, if practicable, allow the suspected person to present his or her views on the alleged offence and the intended transfer, unless that person has absconded or otherwise obstructed the course of justice.

Article 9

The rights of the victim

The requesting and requested States shall ensure in the transfer of proceedings that the rights of the victim of the offence, in particular his or her right to restitution or compensation, shall not be affected as a result of the transfer. If a settlement of the claim of the victim has not been reached before the transfer, the requested State shall permit the representation of the claim in the transferred proceedings, if its law provides for such a possibility. In the event of the death of the victim, these provisions shall apply to his or her dependents accordingly.

Article 10

Effects of the transfer of proceedings on the requesting State

(ne bis in idem)

Upon acceptance by the requested State of the request to take proceedings against the suspected person, the requesting State shall provisionally discontinue prosecution, except necessary investigation, including judicial assistance to the requested State, until the requested State informs the requesting State that the case has been finally disposed of. From that date on, the requesting State shall definitely refrain from further prosecution of the same offence.

Article 11

Effects of the transfer of proceedings on the requested State

1. The proceedings transferred upon agreement shall be governed by the law of the requested State. When charging the suspected person under its law, the requested State shall make the necessary adjustment with respect to particular elements in the legal description of the offence. Where the competence of the requested State is based on the provision set forth in paragraph 2 of article 1 of the present Treaty, the sanction pronounced in that State shall not be more severe than that provided by the law of the requesting State.

2. As far as compatible with the law of the requested State, any act with a view to proceedings or procedural requirements performed in the requesting State in accordance with its law shall have the same validity in the requested State as if the act had been performed in or by the authorities of that State.

3. The requested State shall inform the requesting State of the decision taken as a result of the proceedings. To this end a copy of any final decision shall be transmitted to the requesting State upon request.

Article 12

Provisional measures

When the requesting State announces its intention to transmit a request for transfer of proceedings, the requested State may, upon a specific request made for this purpose by the requesting State, apply all such provisional measures, including provisional detention and seizure, as could be applied under its own law if the offence in respect of which transfer of proceedings is requested had been committed in its territory.

Article 13

The plurality of criminal proceedings

When criminal proceedings are pending in two or more States against the same suspected person in respect of the same offence, the States concerned shall conduct consultations to decide which of them alone should continue the proceedings. An agreement reached thereupon shall have the consequences of a request for transfer of proceedings.

Article 14

Costs

Any costs incurred by a Contracting Party because of a transfer of proceedings shall not be refunded, unless otherwise agreed by both the requesting and requested States.

Article 15

Final Provisions

1. The present Treaty is subject to (ratification, acceptance or approval). The instruments of (ratification, acceptance or approval) shall be exchanged as soon as possible.

2. The present Treaty shall enter into force on the thirtieth day after the day on which the instruments of (ratification, acceptance or approval) are exchanged.

3. The present Treaty shall apply to requests made after its entry into force, even if the relevant acts or omissions occurred prior to that date.

4. Either Contracting Party may denounce the present Treaty by giving notice in writing to the other Party. Such denunciation shall take effect six months following the date on which it is received by the other Party.

* * *

6. Model Treaty for the Prevention of Crimes That Infringe on the Cultural Heritage of Peoples in the Form of Movable Property

ANNEX

Model treaty for the prevention of crimes that infringe on the cultural heritage of peoples in the form of movable property[53]

Conscious of the need to cooperate in the field of criminal justice,

Wishing to add to the effectiveness of the co-operation between their two countries in combating criminal activities which involve movable cultural property through the introduction of measures for impeding illicit transnational trafficking in movable cultural property whether or not it has been stolen, the imposition of appropriate and effective administrative and penal sanctions and the provision of a means for restitution,

---

[53]An alternative title could be "Model treaty concerning crimes relating to the restitution of movable cultural property".

Have agreed as follows:

Article 1

Scope of application and definition[54]

1. For the purposes of this treaty, movable cultural property[55] shall be understood as referring to property which, on religious or secular grounds, is specifically designated by a State Party as being subject to export control by reason of its importance for archaeology, prehistory, history, literature, art or science, and as belonging to one or more of the following categories:

a. Rare collections and specimens of fauna, flora, minerals and anatomy, and objects of paleontological interest;

b. Property relating to history, including the history of science and technology, military history, and the history of societies and religions, as well as to the lives of leaders, thinkers, scientists and artists and other national figures, and to events of national importance;

c. Products of archaeological excavations or discoveries, including clandestine excavations or discoveries, whether on land or under water;

d. Elements of artistic or historical monuments or archaeological sites which have been dismantled;

e. Antiquities, including tools, ceramics, ornaments, musical instruments, pottery, inscriptions of all kinds, coins, engraved seals, jewels, weapons and funerary remains of any description;

f. Materials of anthropological, historical or ethnological interest;

---

[54]Suggested alternatives to article 1, paragraph 1, are: (i) "This treaty covers all items of movable cultural property specifically designated as such by a State Party, and subject to export control by that State Party."; or (ii) "This treaty covers those items of movable cultural property specifically agreed to between the States Parties as being subject to export control."

[55]The categories follow closely the list contained in article 1 of the UNESCO Convention on the Means of Prohibiting and Preventing the Illicit Import, Export and Transfer of Ownership of Cultural Property, of 1970. However, this list may not be exhaustive, and States Parties may wish to add other categories.

g. Property of artistic interest, such as:

i. Pictures, paintings and drawings produced entirely by hand on any support and in any material (excluding industrial designs and manufactured articles decorated by hand);

ii Original works of statuary art and sculpture in any material;

iii Original engravings, prints, lithographs and art photographs;

iv Original artistic assemblages and montages in any material;

h. Rare manuscripts and incunabula, old books, documents and publications of special historical, artistic, scientific, literary or other interest, singly or in collections;

i. Postage, revenue and similar stamps, either singly or in collections;

j. Archives, including phonographic, photographic and cinematographic archives;

k. Articles of furniture, furnishings and musical instruments of more than 100 years of age.

2. This treaty applies to movable cultural property stolen in or illicitly exported from the other State Party after the coming into force of the treaty.[56]

Article 2

General principles

1. Each State Party undertakes:

---

[56]States Parties may wish to consider providing for a period of limitation after which the right to request recovery of stolen or illicitly exported movable cultural property will be extinguished.

(a) To take the necessary measures to prohibit the import and export of movable cultural property (i) which has been stolen in the other State Party or (ii) which has been illicitly exported from the other State Party;

(b) To take the necessary measures to prohibit the acquisition of, and dealing within its territory with, movable cultural property which has been imported contrary to the prohibitions resulting from the implementation of subparagraph (a) above;

(c) To legislate in order to prevent persons and institutions within its territory from entering into international conspiracies with respect to movable cultural property;

(d) To provide information concerning its stolen movable cultural property to an international data base agreed upon between the States Parties;[57]

(e) To take the measures necessary to ensure that the purchaser of stolen movable cultural property which is listed on the international data base is not considered to be a purchaser who has acquired such property in good faith;[58]

(f) To introduce a system whereby the export of movable cultural property is authorized by the issue of an export certificate;[59]

(g) To take the measures necessary to ensure that a purchaser of imported movable cultural property which is not accompanied by an export certificate issued by the other State Party and who did not acquire the movable cultural property prior to the entry into force of this treaty shall not be considered to be a

---

[57]Further developments in this field will provide the international community, particularly potential States Parties, with an opportunity to implement this method of crime prevention. (See also resolution 6 below.) The United Nations Congresses on the Prevention of Crime and the Treatment of Offenders may wish to develop initiatives in this direction.

[58]This provision is intended to supplement, and not be in substitution for, the normal rules relating to good faith acquisition.

[59]This procedure is consistent with the validation procedure described in article 6 of the Convention on the Means of Prohibiting and Preventing the Illicit Import, Export and Transfer of Ownership of Cultural Property.

person who has acquired the movable cultural property in good faith;[60]

(h) To use all the means at its disposal, including the fostering of public awareness, to combat the illicit import and export, theft, illicit excavation and illicit dealing in movable cultural property.

2. Each State Party undertakes to take the necessary measures to recover and return, at the request of the other State Party, any movable cultural property which is covered by subparagraph (a) above.

Article 3

Sanctions[61]

Each State Party undertakes to impose sanctions[62] upon:

(a) Persons or institutions responsible for the illicit import or export of movable cultural property;

(b) Persons or institutions that knowingly acquire or deal in stolen or illicitly imported movable cultural property;

(c) Persons or institutions that enter into international conspiracies to obtain, export or import movable cultural property by illicit means.

---

[60]States Parties may wish to consider adding certain types of offences against movable cultural property to the list of extraditable offences covered by an extradition treaty. (See also sect. A, draft resolution 10 above.)

[61]States Parties may wish to consider adding certain types of offences against movable cultural property to the list of extraditable offences covered by an extradition treaty. (See also sect. A, draft resolution 10 above.)

[62]States Parties may wish to consider establishing minimum penalties for certain offences.

Article 4

Procedures

1. Requests for recovery and return shall be made through diplomatic channels. The requesting State Party shall furnish, at its expense, the documentation and other evidence, including the date of export, necessary to establish its claim for recovery and return.

2. All expenses incidental to the return and delivery of the movable cultural property shall be borne by the requesting State Party,[63] and no Person or institution shall be entitled to claim any form of compensation from the State Party returning the property claimed. Neither shall the requesting State Party be required to compensate in any way such persons or institutions as may have participated in illegally sending abroad the property in question, although it must pay fair compensation[64] to any person or institution that in good faith acquired or was in legal possession of the property.[65]

3. Both parties agree not to levy any customs or other duties on such movable property as may be discovered and returned in accordance with the present treaty.

4. The States Parties agree to make available to each other such information as will assist in combating crimes against movable cultural property.[66]

---

[63]States Parties may wish to consider whether the expenses and/or the expense of providing compensation should be shared between them.

[64]States Parties may wish to consider whether the expenses and/or the expense of providing compensation should be shared between them.

[65]States Parties may wish to consider the position of a blameless possessor who has inherited or otherwise gratuitously acquired a cultural object which had been previously dealt with in bad faith.

[66]Some States Parties may wish to preface article 4, paragraph 3 by the following: "Subject to domestic laws, particularly those concerning access to information and the protection of privacy...".

5. Each State Party shall provide information concerning laws which protect its movable cultural property to an international data base agreed upon between the States Parties.[67]

Article 5

Final provisions[68]

1. This treaty is subject to (ratification, acceptance or approval). The instruments of (ratification, acceptance or approval) shall be exchanged as soon as possible, through diplomatic channels.

2. This treaty shall come into force on the thirtieth day after the day on which the instruments of (ratification, acceptance or approval) are exchanged.

3. Either State Party may denounce this treaty by giving notice in writing to the other State Party. Such denunciation shall take effect six months after the date on which such notice is received by the other State Party.

4. This treaty is intended to be complementary to, and does not in any way exclude, participation in other international arrangements.

* * *

---

[67]It should be noted that G.A. Res. 44/18 of 6 November 1989 and quite a number of resolutions of the General Conference of UNESCO have invited member States to establish, with the assistance of UNESCO, national inventories of cultural property. At the date of the drafting of this treaty, national legislative texts on the protection of cultural movable property from 76 countries have been collected, published and disseminated by UNESCO.

[68]States Parties may wish to consider providing for a process for the resolution of disputes concerning the treaty.

7. Model Treaty on the Transfer of Supervision of Offenders Conditionally Sentenced or Conditionally Released

ANNEX

Model Treaty on the Transfer of Supervision of Offenders Conditionally Sentenced or Conditionally Released

Desirous of further strengthening international co-operation and mutual assistance in criminal justice, on the basis of the principles of respect for national sovereignty and jurisdiction and of non-interference in the internal affairs of States,

Believing that such co-operation should further the ends of justice, the social resettlement of sentenced persons and the interests of the victims of crime,

Bearing in mind that the transfer of supervision of offenders conditionally sentenced or conditionally released can contribute to an increase in the use of alternatives to imprisonment,

Aware that supervision in the home country of the offender rather than enforcement of the sentence in a country where the offender has no roots also contributes to an earlier and more effective reintegration into society,

Convinced, therefore, that the social rehabilitation of offenders and the increased application of alternatives to imprisonment would be promoted by facilitating the supervision of conditionally sentenced or conditionally released offenders in their State of ordinary residence,

Have agreed as follows:

Article 1

Scope of application

1. The present Treaty shall be applicable, if, according to a final court decision, a person has been found guilty of an offence and has been:

   a. Placed on probation without sentence having been pronounced;

   b. Given a suspended sentence involving deprivation of liberty;

c. Given a sentence, the enforcement of which has been modified (parole) or conditionally suspended, in whole or in part, either at the time of the sentence or subsequently.

2. The State where the decision was taken (sentencing State) may request another State (administering State) to take responsibility for applying the terms of the decision (transfer of supervision).

Article 2

Channels of communications

A request for the transfer of supervision shall be made in writing. The request, supporting documents and subsequent communication shall be transmitted through diplomatic channels, directly between the Ministries of Justice or any other authorities designated by the Parties.

Article 3

Required documents

1. A request for the transfer of supervision shall contain all necessary information on the identity, nationality and residence of the sentenced person. The request shall be accompanied by the original or a copy of any court decision referred to in article 1 of the present Treaty and a certificate that this decision is final.

2. The documents submitted in support of a request for transfer of supervision shall be accompanied by a translation into the language of the requested State or into another language acceptable to that State.

Article 4

Certification and authentication

Subject to national law and unless the Parties decide otherwise, a request for transfer of supervision and the documents in support thereof, as well as the documents and other material supplied in response to such a request, shall not require certification or authentication.[69]

---

[69]The laws of some countries require authentication before documents transmitted from other countries can be admitted in their courts and, therefore, would require a clause setting out the authentication required.

Article 5

Decision on the request

The competent authorities of the administering State shall examine what action to take on the request for supervision in order to comply, as fully as possible, with the request under their own law, and shall promptly communicate their decision to the sentencing State.

Article 6

Dual criminality[70]

A request for transfer of supervision can be complied with only if the act on which the request is based would constitute an offence if committed in the territory of the administering State.

Article 7

Grounds for refusal[71]

If the administering State refuses acceptance of a request for transfer of supervision, it shall communicate the reasons for refusal to the sentencing State. Acceptance may be refused where:

a. The sentenced person is not an ordinary resident in the administering State;

b. The act is an offence under military law, which is not also an offence under ordinary criminal law;

c. The offence is in connection with taxes, duties, customs or exchange;

---

[70]When negotiating on the basis of the present Model Treaty, States may wish to waive the requirement of dual criminality.

[71]When negotiating on the basis of the present Model Treaty, States may wish to add other grounds for refusal or conditions to this list, relating, for example, to the nature or gravity of the offence, to the protection of fundamental human rights, or to considerations of public order.

d. The offence is regarded by the administering State as being of a political nature;

e. The administering State, under its own law, can no longer carry out the supervision or enforce the sanction in the event of revocation because of lapse of time.

Article 8

The position of the sentenced person

Whether sentenced or standing trial, a person may express to the sentencing State his or her interest in a transfer of supervision and his or her willingness to fulfil any conditions to be imposed. Similarly, such interest may be expressed by his or her legal representative or close relatives. Where appropriate, the Contracting States shall inform the offender or his or her close relatives of the possibilities under the present Treaty.

Article 9

The rights of the victim

The sentencing State and the administering State shall ensure in the transfer of supervision that the rights of the victims of the offence, in particular his or her rights to restitution or compensation, shall not be affected as a result of the transfer. In the event of the death of the victim, this provision shall apply to his or her dependents accordingly.

Article 10

The effects of the transfer of supervision on the sentencing State

The acceptance by the administering State of the responsibility for applying the terms of the decision rendered in the sentencing State shall extinguish the competence of the latter State to enforce the sentence.

Article 11

The effects of the transfer of supervision on the administering State

1. The supervision transferred upon agreement and the subsequent procedure shall be carried out in accordance with the law of the administering

State. That State alone shall have the right of revocation. That State may, to the extent necessary, adapt to its own law the conditions or measures prescribed, provided that such conditions or measures are, in terms of their nature or duration, not more severe than those pronounced in the sentencing State.

2. If the administering State revokes the conditional sentence or conditional release, it shall enforce the sentence in accordance with its own law without, however, going beyond the limits imposed by the sentencing State.

Article 12

Review, pardon and amnesty

1. The sentencing State alone shall have the right to decide on any application to reopen the case.

2. Each Party may grant pardon, amnesty or commutation of the sentence in accordance with the provisions of its Constitution or other laws.

Article 13

Information

1. The Contracting Parties shall keep each other informed, in so far as it is necessary, of all circumstances likely to affect measures of supervision or enforcement in the administering State. To this end they shall transmit to each other copies of any relevant decisions in this respect.

2. After expiration of the period of supervision, the administering State shall provide to the sentencing State, at its request, a final report concerning the supervised person's conduct and compliance with the measures imposed.

Article 14

Costs

Supervision and enforcement costs incurred in the administering State shall not be refunded, unless otherwise agreed by both the sentencing State and the administering State.

Article 15

Final Provisions

1. The present Treaty is subject to [ratification, acceptance or approval]. The instruments of [ratification, acceptance or approval] shall be exchanged as soon as possible.

2. The present Treaty shall enter into force on the thirtieth day after the day on which the instruments of [ratification, acceptance or approval] are exchanged.

3. The present Treaty shall apply to requests made after its entry into force, even if the relevant acts or omissions occurred prior to that date.

4. Either Contracting Party may denounce the present Treaty by giving notice in writing to the other Party. Such denunciation shall take effect six months following the date on which it is received by the other Party.

* * *